Pacific Northwest Women, 1815-1925

LIVES, MEMORIES, AND WRITINGS

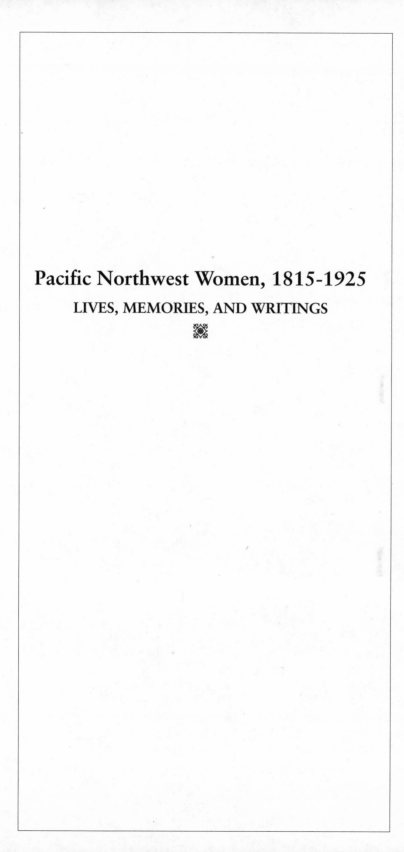

Pacific Northwest Women, 1815-1925

LIVES, MEMORIES, AND WRITINGS

edited by
Jean M. Ward & Elaine A. Maveety

OREGON STATE UNIVERSITY PRESS
CORVALLIS

The paper in this book meets the guidelines for permanence and durability of the Committee on Production Guidelines for Book Longevity of the Council on Library Resources and the minimum requirements of the American National Standard for Permanence of Paper for Printed Library Materials Z39.48-1984.

Library of Congress Cataloging-in-Publication Data
Pacific Northwest women, 1815-1925: lives, memories, and writings / [edited] by Jean M. Ward and Elaine A. Maveety.
  p. cm.
Includes bibliographical references (p.) and index.
ISBN 0-87071-387-6
1. American literature—Northwest, Pacific. 2. Frontier and pioneer life—Northwest, Pacific—Literary collections. 3. Women pioneers—Northwest, Pacific—Literary collections. 4. Women pioneers—Northwest, Pacific—Biography. 5. American literature—Women authors. 6. American literature—19th century. 7. American literature—20th century. I. Ward, Jean M. II. Maveety, Elaine A.
PS570.P33 1995
810.8'09352042—dc20   95-17850
                                                    CIP

Contents

MAKER OF SONGS

Take strands of speech, faded and broken;
Tear them to pieces, word from word,
Then take the ravelled shreds and dye them
With meanings that were never heard.

Place them across the loom. Let wind-shapes
And sunlight come in at the door,
Or let the radiance of raining
Move in silver on the floor.

And sit you quiet in the shadow
Before the subtly idle strands.
Silence, a cloak, will weigh your shoulder;
Silence, a sorrow, fill your hands.

Yet there shall come the stirring. . . Weaver,
Weave well and not with words alone;
Weave through the pattern every fragment
Of glittered breath that you have known.

Hazel Hall
from *Cry of Time*, 1928

Introduction

*When women's true history shall have been written, her part in the
upbuilding of this nation will astound the world.*
        Abigail Scott Duniway, *From the West to the West* (1905)

*Marie Holst
Portsmith,
Oregon
schoolteacher,
doing laundry
in a wooden
tub behind her
home, 1908*

        Pacific Northwest Women gives
both voice and interpretation to the cultural and cross-cultural
experiences of a diverse group of women, all of whom were part of a
particular geographic region—the Pacific Northwest, which we define
as the area now known as the states of Oregon and Washington. In
addition to asking how social constructions of race, class, and gender
affected these women's experiences, we ask what role place—
geographical region—played in shaping their lives.

Throughout the process of collecting, selecting, and interpreting Pacific Northwest women's texts, we have been influenced by the thinking of western historians such as Glenda Riley, Peggy Pascoe, Patricia Nelson Limerick, and Susan Armitage. These historians remind readers of the virtual absence of women of all ethnicities in Frederick Jackson Turner's frontier thesis, as well as the stereotyping of American Indian women as drudges and Anglo women as Saints in Sunbonnets, Reluctant Pioneers, and Gentle Tamers in later "frontier" histories.

Limerick and others argue persuasively for a paradigm shift that moves beyond narrow, obsolete visions of "conquered frontiers" to a paradigm that includes *all* women and recognizes the diversity of women's experiences within and across cultures. In a discussion of prostitution in the early West, Limerick writes: "Exclude women from Western history, and unreality sets in. Restore them, and the Western drama gains a fully human cast of characters—males and females whose urges, needs, failings and conflicts we can recognize and even share" (*The Legacy of Conquest* 52).

Pascoe and Riley contribute to this new paradigm, and their ideas helped guide our development of *Pacific Northwest Women*. Pascoe addresses "the problem of disappearing women of color" and calls for multicultural western history that recognizes western women at the cultural crossroads—"an analytic crossing of three central axes of inequality—race, class and gender" ("Western Women at the Cultural Crossroads" 49). To enrich understanding of western women's experiences and to contribute to comparative regional studies of their lives, Riley urges adding region to critical considerations of gender, race, and class (*A Place to Grow* 12).

Pacific Northwest Women is a step toward regional recovery and interpretation of women's diverse voices, lives, and experiences.

Pacific Northwest Women

The lives and words of the thirty women who appear in this volume, along with the dozens of others we could not include, have sometimes amazed and frequently touched us during the course of this project. They still do, each time we reread them. Only five—Frances Fuller Victor, Bethenia Owens-Adair, Narcissa Prentiss Whitman, Abigail Scott Duniway, and Sarah Winnemucca—appear in *Notable American Women: A Biographical Dictionary, 1650-1950*, but all thirty are "notable" in the study of women's lives in the Pacific Northwest.

Who were these women? They were African American, Euro-American, Asian American, and American Indian. They were single, married, widowed, and divorced. They were missionaries, homesteaders, former slaves, nurses, schoolteachers, historians, architects, homemakers, doctors, migrant harvesters, milliners, newspaper editors, seamstresses, domestic servants, professional writers, poets, artists, suffragists, midwives, social workers, evangelists, and prostitutes. Some were born in the Pacific Northwest; some emigrated from other states or countries. Some were mothers; some were childless. Some were able bodied, others lived with physical impairment. Several survived oppression and even brutality, loss of families and loved ones. Some died young—in childbirth, from illness, or by violence. Others lived long, productive lives. A few just disappeared, and we do not know the end of their stories.

They were women of spirit, courageous and resourceful; they were ordinary and yet extraordinary, each in her own way. They told of living with nature, of coping with challenges, of caring for others, of communicating their messages. They were builders—of schools, hospitals, and orphanages; of homesteads and farms; of families and communities; of novels, stories, and poems. They were recorders and keepers of stories, makers of songs.

All of these women lived, at least for a number of years, in the Pacific Northwest, the vast geographical area now known as Oregon and Washington, twin states created and bonded by nature to share geology and climate, and therefore much of their history and culture. From the beginning, the region was culturally diverse; prior to the arrival of Anglos, a variety of Indian cultures thrived. After the arrival of fur traders—followed by missionaries, pioneers, miners, ranchers, and homesteaders—the landscape began to change. Fertile lands west of the Cascade Range became farmlands; drylands east of the Cascades became ranches and homesteads.

Although we use the term "culture" throughout this work, the women and men who came together in the early Pacific Northwest did not use this word to represent their systems of beliefs, customs, and behaviors, and they would not know the meaning of "standing at cultural crossroads." The concept of culture was a creation of the late nineteenth and early twentieth centuries, and was not a part of the thinking of those who came west in the nineteenth century. From a contemporary point of view, Euro-American visions of the world were typically ethnocentric, and their attitudes—linked to prevailing distinctions between "savagery" and "civilization"—were often racist. "Savagery," Patricia Limerick writes, "meant hunting and gathering,

Ka-Ki-Is-Ilma, Princess Angeline, daughter of Chief Sealth, after whom Seattle was named. She died in 1896, about age ninety.

not agriculture; common ownership, not individual property owning; pagan superstition, not Christianity; spoken language, not literacy; emotion, not reason" (*The Legacy of Conquest* 190).

With the arrival of Euro-Americans in the Pacific Northwest, conditions for Indian women changed dramatically over time. Before the Anglos came, the Colville ancestors of Able-One and Mourning Dove lived in harmony with nature, relatively undisturbed at their hunting grounds in the upper regions of the Columbia River; the Northern Paiute ancestors of Sarah Winnemucca traveled in nomadic bands, hunting and gathering in seasonal rounds that took them to what is now Southeastern Oregon, as well as into Nevada and California. But, as told in the narratives of these Indian women, arrival of Euro-Americans eventually pushed their people to the very edge of survival. Although Sarah Winnemucca, Mourning Dove, and Nancy Perkins Wynecoop (the granddaughter of Able-One) assumed roles as mediators between Indian and white cultures, they could not restore the lost cultures of their grandmothers and their great-grandmothers.

As settlement continued, African-American and Asian-American women came to the cultural crossroads of the Pacific Northwest. Women such as Emma J. Ray, Susie Revels Cayton, and Sui Sin Far acted as what we term "cultural mediators" and addressed issues of race, class, and gender in their writings and interracial community efforts. They, like the American Indian women whose narratives are included in this collection, were what historian Peggy Pascoe calls "intercultural brokers, mediators between two or more very different cultural groups" ("Western Women at the Cultural Crossroads" 55).

For Anglo women, including early missionaries, the Pacific Northwest was also an intersection of contrasting cultural values. Separated by great distance from centers of white culture and sometimes ill equipped to understand or accept the Indians as anything but "other," some women, such as Narcissa Prentiss Whitman, responded by retreating into private cultures of their own creation, literally closing the door to the "other." Emeline Fuller, traumatized by a childhood experience, did not make distinctions as an adult between and among Indians, and she classed all as one hostile group. In Emily Inez Denny's myopic vision, Indians were curious parts of the landscape— interesting figures in her own childhood playground.

For other white women, several of whom became cultural mediators, the Pacific Northwest was a place to learn about and appreciate Indian culture and language—to empathize with and respect indigenous peoples as individuals. This was the case for Mother Joseph of the Sacred Heart, S.P., in her work and travels throughout the Pacific Northwest, and for Susanna Ede, who became matron and interpreter for the Indian School at Quinault Reservation. For Caroline C. Leighton, who shared her understandings with eastern readers, American Indian cultures were not threatening but fascinating and sometimes beautiful—not "savage" or "other" but simply different.

The Women's Texts

For this volume, we have chosen oral histories and writings that illustrate the diversity of women's experiences in the Pacific Northwest during the early period of 1815 to 1925. We have not, however, emphasized overland journals and diaries since these are readily available in collections such as Kenneth L. Holmes's *Covered Wagon Women: Diaries and Letters from the Western Trails, 1840-1890*. And, because of our interest in the effects of geographic region on women's lives, we have not included travel accounts by women who briefly visited but did not live in the Pacific Northwest. Many of the pieces we include have been neglected or overlooked in studies of western women. Some have received limited exposure, and others have never been presented to contemporary audiences.

Our decision to include a few reminiscences in this collection should be clarified. Because some of the women are recalling events that occurred many years earlier, questions about source credibility and the function of memory are appropriate. Although the ability to recall details of early events can be keen in later years, the passage of time can also dim the memory, or the narrator may choose to alter details of events. If the narrator's recollection of fact was in error, we set the reminiscence aside; however, if a narrator colored or altered what *we* saw as her reality, we asked why.

All of the reminiscences we include from women in their seventies and eighties appear to meet the tests of memory and veracity. Elizabeth Sager Helm and Amanda Gardener Johnson, for example, were both in their eighties when they were interviewed, but nothing in Helm's balanced account of life with Dr. Marcus and Narcissa Whitman or in Johnson's brief narrative of her life in and out of slavery suggests failed memory or alteration of fact. Susanna Ede was also in her eighties when she narrated her life story for her family, and the detail she provides about living conditions in the early Pacific Northwest suggests a sharp, rather than dimmed, memory. Esther Lockhart published some of her recollections as early as 1898 and later gave the full story of her life to her daughter. Sarah J. Cummins did not publish her *Autobiography and Reminiscences* until she was eighty-six, but she states that her book was "copied from my diary as written in years long gone by" (7).

Two texts do, however, raise some interesting questions about memory and veracity, and both were written by women in their forties—Emeline Fuller and Emily Inez Denny. Emeline Fuller was only forty-five when she published *Left by the Indians: Story of My Life*. Although Fuller's prejudice toward all Indians strongly colors her narrative, her account of the events of what has come to be known as the "Utter Massacre," including the involvement of white instigators, largely corresponds with what historian Donald H. Shannon (1993) has found.

While Fuller was struggling for survival in 1860, Emily Inez Denny was enjoying what she describes as a carefree childhood in Washington Territory. Denny was only forty-six when she copyrighted her autobiography, yet her description of early years in the Pacific Northwest appears colored already by nostalgia for a lost time. Of all the texts in this collection, only Denny's may fit historian Julie Roy Jeffrey's caution about pioneer and early settler recollections: "Nostalgia for lost youth colored their recollections, and the pioneer period became a golden age marked by youthful simplicity, virtue, and happiness" (*Frontier Women* 202). Even the title of Denny's autobiography—*Blazing the Way*—suggests romanticization of her culture and of the period.

In contrast to Denny's romantic view of the West, the number of separations and divorces that appear in these Pacific Northwest women's writings may surprise contemporary readers. But, as historian Glenda Riley points out, "a proclivity to divorce" existed on the Plains and throughout the West, and census records indicate that "western women sought and received a higher proportion of divorces than women in other regions of the country" (*A Place to Grow* 201). Riley adds that the cause for this high rate of divorce in the West is unclear but might have been related to economic opportunities and western women's desire for independence.

To preserve the authenticity of the women's voices, all selections in *Pacific Northwest Women* are presented in their original form, with the exception of a few paragraphing changes and infrequent use of "*sic.*" Titles for the texts have been drawn from the women's writings and narratives. Ellipses and bracketed information, unless otherwise noted, are our work as editors.

One of our objectives in *Pacific Northwest Women* is to give readers more than snapshots—brief glimpses—of these women. Since most are not well known to contemporary audiences, even in the Pacific Northwest, we introduce them with essays which provide biographical information, introduce the themes we found in the women's writings and narratives, and set their lives and words within historical, social, and cultural contexts. In a few cases, full biographical information has not been found, and we trust that others, intrigued by our beginnings, will continue the process of recovering the lives of "lost" women. To assist in this endeavor, we provide an extensive bibliography for those who wish to pursue the works of women of the early Pacific Northwest.

The Four Major Themes

In the process of reading scores of texts by Pacific Northwest women, we identified four major themes: connecting with nature, coping with circumstances, caregiving to others, and communicating for the self and others. Despite the diversity of backgrounds and life experiences of the women, these four themes emerged again and again in their writings and oral narratives. To illustrate these themes, we selected representative texts from thirty women.

Pacific Northwest Women is arranged in four parts, each of which corresponds to one of the themes, and we introduce each part with an essay that explores questions we asked about the theme. To show each theme across time, texts within the four sections are ordered by approximate dates of the events described, not necessarily by dates of writing or publication. (The one exception to this ordering is Ella Higginson's 1892 essay, "A Mossback to My Very Finger Ends," which concludes Part I.)

In Part I, *Connecting With Nature*, we focus on the importance of nature in the lives of these women—their relationships and connections with the natural world of the Pacific Northwest. Six texts are included in Part I, but the nature theme reappears in many other texts in this volume. To explore this theme, we asked two questions: What does nature in the Pacific Northwest represent to these women? What are the similarities and differences in their responses to nature?

From Able-One's early experiences of walking in balance with nature, to Ella Higginson's passionate appeal for stewardship of the natural world, the six women in Part I speak of living in connection with nature. We found no calls for taming the land, for conquest and subjugation of nature's landscape; instead, these women see themselves as part of—in harmony with—the natural world of the Pacific Northwest.

In Part II, *Coping: Learning by Doing*, we examine accounts of "making do" and doing what needs to be done, a theme we found frequently in texts by Pacific Northwest women. To illustrate the theme of coping, we include texts from nine women. In our exploration of this theme, we posed two questions: What forms does coping take in these women's lives, and how diverse are their experiences? What factors appear to be key in the coping process?

From the letters of Anna Maria Pittman Lee, which give insight into how she coped with early missionary life and a difficult pregnancy, to the writings of Emma J. Ray, which describe racial discrimination in the early part of the twentieth century, these nine women provide diverse accounts of coping. For some, coping with challenging circumstances is achieved in partnership with husbands and in connection with families; for others, coping involves breaking away from family and asserting autonomy.

In Part III, *Caregiving: Family and Community*, we focus on concern for the welfare of others, both within the domestic circle of family and within the expanded arena of community. Although accounts of caregiving are commonly associated with accounts of coping, the two themes can and do appear separately. To illustrate this recurring theme in the experiences of Pacific Northwest women, we include six texts, one of which is fictionalized. As we read the texts, we asked two questions: What are the examples and forms of caregiving in these women's lives and writings? How does one learn caregiving?

From Narcissa Whitman's concern for care of the children in her charge, to Mourning Dove's recollections of acts of caring by her family and others, diverse acts of caregiving are highly valued by the women themselves. The models for caregiving, who are usually older women, are almost as diverse as the acts performed. Throughout these texts, women frequently define themselves and others in terms of their capacity to give care, which includes the ability to create and sustain connections with others.

Arrival in Northeast Washington

In Part IV, *Communicating: From Private to Public,* we address our final theme: communicating for the self and others, wanting to be heard and understood by a public audience. Women throughout this volume were motivated to author autobiographies, to recover the lives and stories of family members, to research and write history, to publish in newspapers, to take to the lecture platform, and to write fiction and poetry.

To focus on this theme, we present a variety of genres from ten women, including two writers of fiction and one poet. To understand the place of communicating in these women's lives, we asked two questions: Why do these women want to be heard and understood publicly? What forms do they choose for their communication?

From Margaret Jewett Bailey, who wrote of her life as a former missionary and an abused wife, to Hazel Hall, who was confined to a wheelchair and wrote poetry acclaimed for its universal significance, the lives and texts of these ten women represent a wide range of communication purposes and forms. Some, particularly those who entertained their audiences and did not challenge cultural norms, found enthusiastic readers. Others, particularly the social reformers and cultural mediators, were constrained by prescriptions for gender, race, and class; they were more controversial and less well received. Whether they shared the personal or challenged the public, all of their texts are woman centered. Some of their messages are reflective, even lyrical; some are argumentative. For some of these women, the objective was self-expression and self-empowerment; for others, the objective included empowerment of others.

Empowerment through Autonomy and Connection

Theoretically, *Pacific Northwest Women* reveals much about woman's empowerment—empowerment of self and of others. Empowerment involves the ongoing processes of self-discovery, self-determination, and self-expression. The empowered person has the capacity—the agency—to act on behalf of self and others, sometimes as an agent for change. To empower means to strengthen, to increase viability. Empowerment is reciprocal, for the act of empowering others does not diminish but strengthens the self. Unlike power, empowerment does not imply the exertion of control, legitimate or otherwise, over others.

Every woman in this volume writes or speaks from a position with the authority or capacity to act. These women reflect on and display their own empowerment, and they often encourage the empowerment of others. When Anne Shannon Monroe writes about her decision to leave the unpleasant confines of the schoolroom to become an author, she is reflecting on her own empowerment; when Sarah Winnemucca takes to the lecture platform and later writes her autobiography, she is displaying empowerment; when Lydia Taylor warns mothers and young girls of the evils of prostitution, she is seeking to empower them.

We came to our conclusions about the centrality of empowerment in Pacific Northwest women's experiences after identifying and exploring the four major themes of the volume, which suggested that both autonomy *and* connection with others were important in these women's lives, especially in the enactment of coping, caregiving, and communicating. This led us to careful examination of the women's lives and texts to determine the less evident, quiescent theme, which we have identified and interpreted as women's empowerment.

Both autonomy and connection—separation and affiliation—are embedded in the empowerment of these women. Their capacities to act—to be agents for themselves and others—are acquired through what we call "autonomy-based empowerment" and "connection-based empowerment." Autonomy-based empowerment involves development of the self through individuated separation from others; connection-based empowerment involves development of the self through relational connections with others. Both forms of empowerment appear in the lives and texts of these Pacific Northwest women, sometimes through accounts of simultaneous separation and connection.

Our interpretations suggest that new questions should be posed about women's experiences in the American West and elsewhere. Rather than simply asking what happened to women's personal autonomy or what supportive networks they enjoyed, we should begin asking how women were empowered or disempowered through autonomy and connection—through processes of separation and affiliation.

Also, the concepts used in exploration of women's experiences need clarification. For example, we believe what historians such as Gerda Lerner have termed "autonomy" is more accurately identified as autonomy-based empowerment. "Autonomy," Lerner writes, "means women defining themselves and the values by which they will live." This involves "moving out from a world in which one is born to marginality" and "moving into a world in which one acts and chooses, aware of a meaningful past and free to shape one's future" (*The Majority Finds Its Past* 161-62). Lerner's definition of women's autonomy implies autonomy-based empowerment but does not speak directly to women's connection-based empowerment.

A country school at the Garrison, Cascades, Columbia River, 1867.

In contrast, psychologist Jean Baker Miller emphasizes the centrality of connection in women's experiences. She argues for a revamping
of the concept of autonomy to include the self-direction and self-
determination that women achieve through affiliation with others.
"Women are quite validly seeking something more complete than
autonomy as it is defined for men," she observes, "a fuller not a lesser
ability to encompass relationships with others, simultaneous with the
fullest development of oneself" (*Toward a New Psychology of Women*
95).

In addition to Miller, developmental psychologists such as Carol
Gilligan, Mary Field Belenky, Blythe McVicker Clinchy, Nancy Rule
Goldberger, and Jill Mattuck Tarule recognize the importance of what
we term connection-based empowerment in women's lives. Gilligan
notes that "women's sense of integrity seems to be entwined with an
ethic of care, so that to see themselves as women is to see themselves
in a relationship of connection" (*In a Different Voice* 171). And,
Gilligan writes, attachment with others, "the ethic of responsibility,"
can become "a self-chosen anchor of personal integrity and strength."
Like Gilligan, Belenky et al. recognize women's quest for self and
voice, for "a core self that remains responsive to situation and context," including affiliations with others (*Women's Ways of Knowing*
138). And, they add, women often gather the "essential wisdom" that
"they can strengthen themselves through the empowerment of others"
(47).

To explore the construct of empowerment in the experiences of the
thirty women in *Pacific Northwest Women*, we asked two questions:
How are these women empowered? What are the examples of
autonomy-based empowerment? of connection-based empowerment?
In our introductions to the texts and experiences of these and other
Pacific Northwest women, we include discussion of autonomy-based
and connection-based empowerment in their lives. Our interpretation
suggests, for instance, that Anna Maria Pittman Lee was empowered
by her autonomous decision to become a missionary *and* by close
bonds with her husband; Tabitha Brown's establishment of an
orphanage and school in Oregon was linked to her independent
resourcefulness *and* to the support she received from friends in
Oregon. The lives, memories, and writings of these and hundreds of
other Pacific Northwest women are rich resources for exploring the
significance of gender, race, class, and place in women's lives; for
discovering the themes that were central to their experiences; and for
testing the construct of autonomy-based and connection-based
empowerment.

Part I: Connecting With Nature

*Yet for me, the wilderness and the solitary place have been glad, and
Nature has not betrayed the heart that loved her.*
    Alice Day Pratt, *A Homesteader's Portfolio* (1922)

The women represented in the six
selections in Part I are diverse individuals who brought varying
degrees of aesthetic sensibility and intellectual curiosity to their
experiences of nature in the Pacific Northwest. What these women
have in common in their writings about nature, however, is the
overriding sense of being in accord, at peace with and happy in the
natural world.

For Emily Inez Denny and Caroline C. Leighton, the natural beauty
of the Pacific Northwest offers sensory and aesthetic pleasure; for
Frances Fuller Victor, the magnificence of untouched nature provides
a spiritual experience. Alice Day Pratt describes her affinity with
animals and the wilderness beauty of Central Oregon. For some,
nature's landscape offers solace and restoration; for all, the connection
with the natural world is powerful. In most of these writings, the
desire for preservation and conservation of the wilderness is implicit,
but we see these principles articulated most clearly by Ella Higginson
and in the stories of Able-One.

Able-One, who lived in what is now Northeastern Washington
before the overland migration began, is an appropriate woman to
open this section, and indeed this volume. Born in approximately
1815, Able-One was the daughter of a Colville chief, the only one of
his five children to live to adulthood. As such, she was strictly trained
for a life of service to her people.

Able-One, whose stories of childhood were recorded by her granddaughter Nancy Perkins Wynecoop, was taught that all things in
nature had purpose, utility, and meaning, and that nature's gifts
should not be taken for granted. Traditional rituals, in which both
women and men had appointed roles, assured an ongoing supply of
what was needed for sustenance; these necessities came from nature's
bounty, and were accepted with ceremonies of thanksgiving. The
Colville ethic of conservation also extended to the women's tradition
of gathering only fallen rather than felled wood for their fires.

In contrast, Emily Inez Denny's childhood memories of life in Puget Sound during the 1850s and '60s emphasize the sensory delights she experienced in nature. Similar in cadence to Dylan Thomas's "Fern Hill," Denny's nostalgic memoir stresses the romance and adventure of her idyllic youth, and the sheer beauty of the "virgin wilderness" where she romped to her heart's content with her friends and siblings.

One of the "first white children born on Puget Sound," Emily Inez Denny was the privileged daughter of one of Seattle's founding families. While privileged status for Able-One meant strict training and adherence to duty, for Denny it meant freedom, after her lessons and gardening chores were done, to play games on the beach or run down the hillsides with the wind whipping through her unbraided hair. In contrast with American Indian conservation practices, it is interesting to note the abandon with which the Denny children, imitating their elders, "hacked and chopped" through the woods with their "little hatchets," and Emily's fond memories of watching her grandfather make shingles from huge cedar trees cut for the purpose.

Emily Inez Denny's observations of Indians are generally sympathetic and well intentioned but, to a contemporary reader, they resonate with ethnocentrism. Denny's tales of a happy childhood spent "close to dear nature," in a new land on the brink of development, are filled with the enthusiasm and joy of youthful discovery and adventure.

Unlike Able-One and Emily Denny, who were born in the Pacific Northwest, Caroline C. Leighton was an adult when she came from Massachusetts to the Washington Territory in 1865. Leighton was immediately captivated by the aesthetic pleasures of her new sur-roundings, and she was receptive to learning the ways of its native people. Leighton had keen powers of observation, cultural sensitivity, and a decided talent for writing effective descriptive prose, all of which she brought to her new home.

During the sixteen years she lived on the Pacific Coast, Leighton kept journals of her many travels and observations, which she later refined and published in book form. Since Leighton thought of the land in relationship to its inhabitants, her writing includes both her observations of nature in the Pacific Northwest and sensitive, respect-ful renderings of Indians and their cultural practices. The selections we have chosen are dated between 1865 and 1873 from Port Angeles and Port Townsend, Washington Territory. The last, though written at Port Townsend, tells of a recently completed trip to Southwestern Oregon.

Frances Fuller Victor, another frequent traveler throughout the Pacific Northwest, was best known as a historian, but was also a "passionate lover" of nature's beauty. Victor also had a passion for truth, a prodigious intellectual curiosity, and a sense of adventure. Between 1865 and 1878, she traveled all over Oregon and Washington by steamer, train, stagecoach, "ambulance," and, if necessary, on foot, interviewing pioneers, collecting historical materials, geological and botanical specimens, and adventures to report in her writing. Her intellectual curiosity extended to the region's natural history, and any account she wrote of her travels contains background and factual data alongside her descriptive prose. One such account is her trip to Crater Lake in 1873, described in "A Font of the Gods." Although she had always loved and revered nature, something mystical occurred when she looked into the blue depths of the lake once called Lake Mystery. Victor movingly describes her soul's spiritual response upon experiencing such incomparable beauty.

Living creatures fed the spirit of Alice Day Pratt, a single dryland homesteader in Oregon during the early 1900s. Pratt's affinity with animals and the beauty of her homestead sustained her when she lacked human companionship. Pratt tells of how she fulfilled her dream of becoming a "creative farmer" with her own piece of soil on which to take "delight in all forms of nature life." In all that she did, Pratt practiced a conservation ethic, disturbing the land and animals as little as possible, always keeping in mind that the intruders—the spoilers—were human.

We conclude Part I with Ella Higginson's passionate appeal for appreciation and protection of the natural beauty and resources of the Pacific Northwest. At the time Higginson published her essay, over one hundred years ago, the development boom in the West was well advanced and the pristine wilderness was already slipping away. Higginson turns the fury of her pen on the invasion of Eastern transplants—men who sought to profit from exploitation of the West's resources, and "homesickly" women, blinded to the beauty of their surroundings, who spent their time complaining because there was no opera.

Through the words they left us, these six women share their individual perspectives and their relationships with nature, each unique and yet each, in her own way, connected with the natural world of the Pacific Northwest.

Nancy Perkins Wynecoop
1875-1939

In 1815, a number of years before the overland migration of white settlers to the Pacific Northwest, Able-One, the treasured daughter of Colville chief Withered-Top, was born in what is now known as Northeastern Washington. No document gives the exact date of her birth, but the story of Able-One's life was lovingly transcribed by her granddaughter, Nancy Perkins Wynecoop.

We were first introduced to Nancy Wynecoop and Able-One when we read Wynecoop's oral narrative in the first volume of *Told by the Pioneers*, the WPA collection published by the state of Washington in 1937. "I have to cry now as I recall those old days," Wynecoop said. "I didn't know those common every-day things would be history" (119). "My grandmother was my best teacher," Wynecoop recalled; it was Able-One who taught her that "the stars, the mountains, the trees and rocks all had a meaning" (117).

After reading Wynecoop's narrative of her Colville mother, white father, and grandmother Able-One, we searched for more information about the family. With the assistance of the Eastern Washington State Historical Society and the Spokane Tribal Council, we were placed in contact with Nettie (Janet) Beryl Wynecoop Clark, the youngest of Nancy Wynecoop's ten children. In several conversations with Nettie Clark, we learned more about the Wynecoop family, and she provided us with a copy of her mother's book *In the Stream: An Indian Story*, completed by Clark and privately published for family members in 1985. Clark has given permission to include selections from *In the Stream* in this volume, the first time they have been made available to a public audience. The selections published here are from Wynecoop's transcriptions of Able-One's childhood, and this introductory essay places Able-One within several generations of her family.

Able-One was a descendant of the Arrow Lake Indians of British Columbia and the daughter of Colville chief Withered-Top (Skie-Yaw-Teekin). Her mother's name is lost and she is referred to as "Mrs. Withered-Top." At an early age, Able-One was taught the history of her people. "By the time Able-One was seven years of age,"

Wynecoop wrote, "her mother had told her many things about the distant past. She began from the time they were a large tribe on their own hunting ground in the upper regions of the Columbia River" (*In the Stream* 16). Religious teachings were also a part of her training: "By the time Able-One was nine years old, the enveloping mystery of life here and hereafter was clearly outlined to her" (74).

The cultural prescriptions for gender roles were not always to Able-One's liking, but her mother reminded her of the importance of accepting her role as a woman. "Oh, mother," said the child, "I wish I were a man so I could steal my way into the heart of life and be filled by pure dew and clean air. Now I will never be anything but an unclean creature of burden." Her mother replied: "But, my daughter, your very discontent must be employed to teach you the true meaning of life and this is to obey and keep in the stream" (22).

In 1832, when Able-One was about seventeen, she became the wife of Shadow-Top (Kee-Kee-Tum-Nouskeen or Ske-out-kin, "tall man"), an adopted Colville who became a Colville chief and later worked as a successful fur trapper for the Hudson's Bay Company. Able-One had known Shadow-Top's first two wives, both of whom had died, and she had a deep love for this handsome leader of her people. Although Able-One was "small and slight of stature," she was "strong and willing" to assume leadership of the women, a role her mother had filled. Able-One bore six of Shadow-Top's children, one of whom was Helena, who became the mother of Nancy Perkins Wynecoop.

Able-One, Nancy's grandmother, clung to traditional ways but often lived with the Perkins family. "We might prevail upon her to sleep in the house during the winter, but as soon as spring came we would miss her," Wynecoop said. "We always knew then that she had set up her teepee not far away and would remain there until winter snows drove her in" (*Told by the Pioneers* 117). Wherever Grandmother Able-One chose to be, Nancy wanted to be at her side.

At age nineteen, five years after the death of Able-One, Nancy Perkins married John Curtis (Curt) Wynecoop, a widower who had first been married to Nancy's sister, Christine. Nancy and Curt Wynecoop had ten children, and also cared for Christine's and Curt's three children.

After Nancy Wynecoop became an adopted member of the Spokane tribe, the Wynecoops moved to reservation lands near the Spokane River. As an active member of the reservation community, Nancy Wynecoop was loved and respected as a nurse and midwife, served as an interpreter in the Presbyterian Church, and became a church elder.

Although Nancy Wynecoop's formal education was limited, she had an abiding desire to record the life and stories of Grandmother Able-One. Two house fires on the Spokane Reservation destroyed Wynecoop's first manuscripts. Nettie Clark recalled that a partially reconstructed manuscript was barely saved, along with Nettie's high school graduation gown, by Curt Wynecoop in a 1932 house fire (Interview, 18 October 1993). Clark wrote that her mother gave "any extra minutes" to rewriting; "to have the story finished and published was the dream of her heart" (*In the Stream* 102).

The last months of Wynecoop's life were marked by illness and pain, but she worked with her daughter Nettie to complete the manuscript. In early 1939, after difficult surgery, Nancy Wynecoop died. In 1985, Nettie Wynecoop Clark fulfilled her mother's wish and privately published the life and stories of Able-One.

The selections below were recorded by Nancy Perkins Wynecoop from Able-One's memories and are taken from Part I of *In the Stream*. Other sections of the book include "The Story-Telling Hour," Wynecoop's transcriptions of stories Able-One heard in her childhood; "Blue Water's Death and Able-One's Growth," written in part by Wynecoop and completed by Clark; and "The Life of Nancy, Able-One's Daughter," written by Clark. Throughout the book, a predominant theme is respect for and connection with nature.

THE SONG OF THE GENEROUS SUPPLY AND ABLE-ONE, MY GRANDMOTHER

The month of March 1815 found the winter quarters deserted and the upper tribes moving upstream while the lower tribes drifted down the river or up the valley streams. Each group had its own leader who was sympathetic and kind but stern and unyielding toward any wrong done in tribal relations. There were young people to give in marriage and train to leadership.

The training of the boys was given in strict confidence by the men in their own quarters. Just as soon as a boy was able to walk alone, he drew away from his mother and any feminine associates, to be literally absorbed into manhood.

The shore line was full of tepees. The families had grouped together, and Withered-Top sat in the long council house and drew all men about him in a late but very necessary council.

The birth of Able-One took place beside a bathing pool warmed by hot stones. Here she had been washed and oiled, wrapped in soft skins well padded with the down of the cattail which every mother kept in a skin bag, and placed in her place on the pillow.

When the news of her birth reached her father, Withered-Top, he answered, "A new hand for her mother, for she will strengthen and increase the supply as well as comfort and cheer our hearts. A son-in-law will sustain like a son but a son is often ruled by a strange woman. Her name shall be Able-One for she covers the space of four children; a sprout of a weakened tribe and my last growth."

There was one thing that must be done by the women at this time, before life started in tree or plant. There must be an invitation demonstration. A sweet and solemn invitation to nature for a generous fruitage. There was no set time for this demonstration, so the day after Able-One was born her mother was thrilled by the Song of the Generous Supply.

The news had been given the day before that a fine dry tree had blown down and this meant wood for all. The high wind was a friend of women for it crushed the trees into small pieces. The women took their straps and started before dawn cast its gleam upon the eastern sky. They had filed up the hill where snow and mud lay frozen. The crumbled tree was about halfway up that long hill. Movable parts of the tree were soon carried down to the campground. By ten o'clock, according to our time, the carriers had gone back to gather the last bits of wood. When one gathered an armful of burrs, she sprang upon the log that was adamant against their puny implements and bare hands. Here she began the Song of Fruitage that swayed and thrilled every woman and girl within hearing distance of her pleading voice. She stroked the burrs saying, "This is the wish of our womanhood. Let the bough bend with fruit and the ground heave up with roots." Then, stooping, she tore a section of bark from the log and waved it back and forth as she sang, "That our bark baskets may overflow and the supplies might flow through our hands." Leaping from the log she swayed into a dancing walk that the other women imitated to the best of their ability, unity being necessary to insure a definite purpose.

In twenty minutes that toiling, sweating and struggling mass of human services became a bounding stream of action, propelled by one desire and motive. Every act was a sign that interpreted a vast meaning which was to capture nature in its most tender age and bind their hopes into its growth. Their message of invitation must be spread before the Gods that govern growth. Their request was launched at the beginning of the time of flowing sap and would be sent through the grass and vegetation until it ended in the empty cone of next year. All the parts were rehearsed time and again as their slowing ranks moved over the crest of the hill, each holding high a pine cone as a symbol of fruitage and a piece of bark to represent baskets for filling.

My great-grandmother, being in isolation, could not take part in the ceremony but, as the wife of the Chief, she must give her consent and signs. Her first act was to take the sign of purity and cleansing by plunging her hands into a pile of ashes kept for all such purposes, pouring it on her arms and rubbing it in. Then, taking her wee daughter from the pillow, she stepped out of her small tepee and walked swiftly to the storehouse where her root digger fashioned from deer antlers was stored in a rawhide case that dangled from a high beam. She moved to a place beside the deep path down which the dancers were passing. Swinging her baby, laced in a snug little sack, she lifted her digger high into the air. This meant a full-hearted wish for plenty of camas and roots. Then, shaking her arm vigorously, as in intercession for strength, she stepped with a quick stride that was to show her willingness to gather that which the Spirits might give. She pressed her child

to her bosom, a sign of careful guardianship over life and strength
and the willingness to make a shelter for her loved ones. Slowly
turning she glanced down the line of tepees where other women
were in retreat. Not a one was in sight, for they were each true to
her sisters.

She lifted her eyes to the hills where the Spirits dwelt and prayed
that her unclean state might not blight the coming crop or diminish the strength of the harvesters. Going into her tepee she placed
the baby on her pillow and passed the horn digger through the
small blaze, following it with her hands. Then, gripping the handle
with her purged hands she came back and placed it in the case,
awaiting the day when roots were ready to be pried from the
ground.

On went the dancers, from camp to camp until every woman
and girl had joined the wide circle that beat in exact step around
the encampment. This dancing commenced about ten o'clock in
the morning, and as the sun sank behind the steep western hill
they were called to the one meal of the day.

As the last rays crept up the gentle eastern slope, they quietly
gathered in the central opening where the men had built a bonfire
and spread green boughs on the chilly ground. They were served
by the men in designation of cooperation, and only the ones who
had been cleansed by the sweatbath were allowed to come near
the sacred food which the season annually supplied. The beautiful
salmon trout which had been impaled on green stakes and roasted
beside the open fire were taken by the men and placed on the
ground before the women who helped themselves by taking what
they wanted on their piece of bark. This meal lasted until every
part had been eaten and the bones were carefully placed on their
plates of bark. They arose as one body, and piling the boughs on
their arms they placed the bark, bones and roasting spits on top
and in one move carried them to the fires to be burned. The women
withdrew while the men painstakingly burned every token of the
day's worship. They left no remains for blight to use in working
its evil spell into their hopes, and they stayed up all night to keep
the fire and watch.

The early rays of the morning sun disclosed a combed and swept
central court, and the men drew away to their own ground where
those who had been unfit for the ceremony had roaring fires burning over red-hot stones. After cleansing and subduing the flesh
with the sweatbath, they wrapped themselves in their fur robes
and lay down beside the fire to sleep until they were refreshed.

The women had left at daybreak to make the short journey across the Low Pass into the Kettle Valley where they built the fires to use in preparing the next catch of salmon.

By noon the able-bodied men had filed over the divide into the valley where the great fish traps were filling with the trout that were schooling upstream. The huge fires were ready and awaiting the landing of the trap's catch and the slaughter of the fish. They were cleaned and dressed, the remains being thrown back into the water as food for the living fish. The heavy willow mats were thoroughly washed after the cleaned meat was packed into coarse grass bags, to be carried across country to the camps on the Columbia River. As soon as a load was ready one of the women would place her straps around it and, swinging it up onto her back, she would take the winding path which led over the rugged pass. The fish were strung on willow boughs and carried slung across the broad shoulders of the tired men. They took the straight and more difficult path but reached camp ahead of the women. Their supplies would be cooked and ready for them by the time they had taken their daily sweatbath.

There were women who kept the fires burning while those in retreat carried wood for the daily usage. They arranged this wood ready for the early morning baths, when the women did their washing in rock-lined pools beside the river.

This meal differed from the simple one of the day before. In every tepee there stood a soup basket, bubbling and steaming a safe distance from the fire. The cooking heat was supplied by hot rocks replacing cooled ones in these baskets. When the fish came there were generous portions placed around the fire. Fresh rabbits, groundhogs and pheasants were brought by the boys to give variety to the meal. These were all trussed on green sticks and stuck into the ground around the bright fire, completing the warm welcome for the weary fishers, hunters and camp wranglers.

When the men entered their homes, a place was cleared at their end of the tepee, and clean mats were placed where they might sit or recline. The women removed their soiled work dresses and donned the soft buckskin in readiness of serving their men. Hot soup was served first, in horn bowls with accompanying horn spoons. The meat spits were placed where all might reach them to serve themselves. In the grass baskets were seen piles of nut and fruit cakes and a clean basket of cool water completed this fare. There were no condiments to tickle the palate nor stimulants to create a thirst. Food was eaten only to satisfy hunger. With the deep sleep that comes from a busy outdoor life and its usual sweatbath they were refreshed. These people lived only to sustain the spirit and to do nothing which might offend or hinder its timely assistance.

Able-One was cradled in this environment. Because of the staggering loss of innumerable children near her age, she was doomed to be spoiled by her saddened parents, or else to be abnormally trained. Her position and name would indicate the latter. Her first summer was spent on her mother's back as they ranged the hills and valleys in search of the various kinds of food. Often swinging from a limb she smiled at her mother as she dug roots or gathered berries and nuts. Mrs. Withered-Top was an active woman and led all the others by gentle example in fidelity, cleanliness and punctuality. This latter virtue meant more in those far-away days than it does now because the meat must be jerked and all food must be saved at the right time, there being no salt or sugar preservatives known. The food must be saved through the processes of fire and sun-drying.

Able-One was her mother's constant companion in those days, and as she grew, her tiny strength was joyfully given in service for the good of the tribe. She was lovingly included in the hardiest games and ceremonial practices among girls older than herself. Thus she was projected into the stern realities of their strict tribal government, while her years would have forced her into the kindergarten of today's educational program.

ABLE-ONE WAS AFRAID

Fear was one thing that would remove anyone from the class race. Able-One, at 5 years of age, was afraid of water and she refused to swim; everyone knew it was time she came out of this pocket. The years were passing, and this trouble might weaken the fiber of her whole nature. Water seemed the essence of life, and she had turned away from this one friend of the tribe. It supplied food in its surging tide, while it seeped life into growth along its banks, cooled the heat of the day, quenched the fire, and cleansed the body. Its courses were the highways of man, and in time of danger there was escape by paddle and stream. Yet here was a daughter who would not venture out of her own depth or trust herself to a teacher. Her mother tried to explain, but the little girl only wept. No harmony could ever come to a coward; one must master fear or be cramped and hampered through life. To fear water was like being afraid of a good friend. Fear can be noble only when it aids you to escape an enemy or a deadly thing.

One day Able-One followed her mother to where some men were gathering a special variety of fish that schooled at the foot of a waterfall in a deep gorge. They crowded in an eddy in the center of the stream. A long swinging platform was slung from heavy cable made of plaited willow withes, interwoven with cross slats to make a ladder approach. A man stood on the platform, speared the fish with a wooden grabhook and passed it to another who took it off. The fish was then sent on from man to man until it finally was placed on clean grass mats at the top of the cliff. Here the women came for them and carried them to fresh mats where they were cleaned and strung on grass switches and drying frames to slowly bake and dry in the sun or by a low fire. These fish were liked for the rich oily soup they provided in the winter. Able-One watched and helped wherever a child was allowed.

Following her mother today, they went farther and gazed at the mid-stream scene and watched the flashing fish wiggle from hand to hand as the men posed on the web-like structure with ease and confidence, unmindful of the swirling waters easing off in a pool below them. Even if one should fall he would take but a short time to swim ashore and go back to work or be replaced by another. There was enough danger to make this method of fishing a real sport and test of endurance. Like all other such tasks these men went first through the regular purification and strict isolation. No women were allowed to touch or even go near this trap while the fish ran. Now the season had just begun and it seemed to promise a good catch.

Mrs. Withered-Top was preoccupied and often sighed as they tramped back to the nearby camps and swiftly slung the load of fish over the fire. On the return trip she seemed to come to a different decision as she dried her hands with apparent determination and went to the side of her husband, the Chief. As he watched her approach, he gathered himself for words that would send him far afield for an answer. This wife was true and interesting but often broke rules because she was his wife and he was the Chief. Yet deep in his soul he confessed that she ruled because she was able to see through the binding customs and often hurdled across the bars to save a life. It seemed proper and fitting to ask a favor that may upset the painstaking preparation for a season of abundant fish. "Now what, my wife?" he asked as she came up to him.

"I want to borrow your swinging platform for one night," she answered. "Able-One must sleep there to seek a release from her fear of the water."

A long silence ensued before he spoke. "I shall make it possible. Go make yourselves clean and ask the fish not to forsake us. We shall intercede for a full catch but we have kept the rule in the women's departments, as you ought to know. Otherwise the fish would have hid away from the unclean men."

Wise woman, ever ready to snatch a boon for womanhood and a new lesson. Able-One shivered inside but knew she must pass this test or die. She seemed to be wrapped in a close and tight binding. She found it hard to breathe, a hard lump was in her throat as she made the many circles of the Prairie Chicken Dance to cause a free perspiration. She took a dip in the stream and a slow turn before the fire before dressing again. She must go to her bed before the sun set if she would have light to find her way. She followed her mother down the ladder and onto the platform. As her mother went back she removed a number of cross bars to make sure that her small daughter must stay in the middle of the stream. A chilling terror held Able-One as her mother walked out of sight on the dry land. She clung to the swaying bed, closed her eyes and moaned. Her mind recalled the carefree men she had seen earlier in the day and she was somewhat comforted. Soon the singing water caught her attention. There seemed to be laughing notes in the powerful surge and roar of glad water. She found a fine reason for her mother's scheme in bringing her in close embrace with this strange fear, and she was determined to overcome it.

Hours were mingled with the old terror that seemed to drag her to the edge of her bed and threatened to cast her into the thundering stream and squeeze the life from her. She slept and dreamed that she was thrown from the platform by a power outside herself, and not being able to swim she went to the bottom. She could feel the cool water singing around her and the fish swarmed close to her asking why she was afraid. She was thrown to her knees and pushed to the bottom of the stream where bubbling shellfish and crawfish murmured reproaches at her fear of the water. "Look at me," said a large shellfish. "I do not swim and I live in the heart of the water." Able-One fearlessly asked the teeming creatures what she would do if she fell into the river while she was still unable to swim. "Do as I do," said the shellfish. "Go to the bottom and walk out." No answer came from the other creatures though she listened intently.

She heard a pebble rattle in the water and as she uncovered her head she saw her mother coming to her in the dark gray of dawn. Quickly the cross bars were replaced and she soon crouched beside the little girl, looking fondly into the calm and happy face. "Come away, my child," she whispered, "before the fishermen come. They have kept vigil the whole night to aid you in your quest, and they have decided that if the fish are offended and shy away it will not matter. It has been worth the effort to cure you of this fear of water."

They soon gained the rocky ridge and met the still-faced men. Shadow-Top was in the lead. Mrs. Withered-Top and Able-One drew away from the narrow path and stood still while the men passed by. The leader looked into the child's eyes and read the calm and gentle peace that rested in her small face. He was satisfied that his adopted people were wise in their methods of training the children.

Emily Inez Denny
1853-1918

Emily Inez Denny loved the
Pacific Northwest; she wrote about it in prose and poetry descriptions,
often illustrated with her drawings and paintings. She was a keen
observer of nature with artistic ability, knowledgeable in the areas of
geology, botany, and local history. These attributes, combined with
her gift for colorful descriptive writing, enabled her to make a significant contribution to Northwest literature.

Denny's book, *Blazing the Way, or, True stories, songs and
sketches of Puget Sound and other pioneers*, was copyrighted in 1899
and first published in 1909 by the Rainier Printing Company, Inc., of
Seattle. In this book, Denny gathered together the "thrice-told tales of
parents and friends who had crossed the plains" and added her own
personal recollections of "over fifty years in the Northwest, acknowl-
edging also the good fortune of having been one of the first white
children born on Puget Sound" (8).

The pioneering families of whom Denny wrote developed lasting
friendships with the Indians of Puget Sound, who are depicted sympathetically, if somewhat patronizingly, in her recollections. Denny
wrote of the experiences of women and children, often neglected in
works of this era, and also provided illustrations for her book.

Blazing the Way was reprinted in 1984 by the Seattle/King County
Historical Society with an introduction by Susan J. Torntore. Our
page references are to the 1984 reprint of the text, but there are no
page numbers for Torntore's introduction to which we are largely
indebted for Denny's biographical information.

Emily Inez Denny wrote little about herself. As Torntore points out,
what is known comes from "scattered fragments recorded in *Blazing
the Way*," a "handwritten memoir of 1915 titled 'Concerning the
Development of Art in Seattle, Reminiscences' by E. I. Denny," her
creative works, and newspaper clippings (introduction).

Emily Inez, the oldest child of David T. and Louisa Boren Denny,
was born December 23, 1853—"the first white girl born in Seattle"
(introduction). Her parents were unmarried when they crossed the
plains with their families in the same wagon train. David accompanied
his father and mother, John and Sarah Latimer Denny, his brothers,

sisters, nieces, and nephews. Louisa Boren was the only unmarried woman in the party; she came west with her brother, C. D., and his wife and daughter. One of David's brothers, Arthur Denny, had married Louisa's sister, Mary. Emily wrote that the two families left "Cherry Grove, Knox County, Illinois, on April 10th, 1851," in four "prairie schooners" (20).

The Denny and Boren pioneers landed at Alki Point in November 1851. Louisa Boren and David Denny were married on January 23, 1853; Emily Inez was the first child of a family which eventually included three sons and four daughters.

Emily's grandfather, John Denny, settled on a farm in Marion County, Oregon, until 1859, when he joined his sons in Seattle. His sons, Arthur and David, took claims on Elliott Bay and were significant figures in early Seattle. Emily recalled that Arthur "represented the territory as delegate in congress and served several terms in the Territorial Legislature," while David "held many responsible public positions, including Probate Judge and Regent of the [Territorial] University" (187).

Emily Inez Denny came from a prominent family and enjoyed a privileged childhood. These are factors which may have cast a rosy hue on her memories of childhood. Her mother had been a school-teacher before coming west, and Emily's education began at home. In

1861, at age eight, she attended preparatory classes for school-age children at the Territorial University. Torntore noted that, as Emily Inez grew older, "she penned compositions, memorized 'pieces,' delivered orations, and studied physical geography, natural history, botany, and geology."

As a child, Emily Inez expressed a desire to study art but, as no teacher was available, she sketched on her own until she had the opportunity to take her first formal drawing lessons from Miss Parsons in Seattle. She later studied with T. A. Harrison, a local landscape painter, and Harriet Foster Beecher, a California artist. Encouraged by her family, Denny carried notebooks everywhere, sketching and painting incessantly. She always delighted in nature, and painting, sketching, and writing provided her with creative outlets for the rest of her life. Susan Torntore says, "Her landscapes varied from expansive views of the Cascades, Olympics, and Puget Sound to limited views of favorite forest groves rich with foreground detail."

She also wrote for several periodicals including *Northwest Magazine* and the *Washington Historian*. Denny was a member of many Seattle groups interested in history and writing, such as the Classic Culture Club, the Washington Pioneer Association, the Scribes, and the Women's Century Club. She was appointed in 1899 to a committee of the Washington State Federation of Women's Clubs, which was dedicated to collecting and preserving the history and relics of Washington State.

Emily Inez Denny never married. Her father lost his fortune in 1894, in the great recession, and she remained devoted to him until his death in 1903. She then cared for her mother, who died in 1916. Two years later, on August 23, 1918, Denny herself died of Bright's disease, at sixty-five years of age.

The following excerpts from Chapter VIII of *Blazing the Way* provide Denny's remembrances of an idyllic childhood spent with a loving extended family. In this chapter, she writes in the first person, and her prose is at its most vivid and lyrical as she takes the reader on an exploration of the sensory delights she experienced in the "virgin wilderness" of her youth—the beautiful surroundings, the flowers and animals of her beloved Puget Sound, where she was born, lived her life, and died.

We Lived Close to Dear Nature

The very thought of it makes the blood tingle and the heart leap. No element was wanting for romance or adventure. Indians, bears, panthers, far journeys, in canoes or on horseback, fording rivers, camping and tramping, and all in a virgin wilderness so full of grandeur and loveliness that even very little children were impressed by the appearance thereof. The strangeness and newness of it all was hardly understood by the native white children as they had no means of comparing this region and mode of life with other countries and customs.

Traditions did not trouble us; the Indians were generally friendly, the bears were only black ones and ran away from us as fast as their furry legs would carry them; the panthers did not care to eat us up, we felt assured, while there was plenty of venison to be had by stalking, and on a journey we rode safely, either on the pommel of father's saddle or behind mother's, clinging like small kittens or cockleburs.

Familiarity with the coquettish canoe made us perfectly at home with it, and in later years when the tenderfoot arrived, we were convulsed with inextinguishable laughter at what seemed to us an unreasoning terror of a harmless craft.

Ah! we lived close to dear nature then! Our play-grounds were the brown beaches or the hillsides covered with plumy young fir trees, the alder groves or the slashings where we hacked and chopped with our little hatchets in imitation of our elders or the Father of His Country and namesake of our state. . . .

When the frolicsome Chinook wind came singing across the Sound, the boys flew home built kites of more or less ambitious proportions and the little girls ran down the hills, performing a peculiar skirt dance by taking the gown by the hem on either side and turning the skirt half over the head. Facing the wind it assumed a baloonlike [sic] inflation very pleasing to the small performer. It was thought the proper thing to let the hair out of net or braids at the time, as the sensation of air permeating long locks was sufficient excuse for its "weirdness" as I suppose we would have politely termed it had we ever heard the word. Instead we were more likely to be reproved for having such untidy heads and perhaps reminded that we looked as wild as Indians.

"As wild as Indians," the poor Indians! How they admired the native white children! Without ceremony they claimed blood brotherhood, saying, "You were born in our 'illahee' (country) and are our 'tillicum' (people). You eat the same food, will grow up here and belong to us."

Often we were sung to sleep at night by their "tamanuse" singing, as we lived quite near the bank below which many Indians camped, on Elliott Bay. . . .

We were seldom panic stricken; born amid dangers there seemed nothing novel about them and we took our environment as a matter of course. We were taught to be courageous but not foolhardy, which may account for our not getting oftener in trouble.

The boys learned to shoot and shoot well at an early age, first with shot guns, then rifles. Sometimes the girls proved dangerous with firearms in their hands. A sister of the writer learned to shoot off the head of a grouse at long range. A girl schoolmate, when scarcely grown, shot and killed a bear. . . .

The wild flowers and the birds interested us deeply and every spring we joyfully noted the returning bluebirds and robins, the migrating wren and a number of other charming feathered friends. The high banks, not then demolished by grades, were smothered in greenery and hung with banners of bloom every succeeding season.

We clambered up and down the steep places gathering armfuls of lillies (trillium), red currant (ribes sanguineum), Indian-arrow-wood (spiraea), snowy syringa (philadelphus) and blue forgetmenots and the yellow blossoms of the Oregon grape (berberis glumacea and aquifolium), which we munched with satisfaction for the *soursweet*, and the scarlet honeysuckle to bite off the honeyglands for a like purpose.

The salmonberry and blackberry seasons were quite delightful. To plunge into the thick jungle, now traversed by Pike Street, Seattle, was a great treat. There blackberries attained Brobdignagian hugeness, rich and delicious.

On a Saturday, our favorite reward for lessons and work well done, was to be allowed to go down the lovely beach with its wide strip of variegated shingle and bands of brown, ribbed sand, as far as the "three big stones," no farther, as there were bears, panthers and Indians, as hereinbefore stated, inhabiting the regions round about.

One brilliant April day we felt very brave, we were bigger than ever before, five was quite a party, and the flowers were O! so enchanting a little farther on. Two of us climbed the bank to gather the tempting blossoms.

Our little dog, "Watch," a very intelligent animal, took the lead; scarcely had we gained the top and essayed to break the branch of a wild currant, gay with rose colored blossoms, when Watch showed unusual excitement about something, a mysterious something occupying the cavernous depths of an immense hollow log. With his bristles up, rage and terror in every quivering muscle, he was slowly, very slowly, backing toward us.

Although in the woods often, we had never seen him act so before. We took the hint and to our heels, tumbled down the yielding, yellow bank in an exceedingly hasty and unceremonious manner, gathered up our party of thoroughly frightened youngsters and hurried along the sand homeward, at a double quick pace. . . .

Not many days after the young truants were invited down to an Indian camp to see the carcass of a cougar about nine feet long. There it lay, stretched out full length, its hard, white teeth visible beyond the shrunken lips, its huge paws quite helpless and harmless.

It is more than probable that this was the "something" in the great hollow log, as it was killed in the vicinity of the place where our stampede occurred. . . .

The shadow of danger always lurked about the undetermined boundary of our playgrounds, wild animals and wild men might be not far beyond.

We feared the drunken white man more than the sober Indian, with much greater reason. Even the drunken Indian never molested us, but usually ran "amuck" among the inhabitants of the beach. . . .

The nearest Indian graveyard was on a hill at the foot of Spring Street, Seattle. It sloped directly down to the beach; the bodies were placed in shallow graves to the very brow and down over the face of the sandy bluff. All this hill was dug down when the town advanced.

The childrens' graves were especially pathetic, with their rude shelters, to keep off the rain of the long winter months, and upright poles bearing bits of bright colored cloth, tin pails and baskets.

Over these poor graves no costly monuments stood, only the winds sang wild songs there, the seagulls flitted over, the fair, wild flowers bloomed and the dark-eyed Indian mothers tarried sometimes, human as others in their sorrow.

But the light-hearted Indian girls wandered past, hand in hand, singing as they went, pausing to turn bright friendly eyes upon me as they answered the white child's question, "Ka mika klatawa?" (Where are you going?)

"O, kopa yawa" (O, over yonder), nodding toward the winding road that stretched along the green bank before them. Without a care of sorrow, living a healthy, free, untrammeled life, they looked the impersonation of native contentment. . . .

For recreation, we went with father in the wagon over the "bumpy" road when he went to haul wood, or perhaps a long way on the county road to the meadow, begging to get off to gather flowers whenever we saw them peeping from their green bowers.

Driving along through the great forest which stood an almost solid green wall on either hand, we called "O father, stop! stop; here is the lady-slipper place."

"Well, be quick, I can't wait long."

Dropping down to the ground, we ran as fast as our feet could carry us to gather the lovely, fragrant orchid, Calypso Borealis, from its mossy bed.

When the ferns were fully grown, eight or ten feet high, the little girls broke down as many as they could drag, and ran along the road, great ladies, with long green trains!

We found the way to the opening in the woods, where in the midst thereof, grandfather sat making cedar shingles with a drawing knife. Huge trees lay on the ground, piles of bolts had been cut and the heap of shingles, clear and straight of the very best quality, grew apace.

Very tall and grand the firs and cedars stood all around, like stately pillars with a dome of blue sky above; the birds sang in the underbrush and the brown butterflies floated by. . . .

So the happy pioneer children roamed the forest fearlessly and sat on the vines and moss under the great trees, often making bonnets of the shining salal leaves pinned together with rose thorns or tiny twigs, making whistles of alder, which gave forth sweet and pleasant sounds if successfully made; or in the garden making dolls of hollyhocks, mallows and morning glories.

Caroline C. Leighton
1838-?

After forty-two days of passage from the Atlantic Coast to San Francisco and surviving a shipwreck, Caroline C. Leighton and her family arrived at Port Angeles, Washington Territory, on July 18, 1865, a time when Seattle was but a small village. At her first sight of Port Angeles, Leighton described it as "the loveliest place" she had ever seen. The Leightons remained on the Pacific Coast until 1881.

In *Life at Puget Sound with Sketches of Travel in Washington Territory, British Columbia, Oregon and California, 1865-1881,* first published in 1883, Caroline Leighton described a life that was a marked contrast to her earlier years in New England. She made detailed journal entries about the flora and fauna, cultural practices, and indigenous peoples of the region. *Life at Puget Sound* reflected the sensitive nature of a poet in combination with the trained eye of an amateur botanist and the thick description of a cultural anthropologist. Her observations in this region provided an introduction to the area for those who were curious about the Pacific Northwest, but had never seen it.

Relatively little is known about the woman who wrote *Life at Puget Sound.* Leighton gave little autobiographical information in her journal entries in *Life at Puget Sound.* She referred, for example, to her husband only as "R," and she hardly mentioned the two babies, both daughters, who accompanied them on travels in the Pacific Northwest. Glen Adams of Ye Galleon Press in Fairfield, Washington, found that "Caroline Leighton was very difficult to research" ("A Lady Travels Our Region" 34).

What we do know is that Caroline C. Leighton was born in 1838 and came from Massachusetts. The "R" for her husband stood for Rufus Leighton, who was born in 1834 and grew up in Boston. Beginning in 1861, Rufus Leighton served on the East Coast as a customs agent for the United States Treasury Department, and he was appointed customs agent in Washington Territory in 1865 (Adams 34). He was paid from six to eight dollars a day by the Treasury Department, but he only worked when he was given a specific assignment (Adams 37). Rufus Leighton's work took him far into

Washington Territory, into Oregon, and even into British Columbia with Caroline as his companion.

Evidently, there were problems in government service, and Rufus Leighton resigned from his post, effective December 31, 1874. He asked for reinstatement but, when none was granted, he sailed with his family for California in March of 1875. Caroline Leighton did not discuss her husband's work in her published journal, but her entry for March 20, 1875, was written from San Francisco: "We reached here last night, after a rough voyage from Puget Sound" (*Life at Puget Sound* 182). The last four chapters of her book described scenes and experiences in California.

The Leightons left California about 1881. *Life at Puget Sound* was published in 1883, by Lee and Shepard of Boston, and in 1884, by Charles T. Dillingham of New York. Caroline Leighton's second work, *A Swiss Thoreau: Henry Frederick Amiel*, was published in 1890, as a thirty-page booklet. Henri Frederic Amiel (1821-1881) was a Swiss writer, and his *Journal intime*, which he maintained from 1847 until his death, has been described as a masterpiece of self-analysis. *Intimations of Eternal Life*, her third work, published by Lee and Shepard in 1891, was reviewed in *Popular Science* in January of 1892.

The excerpts below, which we have titled "A Fit Home for the Gods," are taken from Caroline C. Leighton's *Life at Puget Sound*. The three pieces—journal entries from 1865, 1869, and 1873—are examples of her descriptive prose and provide a sense of her intellectual curiosity, her keen and sensitive skills as an observer of nature, her empathy with and respect for indigenous peoples, and her poetic nature.

A FIT HOME FOR THE GODS

❈

Port Angeles, Washington Territory, July 20, 1865.

We reached here day before yesterday, very early in the morning. We were called to the forward deck; and before us was a dark sea-wall of mountains, with misty ravines and silver peaks,—the Olympic Range, a fit home for the gods.

A fine blue veil hung over the water, between us and the shore; and, the air being too heavy for the smoke of the Indian village to rise, it lay in great curved lines, like dim, rainbow-colored serpents, over sea and land.

I thought it was the loveliest place I had ever seen. The old Spanish explorers must have thought so too, as they named it "Port of the Angels."

We found that the path to our house was an Indian trail, winding about a mile up the bluff from the beach; the trees shutting overhead, and all about us a drooping white spirea, a most bridal-looking flower. Here and there, on some precipitous bank, was the red Indian-flame. Every once in a while, we came to a little opening looking down upon the sea; and the sound of it was always in our ears. At last we reached a partially cleared space, and there stood the house; behind it a mountain range, with snow filling all the ravines, and, below, the fulness and prime of summer. We are nearly at the foot of the hills, which send us down their snow-winds night and morning, and their ice-cold water. Between us and them are the fir-trees, two hundred and fifty and three hundred feet high; and all around, in the burnt land, a wilderness of bloom,—the purple fireweed, that grows taller than our heads, and in the richest luxuriance, of the same color as the Alpine rose,—a beautiful foreground for snowy hills.

The house is not ready for us. We are obliged at present, for want of a chimney, to stop with our nearest neighbor. But we pay it frequent visits. Yesterday, as we sat there, we received a call from two Indians, in extreme undress. They walked in with perfect freedom, and sat down on the floor. We shall endeavor to procure from Victoria [B.C.] a dictionary of the Haidah, Chinook, and other Indian languages, by the aid of which we shall be able to receive such visitors in a more satisfactory manner. At present, we can only smile very much at them.

Port Townsend, Washington Territory, April 4, 1869.
This afternoon we rode past the grave-yard of the Indians on the beach. It is a picturesque spot, as most of their burial-places are. They like to select them where land and water meet. A very old woman, wrapped in a green blanket, was digging clams with her paddle in the sand. She was one of those stiff old Indians, whom we occasionally see, who do not speak the Chinook at all, and take no notice whatever of the whites. I never feel as if they even

see me when I am with them. They seem always in a deep dream. Her youth must have been long before any white people came to the country. When she dies, her body will be wrapped in the tattered green blanket, and laid here, with her paddle, her only possession, stuck up beside her in the sand.

We saw two Indians busy at one of the little huts that cover the graves. They were nailing a new red covering over it. We asked them if a chief was dead. A *kloochman* [woman] we had not noticed before looked up, and said mournfully, "no," it was her "little woman." I saw that she had before her, on the sand, a number of little bright toys,—a doll wrapped in calico, a musical ball, a looking-glass, a package of candy and one of cakes, a bright tin pail full of sirup, and two large sacks, one of bread, and the other of apples.

Another and older woman was picking up driftwood, and arranging it for a fire. When the men had finished their work at the hut, they came and helped her. They laid it very carefully, with a great many openings, and level on the top, and lighted it.

Then the grandmother brought a little purple woollen shawl, and gave it to the old man. He held it out as far as his arm could reach, and waved it, and apparently called to the spirit of the child to come and receive it; and he then cast it into the fire. He spoke in the old Indian language, which they do not use in talking with us. It sounded very strange and thrilling. Each little toy they handled with great care before putting it into the flames. After they had burned up the bread and the apples, they poured on some sugar, and smothered the flames, making a dense column of smoke.

Then they all moved a little farther back, and motioned us to also. We wondered they had tolerated us so long, as they dislike being observed; but they seemed to feel that we sympathized with them. The old man staid nearest. He lay down on the sand, half hidden by a wrecked tree. He stripped his arms and legs bare, and pulled his hair all up to the top of his head, and knotted it in a curious way, so that it nodded in a shaggy tuft over his forehead. Then he lay motionless, looking at the fire, once in a while turning and saying something to the women, apparently about the child, as I several times distinguished the word *tenas-tenas* (the little one). I thought perhaps he might be describing her coming and taking the things. At times he became very animated. They did not stir, only answered with a kind of mournful "Ah—ah," to every thing he said.

At last their little dog bounded forward, as if to meet some one. At that, they were very much excited and pleased, and motioned us to go farther off still, as if it were too sacrilegious for us to stay there. They all turned away but the old man, and he began to move in a stealthy way towards the fire. All the clumsiness and weight of a man seemed to be gone. He was as light and wiry as a snake, and glided round the old drift that strewed the sand, with his body prostrate, but his head held erect and his bright eyes fixed on the fire, like some wild desert creature, which he appeared to counterfeit. The Indians think, that, by assuming the shape of any creature, they can acquire something of its power. When he had nearly reached the fire, he sprang up, and caught something from it. I could not tell whether it was real or imaginary. He held it up to his breast, and appeared to caress it, and try to twine it about his neck. I thought at first it was a coal of fire; perhaps it was smoke. Three times he leaped nearly into the flames in this way, and darted at something which he apparently tried to seize. Then he seemed to assure the others that he had accomplished his purpose; and they all went immediately off, without looking back.

[Port Townsend, Washington Territory] July 1, 1873.
We have just returned from a long, rough journey in southern and western Oregon. We crossed the Coast Range of mountains,— not so high and snow-capped as the Cascades, but beautiful to watch in their variations of light and shade, always the shadows of clouds traveling over them, and mists stealing up through the dark ravines. A Dutchwoman—our fellow passenger—was in ecstasies, exclaiming continually: "How beautiful is the land here! How *bracht* [bright]!"—noticing all the sunlighted places; but I was more attracted by the shadows. I heard another hard-looking woman say to a man, that she cried when she saw the hills, they were so beautiful. There was a deep welcome in them; something human and responsive seemed to fill the stillness. . . .

We crossed the mountain range through a cañon. The road wound round and round the sides of it, sometimes so narrow that it seemed hardly more than an Indian trail. We had a true California driver, who shouted out to us every few minutes, to hold on tight, or all to get together on one side, or something equally suspicious; but dashed on without any regard to danger. We were in constant expectation of being hurled to the bottom; but it quickened our senses to enjoy the beauty about us, to feel that any moment might be our last. . . .

We spent one night in a myrtle-grove. The trees leaned gracefully together, and the whole grove for miles was made of beautiful arched aisles. Coming from our shaggy firs, and the rough undergrowth that is always beneath them, to these smooth, glossy leaves, and clear, open spaces of fine grass, was like entering fairy-land, or the "good green wood" of the ballads. I looked for princes and lovers wandering among them, and felt quite transformed myself. The driver I regarded as a different man from that moment; to think that he should show so much good taste as to draw up for the night in that lovely place. . . .

One day we were accompanied quite a distance through the woods by a female chief, Yaquina. I think that she is a celebrated woman in Oregon, and that Yaquina Bay was named for her. She was mounted on a little pony, and riding along in a free and joyous way, looking about at the green leaves and the sunshine. I thought of Victoria with her heavy crown, that gives her the sick headache, and wondered how she would like to exchange with her.

Frances Auretta Fuller Victor
1826-1902

"**I** am a child of Nature," Frances Fuller Victor wrote in 1873. Victor, who was memorialized by the Portland *Oregonian* as "the Clio of the Northwest," and has also been called "the Mother of Oregon History," was reporting on her journey from Portland to Southern Oregon, and across the Cascade Range to Crater Lake. Her report, "Letter from Mrs. Victor," was published in Abigail Scott Duniway's Portland weekly, the *New Northwest*, on September 5, 1873, and appeared in revised form in Chapter 12 of Victor's *Atlantis Arisen; or, Talks of a Tourist about Oregon and Washington*, published in 1891. We have selected the 1891 version of Victor's narrative, which we have titled "A Font of the Gods," for this volume.

Victor began traveling in the Pacific Northwest in 1865. Her keen interest in the region's history was coupled with curiosity about its natural history. In addition to studying geology, she observed animal life, made botanical sketches, learned to identify the flora, and collected seeds, shells, and insects for identification and further study.

Victor continued her Pacific Northwest travels on a regular basis until 1878, when she moved to San Francisco and joined Hubert Howe Bancroft's historical research group. Her association with Bancroft involved work on his *History of the Pacific States*, an ambitious project of thirty-nine volumes. Bancroft, who directed and edited the project, also claimed authorship of the entire series; however, Victor evidently wrote all of the *History of Oregon* (two volumes), the *History of Washington, Idaho and Montana,* and the *History of Nevada, Colorado and Wyoming,* as well as numerous biographies for the series and parts of the volumes on the Northwest Coast, California, and British Columbia.

In 1890, after resigning from the Bancroft Company, Victor returned to Oregon. Dividing her time between Oregon and her favored city of San Francisco, she continued to write until her death in Portland, at the age of seventy-six. Although less than twenty years of her life had been spent in Oregon, Victor left a rich legacy of Pacific Northwest writings—poetry, narratives, essays, short stories, and histories.

Frances Auretta Fuller was born on May 26, 1826, at Rome, New York, the eldest of five daughters of Adonijah and Lucy A. (Williams) Fuller. When Frances was thirteen, the Fuller family settled in Wooster, Ohio, where she and her sister Metta Victoria (1831-85) attended a female seminary. The two sisters were separated by five years in age but bonded by their shared talent and love for writing. Both published poetry and stories in local papers and in the New York *Home Journal*. Metta's first full-length romance was published in 1846, when she was only fifteen; Frances's first novel was published in 1848, when she was twenty-two.

With aspirations for literary success, Frances and Metta visited New York City in 1848 and 1849, and they were encouraged by critics and editors such as Rufus Wilmot Griswold, who included them as "Sisters of the West" in his 1849 collection, *The Female Poets of America*. On the recommendation of Griswold, the sisters' joint effort—*Poems of Sentiment and Imagination*—was published in 1851.

After the death of their father in 1850, the two sisters joined the Fuller family in St. Clair, Michigan, and served as assistant editors of the newly established *Monthly Hesperian and Odd-Fellows Literary Magazine* of Detroit. Before long, however, Metta experienced literary success, particularly as a reform novelist, and she returned to New York City. In quick succession, three of Metta's novels were published.

When Metta married Orville James Victor, a successful editor, in July of 1856, she entered a marriage that permitted her to continue writing. Although she became the mother of nine children, Metta Fuller Victor assisted her husband in his editorial duties and became editor of *Home*, a monthly published by Beadle and Adams, and *Cosmopolitan Art Journal,* formerly edited by her husband. Orville Victor served for thirty-six years as general editor for Beadle and Adams in New York City, and Metta, under pseudonyms, wrote close to one-hundred books for Beadle's popular "dime novel" series and later wrote serialized novels for magazines. By 1870, she was reported to command the impressive sum of $25,000 for a collection of stories (William R. Taylor, "Metta Victoria Fuller Victor" 520).

In contrast to Metta's lasting marriage and success as a writer, Frances faced a series of personal and professional disappointments. She married Jackson Barritt of Pontiac, Michigan, in 1853, and the Barritts homesteaded for several years near Omaha, Nebraska, before they separated in 1859. Frances joined Metta in New York City. Biographer Jim Martin found that Frances "produced three dime novels and one of the *Pocket Novels* series" for Beadle, and "two other novels written by her were published by the Beadle subsidiary in London as part of the American Library series" (*A Bit of a Blue* 8).

In May of 1862, Frances married Henry Clay Victor, a naval engineer and brother of Metta's husband. As the wife of a navy man during the Civil War, she traveled with her husband to Panama and Mexico, and arrived in San Francisco in 1863. While Henry Victor was on sea duty, Victor took the pen name of "Fanny Fane" and wrote for the *Golden Era*. In one of her columns, she confessed, "There may be something extremely improper in it . . . but I have several times wished to be a man" (*Golden Era,* 25 October 1863). In December of 1864, after her husband's health failed and he resigned from the navy, Victor followed him to Oregon.

Henry Victor was associated with the Oregon Iron Works, and Victor became intrigued with Oregon history. The couple purchased property in Columbia County, Oregon, at the townsite of St. Helens, but failed investments led to financial problems. They separated in 1868, and Victor struggled to support herself by writing. Years later, after Henry Victor had moved to the Puget Sound area, he was drowned in the sinking of the *Pacific*, November 4, 1875. That same year, while she was writing as "Dorothy D." for the San Francisco *Call*, Victor addressed the issue of divorce: "To be yoked for life to one whom we could never really love is hardly worse than being so situated only to find too late that we have a strong capacity for love which we dare not use" ("Wanted, A Divorce," 6 June 1875).

Shortly after Frances Fuller Victor arrived in Oregon, she discovered that history was her forte. With the assistance of governors, judges, and historians, she learned and read Oregon history, collected historical materials, and interviewed early pioneers. But, her search for historical accuracy was not easy. "I had constantly to correspond with people whom I knew or did not know," Victor wrote, "and it did not take me long to find out that memory, like the human heart, was deceitful, if not 'desperately wicked'" (quoted in Powers, *History of Oregon Literature* 772). In her pursuit of "truth, plain and simple," Victor found hearsay, fading recollections, and prejudiced memories inadequate, and she sought evidence in contemporary written and printed records.

Publication of the first volume of Bancroft's *History of Oregon* in 1886 made Victor acutely aware of her status in Bancroft's enterprise. Clearly, Bancroft did not intend to give Victor authorial credit for her work on the *History of the Pacific States* series. In a display of her books at the World's Columbian Exposition in Chicago in 1893, several years after she had resigned from the Bancroft Company, Victor added her name to the spines and title pages of the four volumes she had written for Bancroft and included a special preface explaining her authorship. When the *Oregonian* gave Victor credit for these volumes in 1900, Bancroft claimed that Victor had never written any "finished work" for him; Victor acknowledged Bancroft's role as editor but added: "[W]hatever knowledge of Oregon history Mr. Bancroft possesses, he obtained from me" ("Bancroft's Histories," *Oregonian*, 8 July 1900).

Victor's insistence on being recognized as an author for the Bancroft series was motivated by far more than a desire to see her name in print. As a woman author, particularly as a woman attempting to establish herself as an historian, she struggled for equal opportunity and autonomy in a male-dominated system. In an autobiographical sketch for the Salem *Statesman*, Victor wrote: "[W]hile men, even men of no great intellectual or moral value to society, can create a constituency which will bring them profits of reputation, position, and hard cash by means of which women cannot or will not avail themselves, the woman of no matter how much industry, ability, or moral worth is not recognized because of her refusal to adopt certain of their methods, as well as on account of her inferiority from a political point of view" (16 June 1895).

In contrast to her sister Metta, who had not needed to worry about "hard cash," Frances Fuller Victor was dismayed at how little she earned as a writer. In *Literary Industries*, published in 1890, Bancroft wrote that Victor was "a lady of cultivated mind, of ability and singular application; likewise her physical endurance was remarkable" (237-38); however, at Bancroft's, where she had worked long hours, six days a week, she never earned more than $100 a month. By 1900, Victor estimated that she had received a total of $100 for all her publications in Oregon newspapers. For *The Early Indian Wars of Oregon* (1894), which was commissioned by the state of Oregon, biographer Jim Martin found that Victor was paid a total of $1,306.13 (*A Bit of a Blue* 185).

Fred Lockley, the Oregon *Journal* reporter, knew Victor when she returned to Oregon after working at Bancroft's, and he recalled that "Mrs. Victor was compelled to earn her living at selling face cream and other toilet articles from door to door" (quoted in Powers, *History of Oregon Literature* 312). Some income was generated by writing for publications such as the *Overland Monthly* in California, and Oregon supporters tried to help her financially; however, Victor worried that she would have to give up writing and find some other way to support herself.

Although Victor was not paid for contributions to Abigail Scott Duniway's *New Northwest*, she gained public exposure in the Portland weekly. As an advocate for woman's rights and suffrage, Victor canvassed for the *New Northwest* and helped edit the paper while Duniway was on a lecture tour in the spring of 1874. Although Victor and Duniway agreed on the need for woman suffrage, they had several philosophical and rhetorical differences. Victor argued that women should first learn how to use the vote before launching a major campaign for suffrage; Duniway advocated immediate equal suffrage as the passport to educational and employment opportunities for women. Victor chose not to speak in public and usually had her suffrage convention papers read aloud by someone else, such as Belle Cooke of Salem; Duniway prided herself on public speaking and visible leadership in the suffrage movement. In *The Women's War with Whisky,* Victor sympathized with the women's temperance crusade that swept across the nation to Portland in the spring of 1874; in the pages of the *New Northwest*, Duniway chastised Victor, her "amiable and gifted friend," for publishing "a remarkably one-sided affair" and not accurately reporting "some of the proscriptive and intolerable acts of a few of the crusaders and their self-righteous leaders against the Woman Movement" ("Woman's War with Whisky," *New Northwest*, 11 September 1874). Despite their differences, these two strong-minded women agreed on at least one point: the justice argument for woman suffrage.

A year before their differences over the temperance crusade, Duniway published Victor's first account of travel to Crater Lake as "Letter from Mrs. Victor" (*New Northwest*, 5 September 1873). Victor had been invited to visit Southern Oregon by Jesse Applegate and his nephew, Oliver Cromwell Applegate, to gather material for a history of the Modoc War. The Modocs, under Captain Jack (Kientepoos), had resisted efforts to place them on a reservation, and open warfare escalated to killings of peace commission members on April 11, 1873. In the company of Oliver Applegate, with whom

Victor developed a lasting friendship, she attended the trial of the Modoc prisoners at Fort Klamath. In early October of 1874, four convicted Modocs were hanged.

The version of Victor's journey reproduced here includes elements not found in the original narrative—detailed description of Crater Lake and clear identification of Jesse Applegate as a member of the party. Jesse Applegate (1811-88), who had traveled overland to Oregon Country in 1843, was one of the first pioneers interviewed by Victor when she arrived in Oregon. Noted as an early pioneer, surveyor, legislator and publicist, he had settled on a land claim in the Umpqua Valley in 1849 and became known as "The Sage of Yoncalla."

To accept the Applegates' invitation, Victor traveled from Portland to Roseburg by train, and from Roseburg to Ashland by stagecoach, seated on cushions "a trifle less hard than a rock." In Ashland, she joined "a private party" and traveled over the mountains—sixty-two miles in three days. Because she was unable to ride a "hard-trotting horse," Victor walked the sixty-two miles. This was, Victor said, "the most genuine gypsying I ever did." For the uninitiated camper, she recommended: "[T]o travel in Eastern Oregon requires you to wear stout shoes, a linen duster, a dust-cap, an immense hat; to carry a field-glass and a carbine; to know how to make a hemlock bed, or sleep on a haystack, and to talk jargon. With these accoutrements and accomplishments, if you are a good and indefatigable rider, you will get along" ("Letter from Mrs. Victor").

Stagecoach between Roseburg and Myrtle Point, Oregon

A Font Of the Gods

Some years ago—it was just after the Modoc war—I crossed the Cascades between Ashland and Linkville with a party, of whom the "Sage of Yoncalla" [Jesse Applegate] was one. It was an interesting trip from every point of view. We had an ambulance, a baggage-wagon, and horses, and walked or rode as it pleased us to do, taking three days for the passage. The first night we encamped in the valley of Jenny Creek, from which we took our supper of fish, and, not knowing any better, I left my shoes out in the dew, of the effect of which I became unpleasantly aware next morning; but I had a good sleep, quite undisturbed by grizzlies, of which there were not a few in the mountains. Next day our hunters killed a deer, and while we waited for it to be dressed, being in advance of the hunters, a huge brown bear trotted leisurely across the track in front of us; but the guns were behind, and we quietly watched his departure, thinking it was an escape on both sides. That night we encamped on the summit, and toasted venison on sticks around a blazing log-fire. We told stories, sang songs, and slept well afterwards. There was no dew to wet my shoes this night; but I was awakened about three o'clock in the morning by the voice of the Sage, who, like those of old, called upon me to observe the brightness of the morning star. And it was worth the misery of being wakened at such an hour to behold the great golden clusters sparkling above us,—two or three times as large as when seen through the murky air of the lowlands.

As we walked along next day the Sage told me the story of the opening of this road—the Southern Immigrant Road it was called—by himself and others, in 1846, when it was feared in Oregon that there might be a war with Great Britain, and it behooved them to be surveying out a track for the soldiers of the United States to take in coming to protect the Oregon settlers, which would be safer to travel than the Columbia or Mount Hood routes. He showed me, too, a tree near the crossing of the Klamath River where some of Fremont's exploring party carved their names in 1843.

Linkville was at the time of this trip but a few months old, and most of the settlers in Klamath Land had been driven out by fear of the Modocs—most of those not murdered. I was present at the trial of the Modoc prisoners at Fort Klamath, and spent some weeks at the Klamath Indian Agency, visiting notable places and studying Indian mythology under the tutelage of Captain O. C. [Oliver Cromwell] Applegate, who is a master of Indianology.

But the crowning pleasure of those enjoyable weeks was an excursion to a lake then little known but now famous in the Northwest. It was discovered in 1853 by prospectors from Jacksonville looking for gold, who, deeply impressed by its weird beauty, called it Lake Mystery. Subsequently some gentlemen from Fort Klamath visited it and called it Lake Majesty. Both these names were suggested by the effect upon the beholders. But exploration convinced all that the great rocky bowl containing these beautiful waters, whose rim was eight thousand feet above sea-level, was an immense crater, egg-shaped in form, and six by seven miles in extent of surface. This discovery changed the name to Crater Lake, which it is now called.

According to the belief of scientists and other observers, there once stood here a volcano higher by several thousand feet than any existing mountain, the angle of the remaining mass carrying an imaginary line to a height of thirty thousand feet. . . . There is a crater within the crater, rising in a hollow cone above the water eight hundred and forty-five feet, called Wizard Island, and another similar crater fathoms deep beneath the lake's surface.

The military road from Jacksonville to Fort Klamath runs within about four miles of the lake, and is the route usually taken by tourists. But the approach from the east side is much more easy, being a comfortable afternoon's drive from the Agency to camp at the turning-off point. Our party found bear-tracks close to camp, and deer-tracks in the ashes of our burnt-out fire when we arose from our mosquito tormented slumbers. Our ambulance was taken to the summit, although we walked a good part of the four miles, for the ground was very lumpy with rocks and frozen snowdrifts which July suns had failed to liquefy, and which, to them unaccountable, phenomenon kept our mules in a greatly agitated state of nerves.

On arriving at the summit we found the earth light and ashen, diversified by patches of snow, and by other patches of alpine flowers, some of which were very pretty in form and color. The air was bright and mild; we had left the forest behind us; there was nothing anywhere about more elevated than our position, nor any living thing anywhere near us. We were apparently on the highest point of the earth, for there was nothing to look up to, and it would not have surprised me to have been whirled off into space. *The solitude of the situation was thrilling.*

One cannot, owing to the sunken position of the lake, discover it until close upon its rim, and I say here, without exaggeration, that no pen can reproduce its image, no picture be painted to do it justice; nor can it, for obvious reasons, be satisfactorily photographed. At the first view a dead silence fell upon our party. A choking sensation arose in our throats, and tears flowed down our cheeks. I do not pretend to analyze the emotion, but, if I were to endeavor to compare it with anything I ever read, I should say it must be such a feeling which causes the Cherubim to veil their faces before God. To me it was a revelation.

The water of Crater Lake is of the loveliest blue imaginable in the sunlight, and a deep indigo in the shadows of the cliffs. It mirrors the walls encircling it accurately and minutely. It has no well-like appearance because it is too large to suggest it, yet a water-fowl on its surface could not be discovered by the naked eye, so far below us is it. It impresses one as having been made for the Creator's eye only, and we cannot associate it with our human affairs. It is a font of the gods, wherein our souls are baptized anew into their primal purity and peace.

Alice Day Pratt
1872-1963

When Alice Day Pratt's *A Homesteader's Portfolio* (1922) first came to our attention, we were excited by the fact that it appeared to be a first-hand account of the experiences of a single woman homesteader, slightly fictionalized, but too knowledgeable and detailed to be fiction. Since then, *A Homesteader's Portfolio* has been reprinted (Oregon State University Press, 1993), with a full and well-researched introduction by Oregon author Molly Gloss. And, although the main character in the text is called "Miss Andromeda," the book is, indeed, an autobiographical account of Alice Day Pratt's five years of proving up a homestead on the high desert of Central Oregon during the last homesteading wave of the 1910s.

Although she was near forty, a schoolteacher, and a self-described "old maid" when she took up her claim, it would be difficult to find a woman who was better prepared to take her place alone in Central Oregon as a dry-land homesteader and chronicler than Alice Day Pratt. From childhood, she was spirited and adventurous; she loved animals and plants and working outdoors, and she was accustomed to hard work. Pratt's self-published memoir, *Three Frontiers,* tells of her background and early life in Minnesota and Dakota, all of which helped prepare her for homesteading in Oregon.

Alice's father, William McLain Pratt, was a son of Connecticut's founders, and a man who thrived on adventure. In 1870, he and his wife Sophie and their baby daughter, Sophie Caroline, moved to Mankato, on the Minnesota River. Alice wrote that her mother "did not share [her husband's] adventurousness" and did not want to leave her relatives and friends, but she was "one of those for whom decisions are made" (*Frontiers* x). Alice was born in 1872 on their homestead claim in Minnesota in "a new little cottage" with a "commanding view of the entire settlement and a long stretch of river valley."

The beauty of the prairies experienced in her childhood lingered in Alice Day Pratt's memory. One of the first "pictures" she remembered was of a picnic on a blue lake, her mother spreading a white cloth on the green grass, and lunch of boiled eggs and sandwiches. She remem-

bered her first boat ride, but she also remembered her horror when the little frogs she helped her father catch became fish bait, and the fish he caught "lay gasping and flopping in the boat." She remembered stroking the iridescent feathers, and looking into the "poor dead eyes" of the quail and ducks her father killed on a later trip to the lake (*Frontiers* 2).

Pratt's affinity for all birds and animals became a lifelong passion. She wrote sensitively and lovingly about animals in all five essays she published in the *Atlantic Monthly*, in two children's books, and in large sections of her two memoirs—*A Homesteader's Portfolio* and *Three Frontiers*. When she became a homesteader, Pratt always kept in mind that it was humans who were the intruders. Gloss points out that "[E]ven in her relations with destructive plagues of jackrabbits, and chicken-eating hawks, Alice practiced a compassionate conservation ethic, undertaking to protect her animals and fields by the most minimal, least tortuous methods" (*Homesteader's* introduction xlv). Pratt was keenly aware of the ruin human habitation caused as new settlements were developed: "The beauty of the prairies and the destruction of prairie life! These go together in my memory as they go together in our history" (*Frontiers* 3).

The land along the Minnesota River was rich, and William Pratt's lumber business prospered with the grain crops of the farmers, until clouds of grasshoppers appeared in three consecutive summers, devouring "every green blade and leaf" (13). Pratt had invested all of his inheritance in the business and was wiped out when banks foreclosed on the farmers' lands and they were forced to leave.

In 1877, William Pratt set off for the Black Hills of Dakota, an area just opening to settlement, hoping to re-establish his lumber business in a newly prospering location. Because he considered the country too rough, Pratt left his wife and daughters behind and, although there were summer visits, it was 1886 before his family came to join him permanently. By this time, William Pratt had built a "rough little house of five rooms" and had planted fruit trees and a garden. It was this humble, but beautifully situated house, which became the family's home for the next fifteen years. They were two miles from the country store, twenty-five miles from Pratt's lumber business in Deadwood, and three miles from Piedmont, which was "never more than a few scattered houses: schoolhouse, church, store, bank and railroad station" (36).

At her father's suggestion, Alice took up the study of botany and began a collection of the area's flora. She spent much of her time studying plant books or in solitary excursions in the forest. She wrote: "The thrills of my adolescence became the discovery of a new plant, the nest of a hitherto-unknown bird, the meeting with a wild creature who studied me with that unblinking observation that is characteristic of *his* kind" (49). Although she would wonder in later years whether her time spent in solitary pursuits rather than with other people had been "for good or ill," it was yet another preparation for the lonely life of the single homesteader that lay ahead.

After leaving home, Alice Day Pratt spent about fifteen years studying and teaching. In 1910, she had completed three years doing "social-educational" work in the coal camps of Arkansas when labor troubles closed the camps. As Pratt took stock, she realized how tired she was, both *by* and *of* her work. It was then that she determined to follow a long-repressed dream and claim her "portion of the earth's crust" by becoming a homesteader in Oregon. Since she had no savings, she applied for and obtained a primary teaching position in Athena, Oregon, near Pendleton, in the northeast corner of the state.

Pratt arrived in Athena to take up her position but was soon transferred to the Stanfield Irrigation Project, where she spent a year. Stanfield was a new, privately owned, and thriving agricultural settlement, which had once been an enormous sheep ranch. She would have liked to establish her farm there, but she did not have the capital to buy land and was unwilling to take the risk of borrowing. Instead, she hired a "locator" to find her a desirable homestead.

It was November of 1911, and Alice Day Pratt was in Baker attending the State Teachers' Association meeting, when word came that the locator had found something he wanted her to see. Pratt rushed off to have her first look at what would become Broadview, a homestead she eventually increased from the original 160 acres to 640. The story related in *A Homesteader's Portfolio* is of her first five years, from 1911 to 1916, as she proved up on her land.

Her financial situation was always precarious. As soon as she proved up, she went back east to visit her family and to earn money. She returned to Broadview in 1918, but outside income was always necessary, and she secured a teaching job at Conant Basin, ten miles from Broadview, bringing her Jersey cows, horses, chickens, dog, and cats with her "over the rimrock" (Gloss introduction, *Homesteader's* xiv). Because of drought, hay prices skyrocketed, and prices for dairy products plummeted. Pratt took out a large loan on her herd and, the following autumn, she was forced to sell her herd for the amount of the loan. Alice Day Pratt left Broadview in 1930. She held onto the property for another twenty years, but never returned, and the land was sold in 1950.

Alice Day Pratt lived with her mother and her sister, Marjorie, first in Niagara Falls, and later in New York City. She continued to teach, as did Marjorie, and she continued to write, though not always successfully. Her novel set in Central Oregon—*Sagebrush Fires*—remains unpublished, as do several other manuscripts (Gloss introduction xxix). In 1955, Pratt's brother, Julius W. Pratt, financed the private printing of *Three Frontiers*.

Alice Day Pratt died in 1963, at age 91. Gloss found that, during the last few years of her life, Pratt was confined by crippling arthritis to her room above New York's East River. Marjorie gave up teaching to care for her sister. Although Pratt's body was crippled, her intellect and spirit remained undiminished.

The selections we have titled "Nature Has Not Betrayed the Heart That Loved Her" are taken from *A Homesteader's Portfolio*. We believe these excerpts convey a sense of the determination, courage, and abiding love for nature and its creatures that Alice Day Pratt exemplified, not only during her years as an "old maid" Oregon homesteader, but throughout her entire life.

Nature Has Not Betrayed the Heart That Loved Her

About the year nineteen-ten came to me—teacher and spinster—the conviction that Fate had paid me the compliment of handing over the reins. She had failed to provide for me that ideal relationship which alone is the basis of the true home, and I was by nature obdurate toward accepting anything less at her hands. When a youthful friend was surreptitiously chidden for using the term "old maid" in my presence, the incident gave rise to thought. What now? I asked myself. *Quo vadis,* old maid? What will you do with your life? Perhaps you have known the glory and the dream. Will you subsist henceforth upon the memory thereof or shall life continue to be for you that "ecstasy" "nothing less than which is worthy of the name"?

But by what route, if any, was that ecstasy to be attained? Not in the character of an "unplucked rose on the ancestral tree"—an illustration of the immemorial dependence and subjection of the feminine. Not through that occasional achievement—"fifty years a teacher.". . . Not through social service as I knew it in the great city. . . . One's course, to be most effective, must be in line with one's spontaneous loves and interests.

For some months, while work went on as usual, I reflected deeply, and gradually evolved the determination to be a creative farmer. There recurred to me the longing and ambition—innate but hitherto suppressed—to own a portion of the earth's crust in my own right and to tamper with it unrestrained. I would build a farm, whereon I could exercise my delight in all forms of nature life and to which in time I might bring some little unparented children, on whom to wreak my educational convictions and whom I might hope some day to turn over—a little bunch of good citizens—to my native land.

My fellow teachers wondered somewhat that winter at my unaffected cheerfulness under certain afflictions that visited themselves upon us. They never dreamed that I was all the time afar on the prairies with the wind in my hair and the smell of new-plowed earth in every breath I drew.

From the Department of the Interior I obtained facts as to public lands—for I had no treasure laid up wherewith to buy. Anyway, the virgin soil suited my plan. My farm was to be a true creation.

Gradually the prospective field narrowed itself until I had decided upon Oregon. Then, that I might not be a pauper immigrant, I decided to procure a school in the state and take what time might be required for finding my waiting acres. Through the State Superintendent, rather late, I obtained a position as primary teacher in the little town of Athena, eastern Oregon, and, on one memorable September day, companioned by an inseparable brown dog, I found myself about to embark upon the great adventure.

"Portland, Oregon? To your left. Leaves in twenty seconds." The forbidding gate clanged to behind me and I sped down the track.

"Portland, Oregon? Right here. Mind the step, Madam. All aboard!" The conductor and his little stool swung themselves up behind me and the vast train for the Pacific coast moved noiselessly out of our great metropolis. Behind, what extremes of gayety and misery, what competition, what life at high pressure! Before, what calm, what freedom, what limitless spaces, what hope and opportunity! I had become a homesteader!

Eagerly and nervously I watched the changing landscape. I had a haunting fear that it would be tame. I knew what practical considerations would appeal to the locator. But it was not tame. The Maury Mountains, pine-clad and dignified, in the background, the abrupt, walled Rim Rock skirting the valley, the winding river with its alfalfa fields—but, . . . I loved Friar Butte at first sight. In the days to come, through the doubled and redoubled allowance to the homesteader, it was to become my own, almost entire, my upland pasture. Its shadow already lay across the deep wash land when we reached it—my fields to be.

The spring—the *sine qua non* of the homesteader—was frozen and not flowing, but signs indicated that it needed but a little deepening. It has, in fact, proved unfailing at a lower level. I felt no hesitation. It was predestined. It was mine. For the first time, with the butte and the Maury Mountains at my back, I stood beneath a cone-shaped juniper and looked across the still-luminous valley and the river to those other mountains that were for so long to feed my eyes with their changing colors of slaty-blue, rose-purple, and amethyst. This juniper, for its beauty, should be my dooryard tree, I decided. This view should name my place and the name should be Broadview—and so it was.

People say to me that it must be desolate, living alone at Broadview. I reply that I am not alone. I am conscious of no lack—at least in the region of our simpler and more fundamental thoughts and feelings—of reciprocal understanding and sympathy. To and fro at my side on all of my busy excursions about the farm, trot Bingo and Kitty Kat—interested observers of all my activities, happy in their own digressive explorations and fruitful hunts, ever ready in my moments of rest with eloquent companionship and tender caress, drawing close with me at the close of day by the fireside or on the doorstone, sharing the peace of evening after the busy day.

My chickens gather in little groups about me as I work here and there, engaging me in cheery conversation, essaying little familiarities and friendly overtures, even performing certain stunts with self-conscious gravity, delighting in personal attention. Fly—joy of my life, swift, tireless companion of my larger adventures—accommodates her browsing to my movements, keeping me in sight with that undemonstrative friendliness characteristic of her kind. Bossy—silky-coated Jersey, producer of foamy milk and golden butter—with all her impatient head-tossings and waywardness under control, still feeds the home end of the pasture quite into the ground, rather than follow better grazing out of sight of our domestic circle.

There is that in the gentle response of these calm and friendly creatures that soothes the spirit and leaves the mind free for its own excursions. Not so with the harassing companionship of non-understanding humans. The cheerful care-freedom of the animals is contagious. It harmonizes with all out-of-doors, and engages one's own spirit in the unapprehensive activities of Nature. All Nature is cheerful till calamity befalls, and the calamities of Nature are short and sharp, and cloud the heavens of the immediate victims only.

So it was that, as yellow began to tinge the fields, desperate with the fear of losing what had cost so much, I set to work with a scythe and, working at night in order to avoid the heat of the day—the moon being at the full—I had actually cut about two acres, when a human-hearted rancher bethought him of an old mower that was idle. This was put in repair for me, Fly and her companion bent their willing necks to the task, and my heavy waves of grain bowed obediently before the circling mower. . . . I still had no plan for the raking. It seemed that every hayrake in the countryside was overworked. Once more I set to work by hand, but this time my friends the Nashes stepped into the breach. A hayrake was forthcoming and the day was saved. Could I stack it alone? I confess it looked impossible. I could do no less than begin, however, and begin I did. For one month, "through long days of labor and nights devoid of ease," I tossed and stacked one hundred thousand pounds of hay—twenty-five tons lifted twice—suspending every other activity save milking and chicken feeding, living on boiled eggs, crackers, and milk, while I tossed and tossed and stacked from morn till dewy eve. Nor was I in the end one whit the worse for the experience. When the last load was on the last stack and I realized that I had made a crop from the hauling of the seed to the last folding away of the last straw, I sat down beneath the haystack, while Fly and her mate nibbled unchecked at the heads of wheat, and gave to the world the inspired version that had been turning itself in my head the while I tossed:

> *The Making Of the Hay*
>
> By Friar Butte's rugged hill slopes,
> Out Crooked River way,
> By junipers surrounded,
> There stand three stacks of hay.
>
> And no man stirred the fallow fields
> And no man touched the hay,
> For a lone old maid that hay crop made
> And packed the stuff away. . . .

In this year of our Lord nineteen hundred and twenty-one, ten years since that Thanksgiving Day of glorious hopes, I still cling to the homestead dream. I have known lean years and leaner years, hope and discouragement, good fortune and disaster, friendship and malice, righteousness, generosity and double dealing. . . .

Ah, well! I have said I still cling to the dream. Now and then I have known burdens—most often physical burdens—too heavy for mortals to bear. I have been cold and hungry and ragged and penniless. I have been free and strong and buoyant and glad. Over my six hundred and forty acres—thus increased by a second beneficent allowance—roams a beautiful little Jersey herd. A group of dear white ponies call me mistress. White biddies still dot my hill slopes and cackle ceaselessly. Pax, An Armistice Day puppy, and El Dorado, son of Kitty Kat, have succeeded those earlier friends whose gentle spirits still wander with me on the sagebrush slopes. There is a mortgage. There is still necessity to teach. My little flock of orphan citizens still beckon from the future. Yet, for me, the wilderness and the solitary place have been glad, and Nature has not betrayed the heart that loved her.

Ella (Rhoads) Higginson
1862-1940

A full introduction to Ella Higginson as a poet and fiction writer appears in Part IV of this book. While the following Higginson essay might have been placed in that section as well, we felt that her early appeal for nature preservation was worthy of particular emphasis.

Higginson's passion for the natural beauty of the Northwest was a consistent factor in all her writing. Her poetry is filled with sensuous, romantic descriptions of the marvelous scenery of Puget Sound, which she called "the opal sea"; the play of light at dawn or dusk on the Willamette River; the changing seasons in the valleys and the pine and fir forests of Oregon and Washington. It was in nature rather than in church that Higginson, a deeply spiritual person, found communion with God, as illustrated by the concluding lines of Part II of "Yet Am I Not for Pity," a poem from her 1898 volume, *When the Birds Go North Again*:

> These pearl-topped mountains shining silently—
> They are God's sphinxes and God's pyramids;
> These dim-aisled forests His cathedrals, where
> The pale nun Silence tiptoes, velvet-shod,
> And Prayer kneels with tireless, parted lids;
> And thro' the incense of this holy air
> Trembling—I have come face to face with God.

But Ella Higginson's love for the Pacific Northwest environment is nowhere articulated more clearly and passionately than in an essay she published in the January 1892 issue of the *Overland Monthly*. In this essay, written over one hundred years ago and originally titled "The New West: The Other Side," Higginson laments the lack of attention being paid to the loss of wilderness areas and voices her concern for environmental conservation. This is, to our knowledge, the first appearance of the essay since its original publication. Although the language of today's environmentalist may be less poetic than Higginson's, the topic of conservation versus development remains a subject of heated debate, controversy, and legislation in the Pacific Northwest.

I Am a Mossback to My Very Finger Ends

If to love every inch of this free and noble West with a proud and passionate love, and to hate the money seekers who come here only for gain,—who, with eyes blind to the grand and lonely beauty of our opal seas, our emerald forests, our silver ice-streams, our azure skies fired at sunset with a million blinding tints so exquisite that the very heart is hushed in the breast, our purple hills, and our high and lofty mountains that rear their glistening domes into the clouds,—who, blind to all these things, tear down our forests, rip open our mountain sides, blow out our stumps with giant powder, dam up our water ways, and see in our wide, sea-weeded tidelands only "magnificent places for slaughter houses, b'God," and in our blue, shining sea only so much water that at ebb tide would "carry off the filth, y'know,"—if loving these things and hating these people signifies "moss-backism," then am I a mossback to my very finger ends.

How much has been written about the "great possibilities" of the new West! And how little about her great beauty! Women come here from the East and sit down and sob in a weakly, homesickly way. "The forest almost at your door," they say, whimpering; "and such wild canons and thundering rivers, and such *awful* trees; and no society!" And we who have lived all our lives in this West, and love its every heart beat, and would die for it,— we look at such people with dumb lips and choking throats. What can you say to a woman who sees nothing in a tree but its "awful" size and height; who shrinks in fear from our mighty, deep-tongued, deep-chested rivers, and who, having been so blessed as to be placed in the midst of such beauty and grandeur, weakly yearns for "society"?

To a homesick woman who was fretting for the theaters and operas she had left behind her, I said once: "But you surely have much to console you. It is not every one that has such a grand view of natural scenery."

"The view!" she repeated, looking at me blankly; then, after a moment, limply: "O, the view is all right."

Her home—a pretty and comfortable cottage—was situated on a high and noble bluff which went sheer down to the blue sea of Puget, and which was covered with luxuriant wild vines, wild pink roses, and the flaming red wild currant. Below the shining waves beat, beat forever against the rock walls, and wore huge, creased caves in their grim breasts; farther out lay the low green islands wrapped in purple mist until evening, when the purple changed to silver, and then, fired by the setting sun, to rose, blue, orange, amber, crimson, and gold, rising and falling before the light winds; all about arose the densely timbered hills, and far away the Olympics flushed like a chain of fire-opals, while, still higher, grander,—eternal as the heavens,—stood Mounts Rainier, Baker, and the Twin Sisters. —— And this woman, pining for the false passion of some Bernhardt or Langtry on a mimic life-stage, saw only that "the view was all right."

To another—to whose very door a wide path of gold tumbled nightly across the sea—I said: "But you have the sunsets."

"The sunsets," she repeated vaguely, "are they nice? I have not noticed them." And she had lived there three months!

We who have lived always in the West, and who love each tree, each broken stump overgrown with fringed ferns and pale green thimble-berry leaves, each deeply rutted and forgotten road winding through the dark, wild forest, each stone that has lain, motionless and passionless, since the world began,—we dread and loathe the sleek, sharp, prosperous Easterner, who stands about with his thumbs in the arm holes of his vest, and talks about our great possibilities; who marvels at our push, our progress, enterprise; who writes letters full of untruths and bad grammar to Eastern papers about the amazing number of small towns he finds possessed of such luxuries as electric lights, electric cars, cable cars, stone pavements, immense mills, and so on, but who says never a word about our violet sky that leans down so near to us at night that we can almost put out our hand and touch it; who sees in our ice lakes far up the mountains, wherein speckled trout leap and curve, and the clouds lay their white breasts, only the promise of a fortune in the way of water power, but who never sees how large and mellow the moon comes over those snow mountains at night and reproaches the follies and fevers of human life.

They tell us we have a grand country here, but that we need more *people* and more *society*, and we listen with shut lips and something like grief in our hearts. Is it not people that have planted oyster beds and built ungainly, shrieking mills on our beautiful tide lands—mills into whose hungry throats our noble trees are driven like beasts to be slaughtered?

O, I hate this many-headed thing called Civilization, that is tearing away from us Westerners the things we love!

We are like the Indians; we are crowded on, step by step, inch by inch, until, at last, we can go no farther, and we stand still with rebellious hearts and swelling veins, and hear the blasting of our rocks, the axes beating against our trees, and the crisp crackling of flames on our mountain sides. We drink the water that is carried from our ice lakes in pipes, and we think of a spring that used to gush out of the rocks and where we used to press feverish lips and find peace; we flash through "cleared" woods in electric or steam or cable cars, and we remember lonely, beautiful roads through dim forests where our horse's feet used to ring like bells and the sunlight lay in loops of gold; we toss in couches of down, and we think of nights in the open, fir-scented air with the earth beneath and the sky above, with the indescribable fragrance of the night sea in our nostrils and the wind about our temples,— and we long with the passion of barred in animals for those lost years. We hear pale women say: "But we cannot stand your winds—they are so strong," and we say nothing; but we remember wild nights when the waves broke over these cliffs and we ran down to them and let the spray lash us like hail stones and the winds beat our breath back into our breasts—and again we are like the Indians; we look at them and think: "Weaklings! You have not the Western blood in your veins, and the Western passion in your hearts, and the Western fire in your souls!" We are always grieving to get back to the old times,—as dead women in their graves, with the wet earth piled on their breasts, struggle and yearn to get back to the tender passion of arms that once held them.

Part II: Coping: Learning By Doing

❖

Those women did not see themselves as heroic. They were doing what had to be done.
   Susan Armitage, *The Women's West* (1987)

In this section, we examine the ways in which nine women dealt with problems and difficulties, sometimes in the face of circumstances so unusual or unfamiliar that adequate preparation was impossible. Thus, in order to cope, these women had to call upon whatever resources were available to them to solve their problems, sometimes alone and sometimes through connection with others. We agree with Glenda Riley, who pointed out that "[w]omen's motivations, inner resources, and help from others all contributed to their ability to cope with, and sometimes triumph over, the challenges of western life" (*A Place to Grow* 243). Further, we suggest that the self-confidence gained by coping with challenges frequently led to women's empowerment, and thus to an enhanced willingness and ability to take action in their own or others' behalf.

In *Westering Women*, Sandra Myres writes that women "adapted" to frontier life by making a "realistic adjustment to physical and psychological realities" (165). While this is true, we see adapting as only one form of coping. Adaptation is a process which occurs over time, and time was a luxury some of these women did *not* have. Sarah Cummins, for instance, coped with a near escape from death while crossing the Cascade Mountains in 1845. Cummins exhibited autonomy and strength of will which, in combination with her husband's greater physical strength and resourcefulness, and the help of others who shared what food they had, led to survival, and thus triumph over the fierce and uncontrollable forces of nature. She later adapted successfully and spent the rest of her long life in the West.

Emeline Fuller coped alone with an attack by hostile Indians on the Overland Trail in 1860. She did what she had to do, but the effects of her experience were so extreme that they led neither to triumph nor successful adaptation and Fuller eventually moved back to Wisconsin. The mystery here is how Fuller, at age thirteen, "nerved herself" for an attempt to save her younger siblings instead of giving way to hopelessness and terror.

In her discussion of adaptation to conditions in the West, historian Christiane Fischer has suggested that the more "genteel" a woman's background and education, the more "repelled" she would be by her new environment (*Let Them Speak for Themselves* 13). While we saw no real evidence of repulsion in these texts, class issues surfaced in the writings of Esther Selover Lockhart, who came from a genteel eastern background. Lockhart, a teacher who boarded with pioneer families while her husband tried to establish himself, was appalled by the slovenliness she saw in some of these homes and was considered peculiar for her eastern ways. Lockhart adapted well to pioneer life, but she never sacrificed her own values.

Susanna Maria Slover McFarland Price Ede, on the other hand, was a native westerner, and her experiences provide one of the best examples of coping through adaptation to western life within this group of readings. Cathy Luchetti and Carol Olwell have pointed out that "[i]n the west women experienced an autonomy never before dreamed of, and with this new freedom came the necessity to solve their problems in any way they could. Making do became an art shared by both sexes, and 'women's work' soon came to mean whatever had to be done, whether it was herding cattle, checking trap lines, or seeding the rows with corn" (*Women of the West* 31). This observation applies particularly well to Ede, who was as capable of helping skin a bear as she was of sewing ruffled frocks for her children.

Ede's experience leads us to wonder how much of a factor the willingness to step outside prescribed gender roles may have been for those who successfully met the myriad challenges of life in the early West. Mother Joseph of the Sacred Heart, S.P. (Sisters of Providence), who came to the Northwest from Quebec in 1843, was a woman who, in today's language, we would perhaps characterize as androgynous. Mother Joseph possessed both typically "feminine" and "masculine" skills—she could handle carpentry tools as well as she could sew and spin. Like Susanna Ede, Mother Joseph displayed qualities of resourcefulness and ingenuity as she learned to make do with limited resources and adapted to changing circumstances. She was empowered to act, in part, by her own personal skills and qualities of character. But the most significant source of Mother Joseph's empowerment to overcome adversity was from her dedication to and unfailing faith in God.

The desire to serve God caused Anna Maria Pittman, a single woman of thirty-three, to make the autonomous decision to leave her home and family in Boston and come to the Oregon Country in 1836. With undaunted spirit, a sense of humor, and apparently without regret, Anna Maria coped with the difficulties of the ten-month journey west. After she joined Jason Lee's mission, and then married him in 1837, her loving relationship with Lee reinforced her inner strength and dedication to doing God's work. Although challenged by loneliness, a foreshadowing of death, and the difficult pregnancy she faced in her husband's absence, Anna Maria Pittman Lee's spirit remained undaunted.

Bethenia Owens-Adair was born in 1840, two years after Anna Maria Pittman Lee died in childbirth. Owens-Adair, although pretty and petite, was an inveterate tomboy, and was irritated by the limitations imposed on the female sex—most of which she eventually overcame. From an early age, Owens-Adair expressed an autonomous spirit and a "can-do" attitude; she was adamant that she would not be victimized. Owens-Adair was empowered also by her connection with her family who supported her emotionally and financially during the crisis of her divorce. When she later decided to study medicine, however, she discovered that the support of her family did not extend quite so far beyond the bounds of convention, and further empowerment came through striking out alone to follow her own star.

And when, in 1900, Anne Shannon Monroe made the decision to leave teaching and become a writer, she also found it necessary to separate herself from her family, at least for a time. But Monroe, who went out into the country to find the atmosphere and freedom she needed to write, immediately established an affiliation with a surrogate family. She moved in with an older couple who enhanced, rather than restricted, her self-determined course.

For Emma J. Ray, who was born into slavery, self-determination was more difficult to achieve and came after many turbulent years of confronting adversity. Following a religious conversion, Ray was empowered by developing leadership skills and, in partnership with her husband, identifying a role for herself in interracial social work and evangelism. Her faith in God was instrumental in coping with the racial discrimination Ray was forced to endure in the Pacific Northwest.

Contrary to prevalent images, stereotypes and myths, the women represented here were not passive, downtrodden drudges, nor were they saints. They were active participants in shaping their own lives and reaching out toward the future. Sometimes these women acted autonomously, facing adversity with bravery, humor, resourcefulness, patience—whatever personal resources they could muster. But they were open to accepting the help and support of others, and this meant men as well as other women. Through a combination of self-direction, affiliation and cooperation, these women were empowered to cope, to adapt, to succeed or to fail. More often they succeeded. But if they failed, it was not through lack of trying.

Anna Maria Pittman Lee
1803-38

For Anna Maria Pittman Lee, the first white woman to marry, die, and be buried in the Oregon Country, coping with life's challenges and submitting to God's will were one and the same—her way of life. Hardships were to be met with good humor and piety; losses, including painful separations from family members, were to be endured with abiding love and unflagging faith.

To realize her ambition to carry God's word to the Indians, Anna Maria Pittman, an unmarried woman of almost thirty-three, embarked on a missionary journey that changed her life forever. In the space of less than two years, from July of 1836 to June of 1838, she traveled by sea from Boston to Oregon, met and married the Reverend Jason Lee at the Methodist Oregon Mission, bore a son, and died within a few days after childbirth.

Influences from family, schooling, and religious instruction contributed to Anna Maria's desire to serve her God. She was born September 24, 1803, in New York City, the thirteenth child of George W. and Mary (Spies) Pittman, a financially secure and deeply religious couple who were committed to the value of education for their children. In *Life and Letters of Mrs. Jason Lee*, Theressa Gay writes that Anna Maria was "converted to God" when she was about twenty-five (5), and an interest in the religious conversion of Indians eventually compelled her to apply to the Missionary Society of the Methodist Episcopal Church for an appointment. When no positions with Canadian missions were available, she applied for the Oregon Mission and was accepted in January of 1836.

The Methodist Missionary Society had voted in 1833 to carry their work to the Indians of America. This action was in response to increased public interest in conversion of Indians and the highly publicized request from Flathead and Nez Perce representatives who traveled to St. Louis in 1831. Jason Lee, ordained as a deacon and elder in the Methodist Episcopal Church, was selected to establish a new mission in the Oregon Country. In the fall of 1834, Lee's mission was established about sixty miles from the mouth of the Willamette River. Within a year, Jason Lee asked the Methodist Missionary

Society to send a farmer and his family, a married minister, and some teachers. The Missionary Board chose Anna Maria Pittman as one of "two young ladies as teachers" (quoted in Gay 27). Anna Maria Pittman and twelve others set sail from New York in July of 1836, arriving in May of 1837 at Fort Vancouver.

Although life as a celibate missionary was evidently what Anna Maria Pittman anticipated, she married Jason Lee on July 16, 1837, within two months of her arrival in Oregon. The next year, in her last letter to her husband, Lee confided she used to sing of "the blessings of Celibacy" and had turned her song to "the happiness of Matrimony!"

Following a honeymoon journey to the Pacific Ocean, the Lees returned to their responsibilities at the mission. Lee and the wife of physician Elijah White were in charge of domestic affairs, cooking, baking, making butter each week, teaching a Sabbath School, and sewing clothes for the thirty Indian children who lived at the log Mission House.

In late March of 1838, only eight months after their marriage, the Lees were parted. Jason Lee traveled overland to seek assistance from the Board of Managers of the Methodist Missionary Society to extend the mission work. Lee knew her beloved husband would be gone at least eighteen months, leaving her to go through the last three months of pregnancy and childbirth without him. The letters she wrote to him reveal her concerns about the difficult and painful pregnancy, her attempts to cope calmly in times of crisis, her deep loneliness, and her resignation to God's will. In the first stanza of a poem composed for Jason Lee before his departure, Anna Maria Pittman Lee wrote:

> Must my dear Companion leave me,
>   Sad and lonely here to dwell?
> If 'tis duty thus that calls thee,
> Shall I keep thee? No, farewell;
>   Though my heart aches
> While I bid thee thus farewell.

During the morning hours of June 21, 1838, Anna Maria Pittman Lee fell ill, and Dr. Elijah White was brought to assist her. After several days of difficult labor, Dr. White "was obliged to use instruments" (Gay 84), and he delivered a baby boy on the night of June 23rd. The infant lived only two days, and his mother died the following day, June 26, 1838, at age thirty-five. She and the child were buried together in a grove of fir trees near the mission.

The private letters and poetry written by Anna Maria Pittman Lee—her vital connections with her family and with Jason Lee—were preserved after her death. These writings, collected and edited by Theressa Gay, illustrate why Lee is remembered as "a talented writer of romantic and religious intensity, who was the first poet in Oregon" (Sherr and Kazickas, *The American Woman's Gazetteer* 197).

In the letters we have selected and titled "If My Life Is Spared," some racial stereotypes emerge. Lee was strongly schooled in the prevailing belief of the time that Indians were uncivilized, unsaved souls—"the wasted issue of Adam's sons and daughters." She was prepared to live or die, whether single or wed, in the missionary service of her God among the heathen. A prophetic note—in fact, a foreshadowing and acceptance of death—can be heard and felt in her letters.

Although hardship, loneliness, and physical pain tested and might have broken Lee's strong spirit, her writings reveal that she was empowered by religious and marital bonds; she drew strength and solace from her faith in God and found comfort and passion in a loving relationship with Jason Lee. Anna Maria Pittman Lee's letters provide insight to her capacity for human passion as well as religious piety, and they contradict contemporary stereotypes of missionary women as romantically inexpressive and inhibited from discussing pregnancy and childbirth with their husbands.

IF MY LIFE IS SPARED

June 5th 1837—Oregon Mission Williamate R.r—
My Dear Parents

When I last wrote you I was at Vancouver where we staid a week after which we prepared for our final journey to our long looked for home. On the 25 of May we started in a boat and three Canoes. Capt. H. [Hinkley] and lady accompanied us. I went with Mr. J. L. [Jason Lee] in his canoe. we encamped two nights on shore having with us a tent and provision it seemed like camp meeting we had a delightful sail. the second day we came to the Falls in the Willimatte river I was the first white lady ever witnessed them. . . . we reached the spot where I expect to end my days. . . . Mr. J. Lee assisted us from our horses and conducted us to the house where he bid us a hearty welcome to his humble cottage, a log house with two comfortable rooms a kitchen and school room. it is rough but good enough for the present. . . .We found things in old bachelor style we females soon mad[e] a different appearance in the house. . . . there are several white men Canadians who understand english who attend preaching they have half breed wives their children attend the school. some women come with their babies in their arms. Mr. Lee has 30 children to provide for and has them in his house. . . . I feel as though I had already an important charge. There are 12 members of the mission family 5 children and occasionally laborers hired by Mr. Lee he says he feels now as if he was home with so many females around them, . . . I accompanied Mr. Lee yesterday to see a sick woman who he baptised she is very near death and is afraid to die, her husband is very tender. . . . I know you are anxious to hear from me all that is going on, but I have this request to make, have none of my letters published without my permission—and what I tell you in confidence I hope you will keep—you will be anxious to know if there is any prospect of my having a Protector. let me tell you there is. Mr. J. Lee has broached the subject, it remains for me to say whither I shall be his helpmate in his important charge; I look unto the Lord who has thus far directed me in the path of duty. . . . such a step I would dare not take without wisdom from above. . . . I expect to give my heart and hand to J.

Lee. . . . I am happy here, though I have not forgotten home and all its endearments, and if I can be useful here among these wretched race of Adams sons and daughters here I will toil here I will live and die and be buried. . . .

1838
Mission House, Willamette March 25
My Dear Mother

Before this time I presume you have heard from me by way of England; when I then wrote I did not think the next would be handed to you by my husband whom you will be surprised and gratified to see. . . .

I shall trouble you to purchase some articles for me of which I will give you a list. I wrote you once to send my bed quilts and have them quilted that are not and send me whatever else you please. I have a good feather bed made of two single ones an *old bachelors* and an *old maids*. You may jog Mrs. Martins memory for a pair of fine linen pillow cases she promised me when I should get married, and also yours for the linen sheets and coarse brown towels. I am weary and cannot write much more. . . .

In haste and much love I remain yours as ever
Anna Maria Lee

Mission House April 6th 1838
My Dear Husband

I have taken up my pen to answer yours received . . . . Could you but know what comfort your communications yield to my lonely heart . . ; they are a precious balm—I am now waiting the reception of another. I still feel cheerful, sometimes lonely especially when obliged to lie down in pain, then I feel the loss of the dearest half, though weeping endures for a season joy returns again—as yet I have been out but once since you left, . . . some seem surprised at my cheerfulness. The Dr. [Elijah White] informs me that

Before you receive this if my life is spared I shall have become a mother; and you my mother can realise my feeling when I look forward to that hour when I shall give birth to the first fruit of our union. To be separated from him at that time trembling nature seems almost to shrink. . . . If I cleave unto the Lord I shall be secure and will receive that support I shall need in every trial. . . .

I may hold myself ready before my time, my being in so much pain, he thinks will forward the business.—What do you think? . . . If I were a little bird, I should be most happy to fly to you, and secretly take peep at you, and then fly off again. I would not have to speek. . . . oh my dear, if we never meet again on earth, how pleasing it will be, even in eternity, to reflect on the pleasant life we have led since we became *one*; yes I now look upon the past with delight, and I feel confident if we are spared, we will continue happy in each other, . . . I often at midnight fancy you sleeping on the cold, hard, ground, while I have so good a bed to lie on and surrounded by so many comforts. . . . my mind seems to be gradually preparing for what I must pass through, and I feel to welcome whatever the Lord sees fit to call me to, even if it be unto death; I trust I shall be enabled to say "Thy will be done, . . . I am in much pain while I write, but the subject is pleasing to me; and my mind is in a comfortable frame—I cannot sit long at a time to write—the last I wrote you was part of the time on the bed—It is Saturday and I must see to my bread—April 8 It is now Sabbath, and a pleasant day, our meeting is just out. . . . Nature has put on her beautiful attire, and conspires to make all around us pleasant—I sometimes wish Husband was with me to walk out, and enjoy its sweets—but I walk no where but in the garden. . . . Farewell my dear Husband, believe me ever to be yours in the strongest bonds of love, and increasing affection—

Anna M. Lee—

Mission House April 14. 1838—
My Dear Husband

Though weary with the labours of the day, (it being a buisy [*sic*] day) I do not design closing my eyes to sleep to night, without assuring you of the joy I experienced in the reception of two letters from you to day. . . . every additional one from you, is but a new token of affection, and an evidence to me, that *duty* alone has called you from me, at this time especially. . . . I used to sing, of the blessings of *Celibacy* I have turned my song to, oh the happiness of *Matrimony*! I believe I have the right *one*, and he selected, and given me by my Heavenly Father—I find the old saying in our case is not true, "out of sight out of mind." I know that the heart that truly loves, never forgets and absence only tends to increase affection between two hearts that beat in unison, as *thine* and *mine*. . . . Well, as it respects my health it is about the same; I do not feel in my heart to murmur, but am endeavoring to wait patiently the time, when the *cause* will be removed. I wrote you in my last what the Doctor's opinion was, I think the time is past, and I shall go on to the proper time. I should like to know where you will be about the middle of June, you may guess where your other self will be. I frequently fancy you are near me, and almost hear your foot step, and hand upon the latch of the door, but alas, it is a dream; I often look around the room where we have spent so many pleasant hours together, where we have bowed knee in suplication together, but he who was wont to be with me, is not here in body but I expect is present in spirit. There are many things in our little appartment to remind me of you, but they only say *he is gone* your old chair is where it used to be, when you sat in it to write, it is the seat I ocupy this moment; your white hat hangs just where you left it, to wait the return of the head it formerly crowned; your comb hangs just where you left it and likely to remain there; even your old shoes remain on the shelf in silence, waiting with patience the return of the wearer. . . . and these things make me feel a void in this *lone* bosom, which no other earthly object can fill. . . . Farewell my husband, God bless you, and return you to my embrace again, after a speedy journey—until then I shall endeavour patiently to wait. I remain your affectionate wife, in the strongest bonds of increasing love while life remains,

Anna M. Lee

Sarah J. Lemmon Walden Cummins
1828-1919

Shortly after her arrival in the
Oregon Country in 1845, Sarah J. Cummins, a young bride, survived
an ordeal that challenged her endurance and strength of will to the
limit. The memory of this experience became a part of her *Autobiography and Reminiscences*. The work was popular in its day and went
through at least seven editions between 1914, when it was first
published, and 1919.

From her autobiography, we learn that Sarah J. Lemmon was born
September 16, 1828, in Sangamon, Illinois, the daughter of John
Lemmon and Jane Bourne Crocker Lemmon. Sarah received her early
education from her mother, "a well educated woman of her time and
a student of history and good literature." When her father settled on a
land claim on the site of the future town of St. Joseph, Missouri, one
of Sarah's classmates was Benjamin Walden, who had come to work
in her father's brickyard.

In February of 1845, Sarah, her father, and her brother Lemuel
were seriously ill with "lung fever" (consumption or tuberculosis).
They were advised by the family doctor to leave the Mississippi Valley
and go to Oregon. The Lemmons decided to leave in the spring for the
Willamette Valley, but not before Sarah, age 16, was married to
Benjamin Walden, on April 16, 1845. The Lemmons and Waldens set
out together from St. Joseph, Missouri, in May of 1845, and arrived at
The Dalles, September 14, 1845, after a difficult journey. Their next
challenge was to find a way to cross the Cascade Mountains with Mr.
Lemmon's one-hundred-head of cattle, too many to float downstream
on the Columbia River.

The family decided to transport the Walden-Lemmon goods down
the Columbia in three Indian canoes and yawls that had been towed
up river by the Hudson's Bay Company. Sarah was to travel in one of
the canoes with her mother, brothers, and sisters, and her husband
was to help lead the cattle over the Cascades. "I expressed my determination differently," Sarah recalled (40). Although she was barely
seventeen at the time, weighed less than 80 pounds, and had only
recently recovered from consumption, Sarah insisted on accompanying
her husband over the mountains.

Sarah, Benjamin, and the rest of their party came near death from starvation and exposure as they traveled the Cascades in heavy rain and snow, finally becoming disoriented and lost on the steep slopes of Mt. Hood. Sarah's account of this trip, "We Cross the Mountains and Are Lost for Eleven Days," was written as Chapter 9 of her *Autobiography and Reminiscences,* and an excerpt is given below.

This selection is a strong example of coping with uncontrollable forces. Survival became an issue of will, determination, and resourcefulness. Sarah's strength of will far outdistanced her size and physical strength. She was sustained in coping with this traumatic journey by her connections with others—her husband, her brother, and those who shared food—but also by her faith in God and the solace she found in her love of nature as she sat transfixed by the majestic beauty of Mt. Hood and glimpsed for the first time the vivid green forests and valleys below which would become her new home.

Sarah and Benjamin Walden survived their ordeal and moved on from Oregon City to settle in Salem and later in Eastern Oregon. Benjamin Walden died in 1887, and Sarah married Dr. R. Cummins of Touchet, Washington, in 1894. On August 13, 1919, five years after publication of her autobiography, Sarah J. Cummins died in Chester, Montana.

My Will Was Not to Be Swayed

My husband and Mrs. Welch's three sons were to drive the stock. After some deliberation it was decided that my brother, Lemuel, should accompany them. That decided my case. I, too, would accompany them. To this there was a strong remonstrance but my will was not to be swayed in that matter. Mother wept but I told them of my fears concerning their frail boats to stem the current of that raging river, for we had seen the Celilo Falls. Father and my husband had gone as far as the Cascade Falls. After some consideration of the matter she finally became more reconciled. Soon as all the arrangements were completed we gathered the stock, counted them, and started out on our perilous journey. This was the first day of October, 1845.

I forgot to mention that we were to be assisted by one of father's hired men, the same Marion Poe who had traveled with us from the first day of our journey. On the day of our departure I placed my new Spanish saddle that was bought for me in St. Louis, on my strong and trusty young nag, and, with parting tears and good-byes, we dared the wilderness and the desert.

We were substantially provided with food as a good horse was loaded with all necessary provisions, but on the second day out from The Dalles Poe was left to bring the pack horse while we were rounding the stock in the direction of our destination and again he met a band of straggling Indians. As he attempted to talk to them they deliberately led the pack horse into ambush and half an hour later we returned from the various courses that had called us away and found Poe riding dejectedly along, with nothing to prevent us from starving. We would have returned to The Dalles but the others were already two days journey down the river and we were not prepared to replenish the stores. So it was left us to attempt the mountains without food, except beef.

After another day or two we heard loud hallowing behind us. The sounds were not such as to cause alarm and soon it was seen to come from a party of five young men and one old trapper. These parties were not cumbered with baggage and thought to go on ahead and select camping places and kill game. Learning of our loss the Smith boys kindly divided stores as far as we would permit them, giving me nineteen biscuits and a small rasher of bacon. A small portion of tea and sugar was tied on my saddle so we had a comfortable supper.

The traveling was slow and toilsome. Heavy fall rains were coming on and the steep slopes were almost impassible for man and beast. On the sixth day we became entangled in a thicket of vine-maples and were compelled to turn back to our camping place of the previous night. Next day we found it impossible to proceed through the dense growth of Mountain Laurel. The cattle ate freely of this shrub and were so poisoned that we dared not eat the meat.

The old gentleman, Mr. Carson, had been chosen guide and he was misled by the Indian trails that led to the berry patches far up on the slopes of Mount Hood. So we had been making little progress toward the place of our destination. One morning we awoke in a blinding snowstorm. We toiled along the whole day through without seeing a tree or a spear of grass. Our course seemed to be up a gradual steep slope. As night was coming on it seemed we must all perish, but weak, faint and starving we went on. The stronger men now led the way and left relays to shout back so that we might follow them. My husband and I were the last in the line. The strongest horses had given out before noon and we were compelled to walk and lead our riding nags.

The loose stock became so weak and discouraged that we left them altogether, but the poor lost creatures followed along for most of the afternoon. Our situation was each moment becoming more desperate. The only hope of our lives lay in finding shelter and wood for a fire. The few pieces of bed clothing that were tied on our saddles were wet and our garments were dripping wet through and through with the snow that had fallen on us all day long and had melted. . . . As the evening light illumined the receding storm clouds we realized our hazardous situation as never before and we turned our course down the mountainside. Fortunately for us there were no shadows and the eternal snows cast a white light that was sufficient to guide our feet, even after the day had drawn to a close. We were now crossing the line from the eternal snows into that newly fallen and, as our weary feet sank into the sand that underlay the new snow, hope deserted us, yet on and on we went. At a few minutes before 10:00 o'clock that night we were walking on firmer ground, the wet snow being about a foot deep. I was so faint and weak that I could scarcely put one foot before the other and was dragged along by my husband. One man was leading a fine young horse of which he had taken great care, and leading the animal near my side insisted that I ride. My husband lifted me on the horse but not one step would the poor beast take although I weighed less than eighty pounds at that time. . . . My husband was now leading me along and lifted me over the obstructions of the path. We were of course the last in the line of relays and the welcome sound of "we have found wood," was wafted to our ears. This gave us a renewed energy and by an almost super-human effort we at last reached the assembled group. No sign of a fire was to be seen and most of the men and all the boys were shedding tears. We were told that not a man could be found whose hands had strength to fire a gun, and not a dry thread of clothing for kindling. All were panic stricken and all hope seemed abandoned.

My husband had been exerting all his power in assisting me along and as soon as he realized the situation he seized the gun and fired it into the little bunch of kindling the men had prepared, but no fire resulted. He now made every man present haul off his coat and in the inner lining of Mr. J. Moore's coat a small piece of dry quilted lining was found. This was placed in a handful of whittlings, and as the gun was reloaded all realized that upon that charge depended our lives. With almost super-human effort Mr. Walden succeeded in firing the gun and in an instant the flames burst forth. . . .

I was so exhausted and discouraged that I sat down on a hummock and was perfectly indifferent as to the result. But soon as there was sufficient warmth my husband led me to the fire side. No sooner had the warmth penetrated my wet and freezing garments than such excruciating pains seized me that I was wild with pain and could not forbear the scream that rent the air on that wild mountain. . . .

My saddle horse was the only animal that was brought into the camp and soon my bedding was spread up to dry, and while the great pitch pine trees were consumed with fire the group of weary travelers were soon fast asleep. Mr. Walden presented me with a biscuit, one that he had carried since our morning meal, fearing that some such extremity might overtake us. The morsel of food renewed my strength and as the warm woolen blankets were wrapped snugly around me I reclined near the great heap of glowing logs and felt that God in his great mercy would yet guide us safely into the land of our adoption. We slept soundly and awoke to find the sky cloudless, clear and aglow with the light of the morning sun. The only hope of our lives now lay in the men finding the cattle that one might be used for food, as not a morsel now remained of any sort and some of us had been stinted for more than a week.

All arose and, after due deliberation, it was decided that I should remain with the two boys, my brother Lemuel, and Mrs. Welch's son. All the others were to go in quest of the stock. We watched the weary procession as they disappeared over the distant slope and the boys would have given up to tears, but that hope which precludes despair was ever present in my heart and, after obeying the instruction to "Keep a good fire and smoke going, as it may prove a guide to our return," I proposed that we go to the summit of a near ridge and look beyond and in the direction of our anticipated home. In our wanderings I became separated from the boys.

My attention was wholly devoted to the majestic hue of Mount Hood as seen from that high Southern slope. We were far above the timber line and the prospect was great. We were at the edge of vast snow fields and looking upward towards the summit I saw an unusually black looking spot, and after clambering up many hundreds of feet I came upon what seemed to be an extinct crater, and near what seemed to me to be the summit of a mountain. I anxiously hoped to see smoke issue therefrom. I sat down, lost in thought and admiration of the beautiful and wonderful view that opened before my eyes.

The sky was cloudless. The storms of the previous day had so cleared the air of dust and impurities that my horizon was boundless, and this, my first, prospect of everlasting green forests and their wonderful vividness, green on all the near approaches and changing with wonderful blend from green to ethereal blue, and on the distant margin rested the shade of blue, so intense, so indescribably beautiful that no power of words can express the wonderful panorama of beauty with which my soul was entranced. Seated on eternal snow, looking from over these mountains and hills, across wide valleys into dark glens, above the roar of wind or of water, I was lost in infinity.

Time speeded by without my conscious measurement. It was now about 12:00 o'clock in the day. The descent proved long and tedious. I went in search of the boys and found them busily engaged rolling boulders down the mountainside to hear the crash of their descent and the thud of their landing in the depths of some forested canyon far beneath our feet. By persuasion I convinced them of the dangers of their amusement, and we walked in various directions viewing the curious and wonderful things about us. At some distance from us we saw a curiously colored copse and on approaching nearer we found it to be a dense growth of small green bushes loaded with masses of small purplish berries growing on slender twigs. The fruit was odorous and of a tempting look. I feared to eat them although they were as fragrant as ripe apples, but, venturing a taste, I found them delicious. I plucked some branches and carried them to our camp fire and tested them again and again until I decided they were harmless. The boys and I ate freely of them. Our hunger and thirst was appeased and we realized the nutritious effect. We now carried and laid by the camp-fire a fine stock of the berries to await the return of the weary and starving men folks, should they be so fortunate as to reach us when nightfall should overtake us.

Just before sunset the men and beasts were seen crossing a distant ridge. Instinct seemed to have directed the weary, chilled beasts to climb a distant ridge where they found shelter under a towering cliff. . . . The horses and cattle were in one group apparently afraid to venture out in the snow. The grand rock roof and sandy floor protected them from cold and storm, and but for the tinkle of their bells they might have perished. . . .

Early next morning we resumed our journey, having butchered a beef which we could not eat on account of the poisoned laurel. One of the men had named the fruit which we produced, huckleberries, and from these we made our only breakfast food. My own party had been fourteen days with only nine hard-tack biscuits and four small slices of bacon. The Smith boys and all the others in the crowd were also about out of food, and it was decided to make forced marches in the direction of Oregon City, which, from this treeless height, we judged to be nearly West of us.

We kept the stock with us until we reached the grass lands at the head of Sandy River. Each one then decided to go in quest of food as the men were becoming desperate and had lost all fear of wild beasts so that even the sight of a grizzly bear would not have frightened us. Our horses were now so weak that my husband could not ride any one of them only a few rods at a time. My case now developed the last stages of starvation.

Just after dark we reached the river where it was now quite a broad stream, rolling and tumbling over high boulders. I tried to urge my pet riding nag into the water but it was no use. On the opposite bank we saw a small fire burning and rightfully judged it to be some lagging member of our advanced party. My husband desired to cross, hoping to find something for our starving nags to eat.

After awhile we heard the sound of a human voice. It proved to be Mr. Allen Miner, a young man who had left the party early in the morning and had walked all day in advance of us. He had crossed the river in daylight. He called our horses by name and at this they plunged into the raging stream. My saddle girth broke and I had to hold by the mane and balance myself as Dolly would swim the deep channels, mount the rugged rocks or plunge over the sand bars, but, by the mercy of God, husband and I found ourselves safely across. Allen had a bright fire to welcome us and had killed a bird which he had broiled, and this he shared with us.

We rested until daybreak. The horses had lain all night by the fire and we had great difficulty in getting them up by daybreak. Allen Miner now took the two boys, Mrs. Welch's son and my brother, Lemuel, and forged ahead in search of food. Husband and I went on as fast as our weary limbs would carry us. Most of the party reached the home of Peter Hatch about 2:00 o'clock on that afternoon. They were given some food and were put to bed. Husband and I came in sight of their lights, for Mrs. Hatch kept a tallow candle burning in the window and outside of the house a good fire of logs that we might be guided to their place.

I now took off my blanket dress and put on my spick and span new dress and corded sun-bonnet which I had carried safely on my saddle, and thus arrayed, by my husband's help, I staggered into the door. Mrs. Hatch caught me in her arms and her first words were, "Why dear woman, I supposed your clothing had been torn off your body long ago."

We were seated by the fire. She bathed our weary limbs, and after we had rested a few moments, seeing our starved, wan look, she apologized for having but one potato baked with salt and a little butter for each. She then entertained us with pleasant conversation and put more potatoes to bake. In less than an hour's time we were served with baked potatoes, meat, butter, and a small slice of bread. We then retired for the night.

We awoke early with ravenous appetites. Mrs. Hatch was aware of this, and, knowing the danger of our condition had wisely stinted our meals. Our breakfast was more substantial. They had beef of excellent quality and on this day we were given four meals, and each one recovered from this nineteen days of want with no serious after effects.

Bethenia Owens-Adair
1840-1926

A major crisis in the life of
Bethenia Angelina Owens-Adair was her divorce from LeGrand Hill at
Roseburg, Oregon, in 1859. She had married Hill at the age of
fourteen, bore their only child at sixteen, and found herself a divorced
woman at nineteen. In her autobiography, *Dr. Owens-Adair; Some of
Her Life Experiences* (1906), she recalled: "I was, indeed, surrounded
with difficulties seemingly insurmountable,—a husband for whom I
had lost all love and respect, a divorce, the stigma of which would
cling to me all my future life, and a sickly babe in my arms, all rose
darkly before me" (52).

Bethenia Owens-Adair's future
looked bleak on more than one occasion, but she refused to be a victim. Her
innate optimism, stamina, and strength
of character served her well throughout
her life. The story of how Owens-Adair
left an abusive marriage, provided for
herself and her son, gained an education, earned two medical degrees, and
became one of the first women to
practice medicine in Oregon is the
record of a remarkably resourceful
woman.

Although the majority of her life was
spent in the Pacific Northwest, Bethenia
Angelina Owens was born February 7,
1840, in Van Buren County, Missouri,
the second of nine children born to
Thomas and Sarah (Damron) Owens. When Bethenia was three, the
Owens family crossed the plains in the first major migration to the
Oregon Country. They settled in 1843 on the Clatsop Plains, at the
Oregon Coast, and moved ten years later to the Umpqua Valley,
across the river from Roseburg.

Early in life, Bethenia Owens wished she had been born a boy.
Small in size and not reaching her full height of 5 feet and 4 inches

until she was twenty-five, she was not to be outdone by her brother in wrestling and other feats of strength. Looking back on those years, Owens-Adair wrote: "The regret of my life up to the age of thirty-five was, that I had not been born a boy, for I realized very early in life that a girl was hampered and hemmed in on all sides simply by the accident of sex" (8).

The "accident of sex" also made Bethenia Owens the target of unwanted sexual advances. When she was "just past thirteen," an Englishman, who was working for her father, persisted in trying "to make love" to her. One morning, while Bethenia was doing the family wash and stirring the clothes with a long broom-handle, the man came up behind her. "[C]atching me around the waist," she recalled, "[he] hugged, and tried to kiss me, and then he jumped back and laughed triumphantly" (20). Bethenia turned and gave him "such a whack with the broom-handle that he staggered, and rushed under the stairs, and plunged his head into the cranberry barrel." She continued to beat him until her mother came and pulled her off "by main strength." But, Bethenia had the last word: "You little skunk, if you ever dare to come near me again, I'll kill you" (21)!

Not all men, however, were "skunks" to Bethenia. In 1854, she married LeGrand Hill, then twenty-five and formerly her father's farmhand. Early marriages were not uncommon in the Owens family; Bethenia's sister Diana, "The Beauty of Clatsop," married at thirteen, and Bethenia married at fourteen.

Although Bethenia and LeGrand Hill moved several times during their marriage, LeGrand was more interested in hunting or reading than in working. In 1858, when Bethenia was "broken in spirit and health," she left Hill, and they were divorced the next year. When a friend asked her why she left her husband, Bethenia replied: "Because he whipped my baby unmercifully and struck and choked me,—and I was never born to be struck by mortal man" (53).

When Bethenia left Hill, she knew she would be "protected" by her parents; however, she was determined to be independent—to support herself and her son George. She reclaimed the name of Owens and worked at washing clothes, sewing, and teaching school so that she could complete her own education. After a period of several years in Washington Territory and Astoria, Oregon, Bethenia Owens returned to Roseburg in 1867, where she conducted a successful dressmaking and millinery business for six years.

During this period, Bethenia Owens became involved in the temperance and woman suffrage causes. As a friend of Abigail Scott Duniway, she became a subscription agent and regular contributor to

Duniway's woman's rights newspaper in Portland, the *New North-west*.

After her son attended college, Owens decided to enroll in medical school. She had enjoyed nursing the sick and recalled that she was "always the family nurse." Options for women seeking medical degrees were circumscribed, and once again the "accident of sex" was against her. But she gained admission to the Eclectic Medical College in Philadelphia, one of a number of institutions that trained sectarian practitioners as homeopaths, hydropaths, and eclectics. When she told family and friends of her plans, she was met with a "storm of opposition." Women might be nurses but not doctors! "My family," she wrote, "felt that they were disgraced, and even my own child was influenced and encouraged to think that I was doing him an irreparable injury, by my course" (80). While others "sneered and laughed derisively," only Jesse Applegate, an early Oregon pioneer and her "dear and revered friend," encouraged Owens to study medicine.

After arranging for her son to board with Abigail Scott Duniway and work on the *New Northwest,* Owens went east in 1873. One year later she returned with her medical degree and opened an office in Portland. Her specialty was the care of women and children, and she offered popular water cures, including medicated vapor baths combined with electrical treatments for rheumatism and chronic diseases. But, an irregular medical degree and a limited practice were not enough. In the fall of 1878, she enrolled in the University of Michigan's Medical School. Even Jesse Applegate thought she was foolish to close her profitable eclectic practice and return to school. "Remember, my friend," Applegate told her, "that wealth is power" (89).

Despite the opposition, Bethenia Owens went after what she wanted: a medical degree from a reputable institution. She received her degree from Michigan in 1880, at the age of forty, and then spent a summer of clinical and hospital work in Chicago, did postgraduate work at Michigan, and toured European hospitals. When she returned to Portland, her specialty was established as diseases of the eyes and ears and, not surprisingly for a woman doctor of the period, the majority of her patients were women and children.

Bethenia Owens, M.D., married Col. John Adair, a graduate of West Point, in 1884, and she became Dr. Owens-Adair. Their one child, born in 1887 when she was forty-seven, died within three days. The couple did, however, have two adopted children: Victor Adair Hill, a grandson, and John Adair, Jr. The family lived on a farm near Astoria for eleven years, and Owens-Adair served in general practice as a country doctor.

In 1899, when crippling rheumatism set in, Dr. Owens-Adair sought a better climate for her condition. She moved with her husband to North Yakima, Washington, where her son George was practicing medicine. In 1905, Dr. Bethenia Owens-Adair retired, and the couple moved to Sunnymead Farm, at Warrenton, Oregon. The next year her autobiography was published. Colonel John Adair died in 1915, and Dr. Bethenia Owens-Adair died on September 11, 1926, at the age of eighty-six, in Astoria.

I FELT EQUAL TO ALMOST ANY TASK

Just prior to our marriage, Mr. Hill had bought a farm of 320 acres on credit, four miles from my father's home, for $600, to be paid for in two years.

The improvements on it consisted of a small cabin, 12x14 in dimensions, made of round logs, with the bark on them, each notched deeply enough at its end to dovetail into its neighbors above and below it. The cracks still remaining after this rude fitting were filled with mixed mud and grass, but this cabin had never yet been "chinked." It was covered with "shakes" (thick, hand-made shingles three feet long), which were kept in place by poles, tied down at each end. The door was so low that a man had to stoop to go in and out, and it was fastened with the proverbial latch and string. The cabin had neither floor nor chimney, and the wide cracks admitted both draughts and vermin. Later I gathered grass and fern, mixed them with mud, and filled these cracks, thus shutting out the snakes and lizards, which abounded in that region, and which had made me frequent and alarming visits. The window consisted of two panes of glass set in an opening made by sawing out a section of one of the logs for that purpose. . . .

Our furniture consisted of a pioneer bed, made by boring three holes in the logs of the wall in one corner, in which to drive the rails. Thus the bedstead required but one leg. The table was a mere rough shelf, fastened to the wall, and supported by two legs. Three smaller shelves answered for a cupboard, and were amply sufficient for my slender supply of dishes, which comprised mostly tinware, which, in those days, was kept scrupulously bright and shining. My sugar-bowl, cream jug, steel knives and forks (two-tined) and one set of German silver teaspoons, I had bought with my own little savings before my marriage.

My cooking utensils were a pot, tea-kettle and bake-oven (all of iron), a frying pan and coffee-pot, a churn, six milk pans, a wash tub and board, a large twenty or thirty-gallon iron pot for washing purposes, etc., and a water bucket and tin dipper. All these things, including a full supply of groceries, I got on my father's account, as he had told me to go to the store and purchase what I wanted. This I did in the afternoon of my wedding day, the ceremony having taken place at 10 a.m. He also gave me a fine riding mare, Queen (my saddle I had already earned long before), one fresh cow and a heifer calf, which I selected; also one cow which would be fresh in the early fall, and a wagon and harness. In addition, mother gave me a good feather bed, and pillows, a good straw bed, a pair of blankets and two extra quilts. My husband's possessions were a horse and saddle, a gun, and less than twenty dollars in money; but I considered this a most excellent start in life. I knew what my father and mother had done, and I then believed that my husband was the equal of any man living. . . .

In the beginning of our married life, my father had advised my husband to begin at once to fell trees, and hew them, and put up a good house before winter set in. There was an abundance of suitable timber on our land, near by, but he was never in any hurry to get down to work. In one way and another he managed to idle away the summer, going to camp-meetings, reading novels, and hunting. . . .

It was late in the fall before the logs for the new, 16x20 foot house were even ready to be hauled out. My father had provided two doors, two windows, shingles, nails, and rough lumber for the floor. (No ready planed lumber was to be had in those days. All planing was done by hand.) He had these all on the ground long before Mr. Hill had finished the logs; but at last they were done,—cut the proper length, hewed flat on two sides, the bark removed, and deposited on the building-spot. They were notched to suit, as they were laid together, in building.

When all was ready, father came, with men to raise the house, and mother with him, bringing pies and cakes, and to help me with the dinner. Quilting parties, house-raisings, and hog-killings were always social events in pioneer life.

My father and the other men under his direction soon had the house up, with the openings for one door and windows sawed out; and all departed happy with the sun yet high in the heavens. Father said, before starting: "Now, Legrand [*sic*], go right at it

and put the roof on, for you can look out for a hard rain soon."
Next morning I slipped out of bed at 4 o'clock, and milked the
cow, and when breakfast was almost ready, I skipped in, and tick-
led my husband's feet to waken him, and put him in a good humor
(for he was not pleased with father's advice).

At breakfast I said: "Now we have an early start, and we will
just show father how soon we will have that roof on, and floor
down." I was so excited over the prospect of having a fine new
house, with a floor, and windows, that I felt equal to almost any
task. In two days the rafters were up, and the roof was going
on. . . .

By the time the roof was on, Mr. Hill began to get tired, and
suggested a hunt, but I begged and coaxed for at least one-half of
the floor, so that we could move in, till he reluctantly went
ahead. . . .

When a little over half the floor was done, Mr. Hill stopped to
put in the door, which was not completed when he severely mashed
the thumb of his left hand, which meant the loss of the nail, and a
lay-off for some time.

Oh, dear! This was terrible. November was nearly gone; the
cooking must be done on the old stove in the hut, and we must sit
there, with the rain leaking all around us! The stove could not be
moved into the new house till an opening was made for the pipe,
and we had not sufficient pipe to reach out of it, had there been
one. I was planning to get more pipe with the butter, and few eggs
I could collect in the next few weeks. . . .

I was not yet 15, but, girl as I was, I could but realize that this
condition was due not only to poor management, but to want of
industry and perseverance. I did not then know, however, that a
man with a perfect right hand and a quick and willing wife to help
him, could have gone right ahead and finished the work. My husband now suggested that we go to father's for a "visit." I did not
like this, for I realized that father did not approve of his shiftless-
ness, but I had to consent, for he had begun to exhibit temper
when I objected to any of his plans or suggestions. . . .

I was married in 1854, and a year from that time, in the spring
of 1855, my husband and I started to move farther south, to the
foothills of the Siskiyou mountains, beyond Jacksonville. . . .

At this time there was much gold excitement in and around
Yreka [California], and Mr. Hill decided to go there, and thinking we could not take the cows, he sold them. And now we had
some money. . . .

Unidentified family group with overturned covered wagon, probably in Eastern Oregon.

Mr. Hill had an aunt, his father's sister, a Mrs. Kelly, living there [Yreka]. . . . In March a small, one-roomed, battened house, with a "lean-to" for a kitchen, and a lot, were for sale at $450,— only a block from Aunt Kelly's. That was then a great bargain, and we bought it, paying $300 down, all the money left from the sale of my two cows, heifer and the wagon and horses. My Queen was out on pasture, and continued to be a "bone of contention," as she was only an expense. But I stoutly refused to have her sold. . . .

We moved into our new house in March, with the $150 mortgage hanging over us. On April 17th, 1856, our baby was born, . . .

Mr. Hill neither drank or used tobacco, but, as his aunt said, he simply idled away his time, doing a day's work here and there, but never continuing at anything. Then, too, he had a passion for trading and speculating, always himself coming out a loser; and thus the time dragged on, until September, 1857, when who should drive up, one glad day, but my father and mother. . . .

It did not take them long to understand that we were barely living "from hand to mouth," as it were, with most of the work coming on me, so father said:

"How would you like to go back to Roseburg? It is a growing town. I have several acres in it, and if you think you would like to make the change, I will give you an acre of land, and the material for a good house, which you can put up this fall. The boys can help you, and there will always be plenty of work at carpentering in town."

To say that we were delighted with this proposal expresses it but faintly. We sold our house and lot in Yreka, realizing less than $100 out of the transaction, as the $150 mortgage and interest had to come out of the sum received for the property. . . .

On reaching home, father told me I could go over and select my acre of land, and our building-spot, which I gladly did. He told Mr. Hill he could have the team, and he and the boys could haul the lumber for our house, so that he could get to work on it at once. . . .

Father then told him that he and mother had talked it over, and had decided to deed the property to me and the boy; that he had given us one good start, and now, after three and a half years, we had nothing left but one horse, and that he thought it best to secure a home for me and the child in my own name.

This enraged Mr. Hill, who said he would not build on the lot unless the deed was made to him, as he was the head of his family. Father advised him to think it over, and not to act rashly.

He sulked for a time, and then bargained for a lot in town, after which he hired a team, and hauled lumber off from the acre to the lot, and began to build the house. All this time we were living off father, who said nothing; but furnished the shingles, and told Mr. Hill to get nails, and anything he needed, at the store, on his account, which he did. In time, the roof was on, and the kitchen partly finished, and we moved in. . . .

My health was poor. I had not been strong since the baby came, and I could not seem to recover from the effects of the [typhoid] fever. The baby was ill and fretful, much of the time, and things were going anything but smoothly. A short time before the climax, I went home and told my parents that I did not think I could stand it much longer. Mother was indignant, and told me to come home, and let him go: that "any man that could not make a living with the good starts and help he has had, never will make one; and with his temper, he is liable to kill you at any time."

Father broke down, and shed tears, saying:

"Oh, Bethenia, there has never been a divorce in my family, and I hope there never will be. I want you to go back, and try again, and do your best. After that, if you *cannot possibly* get along, come home." I went back, greatly relieved, for I knew that if I had to leave, I would be protected.

Our trouble usually started over the baby, who was unusually cross. He was such a sickly, tiny mite, with an abnormal, voracious appetite, but his father thought him old enough to be trained and disciplined, and would spank him unmercifully because he cried. This I could not endure, and war would be precipitated at once. A few days before our separation, his father fed him six hard-boiled eggs at supper, in spite of all I could do or say. I slept little that night, expecting that the child would be in convulsions before morning. And thus one thing led to another until the climax was reached.

Early one morning in March, after a tempestuous scene of this sort, Mr. Hill threw the baby on the bed, and rushed down in town. As soon as he was out of sight, I put on my hat and shawl, and, gathering a few necessaries together for the baby, I flew over to father's.

I found my brother ferrying a man across the river, and I went back with him. By this time, I was almost in a state of collapse, as I had ran all the way,—about three-fourths of a mile. Brother, seeing that something was wrong, and always ready to smooth out the wrinkles, took the baby with a smile, saying: "Give me that little 'piggy-wig'; and shall I take you under my other arm? It seems to me you're getting smaller every year. Now, just hang on to me, and I'll get you up the hill, all right. Mother will have breakfast ready, and I guess a good square meal is what you need."

The next day father saw Mr. Hill, and found he had been trying to sell the house and lot. Father told him that he would come with me to get my clothes, and a few things I needed, and that he (Mr. Hill) could have the rest. That he (father) would take care of me from that time on, and that when he (Mr. Hill) sold the house and lot, I would sign the deed, as the lot was not paid for, and the unfinished house would, according to law, go with it.

However, before Mr. Hill found a purchaser, he had repented, and come several times to get me to go back to him. I said: "Legrand, I have told you many times that if we ever did separate, I would never go back, and I never will."

Esther M. Selover Lockhart
1825-1916

Bound for the Oregon Territory in the spring of 1851, Esther Selover Lockhart, her husband, and their baby daughter set out from Ohio with high hopes. Years later, Lockhart recalled that the West had beckoned to them with the promise of "a sort of Aladdin's lamp. We had only to touch or rub it and all our wishes would be fulfilled speedily" (*Destination, West!* 56).

Romantic visions of the West were brought into perspective when Esther Lockhart faced difficult conditions on the Overland Trail and especially when she discovered the rude realities of pioneer life in Oregon. Although she was willing and able to cope with inconvenience, adversity, and danger, Lockhart entered a culture in which she was often viewed as an outsider—the "Yankee" schoolteacher with "eastern ideas" about the virtues of cleanliness and good housekeeping, the equity of husbands and wives sharing household chores, and the evil of "matrimonial abuses" under the Donation Land Act of 1850. To a point, Lockhart was willing to adapt to the pioneer culture, but she was not willing to compromise her values about right and wrong.

Class differences set Lockhart apart and were particularly evident in her early schoolteaching experiences in Oregon. Her advanced education in Ohio not only enriched her life but enabled her to support her family; however, the manners and customs she had acquired in a private female academy did not always match those of a more rustic pioneer culture. In all probability, the fact that Lockhart and her husband were both native New Yorkers also contributed to perceptions of "Yankee" peculiarity.

Esther Lockhart told of some of her experiences in "Recollections of Early Days," a narrative included in Orvil Dodge's *Pioneer History of Coos and Curry Counties* (1898). Lockhart's daughter, Agnes Sengstacken, later published her mother's autobiography as *Destination, West! A Pioneer Woman on the Oregon Trail* (1948).

Born in New York and schooled in Ohio, Esther Mehitable Selover Lockhart might have lived out her adult years as an Ohio schoolteacher or as the wife of a well-established farmer or businessman. She was born January 13, 1825, in Ulysses, Tompkins County, New York, the eighth of nine children of Peter and Elizabeth (Mead) Selover. Her father, who had a successful business transporting passengers and goods on Lake Cayuga, died when Esther was eight and left little for his widow, seven daughters, and two sons. The Selovers, including Esther's married brother Isaac, moved to Ohio (Northwest Territory) about 1835, and settled on a farm.

Esther Lockhart recalled five pleasant years in Ohio, years filled with spelling bees, quilting parties, church meetings, lectures, and visits from the cobbler and the spinster seamstress. All this changed, Esther recalled, when "my little mother died." Esther was fifteen, and she had nursed her mother in six months of illness: "Unaccustomed to such hardships as life in a primitive, new country presented, my mother weakened under them" (*Destination, West!* 25).

After her mother's death, Esther Selover went to live with her sister Lufanny and attended the village school until she was sixteen, when she sought her first teaching position. She had "keen competition," and "there was a slight prejudice to giving the position to a woman, especially if that 'woman' was a slender girl of sixteen" (28). But, unlike her male competitors, Esther was "willing to accept a salary of a dollar and a half a week," and her teaching career was launched in an Ohio village schoolhouse.

Education was valued in the Selover family and, at nineteen, Esther enrolled in Miss Flanders' Norwalk Academy, near Fairfield, Ohio. She was placed in advanced studies in chemistry, French, and botany, in what "might be considered a college course." After one year, Esther accepted an invitation to become vice principal of the academy, and she served in that capacity and continued her academy studies until she was twenty-three. "Then I decided to take a private school," she wrote, "with one pupil only" (29). On March 16, 1848, Esther Selover began her "private school" by marrying Freedman Goodman Lockhart, a childhood friend from New York. Esther wrote that she was deeply in love and "thought him a real Adonis."

Although Freedman Lockhart tried his hand at farming, his wife soon realized that he was not "a 'born' farmer" and that "his tastes were more of the intellectual type." "When his feet were on the ground," she wrote, "his head was among the stars" (31). Possessing "a fine logical mind and nimble wit," Freedman Lockhart "would have made a good lawyer" and "also had an aptitude for medicine" (36). Effective as a lecturer for the Sons of Temperance in Ohio, Freedman later used his "unusually persuasive personality" in Oregon politics.

For Freedman Lockhart, reports of the Oregon Territory held great appeal, and he wanted to break away from the monotony of farming in Ohio to become a part of the New West. He convinced Esther to leave Ohio and, in the spring of 1851, with their fifteen-month-old daughter, they started on "a great adventure." "We had no thought of fear from any source," Esther wrote. "What foolish optimists we were!" (36). Although they planned to return to the East to visit relatives in five years, Freedman never went back, and Esther only returned for a brief visit after thirty years.

After the six-month journey, the Lockharts arrived in Oregon City on September 13, 1851. During their life together in Oregon, Lockhart followed her "globe-trotting husband" in a number of moves. Throughout their years together, Esther and Freedman Lockhart shared intellectual interests, and they had a strong, mutually support-ive relationship. Although Esther made few comments in her autobiography about her husband's political activities in Oregon, Freedman Lockhart was elected to the Oregon State Legislature in 1866 and again in 1870. He died in Empire City, on August 30, 1882, leaving his widow, two sons, and four daughters.

In the excerpts we have titled "It Was Up to Me," taken from *Destination, West!*, Esther Selover Lockhart describes how she coped with "boarding around" as a schoolteacher in the Yamhill area of the Oregon Territory, how she reacted to the marriage boom promoted by the Donation Land Act of 1850, and how she assessed and dealt with a deadly threat to her baby and herself. Her standpoint is that of a well-educated and articulate woman. Uninhibited about discussing her difficulties in adjusting to pioneer ways, Lockhart was able to laugh at herself, and the reader often laughs with her. Good humor, as well as the ability to adapt when appropriate, helped the "Yankee" school-teacher cope with cultural differences and unfamiliar circumstances.

It Was Up To Me

When it became known that I had at one time been a school teacher, I soon had plenty of opportunities to resume this work in my new home. Teachers were very scarce then. As my husband had not yet decided what we were going to do, or where we were going to be located, I finally yielded to the many importunities and commenced a private school in the family of a Mr. Norton, a farmer living near. . . .

I knew that conditions at Mr. Norton's would not be very home-like. But I tried to realize that I was now a pioneer, living under pioneer manners and conditions. Supper the first night at my new home consisted of hot biscuits, very large and coarse, milk, "jerked" beef, the latter prepared on the place, naturally. It was put on the table in large chunks, and each person was supposed to cut off as much of it as he desired. The table was covered with an old colored oil-cloth and tin cups were provided for the milk. There was no butter and it was several days before Mrs. Norton found it convenient to churn some. However, the Nortons were generous providers in their primitive way, but shiftless and extremely poor managers.

When the first Saturday came round, I prepared to do some of my family laundry work. My husband, who had just returned from a fruitless prospecting tour, carried water from the "branch," as the Nortons called the creek, filled the washboiler and placed it over the open fire for me. Mrs. Norton was a deeply interested spectator of these proceedings, and finally she remarked, rather sadly, "The Yankee men are so good to their wives, they help 'em so much!"

After that, I frequently noticed Mr. Norton's way of "helping" his wife. He would stroll in leisurely, after his work or his lounging was over, look around critically, peer into the water bucket, and would then call out loudly, in a tone that brooked no delay, "Mary Jane, I want some water! This bucket's empty!"

And poor Mary Jane, weary and uncomplaining, would stop her dinner getting or put down her fretful baby and run with alacrity to the spring to "fetch" water for her lord and master. Yet her husband was not unkind to her. It was just his way.

Mr. Norton was an illiterate man and therefore much impressed by the "larnin' of the Yankee school-ma'am," as he called me. My school room adjoined the family kitchen, with a sort of Dutch door, separated in the middle, between the two rooms. Nearly every day Mr. Norton would come and lean his big, brawny arms over the lower part of this door, listening in rapt attention to the regular school routine. Often I would see his keen blue eyes gleam with pride and pleasure at one of his children's recitations. Frequently he would slap his plump sides and exclaim in his hearty, genuine way, "Wal, ye do knaow a heap, school-ma'am. I'd give a thousand dollars if I knowed jest half as much!". . .

After teaching at Nortons for four months, I went to another district, where I had a much larger school, nine of the pupils in the former place coming to me in the new location. This time I was to live at the home of Judge Eldon, who had a very large family, not all, however, of school age.

The Eldons were delightful, intellectual people, but extremely poor housekeepers. . . . Of course, this was not a very satisfactory condition of affairs for me, with my strait-laced eastern ideas concerning housekeeping in general.

In this careless household the dishes were always wiped with the same dirty-looking rag with which they had been washed, after it had been wrung as dry as possible. Occasionally, I dried the dishes for the girls and always insisted upon getting a clean white cloth for that purpose, much to the amusement of the entire family, who laughingly declared that "the Yankee women are so particular!"

Every meal I would find half a teaspoonful, or more, of dishwater in my cup. I invariably wiped it out with a corner of my white apron—we all wore aprons in those days—and though my action was plainly visible, as I intended it should be, as I took no pains to conceal it, no apologies or improvements were ever made.

The Eldons had a fine large farm, with many cows, but for the first six weeks of my stay there we had neither milk or butter, simply because they were too indifferent and indolent to attend to the matter. When we finally began having butter, I enjoyed it immensely, until one day when I happened to pass through the kitchen where Mary, one of the girls, was working it with her hands. The sight of the soft, oily substance running through her red fingers sickened me so that I could not taste it again. . . .

Under the bed in my room, which had cracks in the walls so wide that I could almost put my fingers through them, there was a hetereogeneous mass of old boots, shoes and discarded clothing from the different members of the family. These had evidently been accumulating for several years. This accumulation extended from the floor to the straw mattress above, and the odor arising from this mouldy, dirty and decaying rubbish was anything but agreeable or healthful.

One day when I was cleaning the room, I remarked to Annie, one of the daughters, that if she would tell me where to put the things I would take them out from under the bed. Saying that she would ask her mother, she disappeared, returning in a few minutes, however, with the cheering intelligence that "Maw said not to bother, that they were all right there.". . .

According to the Oregon Donation law in force at that time, every citizen—women were not considered "citizens" then—of the United States over eighteen years of age and married, was entitled to "take up" six hundred and forty acres of land, one-half of which was to be his wife's in her own right. If single, a man could take but three hundred and twenty acres. This condition of affairs naturally encouraged every bachelor in the Territory speedily to become a benedict. As a result, many matrimonial abuses developed. Young women of suitable age for marriage were few in the Territory. Thus girls of tender age were sacrificed to greed.

I personally knew of one case where a child of four years was married to a mature man, the "husband" leaving for the mines immediately after the ceremony. Another case that came under my observation was that of a girl of eleven years, who was married to a man of twenty-eight. Several months after this marriage some of my friends spent the afternoon with the little wife, who was a relative of theirs. She helped her husband prepare the supper for their guests, but after the meal was finished she disappeared. Finally she was found in the back yard, having a glorious time with a neighbor's little girl, "teetering" on a board thrown over a log. The husband came back into the house, cleared the table and washed the dishes, remarking as he did so, "Lizzie's young yet!" I'd say that she was!

One Sunday at church my attention was called to a pretty, delicate-looking girl, who also had been married at eleven years of age. She held a baby of four or five months in her arms and another child of about two years stood by her side. These immature marriages, these crimes again nature, as they seemed to me, used to make my old-fashioned "Yankee" blood fairly boil with righteous wrath. . . .

For some time now my husband had been "prospecting" in the country, looking for the elusive gold mine that he always hoped to find. In July, 1852, he came for me and our little girl and we went down to the Umpqua Valley, where he had located a claim of three hundred and twenty acres, at a place called "Camas Swale.". . .

After we moved to Camas Swale, while our log cabin was being built of logs hewed by hand from the virgin forest, we lived for about two months in a tent.

There were many rattlesnakes in the vicinity. I could rarely go to the spring, a few rods distant, without seeing at least one, and frequently I saw several of these venomous creatures. I kept a sharp lookout on my little girl to see that she did not stray far from my side. . . .

While we were living in the tent, I had what seemed to me quite a thrilling experience. No matter how long I live, I shall not forget that little incident. It is not one I would ever wish to repeat, even though it might again end happily. One extremely warm afternoon I put my little girl to bed for her usual nap. As was my custom, I lay down beside her for a few moments. The child soon fell asleep, and as I was about to rise from the bed I saw a sight that seemed to paralyze every nerve and muscle in my body. In the tent, close by the head of the bed stood a large chest that we had brought from Ohio, and which we then used as a table. A foot or so away from this chest, and parallel with it, was an old-fashioned, brass-studded leather trunk, which we had also brought across the plains. This trunk was not as high as the chest by perhaps eighteen inches. As I glanced up, preparatory to rising, the head of a large rattlesnake appeared between the chest and the trunk, scarce a hand's breadth from the bed. I could have touched the creature from where I lay. I seemed absolutely petrified when my astonished eyes first rested on this hideous thing. But it was for a very brief period that I remained in that condition. With startling reality I understood that something had to be done, and done quickly, too, if my life and my child's were to be saved.

There was no one near to help me. My husband was working at our cabin a quarter of a mile away, and could not have reached me in time to save us, even if he had heard my cries for assistance. It was "up" to me to save the situation. . . . But I did not know what to do. All sorts of ideas and schemes rushed through my bewildered brain in a moment, but the main thought underlying it all was that I must somehow get off the bed speedily and find the axe. With this thought uppermost, I began working my way quietly but very rapidly to the foot of the bed, the horrid creature watching me constantly with its bright, beady eyes, its tongue darting angrily back and forth as it hissed its displeasure. It seemed like an eternity to me until I succeeded in getting off the bed. Then I ran like mad to the outside of the tent where the axe lay beside the woodpile. Seizing it, I darted back into the tent.

On the outer side of the low trunk, I could still see some of the snake's tail, and I knew that it could not spring until its body was entirely out in the open space between the chest and the trunk. Now, with the friendly axe held cautiously in my hand, I approached the trunk on the side toward me. Suddenly, the creature put its head down on the ground, drawing the tail out of sight, probably preparing to coil and spring. Instantly, then, I was up on the trunk, axe in hand, and then, nerved to desperation, I brought the heavy end of the axe down on the snake's head, grinding, grinding, grinding slowly and fiercely, literally working for life itself.

I continued to grind heavily upon the reptile's head for several minutes, not daring to stop for fear it might not yet be dead. I knew all too well that a wounded and maddened rattlesnake was far more to be feared than an unharmed one. Finally, after what seemed an interminable length of time to me, I took courage and cautiously lifted up the axe. To my inexpressible joy and relief, I found that the creature was motionless. No need for me to say that I felt like shouting, and then suddenly I grew very faint. . . . But though I had succeeded in destroying the enemy that would have taken our lives, I was not satisfied to have the horrible thing in the tent with me and my child. But how was I to get it out of the tent? I finally evolved a plan that I thought would succeed. I went outside, found a long stick, returned to the tent and gradually drew the horrid creature out into the air. Then, in some way, I never knew just how, I managed to transfer it to a wide board that I stood up against a post where I could watch it from inside the tent to see if the snake showed any signs of returning to life.

It had not hung there more than an hour when two horsemen rode up. They exclaimed in surprise when, in answer to their questions, I told them where and how I had killed the rattler. Dismounting immediately, they counted the rattles, finding seven and a button. However, I am happy to say that this was my first and last encounter with a rattlesnake. I was well satisfied to have it so.

Emeline L. Trimble Fuller
1847-?

For most westward-bound emigrants, the overland journey was a trial lasting five or six months, often involving hardship, deprivation, illness, and sometimes even the death of loved ones. The horrifying conclusion of thirteen-year-old Emeline Trimble's journey with her family from Iowa to Oregon, in 1860, would scar her life forever. Few adult women have coped with more devastating circumstances than those faced by young Emeline.

Some thirty years later, at the urging of friends in her church who thought the story of her experience should be told, Emeline Trimble Fuller agreed to publish her narrative, *Left by the Indians: Story of My Life*. James Hughes, in his introduction to the book, said of Emeline: "Often we noticed her careworn face and listened to her solemn testimony, and heard her weighty words on an important church affair. . . . We noticed also that she did not kneel when she came to the alter [*sic*]. She was deprived of this luxury . . . by previous suffering" (3). Emeline Trimble Fuller was then forty-five years old, and the chilling story she told in her memoirs was her eye-witness account of the "Utter Massacre," an attack by Snake Indians in which twenty-nine people, including all members of her family, were either killed outright or died of starvation.

According to Donald H. Shannon, author of a 1993 chronicle titled *The Utter Disaster on the Oregon Trail*, "the casualty count was the highest of any recorded along the trail" (ix). Although Indian attacks on overland trail migrants were rare, the "Utter Massacre" fueled stereotypes of Indians as bloodthirsty savages. Shannon also underscores the involvement of white men in the massacres of 1859 and 1860. He suggests there is "ample evidence that 'renegade' white men were the instigators and even participants in almost all of these attacks" (introduction 1). The Indians in the "Utter Massacre" were Snakes, about whom Shannon says, "Although Snake was a term used for all Shoshoni, it generally applied to the Northern Shoshoni and Bannocks centered on the Snake River Plains, and also some Northern Paiute of eastern Oregon" (19).

Young Emeline Trimble was one of a handful of survivors rescued by soldiers after living through forty-five days of hell. She was taken

to Fort Walla Walla, after which she was offered a home with some of her father's relatives in Linn County, Oregon. During her school days in Linn County, Emeline relived her trauma: "While in the school-room trying hard to learn, the scenes of the past would come up before me, and it seemed that my heart would break. . . . Many times I was happy with my young friends, and tried to be so; but night would come on, and I would pray for dear mother to come and take me, and cry myself to sleep" (Fuller 35-36).

In 1863, Trimble married John M. Whitman, and they moved to Tillamook County, on the Oregon Coast. Later they lived in Eastern Oregon and Washington Territory. "Here," she wrote, "we took a homestead timber claim, and bought some railroad land adjoining. We farmed, kept a store and stagestand, or travelers home" (39). The couple adopted an eleven-year-old nephew of Mr. Whitman and raised him to adulthood. After her husband's death, Emeline returned to Wisconsin and married Melvin Fuller, a widower with seven children. "We lived together for four years and a few months and then separated on account of trouble with the older children," she explained (39-40). In 1892, when her memoirs were published, she was living with her "uncle Payne" and his family in Marshfield, Wisconsin.

In her narrative, Emeline Trimble Fuller wrote that she was born at Mercellon, Wisconsin, on February 21, 1847, first child of Abagel Payne Trimble and her husband. Two more children were born to the couple—Christopher, in 1850, and Elizabeth (Libbie) in 1852. Also in 1852, Emeline was blinded in her right eye by an accident. She recalled that her father "took a nail and while driving it in a cross-piece under the wagon, the nail flew and struck my right eye as I was looking on, causing almost total loss of vision ever since" (5). Then, shortly after moving to Iowa, Emeline's mother and father both contracted typhoid fever. Her father did not recover, and the family moved back to Wisconsin to live with relatives.

In 1858 the family made a new beginning when Abagel Trimble married Elijah Utter, a widower with three sons and three daughters. Elijah was "a blacksmith by occupation, and a large-hearted, honest man, who proved a good husband to mother, and good father to us children" (7). Thus Emeline's immediate family increased from four to eleven, and then to twelve when a baby girl was born to Abagel and Elijah the next year.

With hope in their hearts for a better future for themselves and their ten children, the Utter family yoked their oxen to the wagons and started for Oregon on May 1, 1860. The family did not travel with a large, organized train, but fell in with other emigrant wagons along the way.

During the 1850s, the relatively peaceful relationship emigrants enjoyed with the Indians along the Snake River routes began to change. The Hudson's Bay Company no longer manned their Snake River posts, and the native people had become frightened at the increasing number of immigrants invading their homelands. According to Shannon, there had been three major attacks on emigrant trains crossing the Snake River plains in 1859 (19). The men of the Utter party must have realized there could be danger, especially for such a small group of wagons—eight according to Shannon, although Emeline Fuller remembered nine.

At Ft. Hall, the Utter party requested an escort of soldiers. Colonel Howe, commander of Ft. Hall, "sent out a small force, with instructions not to go more than half as far with us as those he sent with the train ahead" (Fuller 11). Twenty-two dragoons were assigned to escort the train for six days along the trail and then return, and they were furnished with rations for only twelve days. Also, while at Ft. Hall, five recently discharged soldiers asked to join the Utter train and were granted permission. They were equipped with guns and were to "act as guards or scouts" for the party (Shannon 25).

One of the dragoons, eighteen-year-old Lucius (Charles) M. Chaffee, deserted and joined the Utter party. With the addition of Chaffee, their party now numbered forty-four persons—eighteen men and boys who could bear arms, five women, and twenty-one children between the ages of one and fourteen (Shannon 37). Only fifteen of these people would survive. When the dragoons turned back, Emeline's party was warned they "were just in the edge of danger" (Fuller 11).

Trouble was not long in coming. After they had traveled about a week, a group of five Indians came into camp one night, and "all agreed that the leader among them must be a white man, as his dress and appearance was differant [sic] from the rest. He had a beard, and you could see plainly that he was painted. He wore an old white hat, with the top of the crown gone" (12).

The Utter party was suspicious of the Indians and the painted white man who came to their camp. Emeline wrote, "[W]e all thought them spies, and, I often wish that we had done as our better judgment told us, and killed them and secreted the bodies. . . ." (13). The Indians remained nearby for another two weeks, visiting, selling salmon, and then going away. Later, one night, two yoke of oxen disappeared.

The following section of Emeline Fuller's narrative begins the next morning, September 9, 1860. The site of the Utter Massacre is pinpointed by Donald Shannon as "midway between Murphy and Grand View, Idaho"; bodies of the Van Ornum family were found near Huntington, Oregon (introduction 1).

Sometimes coping is simply facing the reality of the situation with which you are confronted and doing the best you can under the circumstances. The circumstances facing thirteen-year-old Emeline Trimble were as extreme as one could ever imagine. She watched in terror while her stepfather, three stepsisters, a stepbrother, and then her mother, whom Emeline begged to flee, were killed before her eyes.

With her parents gone, young Emeline might have been frozen in grief; instead, she assumed responsibility for her siblings and gathered the remains of her family, five children all younger than she. Emeline Trimble had to make do and empower herself as best she could: "I nerved myself for that terrible struggle for life which I could see was before me."

The raw details of this forty-five day struggle for life are ghastly, almost incomprehensible. Throughout this ordeal, Emeline had only the help of her courageous, eleven-year-old brother, Christy, until he, too, was taken. Little, if any, assistance came from the other immigrants, who were mainly concerned with saving themselves and their own children.

I Nerved Myself

We traveled only a short distance before we came to a grave where a man belonging to the train ahead of us had been buried, and the Indians had dug him up, taken his clothing, and then partly buried him, leaving one hand and foot out of the grave. You cannot imagine what a terror struck to our hearts as we gazed on the awful sight and reflected that we too might share the same fate. For on looking about us we saw a board on which was written an account of his being killed by the Indians, and warning anyone who came that way to be very cautious. But the warning came too late to do good, for we had not gone more than a mile before we were attacked by them. This was the 9th day of September, 1860. As we came up the hill and turned down towards Snake river again, we came in full sight of the Indians, who were singing their war songs, and their shrill war whoop I can never forget. It was too terrible to even attempt to describe, but suffice it to say that although so many years have elapsed since that awful, awful scene, I can never hear a shrill yell without shrinking with much the feelings which I experienced as that terrible noise reached our ears.

We saw at a glance what we must do and corrrelled our wagons as quickly as possible. There were only nine wagons in the train, but we had sixteen men and boys capable of bearing arms, and were well armed. There were also five women, and twenty-one children between the ages of one and fourteen years.

Perhaps it might be of interest to tell you of the families in the train. Elijah Utter and wife, with their ten children, Mr. and Mrs. Myers, with five children, Mr. and Mrs. Vanornam, and five children.

After a short time the Chief rode up and down the road waving a white cloth and motioning for us to go on at noon. Two or three of the Indians came up close to us and motioned that they wished to talk with us. Some of the men went out and met them, and they said they would not hurt us, that they were only hungry, and that we were to go on after noon, but I can tell you that dinner time did not find us with our accustomed appetites that day.

Shortly after noon we started, but did not go by the road as they expected us to do, but kept up the hill from them, and the

last wagon had hardly started before they commenced their terrible war songs and dancing again, and coming toward us all the
time. We correlled our wagons as soon as possible, but before we
could get the last one in place, the man who was driving was shot
dead. . . . We fought them all that afternoon all of that long, awful
night, picking them off as often as we could get a chance. We had
no chance to get way under cover of night, as they were watchful,
and if they heard the least noise would commence whooping and
shooting at us. We talked it over, and made up our minds that we
were all to die, but thought we would try leaving all the wagons
but one for each family, and take some provisions, leave all our
stock and other property, and see if they would not let us go our
way. There were with us three discharged soldiers from Fort Hall,
and . . . [a] deserter. . . . They were mounted on horses and were
to go ahead and clear the way for us to follow with our wagons.
But instead of doing so, the discharged soldiers put spurs to the
horses, which belonged to Mr. Vanornam, and galloped off for
dear life, and left us to our fate. The deserter stayed as long as he
could and stand any chance to save himself, and then taking with
him the Reath brothers, Joseph and Jacob, they left, taking the
one horse with them which belonged to the deserter. In the horrible tumult of the fight we did not see them go, and did not know
but they were killed.

The Indians now seemed to redouble their frenzy and show-
ered upon us a continual fire, until it seemed impossible for one to
escape. . . . As Joseph Reath was helping my oldest step-sister,
Mary Utter, from his wagon, a ball passed through his clothes
and entered her breast. She only lived a few minutes. The next
one to go was my step-father, who had his baby, one year old that
day, in his arms. As I stepped up and took her from him, so he
could the better use his gun, I kissed him and turned to mother,
who was bending over my dying step-sister, Mary, when father
was shot in the breast and fell. He got up, but hardly got up when
he fell close to his daughter Mary, and soon died. We gave up
then. It seemed as though our whole dependance had been taken
from us, and leaving our wagons, we started, each one for himself. I turned to my poor mother who was standing by the dead
bodies of husband and children, and begged her to go with us, but
she said no, there was no use in trying that we were all to be
killed, and that she could not leave father, and when I found that
I could not persuade her to go, I took one last lingering look at
her dear face, and taking my poor little baby sister in my arms

and telling four of the little brothers and sisters to follow me, I started, I knew not whither, but with the one hope of getting away from the wretches who seemed to thirst for the blood of everyone of us. I turned and motioned to my mother, who still stood by the wagon where I left her, with two of my step-sisters and a little step-brother. She shook her head, but the oldest step-sister started to come to me and they shot her down. I turned and ran a little way, and looked back, and they had all been shot down, and were lying with the rest of the dead. I felt then that all that I held dear on earth was dependant upon my feeble care, and child as I was, I nerved myself for that terrible struggle for life which I could see was before me.

Will the reader of this narrative please to pause a moment and reflect upon my situation. A child of barely thirteen years, and slender in build and constitution, taking a nursing babe of one year, and four other children, all younger than herself, and fleeing for life without provisions and barely clothing enough to cover us, into the pathless wilderness or what is worse yet, across the barren plains of the west. It was now the 10th day of Sept., and getting dark, the second day after the attack. Others also fled, and we got to gether as much as possible and made for the river, . . . We decided upon the course that we would keep away from the road and travel in single file, and as near as possible cover our tracks by having a man step in each track.

We traveled by night and hid in the willows that grew along the river, by day. We traveled only a short distance that night and we could see the fire from our burning wagons and such goods as they could not well carry away, and before morning we hid in the willows on the river bank and lay there all day. We saw some of the Indians going past us driving off some of our cattle, for it seemed that they divided up into small bands and dividing their spoil, each one went his way. While they were passing, I held my hand over the mouth of my baby sister, who, frightened, perhaps by the scared faces around her commenced crying. Poor little sister, how my heart did ache for her. Words can not describe my agony as I looked on the faces of my little brothers and sisters, poor orphans now, and heard them cry piteously for father and mother, and if possible worse yet, cry for bread when I had none to give them. . . .

The Indians followed us four days, coming onto us about the same hour each night. . . . They came close, but . . . they did not strike us. . . . After the fourth day we did not see nor hear anything to alarm us, and travelled by day and camped by night.

You will perhaps wonder what we could get to eat. Well, we got so hungry during the third night's travel that we killed our faithful family dog, that had shared our hardships through all that long journey. We also killed Mr. Vanornam's, roasted and ate some of the meat, and carried the rest along for future use.

We kept on our journey through the wilderness until we came to the Oyhee [*sic*] river, near where Fort Boisee used to stand, and all being tired out with travel and weak with hunger, we camped there.

We had found a cow the day before, which had strayed away from the train ahead of us, and was trying to go back home. She was very poor, but we shot her, the first shot which had been fired since we left the wagons. We roasted her, and carried the meat over to the Oyhee [*sic*].

We had traveled more than 100 miles, although it would not have been much over 80 by the road, since leaving the wagons, but so far all were alive, although our sufferings were terrible, both from hunger and exposure. It was getting cold weather, and we were without extra clothing nights, and commenced to suffer from the cold. Our shoes were worn off, and we were barefoot, or nearly so, and nights we would bury our poor bruised feet in the sand to keep them warm. We set to work and built us camps out of the boughs and brush which we could find along the river, for we could see little probability of getting away from there, and tried to make things as comfortable as possible.

Mr. Myers had escaped so far with his whole family, and had it not been for him I think we should have traveled along a little way each day toward the Fort, which was to us the haven of safety, but he begged so piteously for us not to leave him, as he was not able to travel, that we would not go without him.

When we had been in camp some time, my brother Christopher was down by the river fishing one day, when an Indian came to him and seemed much surprised at seeing him, and wanted him to go home to his camp with him, but Christy told him that he had a camp of his own and must go to that. He went away, and Christy came home and told us. In about an hour the same Indian came back and had four more with him, and brought us one fish, but when he saw how many there were of us they went back and brought some more fish for us, and urged us to go to their camp with them, but we would not go. We had a great horror of being taken captive by them. We traded some of our clothes with them for fish, and they wanted Christy to go home with them, and he told us that he would go home with them, as he was afraid that if none of us went they would not like it, and might do us harm. He was a brave little fellow, and . . . only eleven years of age. . . .

Christy said that if the Indians did not let him come back that he could run away the next summer and get in with some emigrant train and reach us if we ever got through, which looked very doubtful. . . .

They [the Indians] went back to camp taking Christy with them, and said they would be back in three days and bring him with them. After they went away we talked it over and thought when they came back they would surely kill us, and Mr. Vanornam and wife, with two sons and three daughters, Mr. Gleason and Charles and Henry Utter, my step-brothers started along to try and reach Fort Walla Walla.

At the end of three days the Indians came back as they had agreed to, and brought Christy with them, and they brought fish again. Mr. Chase ate so much of it that he was taken with the hiccough and died. We buried him, but the Indians dug him up, took his clothes, and buried him again. My poor sister Libbie, nine years old, used to help me gather buffalo chips for fuel, and rosebuds, pusley [pussley, an herb of the purslane family] and other things to eat. She and I went to gather fuel as usual one morning, and she was tugging along with all she could carry and fell behind. I carried mine into camp and went back to meet her. I called her by name and she made no answer. Soon I found her, and I said, "Libbie, why did you not answer?" She said, "I could not talk I felt too bad," and before night she was dead. Soon the Indians came again bringing Christy with them. I did not see him this time as I was away after fuel. Mr. Myers asked him where they camped. Christy asked why he wished to know, and he said "because when the soldiers come we want to come and get you." The Indians, as soon as they heard the word "soldiers" spoken, said it over to each other and talked among themselves and went away taking Christy with them again. I came back with my fuel, and when on my way out quite a ways from camp I heard a frightful noise. It seemed to me more like dogs fighting than anything else I ever heard. I was scared, and made haste into camp, and they told me Christy had been there and gone back again. We waited with as much anxiety as we could feel about anything until the three days were passed and the Indians did not come back, and we felt afraid of them, and we began to talk about trying to start along, but I could not go without finding something of the fate of Christy. We waited a few days and then I went over to

Snake river, about two miles, and I could see their camps, but could not see any living thing around them. I called Christy loud and long, but the echo of my own voice was all the answer I could hear. I went back to camp feeling sure that something had happened to the boy. The next day Mr. Myers took the trail which went from our camp to theirs, and had not gone far when he found where the wolves had dragged something along, and soon he found some of his hair, and then he knew that my brother had been killed by the Indians and his body torn to pieces by the wolves. He came back to camp and told us, and words cannot describe my feelings as I heard of his horrible fate. I knew then that the noise which I heard that day was my poor brave Christy whom I loved so well.

I thought I had passed through all the suffering which I could endure, and God knows how I longed to lie down and die and be at rest, but it was not to be so, nor had I drained the cup to the dregs yet. Starvation was making sad inroads on our little band, and none but those who endured the awful pangs of starvation can have even a faint idea of such horrible sufferings and death. We became almost frantic. Food we must have, but how should we get it? Then an idea took possession of our minds which we could not even mention to each other, so horrid, so revolting to even think of, but the awful madness of hunger was upon us, and we cooked and ate the bodies of each of the poor children, first sister Libbie, then Mr. Chase's little boys, and next my darling little baby sister, whom I had carried in my arms through all that long dreary journey and slept with hugged to my heart, as though if possible I would shield her from all danger. She too had to leave me. In vain had I saved the choicest morsel of everything for her, chewed fish and fed it to her, boiled pusley which we found on Snake river, and fed her the water, and everything which I could plan had been fed to her to keep her alive. Mrs. Myers and Mrs. Chase each had babies about her age, but neither could spare a share of nature's food for our poor little motherless one, for fear of robbing her own. For over forty days I had carried her, but had to give her up at last, and I was left alone. All who had depended upon me had been taken away except the two step-brothers, who had gone on and from whom we had heard nothing. We also dug up the body of Mr. Chase, intending to eat that, but thank God, relief came. . . .

When they [the Reath boys] reached the fort, which was between eighty and a hundred miles from us, one of [them] came back with two companies of soldiers, one of dragoons and one of infantry. They started back immediately and traveled along without resting night or day.

Upon nearing us, they found a sad sight. The company who had gone on ahead when the Indians took brother Christy away, which you will remember consisted of Mr. and Mrs. Vanornam, three daughters and two sons, Samuel Gleason, and Charles and Henry Utter, the Indians had followed and killed Mr. and Mrs. Vanornam, their son Mark, Samuel Gleason, and the last of our family except myself, Charles and Henry Utter. Their bodies lay unburied, showing marks of torture too devilish for any human beings to inflict except Indians. Let those who have neer suffered as I have pity the fate of the noble red man of the forest. My pity all goes out for their poor unfortunate victims, and I can never look even upon one of our poor, degraded, harmless Winnebagoes without such feelings as I do not like to entertain towards any of God's created beings, and I almost doubt if they are a part of our great Maker's work.

Mrs. Vanornam had evidently been tortured too terribly to mention. Her ankles were tied with strong ropes when found, and she had been scalped. Three of the Vanornam girls and one boy had been carried away by the Indians. The next year we heard, by some emigrant trains, something of them. The eldest girl, 13 years old, was killed. In attempting to get away she killed two squaws, and the Indians then killed her. The boy was bought by an emigrant train, and reached his uncle in Oregon. The Indians were seen leading the two little girls with collars around their necks, and chains to . . . lead them by. A thousand pities that they had not all been killed with their parents. . . .

The dragoons commenced to bury the dead, who it was very evident had been dead but a short time but the Reath boy begged of them not to stop there for the night, as it was getting late in the afternoon, but to push on for he told them there were certainly more somewhere, and it was possible they might find them alive. So the infantry traveled all night without resting. I may say here there is no doubt but we owed our lives to that night's work of those brave, tender-hearted men, for we were sure that the Indians were on their way to kill us when scared away by the approach of the soldiers.

About ten o'clock in the morning we saw signal fires off a few miles from our camp, and we knew that either they were coming to kill us, or help was close at hand, and strange as it may seem to my readers my heart was so benumbed by my terrible sufferings that I hardly cared which it was. . . .

I was out after fuel as usual, when I saw the soldiers coming, but was too weak to feel much joy at seeing them. They rode up to me and a few dismounted, and coming to me asked if I did not want something to eat. I answered that I did not care. I shall never forget the pitying looks bent on me by those strong men. Tears stood in every eye as one of the officers gave me a part of a biscuit. I ate that, but did not care for more, but in a few days I was hungry enough to eat anything. I could not have lived many days longer if help had not reached us. . . .

After I arrived at Walla Walla, Washington Territory, I stayed with the family of Lieutenant A. J. Anderson until my cousin came for me from Salem, Oregon. . . . From Salem I went to Linn Co., Oregon, to my only relatives in Oregon that I had ever seen before. . . . The country was beautiful to ride over, and the scenery was lovely to look at. When the snow was three or four feet deep in Wisconsin, I picked wild flowers in Oregon. Everything around me, so far as nature was concerned, was charming to behold. If father, mother, brothers, and sisters had only been with me, my joy would have been complete; but they were gone, and with all that beauty spread before me, I could not help but turn my longing heart toward them, and weep in my lonliness [*sic*].

Mother Joseph of the Sacred Heart, S. P.
(Esther Pariseau)
1823-1902

$\mathbf{M}$any people would be surprised
to learn that the person recognized by the American Institute of
Architects as the first architect of the Northwest was a woman—
Mother Joseph of the Sisters of Providence. Petitioned by people of all
faiths to establish schools, hospitals, and Indian missions in the Pacific
Northwest, Mother Joseph not only raised the necessary funds but
served as architect and construction supervisor for most of these new
institutions.

Mother Joseph gave forty-six years of her life to found and main-

tain the works of charity of the
Sisters of Providence in Washington, Oregon, Idaho, Montana,
and British Columbia. Before she
died in 1902, she established
almost thirty hospitals, schools,
orphanages, homes for the aged,
shelters for the mentally ill, and
Indian schools. In May of 1980,
Mother Joseph became the first
woman from the Northwest to be
immortalized in Statuary Hall,
Washington, D. C., and the
inscription below her statue reads:
"She made monumental contributions to health care, education
and social works throughout the
Northwest."

How could one woman achieve
so much in a single lifetime? Mother Joseph was empowered by her
dedicated faith and distinguished by remarkable ingenuity, energy, and
perseverance. We have chosen to focus on her ability to cope with the
realities of life—to adapt to circumstances of all kinds, to try the
untried, and to make do with limited resources. Heavily dependent on
donations to support their works of charity, Mother Joseph and the

Sisters of Providence found it necessary to conduct "begging tours" under less than ideal conditions. Mother Joseph's chronicle of one of these early tours, which we have selected for this collection, includes vivid description of coping with the difficulties of wilderness travel and camping in 1866.

Mother Joseph was born as Esther Pariseau on April 16, 1823, in a farmhouse at Saint Elzear, Quebec. She was the third of twelve children born to Francoise and Joseph Pariseau. From her father, a successful designer and maker of carriages, young Esther learned the use of tools, and from her mother she learned domestic skills.

The association of Esther Pariseau with the Montreal Sisters of Charity of Providence, eventually known as the Sisters of Providence, began on December 26, 1843, when she arrived at their recently established religious community. In the summer of 1845, Sister Esther Pariseau took the name of Joseph to honor her father and became Sister Joseph, the thirteenth Sister of Providence to take her vows.

By 1847, the order included twenty-seven professed sisters, as well as sixteen novices and postulants. Their work involved some teaching and the care of orphans, mental patients, elderly priests, and aged and infirm women. Sister Joseph assisted with the treasury and the pharmacy, and she worked in the kitchen, garden, and carpenter shop—all important training for her future work in the Pacific Northwest.

Before her death in 1851, Mother Gamelin, the founder of the order, expressed a desire that one day Providence sisters would assist Bishop Blanchet, the new Bishop of Nesqually, and five professed sisters and novices were appointed to travel from Montreal to Vancouver, Washington Territory, in 1856. Sister Joseph, aged thirty-three, was appointed superior of the group and named Sister Joseph of the Sacred Heart. The sisters' journey by land and sea took forty-five days and involved 6,000 miles. They were accompanied by Bishop Blanchet and three associates.

Although the Sisters of Providence in Vancouver encountered many hardships, they persevered in their work. Within the first year, despite limited facilities, the sisters opened a day school, a boarding school, and an orphanage.

Throughout Mother Joseph's correspondence, three practical themes were repeated: financial worries, the need for more sisters to share in the constantly expanding work of the order, and space problems. In January of 1859, after Mother Joseph secured undisputed land for the Sisters of Providence, legal incorporation was approved by the territorial legislature, the second oldest act of incorporation in Washington. The articles of incorporation spelled out the purpose of the religious order: "the relief of needy and suffering humanity, the care of orphans, invalids, the sick and the poor, and the education of youth."

To achieve these goals, the sisters sought donations, held bazaars, and welcomed volunteer assistance. Mother Joseph and her sisters also initiated a series of "begging tours" in 1865, and they traveled at various times to Idaho and Montana mining country, and as far afield as Chile, Peru, and British Columbia. In 1876, Mother Joseph was gone for twenty months to the East Coast and Canada to raise funds for charitable works and special projects.

For their first eighteen years in Vancouver, the Sisters of Providence and their charges were housed in inadequate wooden buildings. St. Joseph Hospital, for example, which opened in April of 1858, was first located in a 20- by 16-foot wooden house originally built as a laundry and bakery for the sisters. In the early 1860s, two cabins provided shelter for the mentally ill. Although Mother Joseph resourcefully collected used building materials from the old Hudson's Bay Company fort, better materials and more permanent structures were needed.

In 1873, when space needs were critical, Mother Joseph designed a large, three-story brick building. J. B. Blanchet, an architect and nephew of Bishop Blanchet, was her assistant and construction superintendent, and they broke ground in Vancouver in June of 1873. In the fall of 1874, before the interior was finished, the sisters moved into the new building with seventy orphans. Mother Joseph "worked into the night painting and finishing window sashes and door frames as she had no money to hire workmen" (Lentz, *The Way It Was* 14). A debt of $20,000 had to be paid, other needs were pressing, and Mother Joseph's plans for a beautiful chapel could not be realized until 1883.

When the twenty-fifth anniversary of the Sisters of Providence in Vancouver was celebrated in 1881, the Elder Foundresses wrote to Mother Joseph and her sisters: "Your little Mission, twenty-five years ago, was but a grain of mustard seed, which rapidly developed and produced abundant fruit." The Foundresses continued: "In the statistics of this remarkable period, you have instructed 1,721 boarding pupils, of many nationalities, and 1,949 day pupils. You have rescued twenty elderly indigent persons and cared for 992 orphans. In your hospitals nursing care was given to 5,930 patients while 2,193 were nursed in their homes. To these last you also made 18,709 visits, while night watches in homes and hospitals were 9,099, and prescriptions dispensed were 15,188" (Letter of 8 December 1881).

In addition to her work in Vancouver, where she established the first hospital in the Northwest, Mother Joseph brought schools, hospitals, and other services to communities throughout the Pacific Northwest. She went to Spokane, for example, and lived in a rough shack while she planned Sacred Heart Hospital, which opened in January of 1887. A partial list of Mother Joseph's other hospitals in Washington and Oregon includes Saint Mary Hospital at New Westminster, Saint Peter Hospital in Olympia, Saint John's Hospital at Port Townsend, Saint Elizabeth Hospital in Yakima, and Saint Vincent Hospital in Portland, the first hospital in Oregon. Some of the schools founded by Mother Joseph were at Colville, Yakima, Colfax, Walla Walla, Tulalip, Steilacoom, Olympia, Cowlitz, Washington, and Kootenay, British Columbia. She also established hospitals and schools at Missoula, Fort Benton, St. Ignatius, and Great Falls in Montana, and at Wallace, Idaho.

Mother Joseph often feared that her confidence and courage were failing, but she found strength and peace in her faith and the work she was doing. Illness marked her last years. On December 23, 1900, she wrote to Mother Mary Antoinette, Superior General, that her right eye was "totally blind, inflamed and painful," and she also made reference to an earlier "operation on the breast." The official cause of Mother Joseph's death was given as a brain tumor, but a reading of her letters suggests she suspected breast cancer and metastasis. Mother Joseph of the Sacred Heart died on January 19, 1902.

Mother Joseph's pioneering spirit and dedication to works of charity are revealed in the selection we have titled "How Fervent Was Our *Te Deum.*" The piece is taken from the Chronicles of the Sisters of Providence, July 23, 1866, in which Mother Joseph related experiences during an early "begging tour" with Sister Catherine, one of the later arrivals from the Montreal Sisters of Providence.

After a successful collection tour of mines in the territories of Idaho and Montana, Mother Joseph, then age forty-three, and Sister Catherine set out for an eighteen-day return trip to Vancouver, Washington Territory. Rather than traveling by more costly stage coach and boat, they made the full trip by horseback. Guided by two priests and a mission Indian, the women rode sidesaddle all day, helped set up camp and cooked in the evening, and shared a tent at night, with saddle-packs for pillows. Frightening encounters with rain storms, heavy forests, falling trees, treacherous passes, a forest fire, and wild animals were offset by enduring faith and friendly meetings with Indian warriors and Mexican packtrainers.

How Fervent Was Our *Te Deum*

This time we were to travel neither by boat nor by stagecoach; only on horseback could we get through the dark forests that lay between us and our own lower Columbia country. To spare us further expense, the sisters at Saint Ignatius loaned us their saddles and riding habits. The Jesuit Fathers furnished us with horses. In the last days of September our little caravan set out. It was composed of Father Louis Saint-Onge, an Indian named Sapiel from the mission, Father Joseph Giorda, S. J., who went with us as far as Missoula, and Sister Catherine and myself. Following our cavalcade were two pack horses with provisions and a tent. So equipped, we pushed ahead into primeval forests and rugged mountain ravines. Except for meeting a few miners now and then, our solitude was unbroken.

Each night we were concerned with the business of making camp. One thing was sure—we all had good appetites. Every evening we would hasten to locate the three things indispensable for a good camp—water, grass, and trees. At a favorable spot we would dismount, and in the twinkling of an eye, every one of us would be busy at the necessary tasks. Father Saint-Onge went hunting for game, Sapiel cared for the horses and collected faggots, and we sisters took charge of the cooking. Very shortly all would be around the kettle, each with his bowl, doing credit to the stew.

Nothing is more congenial than a meal around the camp fire, with each one recounting a story while waiting for the *crêpe* to be made or the meat to broil. After a cheerful supper and a short, fervent evening prayer, each one would wrap up in a blanket, taking saddle or pack for a pillow. The tent was assigned as shelter for Sister Catherine and me. Refreshed after such slumber we would begin again next morning with breakfast at the campfire; then after packing our belongings we were on our way once more until dark. After this fashion we spent eighteen long days and nights out of doors.

As I have said, nothing is more pleasant than such evenings when the weather is fine. But we arose one morning to find that the sun was not shining and the sky was overcast. However, we had to be on our way. We ate breakfast in haste and set out.

A Sisters of Providence begging tour. It is thought that the sister on the right may be Mother Joseph.

Presently it began to rain. After several hours it not only rained but it stormed. When our caravan halted for the night, building a camp was a challenge. By that time we were wet to the bone. Finally we did succeed in getting a small fire going inside the tent, which had been set up with great difficulty. Then we resigned ourselves to lying down in the mud as near to the fire as possible. A few evenings later a great tree fell two or three paces from the tent in which we were sleeping. You can understand how fervent was our *Te Deum*.

Toward the middle of our journey, we spent several days in a particularly dense forest. We had been following a narrow trail which barely kept us from getting lost. When we were simply spent with fatigue we found ourselves between two mountain ranges which lie between the Coeur d'Alene Mission and the Flathead Mission. There was scarcely room to camp. We had a good supper on venison which Father Saint-Onge had killed during the day. We then said an earnest evening prayer and had just wrapped ourselves in our blankets when a terrifying howl frightened us almost out of our wits. Hurriedly Father Saint-Onge took his revolver and Sapiel seized his knife. The Indian quickly cut firewood to start a blaze around the camp. They knew that wolves ordinarily do not pass the line of fire, and that generally they do not attack singly but call out to each other as a signal for attack. The first terrifying call was answered in the distance by another and then another . . . and then on every side. A half-hour after that first howl, we were surrounded by half a hundred of these furious beasts. Our horses were tethered inside the line of fire. I cannot describe the fright of those poor animals.

The spot on which our camp was built had been burned over a few years before so that the trees were very dry. And now the fire which had been meant to keep the wolves at bay began to threaten us as well. A burning forest seemed to surround us. Great branches fell to the ground. This dreadful scene was made worse by the howl of the wolves now redoubled. We battled burning cinders and blinding smoke as best we could, but only prayer saved us. Some of the provisions burned, our tent caught fire several times, and our saddles were damaged. But finally the night of horror passed, and with daylight the wolves left. Although the trees had been too damp for a widespread forest fire, our peril had been very real. We offered humble thanksgiving to Almighty God for having delivered us and protected us in the midst of danger.

As we were preparing to break camp, we heard the beat of horses' hooves trampling the trail nearby. Before we could move, we were surrounded by a troop of mounted Indian warriors. They were in warpaint and ghastly to behold. Our fear was soon dispelled, however, because as soon as they saw our crosses and recognized Father Saint-Onge, they offered their hands in token of friendship and respect. In spite of their determination to be off on a scalping expedition, they treated us well. We gave them some food and were relieved to have them leave us peaceably.

There we were, still in the depths of the interminable forest, in the midst of which the old Mission of the Coeur d'Alenes had been established. Toward evening of another day, we found ourselves on the bank of a small river and prepared to camp there. The horses were put some fifty feet away in an enclosure of fallen trees. They were left untethered in this corral. While raising the tent Father Saint-Onge saw some tracks which aroused his suspicion. He called Sapiel who told him these were the prints of a grizzly bear, known to the Indians as the most dangerous animal in the forest. But what was there to do? It was too late to go farther. They decided to say nothing of our danger but to keep watch throughout the night. Their only weapons, a six-shooter and an ax, were inadequate against such an enemy. They gathered wood and immediately after supper made a large fire because they knew that bears fear fire, and approach only if driven by hunger. Knowing nothing about this threat to our safety, Sister Catherine and I slept peacefully within the tent while our guides acted as sentinels. Thanks to the dear Heart of Jesus, the night passed without incident. Early in the morning Sapiel went to look after the horses. What was his dismay to see a large grizzly bear attacking one of the horses. When the bear saw Sapiel, he jumped the logs of the corral and made for the Indian. Sapiel took to his heels with the bear in pursuit. Twice the animal struck at him with claws outspread, but by a supreme effort the man evaded the attack. Suddenly the bear was distracted by the sound of bells. A pack train of mules loaded with merchandise came in sight and the cries of the Mexicans leading the mules and those of Father Saint-Onge put the bear to flight. Poor Sapiel in his fright had been leading the bear right into our camp! What the consequences might have been, God alone knows. Once more we thanked the Lord for this new deliverance.

Another incident took place on this journey, but not wishing to alarm us further Father Saint-Onge did not tell us about it until we had reached home. One night this good priest was awakened by a sensation of cold and felt something glide across his body. He knew at once that it was a rattlesnake, and had enough presence of mind to lie perfectly still that the reptile might settle down to sleep. After what seemed hours, he sprang to his feet with a bound so that the serpent was forced to fall. It crawled away leaving Father Saint-Onge unnerved and shaken.

Finally on October 16 we arrived in Vancouver, safe but fatigued by our long ride on horseback, grateful for the success of our quest.

Susanna M. Slover McFarland Price Ede
1854-1937

We were attracted to the memoir of Susanna Ede because of the engaging details she gives of her daily life as a pioneer during the 1870s along the lower Chehalis River, Grays Harbor, and Copalis Beach. For example, she describes with precision the 12- by 14-foot cabin in which she lived during her first marriage, the food the family ate, how it was prepared and preserved, and the herbs and roots she used for medicines.

When Ede was in her eighties, she dictated her recollections for circulation within the family. They were published in October of 1976 as "Pioneer Woman in Southwestern Washington Territory: The Recollections of Susanna Maria McFarland Price Ede" in *Pacific Northwest Quarterly*. As her editors point out, Susanna Ede's experiences were not unique. "Mrs. Ede's story is, in many respects, the story of countless American women who . . . established and maintained households in dark, drafty, crowded little cabins, and bore, nursed, reared, and taught a brood of children who arrived with uninterrupted regularity" (introduction 137). Many of these pioneer women were barely out of childhood themselves, frequently marrying and accepting enormous responsibilities at fifteen or sixteen years of age; but accept them they did—and with astonishing supplies of energy and ingenuity.

Like the thousands of other pioneer women whose stories were not recorded, Susanna Ede was a woman who was empowered to cope with whatever came her way. However, we agree with her editors that "there is little in her narrative to suggest that she thought her life was at all remarkable" (introduction 138). Her recollections are notable for their reportorial style, absence of evaluation, and minimal expression of emotion or complaint. This could be due to editing or to the fact that she was recounting long-ago events, or perhaps it is because she was born in the West, and the life she experienced was what she had grown up to expect.

Susanna Maria Slover was born in Oregon in 1854. When she was sixteen, she married a man more than twenty years her senior, William O. J. McFarland—a "man of all work" (introduction 137). She was widowed at age twenty-six, when a visitor accidentally discharged a rifle, sending a heavy lead slug through both of McFarland's legs. He died of blood poisoning on October 16, 1880 (148 n8). Susanna McFarland was left with the care of six children. She owned the homestead at Elma, along with some cattle and stock, and managed to keep her family together.

On a business trip to Olympia, Susanna McFarland met Dr. J. B. Price—a widower, a man of "considerable education, and famed as a physician and surgeon." They were married in 1882, and Dr. Price obtained a position as agency physician at Quinault, where Susanna served as matron of the Indian school and Chinook interpreter. In 1884 they resigned their positions and moved to the Quillayute Valley, where the Prices took up a homestead. The doctor didn't stay in one place for long; Susanna accounted for the many moves during their fifteen-year marriage by explaining that her husband "was badly afflicted with asthma and got relief by moving from place to place."

After a move to Farmington, Susanna Price made an autonomous decision: "I resolved to move no more and the doctor would go and practice in various towns nearby and return to Farmington now and then" (150). In 1897, Dr. Price died at Ellensburg, and Susanna was again widowed. Her third and last marriage, to Walter Ede, ended in divorce.

The portion of Susanna Ede's memoirs we have titled "We Parched Peas for Coffee" concerns the years of her marriage to McFarland and opens at their homestead cabin on the Chehalis River in 1870. One can assume through the tone of her recollections that Susanna and William McFarland enjoyed a companionable and equitable relationship, which would have enhanced her ability to cope.

Susanna Ede displayed remarkable skill, ingenuity, and resourcefulness. She had obviously acquired valuable domestic knowledge from her mother and the other experienced women homesteaders in the Washington Territory community where she was raised. She learned to cook on a hearth, to preserve food, to sew and knit, and to utilize to her family's advantage the healing herbs and other natural resources which were plentiful in the Northwest. As her editors note, "She could deal with Indians, cougars, and wolves, and she could help skin a bear, scrape the hide, and render the bear grease, which she would use for cooking and medicine" (introduction 138). Ede grew up near Indians in both Oregon and Washington Territories, and learned the Chinook language as a child. Clearly there were advantages for the second-generation homesteader, born in the Pacific Northwest for, when expectations match the reality of experience, the level of satisfaction with one's life can be enhanced.

WE PARCHED PEAS FOR COFFEE

The log cabin had but one room, twelve by fourteen feet, built of cedar boards split out, shaved, and nailed to cedar studdings which were also shaved. The floor was of fir planking, unplaned, and six inches in width. The only bed was termed a "wall sticker," having for springs cedar boards split thin to give them a little spring. My mother gave us a feather bed and I later made comforts.

There was a nice little fireplace and hearth and for nearly three years we cooked by it. We soon got a tin reflector 2 1/2 feet long by 1 1/2 feet deep, eighteen-inch-wide open sides, and six inches at closed back. It rested on the hearth in front and on sheet iron legs eight to ten inches high in back. It had a lengthwise shelf on which to set vessels to cook, bake, or roast in. We baked pies, bread, cake, and roasted meat to perfection in it. We also had a cast-iron skillet on four-inch legs used for baking or roasting anything. We always had hardwood to burn. We had an abundance of hot coals to put on top and under skillets and for such salt-rising bread as we could bake.

We had no window so we used oiled wrapping paper and tacked it into place. This admitted light but shut off the view.

At that time, about 1871, we had no glass jars to can fruit in; in fact, airtight sealing of fruit was just becoming known. We bought our kerosene in five-gallon cans and when empty we made a hole in one corner of the top in which to pour the hot cooked fruit. For a seal we used pitch from fir and spruce trees, softened with bear grease to the right consistency, and dipped a cloth big enough to reach well over the hole into the pitch. We put several thicknesses of this sealer on, letting the grease mixture harden before adding the next thickness of cloth.

We usually canned wild blackberries, using the same can for two or three seasons, or until the can discolored the fruit: that is, made the juice black and tasting of the tin. We never thought or knew anything about ptomaine poisoning. . . .

[W]e took a camping outfit and went some twenty miles up John's River where the men cut cedar trees to make shakes . . . We were in a medium-size canoe with bedding, clothing, and a few pieces of cooking equipment. It had grown dark. The ever-present lantern had been lit and placed on a cross seat, about in the middle of the canoe, when the smelt began jumping into the canoe. Some-one said, "Put out the light or the smelt will sink us," which we quickly did. . . .

On this trip the women gathered huckleberries and cranber-ries, and dried some elk and bear meat, and caught fish galore. We had a box, four feet by four feet with one-foot-high sides filled with dry sand for a fireplace, set in the middle of the canoe (scow) where we did all our cooking.

When we were first married, the high waters of the Chehalis River disabled the flour mill on the bank of the river, so we had to grind our wheat in the coffee mill to make our bread. Most of the settlers in the lower half of the county had to do the same. We parched peas for coffee, though some people used rye and barley. The smut was bad in the wheat, and many an afternoon and evening we spent picking over our wheat to be ground. We also cleaned wheat and boiled it in lye water until the hulls cracked, then washed it in many waters. Then we ate it for hominy, which was very good when fried in bacon grease or butter. . . .

In all that large county at that time, and for years later, there was no doctor, and people learned the use and value of many plants for medicine. For instance: for dysentery we used an infu-sion of wild blackberry roots; for a physic, the bark of the chittam tree; for a tonic, the wild or Oregon grape root. The inner bark of the elderberry bush, scraped off and fried in mutton tallow or unsalted butter, made a wonderful healing salve. . . .

During this time at Elma, my husband was taken very ill one night and somehow I sensed the symptoms as brain fever, and I began to look about for something to make a blister on his temple, and I succeeded in getting enough mustard out of the jar which sat on the table to cover a cloth as large as a silver dollar. I applied this poultice to his right temple, and I shall always believe it saved his life for he got better as soon as it blistered.

The older women such as my mother and two aunts carded and spun yarn, and we all knit socks to send to Olympia. There they sold for fifty cents a pair to the loggers and oystermen. This was our means of buying our own clothes, shoes, and sometimes groceries. A good knitter in a long day could knit a pair of socks, the legs being six to eight inches long. The men going to Olympia would purchase calico or muslin when we needed. We sewed ev-erything by hand and made ruffles and tucks with the best. It was not unusual to make a turned-down collar of fine bleached mus-lin and hem ruffles of finest white goods. We often could get Swiss muslin or a bit of linen for a tucked white shirt bosom, and ruffle the collar, then flute the ruffle over the point of a flatiron.

My little girls (I had three) wore two or three ruffles on their print dresses made gabrielle fashion, that is, seamed from shoulder to hem on each side of the neck and flared at the bottom. We made baby shoes from old kid gloves, when we could get them, and we embroidered little merino sacks cut almost round, and flaring sleeves set in armholes. A baby's clothes had to be at least a yard long from neck to hem, and as many tucks above the hem, fine ones, as you had the patience to make—frequently a full dozen. If we went visiting we went early in the morning to spend the day, and we always took our sewing or knitting along. . . .

At one time I never saw a white woman for five months. Now in the early years on the beach we did not go to Elma or up the harbor very often for we were busy hunting, gathering seafood, and related activities to do much visiting.

When on the beach we had to return to the homestead at Elma for we had to spend six months of each year there until we could "prove up" on it, which we did in 1878.

There was a large spruce stump in front of our house that we tried to burn out but could only burn the wood inside the bark and down into the huge roots. We cleaned it all out and stored our winter supplies, such as apples, potatoes, beans, lard, etc., in there, covering it with cedar shakes, straw, and two coats of bear oil. Everything kept nicely until we returned to the beach in the spring.

Another time we had the hams of elk calves, weighing some fifteen pounds each. I cut off the joints and burned the marrow out with a hot iron rod; then I dipped the hams in hot brine and hung them in a chimney. They were smoked with hard wood, mostly alder, and weren't they good! I often prepared the breast of geese the same way.

I earned money to buy my first sewing machine making coats and pants for hunters and waterproofing them with boiled linseed oil, which I bought in five gallon cans. One outfit I finished and hung out but day after day I could not see that it had dried at all. Later I discovered that I had used castor oil from a five-gallon can supposed to hold linseed oil. I had a hard time washing this suit out.

This is the way I learned the Chinook language of the Indians. I was born where both Klamath and Cayuse Indians lived, and we bought game and berries from them and employed squaws to wash for us, so Chinook was as natural to the white children as our own tongue. This was at Oregon City, Oregon, and at Elma, Washington.

The Chinook jargon or language is composed of several languages, such as French, Spanish, English, Indian, and perhaps some others, as used by the Pacific Coast's early settlers, traders, and explorers and seafaring men in communicating with Indians of the Pacific Northwest. . . .

I was quite proficient with the Chinook jargon. Later on I was to draw a fair salary as interpreter at the Quinault Indian Agency for a two-year period. I took the Chinook from the Indians and translated it to English for the government officials. . . .

My husband and I had six children in ten years. The three older ones were girls: Elizabeth, Jessie, Bessie; the latter three being boys: William, John, Joseph.

This is how we taught our McFarland children: from the time they were old enough, that is, from four to six years, we had a short forenoon and a short afternoon school time, and I taught them myself, till later we got set off a school district, comprised of two Campbell children, four of the Damons, three Benn children, and our four McFarlands. We employed young lady teachers, and boarded the children around at different homes, and had three-month terms which continued as long as we lived there. Each family had a separate room set aside for the school. . . .

The children early learned to amuse themselves. We had a pet horse who amused them, carried all who could find room on his back, and when they got too thick, the horse would reach around and lift two or more off with his teeth, and sometimes caught too deep and pinched the flesh. . . .

The girls rode horseback quite a bit, generally with an old quilt or blanket or piece of canvas large enough to reach to the root of the horse's tail, while a surcingle would be strapped just behind the horse's shoulder to hold it on. They never had a saddle, nor did I have a sidesaddle until I was a widow. Then I ordered one from Portland, Oregon, costing eighteen dollars.

On October 16, 1880, my husband passed away at our home on Connor Creek, the result of an accident. Relatives on the harbor wanted to take some of the children to raise but we held them together.

Anne Shannon Monroe
1877-1942

Beginning in 1900, with the publication of her first novel, Anne Shannon Monroe enjoyed a long and productive career as a writer. Monroe was a strong and capable woman with the determination to cope with whatever obstacles stood in the way of what she wanted to achieve. She was in physical pain from a spinal injury throughout most of her life, had little money, was ignorant about publishing, and her family had financial needs which could have tied her to the life of a school teacher. Many would have faltered in the face of such difficulties, but Monroe had the determination, belief in herself, and courage to pursue her dream to fruition. Monroe tells the story of how she became an author in her autobiography, *The World I Saw*, published in 1928.

Anne Shannon Monroe was born in Bloomington, Missouri, the daughter of a physician, William A. Monroe. Her mother, Sarah Louise Hall Monroe, was a granddaughter of George Shannon, youngest member of the 1805 Lewis and Clark expedition. Anne traveled west by railroad in 1887, with her parents, four sisters, and two brothers to settle in Yakima, Washington, a two-year-old town started by the Northern Pacific Railroad. Monroe wrote a vivid account of their trip and arrival in Yakima in her autobiography, and her love affair with the Pacific Northwest continued throughout her life. Though she left for periods of time, moving east to Chicago and New York to further her writing career, she always came back, and much of her writing was set in the sagebrush country of Central and Eastern Oregon.

In Yakima, Dr. Monroe built a new home for his family—the first plastered house in the county—with verandahs all around and large rooms for each of the children. And there was a library, where the family's many "boxes and barrels" of books could finally be unpacked. Young Anne, however, preferred the freedom and activity of being outdoors to reading books, and thought "all the books in the world should be destroyed."

The days of youthful exuberance and hope for the future in a new land were short lived. Within two years, in 1889, Dr. Monroe died. Sadness and worry replaced the family's joy. Shortly thereafter, the

Monroes reluctantly gave up their much-loved home in Yakima and moved to Tacoma, where the children could attend established schools. Around this time, Anne was injured when she jumped from a wagon drawn by a team of runaway horses. Her dislocated hip and fractured shoulder healed with time, but a spinal injury would plague her for years, eventually becoming a source of great pain.

The years in Tacoma were marked by worry and debt. Anne's sister, Wese, went to work teaching school. Anne passed the teachers' examinations and was qualified for student training in the Normal School. Teaching was an occupation Anne disliked intensely, and certainly not what she wanted for her life. Also, long hours on her feet in front of a classroom intensified the pain in her spine.

As a child, Anne had thought she wanted to be a doctor, like her father, but she knew the wish was "more sentiment than anything else." She realized she "had never had but one dream, and that was to be a writer" (*The World I Saw* 60). In the summer of 1899, after her first year of teaching, Anne decided to act on that dream immediately. She announced to her mother that, rather than going to summer school, she would go off into the country and find a place to write.

The section of Monroe's autobiography which we include here, and have titled "I Would Write, and Write, and Write," tells of the summer during which she wrote her first novel, *Eugene Norton: A Tale of the Sagebrush Land,* published in 1900. Without money or connections, Monroe tucked her 60,000-word manuscript under her arm and set off for Chicago to find Mr. Andrew McNally, president of Rand, McNally and Company, whom she had chosen to publish her book. McNally did publish the novel, and it was well received. Anne Shannon Monroe had rescued herself from the schoolroom.

Monroe stayed in Chicago for six years, earning a living as a journalist and editor. She wrote a regular column—"Over the Tea-cups"—for the *Daily News* and she contributed a little "natural history story" to the *Record Herald* for the children's page. To help keep the rent paid, she also worked for a press clipping company.

After several years spent trying to build her career while coping with her spinal injury, Monroe was suddenly, inexplicably, released from pain. She rushed home to her rooms one evening and flung open the windows. With a shock, she realized that her spine didn't ache. "Long I sat," she wrote in her autobiography, "in the wonder of it. . . . I would ask no further boons from life, for I knew I could do what I wanted to do if only that spine would let me alone. And in some way there in that wonderful hour it gave me its word, and it has kept it" (168-69).

Monroe went on to learn the advertising business through editing a trade magazine, *Common Sense*, and returned west in 1907 to establish an all-woman advertising office in Portland, an experience not mentioned in her autobiography. Four years later, she went back east, this time to New York, where she wrote *Making a Business Woman* (1912), and contributed a number of articles and stories to periodicals such as the *Saturday Evening Post, Good Housekeeping, The Delineator,* and *Ladies Home Journal.* Karen Blair notes that during Monroe's time in the Northeast, she was awarded "prestigious residencies" at the MacDowell Colony in Peterborough, New Hampshire, and at the Brydecliffe Art Colony in Woodstock, New York (*Happy Valley* xiii).

In 1913, Monroe, in another period of her life not mentioned in her autobiography, moved back to Oregon. At around age forty, she traveled by horseback and wagon train from Bend into Harney County, where she "proved up on a 300-acre homestead for which she paid sixteen dollars" (*Happy Valley* xiii). Her life among the settlers and cattlemen provided a rich source of material for her writing.

In 1916, Monroe's *Happy Valley* was published. Although the plot meanders somewhat, the novel remains a satisfying one to read because of its well-developed characterizations and details of the difficulties confronting homesteaders in the harsh sage-brush country. Another of Monroe's books with an Oregon setting is *Behind the Ranges* (1925), a fictional account of Central Oregon cattleman and rancher, Bill Hanley. The book proved extremely popular and went through at least eight printings. In 1930, Monroe published *Feelin'*

Fine! Bill Hanley's Book, which was a more straightforward account of the life and wisdom of "the sage of Harney County," based on his notes and his sayings.

Anne Shannon Monroe never married. She implied in her autobiography that marriage would have interfered with her writing. "I know exactly what I want to do while I'm on the earth," she said, "and I can't risk getting sidetracked. I almost was once—I was almost made into a teacher. . . . I don't think it's just teaching that I run from, but from anything at all that might engulf me and keep me from doing the work I want to do" (*The World I Saw* 191).

After leaving Eastern Oregon, Monroe moved to Lake Oswego, near Portland, which she called home until her death in October of 1942. In addition to the dozens of articles she wrote for various periodicals, she published eleven books (one co-authored with Elizabeth Lambert Wood). Monroe was equally comfortable with fiction and nonfiction. Most of her writing has a positive character without being saccharine, and her essays, as well as her fictional works, frequently claim Northwest settings. Through her writing, she encouraged women to pursue careers in male-dominated fields, and she peopled her fiction with strong, capable women characters.

From the time she climbed out of her sick bed in the summer of 1899 to hop a train into the country, Anne Shannon Monroe took control of her own destiny and did what she said she would do—she wrote and she wrote and she wrote. In order to do this, she had to leave home, and she sought the peace and solace of nature as a source of inspiration and a refuge in which to write her first novel. The section of Monroe's autobiography included below recounts that episode of her life when she began her career as a writer.

I WOULD WRITE, AND WRITE, AND WRITE

I decided I would go at once and find a place in the woods—often I had dreamed of it—some ranch house where they would let me board, and I would hide away there, and I would write, and write, and write.

I was suddenly breathless with the idea. I must hurry. Something might stop me. Some wisdom might interfere. Some practical person might advise against it. I must hurry, hurry, hurry.

I went down town immediately and bought a thick roll of news-print, the full-sized sheets, so I shouldn't lose time in turning them. And then I bought a dozen thick editors' lead pencils, the soft kind that do not have to be sharpened often. I returned home and told Mamma and everybody that I was going out into the country somewhere instead of to summer school, and that I would let them know when I had an address.

I took the train that went through the woods between Tacoma and Seattle, and less than an hour out got off at a flag station called "Stuck." The name attracted me. The conductor told me a story about an emigrant train that had got stuck there years and years ago; and one of the men in the train stayed on, and filed on a claim, and he called the place "Stuck," because there he was. But, really, I thought he must have stayed because of the tall pointed firs, so fresh and green and fragrant, and the ferns everywhere. It was as beautiful as fairyland. Right away all problems of living evaporated and I felt in my own world again.

There wasn't a house in sight, but there was a road that wound off into the woods, and I followed it. Pretty soon it began to rain—a soft, gentle summer rain that came down without a bit of fuss; but it wet the road and made puddles and mud. I was picking my way along, my head down, watching my step, when I almost collided with someone, and quickly looking up, I found myself face to face with an elderly lady, plump and motherly, all wrapped up in an old plaid shawl, and carrying a basket of strawberries. "Hello!" she exclaimed with a happy sort of chuckle.

It was the most *illumined* face—gray eyes that fairly shone under a wide brow surmounted by a coil of slate-gray hair. Hardly knowing what I did, I turned about and walked with her. "A beautiful rain," she went on in a rich throaty voice. "Just what the gardens need. Oh, will you look at that robin—he took a strawberry right out of my basket. Help yourself, won't you, just as the robin did."

"I'm afraid I can't repay you with such a sweet song," I said, but helped myself.

"I'm taking them to a neighbour who doesn't raise strawberries," she went on. "At least, that is what I said when I left home, but really I wanted an excuse for a walk. Isn't the air delicious with that fresh, washed, woodsy, fragrance?"

It certainly was delicious. We chatted along till we came to the neighbour's house, a wretched shack in a stumpy clearing, without a single window. "We are going to put in windows for her," she said, sort of tenderly. "Well, good-bye. Enjoy your walk."

But I was appalled at the thought of losing her. "Oh, do let me come live with you," I burst out.

She laughed that funny, throaty chuckle that was so heartening. "Why, my dear, I haven't a place to put you," she said. "We are building and are camped in four walls with a roof over our heads, and that's about all."

"Please let me come! I can sleep just anywhere."

She regarded me amusedly, but much as she might had I merely asked for another handful of strawberries; then she said, "All right, come along."

I could scarcely believe my good fortune: what a simple world it was, after all!

She gave the berries to a sick-looking woman who came to the door—she didn't seem especially sick of anything, just miserable in her dirt and rags and unable to be any different—and we started out again. We talked along as easily as old friends—of the trees and the wild flowers and the funny little squirrels with such bright eyes and straight-up tails; and presently we met Si, her husband, who was on his way to the railway track to light the switches: a thin, narrow-shouldered, town-bred looking elderly gentleman with a tremble in his voice, but brilliant dark eyes that twinkled.

My new friend started to introduce me, but stopped. "What *is* your name, my dear?" she asked.

I told her; neither of us had thought of names before. Her name was Purdy. She finished the introduction then explained to Si about my coming to live with them. He seemed pleased.

The house was a two-story one but without partitions as yet, and everything was very much of a heap, with unpacked boxes and barrels against the walls. But the clutter didn't seem to annoy her. A log was blazing on the hearth, for the house was deep in the woods, and the air was cool. There were several comfortable chairs, a softly cushioned davenport, a long reading table littered with books and magazines, and a general air of comfort and well-being. Right away you wanted to hang up your hat.

"I hardly know where to put you," she said, looking about. "Si and I sleep in that corner back of the screen. We have our old bed and are very comfortable but—"

"Then why can't I have the upper floor?" I asked.

"There's no flooring down yet, but the lumber is up there, and Si could lay some boards, so you wouldn't come through on us."

I ran up the stairs: it was all one big open space with many windows and smelling of the new lumber. "It's perfect," I called back. "And I can lay the boards myself." I ran on down. "And now can I have a table? Some wide boards laid together on horses will do."

"Why, yes, but I can give you a nice little reading stand for your bedside. We unpack things just as we need them, and Si can easily get out the stand. But what did you want it for—books?"

I tiptoed cautiously across to her as though I might be over-heard, put my lips close to her ear, and whispered what no one else in all the world had been told—a great, a momentous secret: "I am going to write a novel."

"Of course, then, you'll want a large table," she said, quite as matter-of-factly as if I'd said I was going to shell peas. "And that will give Si an indoor job for to-morrow. He loves to do cabinet work."

I went on to the reading table. I found Emerson there, and Plato, and Confucius and Swedenborg—writers who held lanterns. And periodicals representing all sorts of cults and ists and isms. "There might be some truth in some of them that we would miss other-wise," Mrs. Purdy said, seeing me go from one magazine hastily to another. The magazines on our reading table had always been literary or scientific. These were new to me. I was curious about them. And yet there was not a preponderance of any one kind, nothing to suggest an adherence to any special brand of belief. I found, before the day was over, that the Purdys' attitude toward life was like that of scientists in a laboratory, seeking only to learn, not caring where knowledge came from. This was the big thing with them, this quest. Those other things—who they were, where they came from, what they were doing here—were unimportant. The facts, as they developed, were that Mr. Purdy had been a manufacturer of pins in New York, until the same panic that had tied us up so tight with property debts had brought on a collapse of business in the East, and dawning old age had found him with little to turn to but this strip of Western timber. They hadn't been able to sell it, so they had packed up their household goods and moved out to it and were now making a new home among the great trees.

They had managed to get an acre cleared and a garden in, and as fast as they could buy lumber were finishing the house. Their closest neighbours were the wretched Icelanders who had drifted south some way, and to whom Mrs. Purdy had been taking the strawberries. There was talk of an interurban line between Tacoma and Seattle, and if this went through, it would bring their land up in value, make it possible for them to sell off some of it, and live on the rest to a peaceful close of their years.

In the meantime, Si had got the job of lighting the switch lamps, and was thankful for the small sum it brought in, this man who most of his adult life had been at the head of his own factory.

That first night under their roof, I lay in the wide, cool bed in a state of absolute harmony. All the tension was gone, all the worry and fret, all the sense of futility and failure. I listened to the wind moaning through the treetops and fell into rhythm with it. I watched the shadows dancing on the walls, and danced with them in spirit. I even talked quietly to Papa: I told him not to be disturbed—that I would go on now and be what I had started out to be; that all his efforts for me would not be wasted, that I would complete my own life and his too. For it came to me in some strange way that I would be able to do that—live out his life as well as my own.

The next morning, immediately after breakfast, I went to work. I had my story well in mind. From the first word it fairly tumbled out. I wished for a faster medium. Hour after hour I wrote with absorbed concentration, concocting a sort of shorthand of my own to save writing all the words in full.

At twelve o'clock I was written out. I ran down the stairs in a state of wild excitement. It was perfectly wonderful, writing a book. The only trouble was that my hand would cramp, and my spine ache, so that I had to stop and rest. I wanted to go on and on, right through the day.

After lunch, I helped Mrs. Purdy with the dishes, then we went out and helped Si. They were like two children playing a game. It was romance to them—clearing the land and building a home when well past sixty. The stumps were like huge teeth with roots that twisted and turned and spread and clung. First Si would dynamite a stump, then he would take his ax and chop out the pieces that stuck, or his spade and dig around the long roots, loosening them. He was not strong, and he trembled a good deal, but all the time he beamed, and sweat, and mopped his brow, and really enjoyed his tussle with the land and the big trees. There's something about clearing land. It does something to you besides making you tired. The Purdys were finding the same sort of exhilaration in it that we had found in taking a piece of sagebrush land and making it into a garden spot. They were having the same experience, only they had great trees to contend with; and then they were growing old.

Mrs. Purdy and I would pick up the pieces of stump left scattered by the dynamite, pile them into the wheelbarrow, and wheel them away to the woodshed to dry out for winter fires. They were full of pitch and would make wonderful flames.

I found that Si didn't use as much dynamite on the stumps as he might have, because of the cost. Every cent was counting with them, and counting big. We had agreed what I should pay, just what a country school teacher would pay, four dollars a week. After I had been there a few days I asked Mrs. Purdy to let me pay more, but she wouldn't consent to it.

Each day it was the same: all the morning I wrote, all the afternoon I helped clear away stumps, and in the evening we all looked proudly at my increasing stack of filled sheets and at the clearing that was so much larger than on the day before, for one stump taken out added a very noticeable area. And then we would cook dinner, and often while Mrs. Purdy stirred something on the stove and Si toasted his feet at the fireplace, I would read aloud from one of the old philosophers, and she would pause while beating the potatoes to hear something from Swedenborg, or Emerson, or some new writer. And Si, toasting his toes, would call out, "What's that?"—not wanting to miss any of it. They were true philosophers, eternally seeking *the way* in everything. And when they found it, they began immediately to follow it. Philosophy was not a thing merely to discuss with them, but a plan to live by. They laid stress continually on how best to *live,* how best to meet the ups and downs, and to turn the downs into ups. They were truly questing people. Even sin had a side to it to be understood; it was not a thing merely to shun. It was well to be good, but just what was good? There might be two answers. Better look into it.

It was the nicest thing the way these two were interested in the same subjects, and in clearing the land, and building the house, and the way they took me into their togetherness and made me a part of their harmony. At the end of two weeks my book was finished. I sat looking at the stack of large sheets, with their 60,000 words, feeling bereft. My child was gone from me. I began turning the pages and looking back, reading a passage here and there, becoming thrilled, reading on to see how it came out. It was difficult to get up and leave it. It was like a beloved child whose curls one can never have done caressing.

"It's finished," I announced, going down to lunch. Mrs. Purdy stopped stirring the soup to receive the big news; and Si, wiping his hands on the roller towel, paused, and his eyes shone extra bright.

"Finished," repeated Mrs. Purdy; and after a moment's silence, while she looked at me with a beautiful tender smile, "And now what?"

"A publisher," I said.

"Of course," agreed Mrs. Purdy, "you must have a publisher."

Si came on to the table: "Have you thought of one?"

"Yes—I've chosen him."

Neither of them asked who he was.

Emma J. Ray
1859-1930

We were introduced to Emma J. Ray through her autobiography. She had wrestled with the question of whether or not to publish her life story but, with "the help of the Lord" and "the assistance of kind friends," *Twice Sold, Twice Ransomed* was published by the Free Methodist Publishing House in 1926, four years prior to her death in Seattle.

Although the book is subtitled the "Autobiography of Mr. and Mrs. L. P. Ray," only one chapter contains "Mr. Ray's Testimony"— the story of his early struggles, eventual conversion, and evangelist preaching with his wife. The other thirty-six chapters constitute Emma J. Ray's first-person narrative. To represent Ray's ability to cope with adversity and racial discrimination in the Pacific Northwest, we have selected an excerpt from her narrative, which we have titled "I Became Disgusted With Portland."

Born into slavery in Springfield, Missouri, on January 7, 1859, Emma Ray was the daughter of two slaves: John Smith and Jennie Boyd. Ray opened her narrative: "I was born twice, bought twice, sold twice, and set free twice. Born of woman, born of God; sold in slavery, sold to the devil; freed by Lincoln, set free by God" (15). When Emma was one month old, she, her eighteen-month-old sister, and her mother were "sold at the auction block to the highest bidder." They were bought by the Smith family, who already owned their father, and their names became Smith.

When General Frémont ordered that slave owners must give up all slaves who wanted their freedom, the Smith family "left with great rejoicing" but, Ray recalled, "We had no place to live; we did not know how to provide for ourselves" (18). A neighboring slave owner, who was sympathetic to the Union, let the Smiths live in "an old log cabin" not far from their old home.

Ray recalled that later, when the Emancipation Proclamation was issued, "such rejoicing and weeping and shouting among the slaves was never heard before" (20). Some slaves stayed on with their masters, but many left their masters immediately and, because they had no place to live, "they dug holes in the ground, made dug-outs, brush houses, with a piece of board here and there, whenever they

could find one, until finally they had a little village called 'Dink-town.'"

After the Civil War, when Emma was only seven, her mother died. "She had been worked hard as a slave," Ray wrote, "and she died in the fall of '68 leaving nine children" (24). Emma's father kept his promise not to separate the children, "to let them 'work out' and always to keep a home for them" (25).

Emma was sent to a doctor's home "to take care of a baby and to wash dishes" when she was nine. Ray remembered that she "cried every day and wanted to go home" because the doctor treated her so harshly. Eventually, she ran away from the doctor's house, and her father agreed to try to find another place for her to work.

During Reconstruction, Emma and one of her sisters attended school taught by missionary teachers from the North. "I did not go very steadily," Ray confessed. "I worked out in the summer and went to school in the winter" (26). Because she was ashamed of her shabby clothing and poor food, Emma often ate apart from the other schoolchildren so they would not see that all she had in her dinner pail was a little cornbread and sorghum molasses, if that. Emma attended school until she entered the fourth grade. She learned "to read, and write, and spell, and that was considered among our people a pretty good education" (28).

Emma met Lloyd P. Ray in Carthage, Missouri, in 1881, and they were married in Fredonia, Kansas, in 1887. Lloyd Ray, born into slavery in 1860, in Kentucky Town, Texas, was one of seventeen children of a white father and a slave mother. His father had never supported him in any way, but Lloyd's mother had always wanted him to be a preacher. Although Lloyd Ray became skilled as a stone-cutter and mason, he found it difficult to settle in one place. The early years of the Ray marriage were unhappy, and their problems were complicated when Lloyd began to drink heavily. "I had a temper equal to a tigress," Emma Ray confessed. "And a drinking man and a woman with a high temper make a home a hell" (38).

After a number of moves, Emma and Lloyd Ray settled in Seattle, in July of 1889, the year Washington was admitted to the Union. Few other blacks lived in the city, but the Rays made friends in the African Methodist Episcopal Church, established in Seattle in 1890. They became involved in the church and were converted. Lloyd overcame his addictions to alcohol and tobacco, and eventually he was baptized in Lake Washington. Emma was elected the first president of the Woman's Christian Temperance Union chapter formed in the A.M.E. Church and later became W.C.T.U. County Superintendent of Jail and Prison Work. When the pastor of the A.M.E. Church objected to the churchwomen's time being diverted to the W.C.T.U., Emma Ray asserted her autonomy and became associated with white chapters of the W.C.T.U.

Despite the personal and social difficulties they encountered, Emma and Lloyd Ray gave years of volunteer service to the needy in Seattle jails, slums, hospitals, and missions. They founded the first rescue mission, an interracial shelter, in 1895. Known as Sister Ray and Brother Ray, they shared religious teachings, music, and material assistance with the poor and unfortunate of the city—the homeless, prisoners, and prostitutes.

Once, when asked by a little white girl why she was black, Sister Emma Ray explained that God had made her that way and she was happy the way she was. She added, however, in her narrative, "The only thing I covet above everything is to have a pure white heart" (317).

I Became Disgusted With Portland

Rev. Purcell and wife, Mennonite evangelists, requested us to go to Oregon and help them in a revival meeting. Brother Ray could not very well go at the time, so I went alone. The place was away up in the mountains some distance from Sweet Home, Oregon. There was a logging camp there with a saw-mill. We labored there for three weeks. It was almost entirely an infidel community except one family. Even the children were infidels.

The family I stayed with had a granddaughter or niece visiting them from Seattle, and they asked me to bring her with me on my return as far as Portland, as the evangelist and his wife were not going that way. We left by the stage in the morning at four o'clock. We rode twenty-two miles and then got the train for Portland. The girl's uncle was to meet her in Portland, and she was to stop over there for a few days and visit them. We were late in arriving at Portland, but her uncle met her and took her home with him. I planned to stop over for a day or two and visit some friends. I did not know where to find them at the time, so thought I would get a room and look them up the next day. Now began a tug of war with me to see where I could get a proper place for the night. There was a colored boy working in the depot, and as I knew it wasn't every place that a colored person could stop, I did not dare venture out until I knew some place where I could go. I inquired of this colored boy for a place where they would accommodate colored people.

He told me to take a bus outside for a certain hotel, as they would take in colored people. When I reached the bus, the driver was calling: "omnibus" for this certain hotel. I offered him my valise and started to step in. He didn't respond, but beckoned me aside, and went on calling "omnibus." It was pouring rain. I wondered where to go. I was perplexed. A cab man came up and said, "Hack for any place in the city." I told him that I wanted a decent place to sleep and asked him if he knew of a place where a colored woman could get a place for the night. He said, "Yes." I gave him my valise and he drove me to a hotel up in the city, but after my other experience I was afraid to get out, and I asked him if he would go in and see if they would take me, as I didn't want to be left outside in a strange city. He came back pretty soon and said they were full. He went to another place and came back with the same reply, and then to another, and then I noticed by the lights and the location that we were getting down towards the slum district. I called to him and asked him if we were not in the slum district. I told him I did not want to stay all night in a place of that kind. Then it came to me that there was a mission somewhere near and that I was acquainted with some of the mission workers, and I thought if I could find them I could find a place for the night. He drove me to the mission hall, but they had moved out a few days previous. I knew it would be an expense to have the driver take me farther, so I decided to walk and find the mission,

Seattle A.M.E. Woman's Christian Temperance Union chapter. Emma J. Ray is fourth from left in back row.

as I did not know what else to do. I had my umbrella, valise, and a Christmas cactus plant in a basket I was bringing home. I struck out down the street, inquiring as I went, for the mission hall. One person would say, "Go two blocks and then turn the corner," and the next person would send me back in the other direction. I walked until I was cold and tired. Then I met a man who knew where they had moved, but when I got inside, there was no one there I knew. A lady came up and asked me if I could give them a song. I told her I couldn't sing now until I knew where I was going to sleep for the night, and asked if she knew a place.

She told me of a widow who kept roomers, and who lived about four blocks away. I left my flower there and went down the street looking for this place. I would go up one flight of stairs and would be in the wrong place. I would come down and go up the next place. Sometimes I would go up four flights of stairs to be refused. I was so tired. I asked another lady if she would let me have a room for the night, but her rooms were all full. I could see readily that she did not want to accommodate me. I came down and went across the street to where it said "Hotel and Lodging." I noticed that it said office on a door. When I went into the office, I found myself in a saloon, but I thought I would take a chance anyway.

The man said he had one room left upstairs with two beds and that he was expecting some one else to take one of the beds unless I would pay for both of them. This made me suspicious of the place and my heart failed me. I went around the corner, and it said "Furnished rooms for rent upstairs." I began my tiresome climb up to the third floor. This was not the place I was hunting, but I asked for a room. As I turned away I felt like crying, and I began to pray for help. I put my valise down and got right down on my knees in the hallway and asked the Lord to help me find a place for the night. I went to another place. There was a lady standing in the hall looking over the banister. When she saw me coming up the steps she said, "Come on up, I'm your friend." And I thought, "Thank the Lord for a friend." As I got to the top of the steps I saw that she had been drinking, but by this time I was very tired and weak. I asked for a room with a stove, as my clothing was wet through. She said she had one, and gave me a very nice corner room, well ventilated, clean, and fresh. She said, "Your friend can come and stay with you, if you have one."

I told her that I had no one that I wanted to stay with me; that I was an evangelist. This gave me a chance to talk with her. I told her that I had been down in the country helping in a revival. When she discovered that I was a Christian she was anxious to talk with me. She told me her tale of woe and it was a sad one. The thought came to me that this must be the place the Lord wanted me to come to. She was very kind and listened attentively to all that I said to her. She seemed to be hungry for the Lord and tired of the life she was living, although she was drinking some. As I sat there and found out where I was, I became disgusted with Portland and asked her what time the train left in the morning. I went back to see if the mission was open. I found it was and I got my basket and plant. The landlady said she would see me when I came back, as she wanted to continue the conversation, but she seemed to have other business on hand. I saw her no more until the next morning as I was going away. I had hoped to be able to pray with her that night. Before going to bed I dried my clothing and prayed the Lord that in some way He would save this poor soul. She had a kind and tender heart.

I went away in a hurry the next morning. The train was late in arriving in Seattle, and I got home just at twilight. I looked through the window and saw my husband sitting by the table reading, and right there I looked up to heaven and thanked God for a HOME.

Part III: Caregiving: Family and Community

❖

[I]n the different voice of women lies the truth of an ethic of care, the tie between relationship and responsibility, . . .
Carol Gilligan, *In a Different Voice* (1982)

The lives and writings of the six Pacific Northwest women who appear in Part III reveal the centrality of their commitments to care for children, the sick, helpless, and needy. Their notions of human relations—of interdependence— produce weblike images of human connection that can strengthen and support both family and community. Rather than defining this theme as care*taking*, we use care*giving* to represent these women's enactments and descriptions of *giving*, rather than *taking*, care.

These women valued and practiced what developmental psychologist Carol Gilligan describes as "the ethic of care," an ethic grounded in "a morality of responsibility" for the welfare of others. They, like the contemporary women Gilligan interviewed, often defined themselves "in a context of human relationships" and judged themselves "in terms of their ability to care" (*In a Different Voice* 17).

The selections that open Part III present two perspectives on the care given to the Sager orphans, seven children who, after they lost their parents during an 1844 overland journey to the Oregon Country, were adopted by Marcus and Narcissa Whitman at the Waiilatpu Mission. Narcissa Prentiss Whitman, who failed to extend her caregiving to the Indians at the Mission, cared for several mixed-blood children and became mother to the seven white orphans, including Elizabeth Sager Helm. These related accounts of women's caregiving come from two voices and two genres—a letter written to family and an oral history narrative. Common to both perspectives is the virtue they assign to the ethic of care.

The first selection, an 1846 letter written by Narcissa Prentiss Whitman to her sister Harriet, illustrates Whitman's self-definition as adoptive mother for the Sager children and details her experiences and expectations as their primary caregiver. In the second piece, published in 1923, Elizabeth Sager Helm recalls daily life in the household, including her view of Whitman's role as a mother and model of

"Constance Crookham works in her kitchen." Oregon, ca. 1910. Photograph by Myra A. Wiggins (1869-1956) of Salem, Oregon.

caregiving. Helm also describes acts of care she saw and took part in during the days surrounding what history has called the "Whitman Massacre" of November 29, 1847.

In late 1846, a year prior to Narcissa Whitman's death at Waiilatpu, a sixty-six-year-old widow named Tabitha Moffat Brown arrived in Oregon Country and settled at what is now Forest Grove, Oregon. In her 1854 letter to relatives in Ohio, Brown relates how she coped with the difficult last stages of her overland journey, the care she gave to her feeble brother-in-law, and the resourcefulness with which she established the Oregon Orphans' Asylum and School, creating a new family for herself and others. Close to penniless when she arrived in Oregon, Brown might have turned to her adult children for assistance; however, she valued her autonomy. With establishment of her school in 1848, Brown found a way to combine her desire for financial independence with her wish to care for and educate children.

While Tabitha Brown's empowerment of self and others involved caregiving to children at her school, Amanda Gardener Johnson practiced the ethic of care within seven generations of the Corum-Deckard family—the only family she ever knew. Johnson, a former slave, continued her caregiving relationship with descendants of her former owners and defined herself in terms of these familial connections.

Amanda Johnson arrived in the Oregon Territory as a free woman with her former owners, the Deckards, in 1853. Throughout her long life in and near Albany, Oregon, she appears to have put responsibility to this family above all else. When members of the Deckard family became ill, Amanda even postponed her marriage to return and care for them.

Although twenty years of slavery deprived Amanda Johnson of what could have been fuller development of her autonomy-based empowerment, interdependent relationships with the Deckards and their descendants gave her connection-based empowerment. At the time of her oral history narrative, Amanda Johnson was eighty-eight and evidently living with the Deckard granddaughter she and her husband had once cared for in their home.

Amanda Gardener Johnson's commitment to caring for family is strikingly similar to that of "Sallie," the title character in Susie Revels Cayton's short story, "Sallie the Egg-Woman," published in 1900. Sallie, also a former slave, carries out her pledge to care for Clarie, the daughter of her former owners. In both cases, the ethic of care and moral responsibility for the welfare of others prevail.

Although Susie Revels Cayton and Amanda Johnson were both African-American women living in the Pacific Northwest, their life experiences were decidedly different. For years, Susie Revels Cayton, daughter of the first black U.S. senator from Mississippi and an educated woman, was associate editor for her husband's newspapers. She became a leader in Seattle's small African-American social set, and an activist for social, economic, and political change. Cayton committed her life to acts of caring for humanity, regardless of race, class or gender. Empowered by both her own sense of autonomy and her connections with others, Cayton served as a cultural mediator in what she termed "striving for the uplift" of humanity.

While Susie Revels Cayton enjoyed an early life of comparative class privilege, Mourning Dove (Christine Quintasket) grew up with poverty in the Pacific Northwest. In her autobiography, which was only recently published, Mourning Dove describes her childhood in Northeastern Washington at the end of the nineteenth century. Within her narrative, Mourning Dove emphasizes the ethic of care practiced by her parents and other Salishan relatives, both within and outside the family.

Mourning Dove was the first Indian woman to author and publish a novel—*Cogewea*—which was followed by collections of Indian tales and her autobiography. In her attempts as a cultural mediator, Mourning Dove found her early writing frequently altered and even censored by white "collaborators," but her autobiography stands essentially as found. Despite the economic hardships, racism and sexism Mourning Dove faced throughout her life, the compassion and understanding she learned from family were her keystones.

The models for caregiving in these women's lives were frequently, but not always, maternal figures. Mourning Dove found models of caring in her parents, particularly her mother, and recalled her family's extension of care to those less fortunate than themselves. Although Narcissa Prentiss Whitman was not disposed to give care to the "savage" Indians, she followed her own mother's example and cultural prescriptions to become a "true mother" for the Sager orphans. For Elizabeth Sager Helm and her older sister, Narcissa Whitman served as a model of family-centered caregiving, even in times of crisis.

In the lives and texts of the six women represented in Part III, the central theme of caregiving to family and community—a theme of concern for the welfare of others—is not only valued but practiced. These women sought and found models for caregiving, sometimes creating new ones through works of fiction; in many cases they became models for future generations to emulate. And, through their diverse practices of giving care, the women in Part III empowered themselves *and* others. They are similar to many contemporary women who, as they approach adulthood, typically understand "that the care and empowerment of others is central to their life's work" (Belenky et al., *Women's Ways of Knowing* 48). And, as they listen and respond to others, drawing out "the voices and minds they help to raise up," they "come to hear, value and strengthen their own voices and minds as well."

Narcissa Prentiss Whitman
1808-47

In October of 1844, after eight difficult years in the Oregon Country, Narcissa Prentiss Whitman's household at Waiilatpu, the Whitman Mission, was increased substantially by the arrival of the seven orphaned children of Henry and Naomi (Carney) Sager, both of whom had died on the Oregon Trail. Although Narcissa's physical and emotional health had been poor, she responded positively to the parental role of caregiving that gave her a sense of purpose, control, and achievement.

Julie Roy Jeffrey suggests in *Converting the West*, a biography of Narcissa Whitman, that the establishment of this family circle at Waiilatpu allowed Narcissa to channel her energies into the domestic world—a private sphere she "could better shape and control" than "the disorderly world" she did not understand and feared outside her doors (188). Jeffrey found that, "like most Protestant missionaries and many later apostles for the American way of life, Narcissa was so tightly enmeshed in her own culture and so sure of its verities that she was ill-prepared for the realities of working in another with very different values and mores" (64).

On April 13, 1846, Narcissa Whitman wrote from Waiilatpu to one of her sisters, Harriet, informing her of the Sager children "under our care." Whitman noted her moral responsibilities as the children's teacher and religious instructor, proudly detailed her care of baby Henrietta, shared her beliefs about child rearing and, as usual, encouraged family members to leave the East and join the Whitmans in the West. The letter, which we have titled "This Orphan Family Under Our Care," is included in this collection as an expression of Narcissa Whitman's definition of self and her empowerment through caregiving, a role for which she had been prepared within the cult of domesticity of the early nineteenth century and by her own mother's example.

Narcissa Prentiss Whitman was born March 14, 1808, in Prattsburg, New York, the first daughter and third of nine children born to Stephen and Clarissa (Ward) Prentiss. Not long before Narcissa's birth, Clarissa Prentiss had undergone a religious conversion, and she developed strong Presbyterian convictions linked to firm

Narcissa Prentiss Whitman, drawn after her death by Oliver W. Dixon

ideas about the importance of child rearing—convictions and ideas that were eventually shared by Narcissa. Clarissa's evangelicalism influenced Narcissa, who was converted at the early age of eleven, during Prattsburg's first revival. Julie Roy Jeffrey concluded that Narcissa's thoughts of work as a missionary followed conversion as "a noble and attractive alternative to the predictable course of marriage and domesticity" and was "likely to win her mother's approval" (20). Although Narcissa may have dreamed of missionary service overseas, her interest in missionary work with Indians was stimulated when she heard the Reverend Samuel Parker, a Congregational minister, speak of the needs of Indians in the Oregon Country, then held jointly by England and the United States. Narcissa Prentiss was prepared to answer Parker's call for missionaries in Oregon.

Narcissa applied to the American Board of Commissioners for Foreign Missions (ABCFM) but, as an unmarried woman, she received limited encouragement. Then, through the recommendation of the Reverend Parker, she was visited by Dr. Marcus Whitman, who had traveled with Parker to the fur traders' rendezvous in Wyoming. Whitman intended to establish a mission in the Oregon Country and was looking for a suitable missionary wife. After a brief courtship of a few days in 1835, the couple reached an agreement and became engaged. They were married in February of 1836, and began their journey to the West the next month.

The Whitmans were joined in Cincinnati by the Reverend Henry Harmon Spalding and his wife, Eliza Hart Spalding. Ironically, Narcissa had once refused a marriage proposal from Spalding, a former classmate from Franklin Academy. Evidently, Spalding's illegitimate birth and inferior social standing clashed with Narcissa's middle-class values and made him an unacceptable candidate for missionary husband. In turn, prior to joining the Whitman party, Spalding had said in public: "I do not want to go into the same mission with Narcissa Prentiss, as I question her judgment" (quoted in Jeffrey, *Converting the West* 60).

Throughout the journey to Oregon, Narcissa Prentiss Whitman maintained a journal which was eventually published by her sister Jane. When letters to her family in the East were circulated, Whitman assumed the role of public correspondent and became an inspiration for revival work. Jeffrey found that, "as a female missionary, Narcissa realized she had become a public figure of sorts and that her correspondence would not be private" (*Converting the West* 63). Rhetorically, Narcissa Whitman was "conscious of an audience" and "shaped material with some of her readers in mind."

While their husbands constructed a rude house at the site for the mission at Waiilatpu (the Place of the People of the Rye Grass), Narcissa Whitman and Eliza Spalding stayed in Fort Vancouver as the guests of Dr. John McLoughlin, chief factor of the Hudson's Bay Company. At the McLoughlin home, the two women enjoyed comforts and meals that they had not experienced for months. This ended, however, when the Whitmans were established at Waiilatpu, to work among the Cayuse, and the Spaldings moved on to their new mission at Lapwai, to work among the Nez Perce.

Within a year, children were born at both missions. Alice Clarissa Whitman was born on Narcissa Whitman's birthday, March 14, 1837, at Waiilatpu, and Eliza Spalding was born November 15, 1837, at Lapwai. With the birth of Alice Clarissa, Whitman became particularly concerned about the responsibilities of raising a child in what she perceived to be an uncivilized environment. Living in what she referred to as "heathen lands, among savages," Narcissa Whitman worried that little Alice, her "great comfort" in the wilderness, would be influenced by the Cayuse. To prevent what she feared as harmful, "heathen" influences, Whitman tried to keep the Cayuse at a distance from Alice, a practice she also followed for the three mixed-blood children and the Sager orphans who later became part of the Whitman family.

At the age of twenty-seven months, Alice Clarissa Whitman died by drowning in the Walla Walla River. She was the first white child born in the Pacific Northwest to parents from the United States. Although the Whitmans took in mixed-blood children at Waiilatpu, it was not until the arrival of Henrietta Sager that Narcissa Whitman once again had full responsibility for the care of a white infant.

Alice's death took a serious toll on Whitman's emotional and physical health, and evidently she withdrew even more from life at Waiilatpu. Never comfortable with the role of missionary and always wary of the "heathens," she could not reach out to the Cayuse and left the real missionary work to others at Waiilatpu. Her relationships with other missionary women in the Oregon Country had never been close, and it was not in her disposition to seek comfort from missionary wives such as Eliza Spalding, Mary Walker, or Mary Gray, women who had already experienced the sting of her sharp tongue, unbending ways, and erratic behavior. With the exception of her dependent relationship with a busy husband and her responsibility for three mixed-blood children, Whitman appears to have been quite alone at Waiilatpu.

The arrival of the Sager orphans in the fall of 1844 was the beginning of a new chapter in Whitman's life. Although her health was not fully regained until about 1847, child rearing became her salvation—both privately and publicly. Her lack of involvement in missionary work at Waiilatpu could now be explained as the personal sacrifice she was making for seven untutored, neglected, white children. She saw herself as following God's plan and wrote in 1846 to *Mother's Magazine*: "I was led to see the hand of the Lord was in it" (quoted in Jeffrey 188). The seven Sager children—John, thirteen; Francis (Frank), eleven; Catherine, nine; Elizabeth, seven; Matilda, five; Hannah (Louisa) three; and the baby—were the family she was intended to manage; their welfare was her mission.

The writings of Narcissa Whitman and those who lived with the Whitmans at Waiilatpu indicate that she had clear ideas about how the children in her charge should be raised. The Sager orphans found themselves in a loving but strictly disciplined household. Henrietta Naomi Sager, the baby, held a special place in Narcissa Whitman's heart.

In Narcissa Whitman's letter to her sister Harriet, written about eighteen months after the arrival of the Sager children, she defined maternal caregiving and underscored the importance of combining spiritual instruction with good health—the "immortal" with the "physical." In comparison to Henrietta, almost a surrogate for the deceased Alice and possibly the easiest to bend to Narcissa's will, the older Sager children were referred to only as "our children," "my girls" and "the boys." Typically, Narcissa Whitman did not mention the Cayuse, and her report of events at Waiilatpu focused on the private world she had created for herself—a world of maternal responsibility and caregiving.

This Orphan Family Under Our Care

Waiilatpu, April 13th, 1846.
My Dear Harriet:—

I believe I have not written you since the Lord brought this orphan family under our care. How could I, for I have been so unwell and had this increase of care upon my mind, that I have written to no one in the States, as I recollect. I find the labor greater in doing for so many, especially in instructing them—where they come in all at once—than if they had come along by degrees and had received a start in their education, one before the other; whereas all their minds appear to be alike uninstructed, especially in the great truths of Christianity.

I would like to know how you and Clarissa get along in unfolding the minds of your little ones. I hope you both feel that the immortal part is of the greatest moment in all your strivings for them, and to educate the physical in such a way as to give the immortal part the utmost vigor and energy possible.

I used to think mother was the best hand to take care of babies I ever saw, but I believe, or we have the vanity to think, we have improved upon her plan. That you may see how we manage with our children, I will give you a specimen of our habits with them and we feel them important, too, especially that they may grow up healthy and strong. Take my baby, as an example: in October, 1844, she arrived here in the hands of an old filthy woman, sick, emaciated and but just alive. She was born some where on the Platte river in the first part of the journey, on the last day of May. Her mother died on the 25th of September. She was five months old when she was brought here—had suffered for the want of proper nourishment until she was nearly starved. The old woman did the best she could, but she was in distressed circumstances herself, and a wicked, disobedient family around her to see to.

Husband thought we could get along with all but the baby—he did not see how we could take that; but I felt that if I must take any, I wanted her as a charm to bind the rest to me. So we took her, a poor distressed little object, not larger than a babe three weeks old. Had she been taken past at this late season, death would have been her portion, and that in a few days. The first thing I did for her was to give her some milk and put her in the cradle. She drank a gill, she was so hungry, but soon cleared herself of it by vomiting and purging. I next had a pail of warm water and put her in it, gave her a thorough cleansing with soap and water, and put on some clean clothes;—put her in the cradle and she had a fine nap. This I followed every day, washing her thoroughly with tepid water, about the middle of the forenoon.

She soon began to mend, but I was obliged to reduce her milk with a little water, as her stomach was so weak she could not bear it in its full strength.

Now I suppose you think such a child would be very troublesome nights, but it was not so with her; we put her in the cradle and she slept until morning without waking us more than once, and that only for a few of the first nights. Her habits of eating and sleeping were as regular as clock-work. She had a little gill cup which we fed her in; she would take that full every meal, and when done would want no more for a long time. Thus I continued, giving her nothing else but milk, she only required the more until her measure became half a pint. In consequence of the derangement of her digestive powers, which did not recover their healthy tone, she had a day of sickness some time in Dec. when we gave her a little oil and calomel; this restored her completely, and since that time, and even before, she has nothing to do but to grow, and that as fast as possible; she is as large or larger than her next older sister Louisa was when she came here, then nearly three years old. She now lacks a month and a half of being two years old. She is strong, healthy, fleshy, heavy, runs any where she is permitted, talks everything nearly, is full of mischief if I am out of the room. She is energetic and active enough and has a disposition to have her own way, especially with the children, if she is not prevented.

She contended sharply for the mastery with her mother before she was a year old, but she, of course, had to submit. Since then she has been very obedient, but frequently tries the point to see if her parents are steadfast and uniform in their requirements or not. She will obey very well in sight, but loves to get out of sight for the purpose of doing as she pleases. She sings a little, but not nearly as much as Alice C. did when she was of her age. Thus much for my baby, Henrietta Naomi Sager. She had another name when she came here, but the children were anxious to call her after her parents. Her father's name was Henry and her mother's name was Naomi—we put them together.

What I call an improvement upon mother's plan is the daily bathing of children. I take a child as soon as it is born and put it in a washbowl of water and give it a thorough washing with soap. I do this the next day and the next, and so on every day as long as the washbowl will hold it; when it will not, then I get a tub or something larger, and continue to do it until the child is able to be carried to the river or to go itself. Every one of my girls go to the river all summer long for bathing every day before dinner, and they love it so well that they would as soon do without their dinner as without that. In the winter we bathe in a tub once a week at the least. This is our practice as well as the children. I do not know but these are your habits, but if they are not, I should like to have you try them just to see the benefit of them. I never gave Henrietta any food but milk until she was nearly a year-and-a-half old. She never wanted any thing else. I avoid as much as possible giving my children candies, sweetmeats, etc. such as many parents allow their children to indulge in almost all the while; neither do I permit them to eat cakes and pies very often.

It is well to study these things with regard to our children, for it saves many a doctor bill; and another thing with our children, we never give medicine if we can help it. If children complain of the headache, or are sick at the stomach, send them to bed without their supper or other meals; they are sure to get up very soon feeling as well as ever.

My husband says many times when a physician is called to see a patient he finds nothing ails him but eating too much. If he is told this he will be offended, so he is obliged to give him something, when all he needs is to do without a meal or two and to fast a day or two and drink water gruel.

Doubtless you will think this a strange letter, Harriet, but you must take it for what is worth and make the best of it.

We sleep out of doors in the summer a good deal—the boys all summer. This is a fine, healthy climate. I wish you were here to enjoy it with me, and pa and ma, too. We have as happy a family as the world affords. I do not wish to be in a better situation than this. . . .

O, how I wish you were all here. I could find work enough for you all to do; and every winter we have a good school, so that our children are learning as fast as most children in the States.

Harriet, I do want you and that good husband of yours to come here and bring pa and ma. I know you will like it after you get here, if you do not like the journey. There are many of the last immigration that came without their families, that are now going back to bring them as quick as possible, and are only sorry they did not bring them last year. Bring as many girls as you can, but let every young man bring a wife, for he will want one after he gets here, if he never did before. Girls are in good demand for wives. I hope Edward and Jane will come. I have written to them to come. Judson wants to come, too. I hope he will, and many other Christians. . . .

Love to all, and a kiss for all those little ones.

Narcissa

Elizabeth Sager Helm
1837-1925

Although Narcissa Prentiss Whitman was apparently neither prepared nor suited for the role of missionary among the Cayuse, she unmistakably defined and embraced her role as mother for her immediate family at Waiilatpu. In the selection below, which we have titled "Stay Close to Me," Elizabeth Sager Helm, one of the Sager orphans, recalled what it was like to be a child in the Whitman household and described Narcissa's caregiving role and eventual death in what is known as the "Whitman Massacre" of November 29, 1847.

A seemingly selfless concern for the welfare of her family and an ability to remain calm in the face of life-threatening circumstances are qualities frequently attributed to Narcissa Whitman in the oral narratives and writings of survivors of the Cayuse attack. In particular, for her oldest adopted daughters—Catherine (Katie) and Elizabeth Sager—Narcissa Whitman was a woman of resource and ingenuity, and served as a model for caregiving and coping in crisis.

Elizabeth Sager Helm was a child of ten at the time of the attack on the Whitman Mission and a widow of eighty-six when she shared her recollections with Fred Lockley of the *Oregon Daily Journal*. She did not lapse into eulogistic rhetoric about the Whitmans but gave, instead, a relatively balanced description of Narcissa Whitman. Questions can certainly be raised about the function of memory and the passage of time, but contemporary research reminds us that childhood events can be remembered vividly and accurately by the elderly. Helm's account of Whitman's caregiving role during the attack appears to correspond with those of other survivors.

At the time of the "Whitman Massacre," John Sager was seventeen, Francis (Frank) was fifteen, Catherine (Katie) was thirteen, Elizabeth was ten, Matilda was eight, and Hannah (Louisa) was six. Henrietta Sager, the baby of the family, was only four. When the attack came, the Whitmans had been at Waiilatpu since 1836, the date of establishment of their Presbyterian Mission, located about twenty miles east of Fort Walla Walla. The Whitmans and the Cayuse were suspicious of one another, few Cayuse sought conversion, and competition with the Roman Catholics had increased. Narcissa Whitman, who was consid-

ered "haughty" and "very proud" by the Cayuse, had cloistered herself and her children away from the Indians and their culture. In contrast, the Reverend Henry Harmon Spalding and his wife Eliza Hart Spalding, who had accompanied the Whitmans to the West in 1836, established a relatively successful mission for the Nez Perce at Lapwai, some seventy miles east of Waiilatpu, but both missions had experienced threats and difficulties with the Indians prior to the attack.

Certainly, the increasing numbers of immigrants who passed through or wintered each year at Waiilatpu were of concern to Indians who saw this as a white invasion of their lands, encouraged by the Whitmans. An epidemic of the measles in the fall of 1847, which may have been carried by Indians returning from California, brought serious illness and death to Indians and whites alike. Rumors circulated that some angry Indians held the whites responsible for the plague and might take action against Dr. Whitman. Possibly, Whitman was seen by some Cayuse as "an evil shaman" who had misused his spirit power and "was using measles to kill people" (Kirk and Anderson, *Exploring Washington's Past* 187). Moreover, it was rumored that Dr. Whitman's medicines were actually poisoning the Indians. At the same time, at least eleven people at the mission, including members of the Josiah Osborne family, were sick in bed when the attack came. The Osbornes, who hid under the floorboards and later escaped, had lost their baby on November 14th, and a daughter, age six, had died on November 24th.

Differing figures have been given for the total number of people residing at Waiilatpu in November of 1847. Frances Fuller Victor, who devoted two chapters of *River of the West* to the Whitman Massacre, gave the figure as seventy-one; Fred Lockley gave the number as seventy-two in *Conversations with Pioneer Women*; and Ronald Lansing calculated seventy-five in *Juggernaut: The Whitman Massacre Trial*.

A total of thirteen people, including the Whitmans, died in the uprising at Waiilatpu, but Narcissa Whitman was the only white woman killed. Those who survived the attack to be held as captives were released through the efforts of Peter Skene Ogden, then chief factor of the Hudson's Bay Company at Fort Vancouver.

Two-and-a-half years after the attack, the Cayuse accused of the murders were brought to trial in May of 1850. All five—Telokite, Tomahas, Clokomas, Isiaasheluckas, and Kiamasumkin—were convicted and sentenced to death by hanging, and Joseph Meek, Marshal of the District of Oregon, was placed in charge of the execution, a public event that drew a large crowd to the gallows at Oregon City on June 3, 1850 (Lansing 90-91). Jane Straight Bingham, a child at the time, recalled her impressions in an interview with Fred Lockley: "In those days people did not have grand opera, or even the movies, so they came from all over the country to witness the hanging of these Indians" (*Conversations with Pioneer Women* 116).

The four Sager girls were placed in various homes. Elizabeth Sager, who was called as a witness in the trial, moved from place to place, working for several different families. When her sister Catherine married Clark Pringle, Elizabeth lived with them. At the age of eighteen, on August 9, 1855, Elizabeth Sager married William Helm, an Oregon farmer and son of the Reverend William Helm, and nine children were born to their marriage.

Helm's narrative of life and death at the Whitman Mission was published in the *Oregon Daily Journal*, July 23-27 and September 4-6, 1923. Two years later, on July 19, 1925, Elizabeth Sager Helm died in Clackamas County, Oregon.

The reportorial nature of Elizabeth Sager Helm's narrative involved brief glimpses of humor, limited use of dialogue, and few asides. She let the facts as she remembered them speak for themselves, and she did not embellish her narrative with comment on the dangers she faced during and after the attack at the Whitman Mission.

STAY CLOSE TO ME

Captain Shaw drove us to Dr. Whitman's mission. . . . [A]nd I saw, coming from the house, a tall, matronly woman, whose yellow hair had a tint of copper. It was Narcissa Prentiss Whitman. People who didn't like her said she was stuck up, said she had red hair, but she was not stuck up and she did not have red hair. She was rather reserved, and her hair was a coppery gold. She was rather plump, weighing about 150 pounds or more. . . .

Mrs. Whitman had us all come in to supper, and Dr. Whitman walked around the table and waited on us. We had baked pork and lady finger potatoes for supper. . . . When we all sat down to the table there was a table full. There were Dr. and Mrs. Whitman, Dr. Whitman's nephew, Perrin Whitman, who was about 16, David [Malin], a little half-breed Spanish and Indian boy; Helen Meek and Mary Ann Bridger, both of whom had white fathers and Indian mothers, and we seven children.

Dr. Whitman was a very genial, kindly man. He was fond of romping with us children, and we did not feel at all in awe of him as we did of Mrs. Whitman. She did all the disciplining in the family. Dr. Whitman was fairly tall, had dark hair a little tinged with gray, blue eyes rather deeply sunk, and heavy eyebrows, and he stooped a little. He never strolled or sauntered, he always walked as if interested in getting to where he was going. . . .

We went to live with the Whitmans on October 17, 1844, and they were killed on November 29, 1847, so we lived with them for more than three years. I told you the agreement was that we children were to stay at the Whitman Mission during the winter of 1844-45. We had been there only a few days when Dr. Whitman started off on horseback to overtake the wagon train and tell Captain Shaw he need not come back in the spring to get us, as he and his wife had decided to keep us. We were with the Whitmans nearly three years before we were legally adopted. You will find certain so-called historians who dispute this because we cannot produce written papers of adoption. . . .

The morning of the massacre I heard Dr. Whitman say to Mr. Kimball [Kimble], who had come into the kitchen, "Yes, the situation looks pretty dark, but I think I shall be able to quell any trouble." A few hours later one of the best friends the Indians ever had was dead by their own hands.

My brother [Francis] had shot a beef for the use of those at the Mission. After shooting it he came into the house to go to school. Nathan S. Kimball and Jacob Hoffman were skinning the beef and cutting it up. This was Monday morning. The school had been closed for some days on account of the measles, but it had started up again.

Mary Ann Bridger, the half-breed daughter of Jim Bridger the scout, was working in the kitchen. Two Indians, Telekaut and Tamsuky, came to the kitchen door and, walking into the kitchen, asked for Dr. Whitman. Dr. Whitman came out into the kitchen, shutting the door into the next room, where Mrs. Whitman was feeding my sister, Henrietta. My brother, John Sager, was sitting in the kitchen winding some twine. The two Indians began talking to Dr. Whitman.

Mary Ann [Bridger] told me that Telekaut was the one who killed Dr. Whitman and that Tamsuky shot and killed my brother [John]. Mary Ann jumped behind the stove and then, running around the side of the house, came and told Mrs. Whitman that the Indians were killing Dr. Whitman.

In a moment everything was in confusion. The children were terrorized, though Mrs. Whitman seemed calm. Mr. Kimball, holding one arm, which had been shot and from which the blood was running, came running into the room and said, "The Indians are killing us. I don't know what the d——d Indians want to kill me for. I never did anything to them. Get some water."

Mrs. Whitman got a pitcher of water for him. Mr. Kimball was a religious man and ordinarily would not have sworn, but he was very much excited. Serious as the situation was, I giggled when he said, "I don't know what the d——d Indians want to kill me for," for I knew Mrs. Whitman would reprove him for swearing, particularly in the presence of the children.

Mrs. Whitman and Mrs. Hall brought Dr. Whitman into the sitting room. Mr. [Andrew] Rogers had come in and said, "Is the doctor dead?"

Dr. Whitman answered, "No."

Mrs. Whitman went to the fireplace to get some ashes to stop the bleeding in the doctor's head where he had been struck with a tomahawk. Looking out of the window I saw the Indians shooting and I said, "Mother, they are killing Mr. [Luke] Saunders." The upper part of the door in the sitting room was of glass. Mrs. Whitman came to the door and looked out.

An Indian that we called Frank was standing on the schoolroom step and, seeing Mrs. Whitman looking out, shot at her, the bullet striking her in the shoulder. My sister, Katie, stooped over Mrs. Whitman, who had fallen to the floor, and tried to help her up. Mrs. Whitman said, "Go and take care of the sick children, Katie. You can do nothing for me." In the room where Dr. and Mrs. Whitman were, were myself and my four sisters, with Mary Ann Bridger, Helen Meek, Mrs. Hall, Mrs. Hays, Miss Bewley, and Mr. Kimball.

When Mrs. Whitman was wounded, she began praying out loud. She said, "Lord, save these little ones."

Dusk came early and as the Indians began breaking the windows, Mrs. Whitman thought we had better go upstairs to Miss Bewley's room. Mr. Rogers helped Mrs. Whitman go upstairs. While Mrs. Hall and those who could helped carry the sick children up to Miss Bewley's room, Mrs. Whitman lay down on the foot of the bed.

Mrs. Whitman said to Mr. Rogers, "There is a gun barrel in the corner. Hold the end of the muzzle of the gun barrel over the top of the stairs so the Indians will think you have a gun."

The Indians broke into the house and mutilated Dr. Whitman and my brother. The Indians then broke the door to the upstairs room and Tamsuky called to Mr. Rogers to come on down, that he would take care of us. Mr. Rogers told him to come on up, but when Tamsuky saw the gun barrel, he was afraid.

Finally, Mr. Rogers went downstairs and talked to Tamsuky and Joe Lewis [part Indian]. Tamsuky told Mr. Rogers that the Indians were going to burn the house and that he wanted to save Mrs. Whitman and the others. Aunt Lucinda Bewley, who was Mrs. Whitman's hired girl, and Mr. Rogers, helped Mrs. Whitman downstairs. She said to me, "Come with me, Elizabeth." When we got into the dining room she said, "Stay close to me."

Mrs. Whitman was so weak from loss of blood that she lay down on the sofa. . . . Joe Lewis put his gun by the kitchen door and took the foot of the sofa to help carry Mrs. Whitman out. When Mrs. Whitman saw Joe Lewis she said, "Oh, Joe. You too?"

They carried Mrs. Whitman on the sofa, through the kitchen door. Just before they had gone out, one of the Indians had told my brother, Francis, to go along with Mrs. Whitman. As we went out of the kitchen, Joe Lewis dropped his end of the sofa, on which Mrs. Whitman was lying and at the same time the Indians standing around fired. Mr. Rogers raised his hands and said, "Oh, my God," and fell. My brother also fell and Mrs. Whitman, who was shot through the cheek and through the body, fell off of the lounge onto the muddy ground.

When the Indians fired at Mrs. Whitman as Joe Lewis and Mr. Rogers were carrying her out of the house, I ran back into the house. I saw my brother [Francis] fall and also Mr. Rogers, and I saw Mrs. Whitman roll off the lounge on which they were carrying her and fall on the muddy ground. My sister Matilda also saw the killing of these three. She said she saw one of the Indians reach down, catch Mrs. Whitman by the hair, and raise her head and then strike her across the face several times with his leather quirt.

We children stayed upstairs that night in the house where Dr. Whitman had been tomahawked. He lived for some time, for he was breathing heavily when Mrs. Whitman was carried out to be killed. Mr. Kimball had been overlooked by the Indians. He was suffering from his wound. He also stayed in the upper room with us that night.

The children who were sick cried for water during the night, so early the next morning I went down to see if I could get some water. The body of Mrs. Whitman was lying near the kitchen door. The body of Mr. Rogers was lying not far away. I saw Edward Telekaut and asked him if he would get some water for me. He got a bucket of water and brought a dipper. As the Indians seemed to have quit their killing, I decided to go over to the Mansion House and see what was going to become of us. Mrs. [Mary] Saunders met me and said, "The Indians have promised not to kill us." At about 10 o'clock that morning my sister Katie took the children over to the Mansion House. . . .

We stayed at the Mansion House a month. Eliza Spalding [daughter of Henry and Eliza Spalding] understood the Indian language and I did also, but not so much as Eliza. Joseph Smith and James Young worked at the mill, grinding wheat for the Indians. The Indians had Eliza stay at the mill to interpret for them. I stayed with Eliza most of the time. It was cold in the mill, so we dug a hole in the straw stack near the mill and put a blanket in front of it. Eliza and I crawled in there, where we would be out of the wind, and when the Indians wanted us they would come and raise the blanket and tell Eliza to come and talk for them.

During that month (December, 1847) the women made up several bales of calico and flannel into shirts for the Indians.

One day Edward Telekaut came in. He had taken a bedpost and trimmed it up to use for a war club. Eliza Spalding and I and some of the older children were in the room where Crockett Bewley and Amos Sales were lying in bed. Crockett Bewley had typhoid and Amos Sales was also sick. Edward raised his club and hit Crockett Bewley on the head. We children screamed and ran out of the room. Edward came out and told us we must come back. The Indians with Edward beat Amos Sales and Crockett Bewley over the head till they had killed them, and then they dragged their bodies out into the yard.

The next day Joe, who had worked for the Whitmans several years, came with a wagon and a yoke of oxen and took the bodies away and buried them. Some days after that Joe came to the Mansion House and said the wolves were digging up the bodies of Dr. Whitman and Mrs. Whitman and the others. I went with Joe, because my brother was buried with Dr. Whitman, Mrs. Whitman, and Mr. Rogers. . . .

Joe showed me where the wolves had eaten all the flesh from Mrs. Whitman's leg from the knee to the ankle. He shoveled the grave full of dirt. Later the wolves dug up all of the bodies and when the Oregon soldiers came from the Willamette Valley they put them into a new grave near the grave of little Alice Whitman, the daughter of Dr. and Mrs. Whitman. Later, the bodies were taken up and buried in a casket, and a monument was put over them.

Tabitha Moffat Brown
1780-1858

In the spring of 1846, at the age of sixty-six, Tabitha Moffat Brown left her Missouri home to immigrate to the Oregon Country. She was accompanied on the overland trip by a son and daughter, their families, and Captain John Brown, the aged brother of her deceased husband. The vicissitudes Brown encountered on her overland journey to Oregon, the resourceful manner in which she turned a coin from the finger of her glove into self-sustenance, and her establishment of a home for orphans and a school in Oregon amply demonstrate that she performed remarkably when faced with challenges.

The known details of her early life are few. Tabitha Moffat Brown was born May 1, 1780, in Brimfield, Massachusetts, the daughter of Dr. Joseph Moffat, a physician. She was married to the Reverend Clark Brown, an Episcopal minister, and they had three children, Orus, Mathano, and Pherne. After her husband died in Maryland in 1817, Brown taught school and lived in Virginia and Missouri.

When the Brown family emigrated from Missouri, Orus Brown, her son, was their pilot. Orus had crossed to Oregon in 1844, and he returned to Missouri in 1845 to bring his family west. When they reached Fort Hall, the Brown family decided to follow the advice of a person Tabitha Brown calls "a rascally fellow"—actually, Jesse Applegate—that they could make better time to the Willamette Valley by taking a new cutoff that crossed the southern Cascades and avoided the difficult old route across the Blue Mountains and down the Columbia River. This new route, the South Road, was later called the "Scott-Applegate Road," or "Applegate Trail." Eventually, the survey for the Scott-Applegate Trail was modified and improved, and became the standard route; however, as noted by historian Malcolm Clark, Jr., "[F]or the roughly one hundred wagons who took it in 1846 it was the road to near calamity" (quoted in S. Applegate, *Skookum* 57). Tabitha Brown writes about this "near calamity" in the following selection.

When the Brown party finally reached what Brown described as "the beautiful Umpqua Valley," in Southern Oregon, winter was setting in, and no white settlement was near. In an attempt to reach help, Tabitha Brown set off with her seventy-seven-year-old brother-in-law, eventually met up with other emigrant wagons, and rejoined her family. Provisions ran out, but Tabitha Brown retained her trust "in the blessings of kind Providence," and she reached the shelter of a Methodist minister's house on Christmas Day, 1846, nine months after beginning her overland journey.

Tabitha Brown supported herself through needlework and later opened the Oregon Orphans' Asylum and School at Tualatin Plains (later Forest Grove). With the assistance of the Reverend Harvey Clark, who had come to Oregon as an independent Congregationalist missionary and owned the site of the future town of Forest Grove, Brown opened the doors of a log meeting house to "receive all the children, rich and poor." The school later expanded to become Tualatin Academy, the forerunner of Pacific University at Forest Grove.

In 1846, when Tabitha Brown confronted dire adversity on the Overland Trail, her grit and her faith in God only grew stronger and, though near starvation, she found the strength to save both herself and her elderly brother-in-law. Mere survival, however, was not the end of her story, but the beginning. Caring for others—being a mother to poor and orphaned children—was her ultimate goal, and one she ably accomplished with financial help from Reverend Clark and the cooperation of neighbors. Her story is related in excerpts from a letter she wrote, dated August of 1854, to her brother and sister-in-law, Mr. and Mrs. Charles Moffat of Claridon, Ohio. This letter, written four years before Tabitha Brown's death on May 4, 1858, was later published in *Congregational Work* (June 1903) and in the *Oregon Historical Quarterly* (June 1904).

I Have Labored For Myself and the Rising Generation

Forest Grove, Oregon Territory, August, 1854
My Brother and Sister:

Our journey, with little exception, was pleasing and prosperous until after we passed Fort Hall. Then we were within eight hundred miles of Oregon City, if we had kept on the old road down the Columbia River.

But three or four trains of emigrants were decoyed off by a rascally fellow who came out from the settlement in Oregon assuring us that he had found a new cut-off, that if we would follow him we would be in the settlement long before those who had gone down the Columbia. This was in August. The idea of shortening a long journey caused us to yield to his advice. Our sufferings from that time no tongue can tell. He said he would clear the road before us, so that we should have no trouble in rolling our wagons after him. But he robbed us of what he could by lying, and left us to the depredations of Indians and wild beasts, and to starvation. But God was with us. We had sixty miles of desert without grass or water, mountains to climb, cattle giving out, wagons breaking, emigrants sick and dying, hostile Indians to guard against by night and day, if we would save ourselves and our horses and cattle from being arrowed or stole.

We were carried hundreds of miles south of Oregon into Utah Territory and California; fell in with the Clamotte [Klamath] and Rogue River Indians, lost nearly all our cattle, passed the Umpqua Mountains, 12 miles through. I rode through in three days at the risk of my life, on horseback, having lost my wagon and all that I had but the horse I was on. . . .

After struggling through mud and water up to our horses' sides much of the way in crossing this 12-mile mountain, we opened into the beautiful Umpqua Valley, inhabited only by Indians and wild beasts. We had still another mountain to cross, the Calipose, besides many miles to travel through mud, snow, hail, and rain.

Winter had set in. We were yet a long distance from any white settlement. The word was, "fly, everyone that can, from starvation; except those who are compelled to stay by the cattle to recruit them for further travel." Mr. Pringle and Pherne [Brown Pringle] insisted on my going ahead with Uncle John to try and save our own lives. . . . Near sunset we came up with the families that had left that morning. They had nothing to eat, and their cattle had given out. We all camped in an oak grove for the night, and in the morning I divided my last morsel with them and left them to take care of themselves. I hurried Captain Brown so as to overtake the three wagons ahead. . . . In the afternoon Captain Brown complained of sickness, and could only walk his horse at a distance behind. He had a swimming in his head and a pain in his stomach. In two or three hours he became delirious and fell from his horse. I was afraid to jump down from my horse to assist him, as it was one that a woman had never ridden before. He tried to rise up on his feet, but could not. I rode close to him and set the end of his cane, which I had in my hand, hard in the ground to help him up. I then urged him to walk a little. He tottered along a few yards and then gave out. I then saw a little sunken spot a few steps ahead and led his horse to it, and with much difficulty got him raised to the saddle. I then told him to hold fast to the horse's mane and I would lead by the bridle. . . .

The sun was now setting, the wind was blowing, and the rain was drifting upon the sides of the distant mountain. Poor me! I crossed the plain to where three mountain spurs met. Here the shades of night were gathering fast, and I could see the wagon tracks no further. Alighting from my horse, I flung off saddle and saddle-pack and tied the horse fast to a tree with a lasso rope. The Captain asked me what I was going to do. My answer was, "I am going to camp for the night." He gave a groan and fell to the ground. . . . His senses were gone. Covering him as well as I could with blankets, I seated myself upon my feet behind him, expecting he would be a corpse before morning

Pause for a moment and consider the situation. Worse than alone, in a savage wilderness, without food, without fire, cold and shivering wolves fighting and howling all around me. Dark clouds hid the stars. All as solitary as death. But that same kind Providence that I had always known was watching over me still. I committed all to Him and felt no fear. As soon as light dawned, I pulled down my tent, saddled my horse, found the Captain able to stand on his feet. Just at this moment one of the emigrants whom I was trying to overtake came up. He was in search of venison. Half a mile ahead were the wagons I had hoped to overtake, and we were soon there and ate plentifully of fresh meat.

Within eight feet of where my tent had been set fresh tracks of two Indians were to be seen, but I did not know that they were there. They killed and robbed Mr. Newton, only a short distance off, but would not kill his wife because she was a woman. They killed another man on our cut-off, but the rest of the emigrants escaped with their lives. We traveled on for a few days and came to the foot of the Calipose Mountain. Here my children and my grandchildren came up with us, a joyful meeting. They had been near starving. Mr. Pringle tried to shoot a wolf, but he was too weak and trembling to hold the rifle steady. They all cried because they had nothing to eat; but just at this time their own son came to them with a supply, and all cried again. Winter had now set in. We were many days crossing the Calipose Mountain, able to go ahead only a mile or two each day. The road had to be cut and opened for us, and the mountain was covered with snow. Provisions gave out and Mr. Pringle set off on horseback to the settlements for relief, not knowing how long he would be away, or whether he would ever get through. In a week or so our scanty provisions were all gone and we were again in a state of starvation. Many tears were shed through the day, by all save one. She had passed through many trials sufficient to convince her that tears would avail nothing in our extremities. Through all my sufferings in crossing the plains, I not once sought relief by the shedding of tears, nor thought we should not live to reach the settlement. The same faith that I ever had in the blessings of kind Providence strengthened in proportion to the trials I had to endure. As the only alternative or last resort for the present time, Mr. Pringle's oldest son, Clark, shot down one of his father's best working oxen and dressed it. It had not a particle of fat on it, but we had something to eat—poor bones to pick without bread or salt.

Orus Brown's party was six days ahead of ours in starting; he had gone down the old emigrant route and reached the settlements in September. Soon after he heard of the suffering emigrants at the south and set off in haste with four pack horses and provisions for our relief. He met Mr. Pringle and turned about. In a few days they were at our camp. We had all retired to rest in our tents, hoping to forget our misery until daylight should remind us again of our sad fate. In the stillness of the night the footsteps of horses were heard rushing toward our tents. Directly a halloo. It was the well-known voice of Orus Brown and Virgil Pringle. You can realize the joy. Orus, by his persuasive insistence, encouraged us to more effort to reach the settlements. Five miles from where we had encamped we fell into the company of half-breed French and Indians with packhorses. We hired six of them and pushed ahead again. Our provisions were becoming short and we were once more on an allowance until reaching the first settlers. There our hardest struggles were ended. On Christmas day, at 2 P.M. I entered the house of a Methodist minister, the first house I had set my feet in for nine months. For two or three weeks of my journey down the Willamette I had felt something in the end of my glove finger which I had supposed to be a button; on examination at my new home in Salem, I found it to be a 6 1/4-cent piece. This was the whole of my cash capital to commence business with in Oregon. With it I purchased three needles. I traded off some of my old clothes to the squaws for buckskin, worked them into gloves for the Oregon ladies and gentlemen, which cleared me upwards of $30.

Later I accepted the invitation of Mr. and Mrs. Clark, of Tualaten Plains, to spend the winter with them. I said to Mr. Clark one day, "Why has Providence frowned on me and left me poor in this world. Had he blessed me with riches, as he has many others, I know right well what I would do." "What would you do?" "I would establish myself in a comfortable house and receive all poor children and be a mother to them." He fixed his keen eyes on me to see if I was in earnest. "Yes, I am," said I. "If so, I will try," said he, "to help you." He purposed to take an agency and get assistance to establish a school in the plains. I should go into the log meetinghouse and receive all the children, rich and poor. Those parents who were able were to pay $1 a week for board, tuition, washing, and all. I agreed to labor for one year for nothing, while Mr. Clark and others were to assist as far as they were able in furnishing provisions. The time fixed upon to begin was March, 1848, when I found everything prepared for me to go into the old meetinghouse and cluck up my chickens. The neighbors had collected what broken knives and forks, tin pans, and dishes they could part with, for the Oregon pioneer to commence house-keeping with. I had a well-educated lady from the East, a missionary's wife, for a teacher, and my family increased rapidly. In the summer they put me up a boarding-house. I now had 30 boarders of both sexes, and of all ages, from four years old to twenty-one. I managed them and did all my work except washing. That was done by the scholars. In the spring of '49 we called for trustees. Had eight appointed. They voted me the whole charge of the boarding-house free of rent, and I was to provide for myself. The price of board was established at $2 per week. Whatever I made over my expense was my own. In '51 I had 40 in my family at $2.50 per week; mixed with my own hands 3,423 pounds of flour in less than five months. Mr. Clark made over to the trustees a quarter section of land for a town plot. A large and handsome building is on the site we selected at the first starting. It has been under town incorporation for two years, and at the last session of the legislature a charter was granted for a university to be called Pacific University, with a limitation of $50,000.00. The president and professor are already here from Vermont. The teacher and his lady for the academy are from New York. I have endeavored to give general outlines of what I have done. You must be judges whether I have been doing good or evil. I have labored for myself and the rising generation, but I have not quit hard work, and live at my ease, independent as to worldly concerns. I own a nicely furnished white frame house on a lot in town, within a short distance of the public buildings. That I rent for $100 per year. I have eight other town lots, without buildings, worth $150 each. I have eight cows and a number of young cattle. The cows I rent out for their milk and one-half of their increase. I have rising $1,100 cash due me; $400 of it I have donated to the University, besides $100 I gave to the Academy three years ago. This much I have been able to accumulate by my own industry, independent of my children, since I drew 6 1/4 cents from the finger of my glove.

Amanda Gardener Johnson
1833-1927

For Amanda Johnson,* caregiving
was a way of life, first as a slave and later as a free woman. Born into
slavery in Missouri in 1833, Amanda started across the plains with her
owners, the Anderson Deckard family, in 1853. Less than a month
before arriving in the Oregon Territory, she accepted freedom as a
twentieth birthday gift; however, she maintained close ties with her
previous owners and their descendants.

We were first introduced to Amanda Gardener Johnson by reading
her narrative, which was published in Fred Lockley's column in the
Oregon Daily Journal, October 23, 1921. Lockley had interviewed
Johnson in Albany, Oregon, and we were eager to learn more about
her. With the assistance of staff at the *Albany Democrat-Herald* and
the Albany Public Library, we found her in census listings, marriage
records, and obituary notices. We also discovered that she had been
the subject of a feature article written in 1924 by Everett Earle Stanard
for the *Albany Democrat-Herald.*

The selection below, which we have titled "My First Duty Is to My
Family," is taken from Fred Lockley's 1921 oral history interview
with Amanda Johnson. Although she was eighty-eight when she
provided this narrative, her memory for detail, including Deckard
family history and relationships, was clear. Throughout the interview,
Johnson stressed the importance of the Corum-Deckards in her life,
referring to them as "my family," "our family," and "my people."

In 1853, when Johnson crossed the plains from Missouri, to Linn
County, Oregon, few other African Americans resided in the Oregon
Territory. The U.S. Seventh Census, 1850, listed no blacks or mulattoes for Linn County and, for the entire Oregon Territory, only 207
blacks and mulattoes were identified. This number, however, was
inflated by inclusion of mixed-blood Indians, Hawaiians, and others.
The adjusted figure for the 1850 black population in the Oregon

---

*We have referred to Amanda Gardener Johnson by her married name
throughout, since her maiden name is in doubt. Three sources give it
variously as Robinson, Robeson, and Robbins. No explanation has
been found for her use of the name Gardener.

*The only known photograph of
Amanda Gardener Johnson, from the
Albany Democrat-Herald, 1924,
accompanying an interview with
Everett Earle Stanard.*

Territory has been calculated at 54 by Elizabeth McLagan, author of
A Peculiar Paradise (17), and at 56 by K. Keith Richard, author of
"Unwelcome Settlers" (I: 36). Richard's adjusted figure for the 1860
state of Oregon Census is 124 blacks and mulattoes, more than a
doubling in ten years, but still a small number.

Beginning with the laws of the provisional government in 1843,
slavery was always prohibited in Oregon, but the immigration of
blacks was not encouraged. Did Amanda Johnson know that slavery
was outlawed in Oregon? Did she know of Mommia Travers, a slave
who was freed by her owner at Fort Vancouver in 1851? Did she
know of Rose Jackson who was hidden in a wooden box when the
Allen family brought her to Oregon in 1851? Did she hear of Robin
and Polly Holmes who were brought from Missouri to Oregon in
1844, to be housed by Nathaniel Ford in slave quarters in Polk
County? Even Louis Southworth, a slave who traveled in the 1853
wagon train with Johnson, had to pay $1,000 for his own freedom,
two years after arriving in Oregon.

Oregon sent mixed messages to African Americans. As Richard
observed, "White attitudes were peculiar to the time and place: blacks
and mulattoes were excluded—but those already present in Oregon
could stay. Slavery was outlawed—but it existed" (I: 29). Some white
settlers wanted to avoid involvement with the slavery issue by exclud-
ing blacks; some wanted to preclude competition from black labor,
whether slave or free; and others, particularly during the years 1844-

49, feared the possibility of hostile actions if Indians and blacks combined forces.

To discourage black settlement, a number of exclusion laws were passed. An 1844 law, intended to take effect in 1846, required that all slaves be freed *and* removed from Oregon within three years. Free blacks were to leave within two years, or they would be flogged every six months. The flogging clause was modified in 1844, and the entire law was repealed in 1845. When Oregon was organized as a territory in 1848, slave keeping was prohibited; however, the exclusion law of 1849, which allowed black settlers already living in Oregon to remain, banned new black settlement. In 1853, the year of Amanda Johnson's arrival in Oregon Territory, the law was repealed.

Johnson told Stanard that the wagon train in which she and the Deckards traveled reached the Willamette Valley on September 18, 1853. She explained that she lived with the Deckards, "much like one of the family, until 1858, when I went to Albany and secured work at the J. H. Foster home." (We found her in the 1860 Linn County Census listed as a "female mulatto" and "servant.")

In 1857, the year of the Dred Scott decision and one year before Johnson went to work for the Fosters, a constitution for proposed statehood in Oregon was approved. The constitution carried an exclusion clause and, in 1859, Oregon became "the only free state admitted to the Union with an exclusion clause in its constitution" (McLagan 57). Although no enforcement was provided and all exclusion laws were voided by the Thirteenth and Fourteenth Amendments, this section of the Oregon Constitution, which excluded blacks and mulattoes from Oregon, remained on the statute books until repealed by a general election in 1926, only one year before Amanda Johnson's death.

At the age of thirty-five, she became engaged to Benjamin Johnson, a blacksmith, and a wedding date was set; however, unexpected events delayed their marriage. Illness struck the Deckard household, and Johnson left the Fosters' home in Albany to nurse the Deckards. Stanard reported: "Within nine days Mrs. Deckard had passed to the other shore and four other members of the family followed." Anderson Deckard was left a widower with a daughter and son to raise, and Johnson remained to help the family.

Two years later, on April 12, 1870, she married Ben Johnson "at the aristocratic home of the Fosters in Albany." Sixty guests and friends were present at "the gala event," and the Reverend T. J. Wilson of Eugene performed the ceremony. "I remember that I was married in a brown silk dress," Amanda Johnson told Stanard, "and that I wore brown silk gloves. There was a magnificent wedding cake, too."

After their marriage, the Johnsons took a house on the corner of Seventh and Elm streets in Albany, and this was their home for over thirty years. Apparently they had no children, but the 1880 census for Linn County suggests that a white child lived with them in Albany. The census lists Benjamin Johnson, age 43, born in Alabama, as head of household; Amanda Johnson, age 43, born in Missouri, as his wife; and Maud L. A. Henderson, age 11, born in Oregon. The ages for Benjamin and Amanda are in error, but other information for them appears to be accurate. Maud Henderson, the child living with the Johnsons, was probably the granddaughter of Lydia and Anderson Deckard and the person with whom Amanda Johnson spent the last years of her life. Johnson's obituary in the *Albany Democrat-Herald* of March 28, 1927, stated that she died the previous day at the Calapooia Street residence of Maude Henderson, granddaughter of Lydia Corum Deckard.

In all of the material we have located by and about Amanda Johnson, including the narrative below, her commitment to family and her dedication to caregiving are remarkably strong. Slavery had deprived her of close and lasting associations with biological family members, and she clung to familial bonds with the Deckards. Amanda Johnson clearly defined herself in this context of permanent connections with the Deckards—interdependent connections that both she and the Deckards had woven across seven generations.

My First Duty Is to My Family

Calapooia Street is in Albany, Oregon. In the center of a block, beside a crystal-clear stream, stands an old-fashioned house—a house of the middle '70s. Thick-branched odorous cedars surround the house. Beside the walk, like green-painted golf balls, are newly fallen black walnuts, still in their protective coverings, which, when crushed smell like woodland incense. I knocked at the door. A pleasant-faced woman answered the summons and, responding in the affirmative to my question as to whether Amanda Johnson lived there, she invited me into the parlor, where enlarged photographs hang on the wall, and called to someone in the kitchen, "Amanda, there is a gentleman here

to see you." A moment later Mrs. Johnson came in, with brisk step. Her eyes were clear, her hair was white, and she was the personification of neatness. [Fred Lockley]

I am not much accustomed to being interviewed, but I will do the best I can do to answer your questions. I was born at Liberty, Clay County, Missouri, August 30, 1833. My father and mother were born at Louisville, Kentucky.

No, sir. I was never sold nor bartered for. I was given as a wedding present to my owner's daughter. I belonged to Mrs. Nancy Wilhite. She was married, after her first husband's death, to Mr. Corum. Mrs. Corum was the grandmother of Miss Maud Henderson, who answered your knock at the door, and the great-great-grandmother of Mrs. E.M. Reagan, whose husband owns the *Albany Herald*.

I have known seven generations of the family. I knew [my] owner, Mrs. Corum, and her father. Mrs. Corum gave me to her daughter, Miss Lydia, when she married Anderson Deckard. My new owner was the third generation and I helped rear her children and grandchildren. That is five generations, and yesterday I held a baby in my arms that is the grandson of one of these grandchildren, so that makes seven generations I have known.

I had five brothers and six sisters. None of them was sold like common Negroes. They were all given as wedding presents to relatives of the family when the young folks got married.

The thought of being "sold down South" was always a cloud that shadowed the happiness of the slaves. A man would drink and lose his money or he would be unlucky at cards and would have to sell some of his slaves. I have often attended auctions of slaves when I was a girl, back in Missouri. They are very much like auctions of any other stock, except that the men that were buying the Negroes would ask them questions to see what they had done and were best fitted for. They would feel their muscles and look them over to see that they were sound. Usually the slaves sold for $500 to $1500, depending upon age and condition. A strong young field hand would bring $1000 to $1200, while a handsome young Negro woman would often sell for $1200 to $1500 if she had attracted the liking of some white man. Usually house servants commanded a better price than field hands.

In 1853 my owners decided to come to Oregon. A merchant, hearing that my master was to go to Oregon Territory, where slaves could not be held, came to Mr. Deckard and said, "I will give you $1200 for Amanda. You can't own her where you are going, so you might as well get what you can out of her."

I had been given to Miss Lydia, his wife, when I was seven, and I was 19 then. Mr. Deckard said, "Amanda isn't for sale. She is going across the plains to the Willamette Valley with us. She has had the care of our four children. My wife and the children like her. In fact, she is the same as one of our family, so I guess I won't sell her."

Mr. Deckard asked me if I wanted to be given my freedom and stay where I had been raised, and where all my people lived, but I was afraid to accept my liberty, much as I would have liked to stay there. The word of a Negro, even if a free Negro, was of no value in court. Any bad white man could claim that I had been stolen from him and could swear me into jail. Then, in place of keeping me in jail, he could buy my services for the time I was sentenced for, and by the time I had served my time for him he could bring up some other false charge and buy my services again, and do whatever he wanted to me, for Negroes were the same as cows and horses and were not supposed to have morals or souls. I was afraid to accept my liberty, so I came to Oregon with my owners.

It took us six months, to a day, to travel by ox team from Liberty, Missouri, to Oregon City. We started from Clay County, March 13, 1853, and got to our destination September 13. When I think back nearly 70 years to our trip across the plains I can see herds of shaggy-shouldered buffaloes, slender-legged antelopes, Indians, sagebrush, graves by the roadside, dust and high water and the campfire of buffalo chips over which I cooked the meals.

Lou Southworth, also a slave, crossed the same year I did. So did Benjamin Johnson, another slave, who later became my husband. . . . We camped at Oregon City until October, while Mr. Deckard went on horseback down through Linn County looking for a donation land claim. He took one between Albany and Peoria. In those days, when the boats ran down the river, Peoria looked as if it would be a good-sized town.

I went to work for a man named James Foster. He was a merchant, but later started the Magnolia Mills and made flour. When I left Missouri you could buy eggs for three to five cents a dozen, bacon at five to six cents a pound, butter at twelve to fifteen cents a pound, and corn for twenty cents a bushel, and you could hire men for fifty to seventy-five cents a day, so when I was paid $3.50

a week I decided I had come to the land of promise, a land that was flowing with milk and honey.

I was baptized when I was 14 years old by Mr. James, a Baptist minister. You have often heard of his son Jesse. Jesse James got into trouble holding up trains and doing all sorts of other mischief.

On April 12, 1870, a little over 50 years ago, I married Ben Johnson. The Reverend T. J. Wilson, who now lives at Eugene, performed the ceremony. I was married at Mr. Foster's house and they gave me a fine wedding.

Yes, I never get over feeling that my first duty is to my family. Whenever any of the Deckards are sick I always go to nurse them and take care of them, for you see, they are my people, and the only I've got. I am 88 years old, but I am strong and well. Most of our family have done themselves proud. Mr. Reagan, the editor of the *Albany Herald*, married into our family. I ate dinner there a few nights ago.

No, I don't suppose there are many other colored people in Oregon who have been slaves, but I have been free since I was 20, and that's nearly 70 years ago.

Susie Sumner Revels Cayton
1870-1943

The objective of Susie Sumner Revels Cayton's life was to strive for the uplift of humanity. As a well-educated African American who had experienced both the privileges of plenty and the harsh realities of poverty, Cayton was well positioned to identify and comment on the potential for care, as an alternative to oppression, in human relationships and political systems. Through her writing, lecturing, and activism, Cayton extended her philosophy from the private sphere to the public arena, addressing the need for a morality of responsibility and ethic of care in all human connections, regardless of race, class, and gender.

To illustrate Susie Cayton's ethic of care, we have selected "Sallie the Egg-Woman," a short story first published in the *Seattle Post-Intelligencer* (3 June 1900). Although "Sallie" is apparently fictional, her physical appearance, voice, and manner are suggestive of Sojourner Truth (ca. 1797-1883), the abolitionist and woman's rights advocate.

Born in Natchez, Mississippi, the fourth of six daughters of Hiram Rhodes Revels and Phoebe Rebecca Bass Revels, Susie Revels spent most of her childhood on the campus of Alcorn University, where her father, the first black U.S. Senator from Mississippi (1870-71), served as president. At the age of sixteen, after completing her schooling at Alcorn, Revels taught for ten years. Correspondence with Horace Roscoe Cayton, a former Alcorn student, led to a marriage proposal.

Susie Revels, the daughter of free African Americans, and Horace Cayton, the son of a white plantation owner and a black slave, were married in Seattle on July 12, 1896. The lure of the West as a land of opportunity for blacks had drawn Horace Cayton first to Kansas and eventually to Seattle, where he began his own paper, the *Seattle Republican*, in 1894, followed by *Cayton's Weekly* (1917-21) and *Cayton's Monthly* (1921).

The spirit of reform prevailed in the lives and work of Susie and Horace Cayton. Through the pages of the *Seattle Republican*, aimed at both white and black readers, Horace Cayton communicated his political views, attacked prejudice and discrimination, and wrote of accomplishments of the "New Negro." He rose to prominence in the

Photograph of Susie Sumner Revels Cayton from the Seattle Republican, 23 July 1909.

Republican Party, directly confronted political enemies, and launched bold attacks against graft in government, segregation, and lynching. Although Susie Cayton had domestic responsibility for the three daughters and two sons born to her marriage, and also for her grand-daughter Susan Cayton (Woodson), she found time to write and assist her husband with his journalistic efforts. Beginning in 1900, her name was listed as associate editor of the *Seattle Republican*, and she also served as associate editor of *Cayton's Weekly*.

An abiding force in Cayton's life was her commitment to helping others, regardless of race or class. Revels Cayton, one of her sons, remembered that his mother called this "striving for the uplift." In an interview with Richard S. Hobbs, Revels recalled his mother's advice: "Son, you must always strive for the uplift, . . . try to do good, try to do what uplifts humanity" (quoted in Hobbs, "The Cayton Legacy" 344).

Hard times came to the Caytons when their newspaper and publishing enterprises failed. In a climate of increased anti-black attitudes, the Caytons moved from their two-story residence on Capitol Hill, no longer the most prominent African American family in Seattle. Cayton stood by her husband when poverty knocked at their door, providing financial and spiritual support for the family, and extending her caregiving to the larger community. During the Great Depression, while her husband stood in the dole lines, Cayton assisted Seattle's unemployed. As Secretary of the Skid Road Unemployed Council, where she was the only woman, she was known as "Mother Cayton."

No longer convinced that education was the passport to human equality, Cayton became more politically radical and, in the mid to late 1930s, she joined the Communist Party (Hobbs 251). On one of his visits to the Caytons, Paul Robeson found his friend Susie Cayton engaged with one of her sewing/quilting groups, which she described as a forum for political discussion and for "educating the neighborhood" (quoted in Hobbs 252). In a 1936 letter to one of her daughters, Susie Cayton reported: "I'm having the time of my life and at the same time making some contribution to the working class I hope" (Letter to Madge Cayton, December 1936).

*Susie Sumner Revels Cayton,
painted shortly before her
death by Eldzier Cortor.*

After her husband's death in 1940, Susie Cayton remained active until her health failed in the spring of 1942. The last sixteen months of her life were spent with family members in Chicago. From her bed, she talked with notable friends such as Richard Wright, Langston Hughes, and Paul Robeson (Hobbs 313). After her death, Byrd Kelso, who had worked with Susie Cayton in Seattle's Skid Road Unemployment Council, wrote that she was "one of the GRANDEST LADIES" he had ever known, "always such an inspiration to all of the poor folks here, no matter their color, religion, or nationality" (Letter to Madge Cayton, 23 August 1943). Kelso calculated that together they had helped "HUNDREDS if not THOUSANDS of poor people" in Seattle "and actually kept them from starving to death."

Cayton's short story, "Sallie the Egg-Woman," is set in a small town after the Civil War. Sallie, a former slave, assumes full care and responsibility for Clarie, the seriously ill daughter of a Confederate family. The human connection between the two women blurs social constructions of race and class. The townspeople, however, exhibit subtle to not-so-subtle forms of race and class prejudice, preferring not to assume responsibility for the human condition of Sallie or Clarie. Even the minister distances himself from their circumstances until Sallie breaks the silence and tells her story.

SALLIE THE EGG-WOMAN

Sallie the Egg-Woman was the name by which she was known, and had more than some one or two persons in the village in which she lived been asked her name in full they could not have told it. Sallie the Egg-Woman seemed to fill all requirements, and no one asked to know more. Sallie was taller than the average woman, with a rather masculine form much in keeping with her voice and carriage, neither of which indicated anything like womanly tenderness. Sallie was a black woman, black as a human being ever gets to be, and each Saturday, rain or shine, her usual customers could count on seeing her black face wreathed in smiles as her ample figure blocked the doorway, a large basket on either arm. "Eggs this morn'nig?" she would ask in a voice which to a stranger might sound rather repulsive, but which closer acquaintance had softened to her customers, for they had found that black Sallie's heart was as white as the beautiful snow, . . .

The profit from her eggs was not Sallie's only means of support, for she also ran a farm on a small scale. Where she came from and when puzzled all who knew her, . . . Apparently, she lived alone, and yet had often been overheard talking as one would to a very small child. Time, assisted by busybodies, disclosed the fact that Sallie the Egg-Woman, who was thought to be so far above earthly sins, had concealed in her home, and had for years, a slim woman with sallow face and great glowing eyes, a woman whose raven black hair fell in laughing ringlets quite below her waistline, a woman of about twenty-eight years of age—a white woman—whom she had chained to the iron railing which formed an inclosure in the room in which they slept.

That part of the Southland went wild over the stunning news that spread like wild fire, and an indignant people went at once to demand of her to give the woman up, a thing she stoutly refused to do. The matter was taken into court, and great was the amazement and a hush fell over the eager throng when Sallie took the stand and admitted that she had in her home and had had for some time, the woman; that she at times confined her to her room because she was absent-minded and might wander from home, but when asked, where she got her, who she was, and similar questions, her only answer was "I borned her." "Is she a white woman?" the judge asked, and Sallie's black face on which was depicted the defiance of despair, seemed blacker than usual as she answered, "Whatever she is, I borned her."

The case was finally dismissed and Sallie allowed to keep her charge, perhaps, mainly so, because the white woman was poor and unknown. And then, who could prove that Sallie did not, as she said, "born her," and that too regardless of the fact that if she did it was contrary to all previous laws of nature.

One Saturday morning about two years later Sallie's customers missed her. Their usual supply of eggs did not come, for early that morning Sallie had gone for a minister to come with her to lay in her last resting place in a quiet corner on her own farm, the woman whose name she said was "Clarie." A few of the curious, who are never absent when anything to be seen or heard is going on, gathered at a respectful distance, and with Sallie as chief and only mourner the last sad words of the funeral rite were said. . . .

When all was ended the minister spoke a few sympathizing words to Sallie, and turned to depart, but she stayed him, saying: "I wish you would wait till they is all gone, and we is alone. I have something to say to you about that poor child who lies there," and she pointed to the newly made mound which the men were just leaving. "Here," said Sallie, "right here by her side, as has ever been my place since I've knowed her, I wants to tell you the story of her sad life. When the civil war broke out her father, who was the only living kin she had in the world, joined the 'federate army. During the first year he was killed. That same year the soldiers, when passing the little town where we lived (I was then what was called a house servant), had a skirmish and a flying bullet hit Miss Clarie, this poor girl. It struck her head and she fell at my feet. The doctors probed for it, but could not find it. She got better for a while and all was well, but I soon noticed a growing nervousness in her manner and a kinder twitching of her limbs which she could not stop. One night about 12 she crawled in my bed, she was just sixteen and good to look at. Shaking me easy like she said:

"'Wake up, Aunt Sallie. I wants to talk to you.'

"'Lord, child, what is it you wants at this time o' night?' I asked.

"'Sallie,' she said, 'they cannot deceive me; that bullet is in my head. I can feel the weight of it and I am slowly losing my mind. No, you cannot fool me,' she said, as I tried to tell her she was wrong, but the great tears were running down my face, for that many a day had I seed that her mind was going from her.

"'Now, Sallie,' she went on, 'I have sold this place, settled up everything here. You know father left everything to me, which includes a small place in the adjoining state, and we will make our home there, you and I. You will go with me, won't you, Sallie?'

"For answer, I threw both arms around her small body and amidst great sobs I said, 'Miss Clarie, I would not leave you, child, in your great trouble for anything. Didn't I promise your mother, who died when your little eyes opened in this world, that I would stay with you, and didn't I promise your father 'fore he went to war that I would never leave you? Yes, child, just you count on Sallie,' said I, and as I looked at her sweet face in the moonlight, which was then shining in the window, I felt that I would just like to stand between her and the whole world. Yes, I'd have died to keep my promise to those two dead ones, who left her in my keer.

"'Now, Sallie,' she said, taking my arms down and holding one of my hands in both of hers, 'there is one thing more I want you to promise me—when I lose my mind they will want to send me to the asylum. I have a horror of that. I do not want to go there, and so you must hide me, Sallie, hide me in our new home and never let anyone see me, and if I do not get so wild that you are unsafe with me you must keep me there till the end. This new home I'll make over to you while I yet have my mind, and we will live there together. Do you promise?' she asked.

"'I do,' said I, 'God helping me, I do.'

"She turned to go, but came back to me and kneeling by the bed whispered, 'Sallie, do crazy people go to heaven?'

"'Well, Miss Clarie, if they is good before they gets crazy, I thinks they does.'

"She did not speak for some time, then she said:

"'I think so too, Sallie, and I do not know what the end will be, but I say to you on my bended knees and in His holy presence that I believe in God.'

"Her soft nightdress fluttered by me, my door was shut gently and I was left alone with my thoughts, which kept going on and on till I got up and set by the winder in the moonlight, and at last I fell asleep.

"The next day we went to our new home, and after fixing up the papers and having the iron railings put up in a back room of our home, Clarie never went out no more, save some of nights when I walked with her in our little garden, but sat there and waited for the end. The change soon came, for in six months she did not even know me, but she was never wild, just sat there and rocked and rocked and rocked. I put her to bed nights and dressed her mornings, cut up her food for her and waited on her as one would on a baby."

"How long has she been like this?" the minister asked.

"Clarie were sixteen when she was shot, and were 30 last week. Yes, we have been here fourteen years and, since the first six months, she has never spoken a word—never as much as turned her head when I replied to her; could not even thank me when I quit work in the fields and walked home in the hot sun for to take her a cool drink of water. Being as she was, she aged quicker than she would have otherwise, and, as the years went by, I could hardly believe that the hard-featured, sallow-faced woman who sat silently rocking in her little iron-bound room could have been my Miss Clarie, bright and cheerful before the war. Sometimes it seemed that the creaking of that chair, as she rocked to and fro, to and fro and to and fro, would drive me crazy, too, but I would say to myself, 'Come, Sallie, it would never do. You must stay by her; keep your mind and stay by her,' and I would get up and brush out her long black hair, which seemed to ease her head in some way, for she'd quit rocking so regular like.

"The end came last Friday night. I heard a strange noise in her room, and unlocking the iron door, which was made so that I could see her from my bed, I found that my duty was ended, for Clarie had been claimed by Him as rules the heavens and earth and don't take 'no' from none of us.

"Now," concluded Sallie, as she laid a sprig of cedar on the mound by which he stood, "I want to come under the keer of your church is why I have told you all of this. The world don't keer nothing about it, so you and me will just cover over it again, but I'd like for you to do her and me the kindness as to get a big white stone to put up for her."

"I will," the minister replied, as he wiped away a great tear which had unconsciously crept into his eyes of tenderness.

"Here," said Sallie, "is what you are to get it with. It's money I have saved up from my eggs for just such a time as this."

"What shall I have carved on it?" he asked.

"You see," said Sallie, "when this poor child came to this world the doctor was late getting there, and I was alone with her mother—that's how I borned her, so you can have put on there: 'Clarie, borned of Sallie the Egg-Woman,' and then under this in big letters put: 'She believed in God.'"

Mourning Dove (Christine Quintasket)
1888-1936

Mourning Dove (Humishuma) was the Okanogan pseudonym of Christine Quintasket, the first Indian woman known to write and publish a novel. Until the recent publication of her autobiography, *Mourning Dove: A Salishan Autobiography*, relatively little was known about Mourning Dove's life, particularly her early years. She died on August 8, 1936, in the state hospital at Medical Lake, Washington, but her manuscript did not surface until the 1980s, and was not published until 1990. Because of the richness of this autobiography, including its many instances of the ethic of caring for others, we have chosen to include excerpts from *Mourning Dove* in this volume.

Her novel, *Cogewea, the Half-Blood: A Depiction of the Great Montana Cattle Range*, first published in 1927, is the story of a woman of mixed Okanogan and Anglo blood, who struggles to find an identity for herself while she mediates between Indian and white cultures. In addition to Cogewea's story, Mourning Dove incorporated three tales related by Stemteema, Cogewea's revered grandmother and a representative of a passing traditional culture.

Although *Cogewea* drew little attention when it was published, contemporary critics have recognized its significance. Alanna Kathleen

Mourning Dove picking huckleberries at Mt. Hood, 1932

Brown, in her *Legacy* profile of Mourning Dove, observed that she "chose to do an extraordinary thing: she chose to write a spiritual autobiography in the form of the popular Western romances of the 1900s. In doing so, she became the first Native American to organically include Indian culture and oral literature, as well as Indian social dilemmas, in a novel" (51). Dexter Fisher, in an introduction to the 1981 reprint of the novel, wrote that *Cogewea* "stands as the first effort of an American Indian woman to write a novel based upon the legacy of her Indian heritage" (xxvi).

Most critics and readers of *Cogewea* have accepted Mourning Dove's claim that her paternal grandfather was a white man—a Scot or Irishman who worked for the Hudson's Bay Company, and that she, like her protagonist Cogewea, was of mixed blood. No evidence has been found for this claim, and Jay Miller, editor of Mourning Dove's autobiography, believes she may have "provided a white ancestor to appeal to her readers" (*Mourning Dove* xvi). Based on his research, Miller concludes: "Her appeal to a white ancestry, denied by her family and the tribal census, indicates how strongly she saw herself as a mediator between Indian and white" (xxxviii).

By all accounts, Mourning Dove was born in a canoe while her mother was crossing Idaho's Kootenai River, near Bonners Ferry. The year of her birth is usually given as 1888 or 1887; however, Jay Miller suggests it may have been as early as 1885 (*Mourning Dove* xii). Her parents were Lucy Stukin, a Colville born at Kettle Falls on the upper Columbia River, and Joseph Quintasket, an Okanogan born at Penticton, in the upper Okanogan country of British Columbia. Her early years were spent with her family in Northeastern Washington, about twenty miles from the Canadian border. In 1902, not long before the death of her mother, the family moved to the Flathead Reservation in Montana, and lived there for about ten years. While there, Mourning Dove witnessed the federal government's round-up of the last buffalo herds in 1912. The buffalo were the "last link connecting him [the Indian] with the past," she wrote later in her novel, "and when one of the animals burst through the car, falling to the tracks and breaking its neck, I saw some of the older people shedding silent tears" (*Cogewea* 148).

Mourning Dove was married twice but had no children. While she was in Montana, she met her first husband—Hector McLeod, a Flathead. They were married in 1909, and lived at Polson, near the southern tip of Flathead Lake. McLeod, who was sometimes violent and abusive, lived a fast life in association with bootleggers and gamblers. Their rocky marriage ended after a few years.

Her second marriage was in 1919 to Fred Galler, a Colville with some white ancestry. The Gallers lived on the Colville Reservation and worked as migrant harvesters in Washington hop fields and fruit orchards. Mourning Dove and Fred Galler had some stormy times, in part due to Galler's drinking, but he was "tolerant of her career" (Miller xxii).

While she was in Portland in 1912, Mourning Dove completed the draft for her novel, but fifteen years would pass before it was published. She was particularly interested in providing a sympathetic portrait of Indians and their culture, all drawn from the perspective of an Indian. In an interview for Spokane's *Spokesman Review*, she said: "It is all wrong, this saying that Indians do not feel as deeply as whites. We do feel, and by and by some of us are going to be able to make our feelings appreciated, and then will the true Indian character be revealed" (19 April 1916).

Mourning Dove's meeting with Lucullus Virgil McWhorter in 1914 was the beginning of a twenty-year collaboration. McWhorter was a white businessman, an advocate of Indian rights, and founder of the *American Archaeologist*. Adopted by the Yakama* and known to them as "Old Wolf," McWhorter had authored *The Crime against the Yakima* (1913), and he was intrigued by the possibility of seeing her novel published as soon as possible. He edited it, and added notes and a biographical sketch. Mourning Dove and McWhorter completed their collaboration on *Cogewea* in 1916, but many years passed before a publisher could be found. World War I altered reader preferences, and "Western romances" were no longer in vogue. Once a publisher was found, Mourning Dove had to do extra work in Washington apple orchards to help finance the project.

Ultimately, the collaboration of Mourning Dove and McWhorter resulted in two major works: *Cogewea* (1927) and *Coyote Stories* (1934), edited by Heister Dean Guie, with notes by McWhorter and a foreword by Chief Standing Bear. A third work, *Tales of the Okanogans,* based on Mourning Dove's *Coyote Stories*, was edited by Donald M. Hines and published in 1976.

The published version of *Cogewea* was clearly the work of more than one author. In her *Legacy* profile of Mourning Dove, Alanna Brown describes the novel as "a splintered work." According to Brown, McWhorter, "out of his need to preserve Indian culture and

---

*The Yakama Nation has asked that, as from 1994, it be referred to in this way, rather than by the older spelling, "Yakima."

his rage at those who would destroy it, edited her novel to the point that he became a constant interruptive voice" (53). In a letter to McWhorter, dated June 4, 1928, Mourning Dove wrote that she had just read the published novel and was "suprised at the changes" McWhorter had made. She thought the changes were "fine" but added: "I felt like it was some one else's book and not mine at all. In fact the finishing touches are put there by you, and I have never seen it."

Mourning Dove's autobiography was written, at least in part, as a response to critics who claimed *Cogewea* was not her own work. Little was done with the manuscript until the 1980s, when Jay Miller, who had worked for years with Colville elders, was asked to prepare the various parts of the autobiography for publication. Miller found Mourning Dove's autobiography to be "the most sustained discussion of Interior Salishan life by an insider that I had ever seen, full of historical and ethnographic gems, but badly disjointed and ungrammatical" (*Mourning Dove* xxxii). With all its faults, Miller describes the autobiography as a "personal ethnography of lasting value," for the "descriptions are detailed, and her sense of history is unique" (*Mourning Dove* xxxiv).

In the selections we have titled "Helping the Needy," taken from Mourning Dove's autobiography, she describes her early childhood at Kettle Falls, her adopted grandmother Teequalt, and the difficult winter of 1892-93. We were impressed by the many ways in which caring for others is a part of these childhood memories. No matter how little her parents had, they were always willing to share with others who had less. In her chosen role as cultural mediator, Mourning Dove maintained the caring attitude she had seen modeled as a child. She eschewed bitterness against whites and sought instead understanding and tolerance of her people and their traditional ways.

Bracketed portions in the text below are Miller's editorial additions.

HELPING THE NEEDY

My own spiritual, moral, and traditional training was supervised by a woman called Teequalt, whom we came to adopt as a grandmother. She was my tutor during her later years.

I had come upon an old woman sitting all by herself. I came up to her full of eagerness. Seeing me, she gathered up her heavy load and got to her feet with the help of a cane. In a loud tone she scolded me, on the verge of sobbing, "Leave me alone. I am walking, walking until I die. Nobody wants me." She waved me away and cried, "Leave me alone." She left our trail and wandered into the chokecherry thicket on the hillside.

I stood there embarrassed. I just could not understand why this woman wanted to die when the land was beautiful, covered with flowers in many hues and shapes. The songs of the meadowlarks mingled with the robins scolding from the treetops, where their nests were. Crickets added their own tunes. It was wonderful to be alive and inhale the clear spring air. My childish mind saw the large world as all happiness. But this woman was sad, weeping and wanting to walk until she died.

Abruptly, I turned on my heel and ran uphill to tell Mother. Reaching the door, almost out of breath, I said, "Mother (toom), I have found a new grandmother, and she wants to die." This so startled Mother that she almost dropped the new baby she was lacing into the cradleboard. Without a pause, she handed me the baby and went swiftly down the trail to find the old woman. She did find her and offered her our home for as long as she wanted to stay. Thereafter Teequalt was always with us, and we stayed closer to home because she could not travel very far.

She was a wonderful storyteller. She was twelve when she first heard of the new people (whites) coming into our country in boats (bateaux) instead of canoes. When my parents went for game or berries, we children took care of her. We prepared meals according to her instructions, then we would sit at her feet and listen to her wonderful stories.

With our adopted grandmother, we became like the other children. Our own grandmother lived far off, and we had always envied other children who were blessed by having elders in their home.

Early one morning I overheard my parents talking. They decided the family should stay in the winter camp while Father went across the river to the white towns to seek work. This was necessary because we had no horses or ponies to carry all of us to another place. The rest of the day, he prepared for his departure. The next morning he put on clean clothing and gave what few coins he had to Mother. He had no blankets or food, nor did he have a destination. He was desperate and in need of food for his family.

After he left, Mother held Keleta to her breast and cried in silence. Sulee and I did not understand any of this and so played around the dying embers of our fire. She had always been generous to the poor and needy with our food. All winter long she had given away some of the food Father had saved the previous summer. Father said nothing because he also believed in helping the needy. That was the reason we were short of food before the spring plants were ready.

It was only when I was much older that I realized the sacrifices made by my gentle mother. She would cook a very small piece of venison and divide it equally into three pieces. Sulee and I would swallow ours almost whole. Mother would then divide the third piece again and go without any food for herself. I did not stop to wonder why she fed the baby after each meal with tears in her eyes. It was because she was hungry. Our childish selfishness did not understand that our mother was going without to keep us alive while she yet had to nurse a third. My heart aches with remorse as I write this. She died long before I realized any of this, and now I cannot ask her to forgive me for being so selfish. When we cried for food, she could only turn her back to the fire, away from us, and weep quietly. . . . She never complained of her ailments or misfortunes and never aired her troubles in public.

Mother was a reserved woman, almost to the point of coldness, and many people misunderstood her aloofness and the hidden warmth of her character. She had a heart of gold that showed only to the poor and unfortunate. I knew her to give away our own food to the needy so that we went without for a time. It was the way she and Father were raised, and they had watched their own parents do the same.

When all our food was gone, Mother did the next best thing. She dressed us each morning and bathed the baby before lacing her into the cradleboard. She took her digging stick and led us to the hillsides to dig up the tender shoots of the balsam sunflower and feed them to us. We did this for two weeks until the shoots were high enough to develop a thin skin that had to be peeled off. These shoots were called "famine food" because they were the first fresh food available each spring. It tasted like celery and was considered an aid to digestion. It was best mixed with other food and meat because a steady diet of it was not healthy.

One day Mother led us up the Kettle River to gather mussels from the shoals to eat with the shoots. Back home she buried the shells under the fire to bake in the sandy loam. Even so, they were tough and we had to work very hard to chew them. Still, we enjoyed this change of food.

Mother trapped ground squirrels when they first emerged from their burrows after winter hibernation. Groundhogs were fatter but had a stronger scent than the squirrels. They were a luxury we all enjoyed. As always, Mother divided our catch with the old people in camp. We also ate tree squirrels and all kinds of birds Mother snared with a hemp string.

That spring of 1893 everyone was starving. Those who were ablebodied had moved on in search of food, work, or money. We were stranded in camp with the old and feeble because of our lack of horses.

Early one morning I awakened to hear the singing of meadowlarks. I had had no supper, and my stomach ached for food. I could not abide the happy sound of the "tattler" of legend and began to cry quietly to myself. By now I had learned to be patient and not complain, for it was useless to share my grief with Mother. She remained true to her education and was stoic with everyone. Mother did this even with her own children, never cuddling us or saying soft words. I was [a bit] afraid of her and in consequence held her words in great respect.

Yet that day, my mother was very kind and understanding. She interrupted my tears by saying, "What is the matter Kee-ten?" using my pet name. It was too much to bear, and I told her I was hungry and lonesome for Father. I heard her sigh as she got up to start the fire. I got up quickly, dried my eyes, and warmed myself at the fire. We said nothing else, but we had shared our sorrow.

Mother dressed Sulee and the baby in clean but worn clothes, better than we wore for every day. I wondered why we were wearing them but was afraid to ask. My questions or inquisitiveness were always rebuked because it was not the Indian way to learn anything.

Instead, I waited to see what would happen. When we were dressed and ready, Mother placed the cradleboard with Keleta on her back, and we went directly across the river in a fragile canoe lent to us for the trip to Marcus. Mother placed her daughters on the bottom and paddled from the stem. With each dip of the oar, the boat leaped forward. Mother was expert with a canoe, and we went in speedy safety.

At the little city of Marcus, we followed Mother from one house to another as she knocked on the back door to ask for food for her family. At each door she was refused admittance and would silently leave while Sulee begged and cried for food in our language. Perhaps this prevented whites from learning the true nature of our distress. By afternoon the sun beat on my bare head and I felt weak [from hunger]. Mother stopped in the shade of some jack pines near three lone houses set in this shade. She rested there for some time before she determined to go to the door of a house where we could hear men and women laughing hilariously.

A woman came to the door wearing a long dress with many ruffles along the bottom and her hair curled and piled high in a roll behind her head. Her smile was sweet and dimpled. She was beautiful, with pink skin, red lips, eyes as blue as the sky. Mother talked to her and she nodded. She came outside and shut the door, giving each of us children a pat on the head. Then she went back inside and returned with some fluffy, lacy clothing for my mother to wash and mend. She also brought out some bread and food that Sulee and I ate in haste under the jack pines.

Out of respect for the dead and their kind deeds, I will not use the real name of this woman but will supply a substitute. The city of Marcus was filled with nice churchgoers who did not believe in associating with a prostitute like Nellie. She made her money from providing the nightlife in the sleepy little burg of Marcus, a character of the Gay Nineties with a kind heart who was shunned by the decent society of this pioneer town. Yet she alone was willing to help and provide our salvation until Father returned. Every week Mother went to get washing and mending from Nellie and returned with food and spare clothing. Mother had no idea where or how Father was. She could only wait for him patiently and continue to support the family by digging roots, trapping animals, and doing laundry. She never stopped dividing our food with those less fortunate, even though the worst was yet to come.

Part IV: Communicating:
From Private To Public

When your own share of sorrow has worn itself to slumber,
Then every woman's sorrow is your own.
Hazel Hall, "Inheritance" (1928)

The fourth major theme in the lives and writings of these Pacific Northwest women is the theme of communicating for self and others. Motivated by the desire to be heard and understood by public audiences, the ten women in Part IV consciously moved from private reflection to public attention, a move we refer to as "the rhetorical turn." As writers, and sometimes as speakers, these women and many others included in this volume sought voice and agency as public rhetors; the overriding goal of their rhetoric was empowerment, sometimes of self and frequently of others. To illustrate the variety of forms their communication took, selections included in Part IV are drawn from published autobiographies, public letters and essays, fiction, and poetry.

Although the specific rhetorical exigencies of their stories varied, all four women whose autobiographies are excerpted in this section defended themselves against public criticism, and three—Mary Sawtelle, Sarah Winnemucca and Lydia Taylor—directly addressed the need for social reform. By pointing out personal injustices in their own lives, they appealed to a public sense of justice; by calling for social reform, they sought to empower themselves and others.

Both Margaret Jewett Bailey's *The Grains* (1854) and Sawtelle's *The Heroine of '49* (1891) are autobiographical novels that focus on injustice to women in marriage and in divorce. For Bailey, who was divorced in 1854, writing and publishing her early autobiography as the story of "Ruth Rover" was both a defiant and constrained act. Bailey wanted the public to know she had been maligned, first by false accusations from former associates at the Methodist Willamette Mission, and later by her abusive husband and his friends. Although she used a pseudonym, created fictitious names for most of the people she portrayed, and wrote mainly in the third person, she did not distance herself entirely, and many readers, including the *Oregonian*'s hostile critic, apparently knew whose story was told in *The Grains*.

Mary P. Avery Sawtelle was also motivated to clear her name by telling readers about the domestic violence she experienced at the hands of her first husband, as well as the injustice she suffered in 1858 when the divorce court took away her parental rights. Sawtelle, who had remarried and established her medical practice by the time she published her autobiography, wrote under her own name, but she felt constrained to write in the third person and to use fictitious names. From a comparatively strong position of autonomy-based and connection-based empowerment, Sawtelle extended her concern from the personal to the universal, seeking empowerment for other women through improvements in education, health care, and legal rights.

In contrast to Bailey and Sawtelle, Sarah Winnemucca wrote her autobiography, *Life Among the Piutes: Their Wrongs and Claims* (1883), in the first person and used actual names throughout. She responded to sexist and racist attacks, presenting herself as part of a caring but threatened Indian culture. In her writings and from the lecture platform, Winnemucca, a cultural mediator, asked for compassion from her white audiences and, through arguments based on justice, advocated for Indian rights and restoration of the vanishing culture she loved.

In the last autobiography excerpted here, *From under the Lid: An Appeal to True Womanhood* (1913), Lydia Taylor told her first-person story of an abusive childhood and the ugliness of poverty —experiences that led her to prostitution. Using her own life as a graphic example of the injustice of women's oppression, Taylor made an appeal for moral and social reform to end the sexual victimization of women.

The rhetorical purposes of the three authors of public letters and essays in this section were also varied, ranging from information and entertainment to self-defense and social reform. Two of these writers—Abigail Scott Duniway and Minnie Myrtle Miller—also used the lecture platform to communicate their messages. The third, Louise G. Stephens, treasured her privacy, avoided interviews, and wrote under pen names.

Abigail Scott Duniway, who is best known for her woman suffrage efforts, used her position as editor of the *New Northwest*, a "human rights" newspaper, to focus on the exigence for woman's rights and to empower other Pacific Northwest women. Duniway's "Editorial Correspondence," from which we have taken several selections for this volume, is an interesting combination of entertaining travel accounts

Eva Emery Dye (right) interviewing Se-Cho-Wa (seated) about her memories of Lewis and Clark. The woman standing is Pe-Yow-Ya, the interpreter. Photograph by Major Lee Moorehouse, ca. 1900, Umatilla County, Oregon.

and advocacy. Her kernel examples of the injustices women suffered throughout the Pacific Northwest are placed within the non-threatening contexts of vivid, often humorous, travel descriptions from the 1870s and 1880s.

Minnie Myrtle Miller (Theresa Dyer) published two contrasting pieces in 1871 issues of Duniway's *New Northwest*. The first, an essay on one of Susan B. Anthony's lectures in Salem, Oregon, includes Miller's entertaining observations of men in the audience as well as her own justification for equal suffrage. Her arguments are examples of what Aileen S. Kraditor describes as the "justice" and "expediency" arguments that were typical of woman suffrage rhetoric (*The Ideas of the Woman Suffrage Movement*). The argument from justice, drawn from natural rights philosophy, held that all persons (including women) had rights as citizens; the argument from expediency, based on assumed differences between women and men, held that, if women had the ballot, the purity of true womanhood would improve the world.

In the second selection by Miller, an open letter to the public, she responded to questions and criticisms about her separation and divorce from poet Joaquin Miller. But, beyond her stated purpose, Miller may have been sending another message intended for her former husband—a covert message he could choose to accept or reject.

In sharp contrast to Miller's public, yet personal, correspondence, the fictionalized letters of Louise G. Stephens were written as joyful expressions of love for the natural world of the Pacific Northwest and to entertain readers with delightful accounts of beginning a new life in rural Oregon. First published as a popular series of letters in the *Oregonian*, Stephens's work was published in 1905 as *Letters from an Oregon Ranch*, by "Katharine."

Fiction and poetry were genres that Pacific Northwest women could use to code their messages without necessarily offending their audiences. Sui Sin Far (Edith Maud Eaton), who described herself as a "connecting link" between the cultures of her Chinese mother and her English father, used fiction to mediate understanding between Chinese and American cultures. In "The Americanizing of Pau Tsu," one of her short stories set in Seattle and reprinted here, Far explored the complexities of gender and intercultural relationships.

Ella Higginson, whose early argument for conservation of the Pacific Northwest appears in Part I, was also the poet laureate of Washington and authored fiction as well. Her fiction frequently illuminated the artificiality of class distinctions and western women's need to develop their sense of selfhood. To illustrate these themes in Higginson's writing, we include "Esther's 'Fourth,'" a short story, and an excerpt from *Mariella; of Out-West* (1902), Higginson's only novel.

We conclude Part IV and this volume where it began—with the artistry of Oregon poet Hazel Hall—"maker of songs." Although most of her life was spent in a wheelchair and her eyesight grew too weak for the intricate needlework with which she supported herself, Hazel Hall was empowered by writing poetry until her early death in 1924. Hall's finely crafted poetry endures as her legacy, and so, we hope, will the words and lives of the other Pacific Northwest women in this volume. We have come to know them well in the course of writing this book and, for us, they were all "makers of songs."

Margaret Jewett (Smith) Bailey
1812-82

Margaret Jewett Bailey understood the power of the written word to praise and to cast blame, to establish character and to destroy credibility. For Bailey, the clouded record of her past association with the Methodist Willamette Mission and rumors about her divorce from Dr. William J. Bailey required clarification and refutation. In an independent attempt to clear her name by defaming others, Bailey made her side of the story public.

Writing under the *nom de plume* of Ruth Rover, Bailey authored one of the earliest works in Oregon—*The Grains, or Passages in the Life of Ruth Rover, with Occasional Pictures of Oregon, Natural and Moral,* published in 1854 by Carter & Austin, in Portland. Intended "to be published in monthly numbers—till completed," the extant work appeared in two parts in August and September of 1854. A reconstructed reprint in one volume, edited by Evelyn Leasher and Robert J. Frank, was published by Oregon State University Press in 1986. The excerpts we have titled "What Have I Married?" and our references to *The Grains* are from this reconstructed reprint.

Although difficult to classify under a single genre, *The Grains* is one of the first examples of a Pacific Northwest woman seeking to empower herself publicly through a thinly veiled personal narrative. In the foreword to the 1986 reprint, historian Edwin Bingham observed that *The Grains* is an unusual document because it is "part autobiography, part religious testimonial, part history and travelogue" (v). He added, "By stretching the definition, *The Grains* may be called a novel, the first novel written and published on the Pacific Coast."

In Chapter One of *The Grains*, Bailey, in the persona of Ruth Rover, made her rhetorical exigence clear: "I am avoided and shunned, and slighted, and regarded with suspicions in every place till my life is more burdensome than death would be. I have, therefore, in this conclusion [to publish the book], been impelled by a sense of justice due to myself and a wish that my future life should not be overshadowed by the gloom of the present" (27). Her objective was to convince her Oregon audience of the injustices she had suffered, thereby opening the door to future possibilities to write, teach, and perhaps remarry.

When Part I of *The Grains* was released, negative reviews in the Portland *Oregonian* added to the constraints Bailey faced. With the exception of favorable comments about the "very neat and immaculate" typography and "considerable piety" he noted in Part I, the anonymous "Squills" of the *Oregonian* went after the author with the invective that characterized what was known as "the Oregon style" of journalism. "We seldom read books of feminine production," Squills wrote, "believing *their* (the females) province to be darning stockings, pap and gruel, children, cookstoves, and the sundry little affairs that make life comparatively comfortable and makes them, what Providence designed them 'Helpmates'" (*Oregonian*, 5 August 1854). Squills went on to say, "To call it trash, would be impolite, for the writer is 'an authoress.'" Moreover, observed Squills, this was not the biography of a Napoleon or a Byron, but the biography of a mere woman: "[W]ho the dickens cares, about the existence of a fly, or in whose pan of molasses the insect disappeared."

What we know about Bailey's life comes partly from Ruth Rover's story, including the letters and journal entries Bailey included in *The Grains*, and partly from the work of scholars such as Janice Duncan, Leasher, and Frank. Bailey was born as Margaret J. Smith, about 1812, in Saugus, Massachusetts, and she was converted at a Methodist camp meeting when she was seventeen. Her dream was to become a missionary among the Indians and, despite admonitions from family members and her father's threat to disinherit her if she left him in his old age, she asserted her independence and enrolled in the Wesleyan Academy at Wilbraham, Massachusetts.

Margaret Smith applied to church officers and was offered an opportunity to go to Oregon, as a teacher, in the company of the Reverend David Leslie (D. Leland in *The Grains*), his family, and H. K. W. Perkins. She sailed from Boston in January of 1837, traveled to Oregon via the Sandwich (Hawaiian) Islands, and became part of the Oregon Mission established by the Reverend Jason Lee in 1834.

Smith's outspokenness and quarrels with the Reverend Leslie created serious problems with the mission family. Her oldest brother had warned her that missionaries were "overzealous, enthusiastic fanatics" (*The Grains* 52), and she began to question their motives. She was relatively sympathetic to Jason Lee and described him as "a *good* man" who "possessed the true missionary spirit" but was "deficient in judgment" and unable to manage efficiently (137). Clearly, Smith was not pleased with Lee's suggestion that she assist Mrs. Lee in the kitchen because he "already had more females in the family than could be well employed" (89), and she was concerned that the Indians were not given clothing by the mission but charged for it.

Although she was finally allowed to teach, she continued to argue with the Reverend Leslie and Cyrus Shepard about her authority as a teacher and her place in the mission family.

When Smith received a marriage proposal from William H. Willson (Wiley in *The Grains*), her problems became more complicated. Smith, the only unattached white woman at the mission, was under considerable pressure from the mission family to marry Willson. Moreover, Willson's "attentions to her had been unremitting—in sickness and in health he was her constant associate—and in all her troubles with other members of the mission family he was apparently her only friend" (*The Grains* 151). She finally consented to marry him; however, when she learned that he had written earlier to the States and asked Chloe Aurelia Clark (Miss J— in *The Grains*) to come to Oregon and marry him, Smith refused to marry until an answer was received. Willson promised to send a messenger to destroy his letter of proposal, which was being carried to the East by Jason Lee, and Smith allowed him to spend the winter of 1838 as her boarder.

Willson continued to press Margaret Smith for an immediate marriage. After a quarrel in which she said she would "never become his wife under any circumstances," Willson turned to the Reverend Leslie, saying that he and Smith had been intimate, and the two confronted her. Smith denied the charge, but Leslie and the mission family exerted such pressure that Smith, in the hope of avoiding expulsion, finally agreed to sign a confession that she was "guilty of the crime of fornication." She soon discovered Leslie had lied to her when he promised the incident would be forgotten if she signed the confession. Her reputation within the mission was ruined, she was shunned, and her years as a mission teacher were over. Willson, however, went on to become a church leader, established a mission at Puget Sound in 1839, and married Chloe Aurelia Clark, who did come to Oregon Country, in 1840 (Duncan, "Ruth Rover" 246).

When Smith received a marriage proposal from Dr. William J. Bailey (Dr. Binney in *The Grains*), she accepted. Dr. Bailey was from outside the mission, and this could be a new life for her. After the wedding, on March 4, 1839, the newlyweds moved to a farm near French Prairie.

Within a short time, however, Margaret Bailey discovered that her husband had a violent temper, particularly after drinking. For years, she stayed with him, believing that he might change his habits and behavior toward her, but their relationship went from bad to worse. In a revealing metaphor, Margaret Jewett Bailey suggested that, just as frost turned her spring garden "all black with wrath," her husband's verbal and physical abuse finally destroyed their marriage. Although

Dr. Bailey achieved prominence in politics, his intemperance, involvement with other women, and mistreatment of his wife led to a divorce on April 12, 1854, the same year *The Grains* was published.

Although she married again, we found no evidence that Margaret Jewett Bailey's life improved after publication of *The Grains*. She married Francis Waddle in Polk County, Oregon, on September 4, 1855, and they were divorced on September 6, 1858. She then moved to Washington Territory and married a Mr. Crane (first name unknown), and she died in poverty, May 17, 1882, in Seattle. Dr. Bailey, Margaret's first husband, married Julia Nagel Shiel, November 2, 1855, and continued his medical practice in the French Prairie area. He became a member of the Catholic faith in 1870 and died February 5, 1876 (Duncan 251).

In the excerpts below, which we have titled "What Have I Married?," Margaret Jewett Bailey, through the persona of Ruth Rover, recalls her decision to marry outside the mission, her attempts to cope with loneliness, and the abuse she received from her husband. No one at the Methodist mission approved of Smith's marriage to Dr. Bailey, and she was warned about his character.

WHAT HAVE I MARRIED?

But let us to the wedding. . . . The only witness to the ceremony, besides the parson's family declared he thought he was at a funeral. . . .

Ruth was herself very sad. A few minutes before the ceremony was to be performed, one of the mission family—the same officious person who had wished her, when she first arrived, "to marry,"—had said to her, "not one of this mission family approves of your union with Dr. Binney."

"For what reason?" she asked.

"Why they say that you'll not live together long—they know his character and temper, and think that *you* are too independent to bear with him—and that your separation will be a disgrace to the mission." . . .

"Well," said Ruth, "I'll not disappoint the man now, at this late moment, even if I sacrifice myself to fulfill my engagement."

Immediately upon this she went to the altar.

Dr. Binney's religion lasted during two seasons of prayer with his wife. He then told her he *could not* pray; and shortly after told her, when she was entreating him most fervently to continue his efforts to be religious, that he did not mean to pray, and furthermore he did not intend to remain a member of the church, and she might make herself easy.

The third morning after their marriage he told her she was a *pest*, in consequences of her having made an enquiry relative to a friend of his, . . .

In a week he was cursing his horse, notwithstanding the profession of religion; and, as an evidence of the precipitancy of his temper, in *three weeks* after marriage he attempted to strangle his wife, by seizing her by the back of the neck, and for which she was entirely off guard, not having yet learned his disposition. . . .

The impetuosity of his temper was equally apparent in shooting his horses and hogs—in breaking his furniture—in destroying his clothing—as in mistreating his wife; with this difference, however, that while an animal could die, or furniture be repaired, or clothing be restored, his wife had to endure her griefs uncomplainingly, or breathe them only to herself with the oft-repeated exclamation: *"What have I married?"*. . .

[For six years, Ruth hoped her husband would be cured of intemperance, but Dr. Binney continued drinking. On one occasion, he returned home at daylight on Sabbath morning after a night of drinking and gambling.]

Ruth rose as usual and attended to her cows and duties about [the] house, and having promised two half-breed girls she had living with her that they should go to meeting that day at a neighbor's, she prepared them to go. Dr. Binney, somewhat recovered from a state of inebriation, said they should not go. Ruth ascertained that his only objection was that he hated the man at whose house the meeting was to be held, and . . . replied to Dr. Binney that his wish to keep her and the children from indulging in recreation of that kind could not be always indulged—that she stayed away herself to gratify him, but the children could do no harm by going, and it was her intention to have them go to meeting sometimes when there was opportunity.

He became enraged, and thrust them and her out of the door, telling her to go with them, and never enter his house again.

The children went to church, and found, on their return, they were not permitted to enter the house. Mrs. Binney had gone from the sun, and from the gaze of strangers, to the hospital, an unfinished log house on the place.

Some time after, the children were told to go into the house, and Dr. B. going to the house where his wife was, told her to leave it and the place, or he would burn it down over her head. She remained all night without bedding or covering, having attended to her cows and calves as usual. In the morning Dr. Binney called at her door, and told her if she wanted her clothing to go for it, for he was going away and wished to shut up the house. She went, and took a few articles, which were taken from her again as he went out of the door—her husband saying, "No, I'll be d——d if you'll come that game over me." When he had gone away, she secured some clothing and some bedding and concluded to remain where she was if the children would bring her food; and attend her garden, and milk her cows, make the butter, &c., all of which she could do without going into the house where Dr. Binney was, . . . At evening, after having milked the cows, and being about to carry the milk to the dairy, she saw Dr. Binney leaving her house with the clothing and bedding she had carried there, and her bundle of manuscripts and journals which she feared he would destroy. She wept for those, and he refused to give them up. He told her again she should leave the place—or he would take straw and burn the house over her head—that "not a d—d article of her clothing should she have"—and that the girls should bring her "no more food, for if he caught them at it he would break their heads." Ruth passed another uncomfortable night—having eaten nothing since dinner but some strawberries; and pondering on the course which appeared most proper for her to pursue, she could not think it right for her to remain there, for certainly she could not subsist without food; . . . Early in the morning she walked on foot through the dew to an acquaintance's house in Champoeg, and from thence found her way to the Falls. After she had gone, Dr. Binney went to Champoeg and posted upon the blacksmith's shop there, a notice for no one to harbor or trust his wife on his account for he should pay no debts of her contracting, which notice the young man tore down the moment he was away. . . .

At Portland Ruth Rover was subjected to a very unpleasant occurrence, and as it very clearly reveals the suspicious character of her husband, we shall enter somewhat into details.

The second day at her boarding-house, having no employment, she asked a Miss Wood, who was sewing, if she should not assist her. Miss W. replied, "I would be very glad if you would; and if you please you may make these collars which I'm to have finished before Christmas." Ruth busied herself, and by evening had made two, and was working on the third; the two that were finished lying upon the table before her when her husband came in. He stopped before the table a moment, looking first at Ruth and then at the collars, and finally, taking them in his hands, he said:

"Who are these for—are they for me?"

"No," replied Ruth, "they are for *Miss Wood.*"

His scarlet face became crimson; his small deep eyes brightened and contracted at the corners, as if to say, *Now I've caught you!* He threw them upon the table, but said nothing, as there were three of the gentlemen boarders present, and went quickly to his room. Ruth, soon after, finding herself alone with the gentlemen, and having finished her work, went into the dining-room, and taking a book sat down by the fire.

Presently Dr. Binney entered, and giving her a tap on the shoulder, said: "Here! go into your room!"

She rose, and as her only course then was to "obey," she walked on before him.

When they were inside the room, Dr. Binney locked the door and put the key into his pocket.

"Now sit down *there* and read," said he, "or else go to your bed."

"What is the matter with you?" asked Ruth.

"I'll let you know presently, d—n you," he answered.

Ruth read some time, while he sat and looked at her, his eyes sparkling and contracting, and his breathing becoming laborious, as if meditating something of importance.

The evening being very chilly, Ruth told him she wished to go out to the fire.

"No," said he, "you will not leave this room again to-night."

"Why, what ails you?"

"Don't speak to me, you d—n w—e of h-ll," said he.

Ruth saw it was useless, and retired to her bed. In the morning, when she thought he might be in a better temper, she asked him what the cause of his ill feelings toward her, when he, in great anger, replied—

"G-d d—n you, shut up, or by G-d I'll kill you!" at the same time raising a stick of wood from the hearth over her head in a threatening attitude.

Mary Priscilla Avery Sawtelle
1835-94

Like Margaret Jewett Bailey's *The Grains* (1854), Mary P. Avery Sawtelle's *The Heroine of '49* (1891) was a rhetorical effort to set the record straight. Both had been divorced—Bailey in 1854 and Sawtelle in 1858—and both were publicly scorned for leaving their husbands. Unlike Bailey, however, Sawtelle was a mother, and she was denied parental rights by the court.

Only those close to Sawtelle knew why she left her first husband and how the children were taken from her. She was not present at the courtroom trial presided over by Matthew P. Deady, a circuit-riding judge who later became a U.S. district court judge. What refutation could Sawtelle provide to hearsay evidence that she was an adulteress and therefore an unfit mother? How could she explain the circumstances that led to her divorce, and how could she vindicate herself in the eyes of her children and the public?

Like Bailey, Sawtelle turned to writing a thinly disguised autobiography to accomplish her rhetorical purpose. Unlike Bailey, who published *The Grains* during the year of her divorce, Sawtelle waited until 1891, thirty-three years after her divorce, to publish *The Heroine of '49*. Possibly, she recognized the strategic advantage of waiting to bring out her work until after the death of her first husband in 1890.

Within the pages of *The Heroine of '49*, Sawtelle presented her rhetorical apologia—her public explanation of why she left her first husband and how her children were taken from her. At the same time, she used the book to argue for justice for all women, particularly in the areas of legal rights, education, and health care. In the selections we have titled "Your Blows Have Divorced Us!," Sawtelle discussed the practice of hasty marriages under the Donation Land Act of 1850 and described the circumstances of her own marriage at the early age of fourteen.

Although some readers of *The Heroine of '49* thought the book was fiction, Sawtelle's friends knew it was based on her life. In the preface, Sawtelle wrote: "The characters in the story are drawn from real life. No living author could have produced them without witnessing the scenes depicted in this work" (7). As noted by the late Lavola J.

Bakken, in her published and unpublished studies of Sawtelle, an examination of Sawtelle's life underscores the parallels with *The Heroine of '49*. Mary Avery was born in the state of New York in 1835, the daughter of Benjamin Green Avery, a Methodist minister, and Lucretia Ellis Avery. The Avery family, which included two sons and four daughters, settled on a rented farm in Illinois. After the death of Benjamin Avery in 1844, Lucretia Avery married John Stipp, a Baptist minister and widower with five children (Bakken, *Lone Rock* 13).

When Mary Avery was thirteen, the Stipp family set out for Oregon and settled on a claim of 640 acres in Marion County, near the Waldo Hills and about three miles east of the site for Salem. One of their neighbors was Carsena A. Huntley (1814-90), who staked out an adjoining claim in 1848. After prospecting for gold in California, Huntley returned to Oregon in 1849 as a wealthy man, and he soon consulted with John Stipp about marrying his stepdaughter, Mary. Although Huntley was twenty-one years her senior, Mary's parents apparently gave their consent under the conditions that Mary would remain at home with the Stipps until she was seventeen and that she would bear no children until she was twenty-five. Later, under the Donation Land Act of 1850, this arrangement would allow Huntley to file for another 320 acres under his wife's name. On October 7, 1849, at the age of fourteen, Mary Avery married Carsena Huntley and, within a short time, she was persuaded by her husband to live with him. She bore her first child before she was fifteen.

The troubled marriage lasted nine years and ended in divorce in Roseburg, Oregon, in November of 1858. According to court records, Mary Huntley filed her petition for divorce in Douglas County, in July of 1858, and alleged that Carsena Huntley had subjected her to "most humiliating and cruel treatment" (Bakken, unpublished typescript). For the period from 1852 to 1857, she cited severe beatings from Huntley, including blows with "a gun stock or ramrod of his rifle." She also charged Huntley with using "the most opprobious and contumelious language" and for "falsely and maliciously" accusing her of "lewd and unchaste conduct" which he knew "to be false and unfounded." She claimed that, about the middle of October of 1857, when Carsena Huntley became "violent and threatening," she feared for the lives of her children and herself, and she left him. She admitted that, in April of 1858, upon Huntley's "urgent request" and "his promises to treat her kindly," she returned to live with him, but within a short time he ordered her to leave.

Carsena Huntley, who had successfully removed the children from his wife's care, denied all of his wife's allegations. He believed that "her object was to obtain a divorce and by conniving or otherwise get a large share of his property." He charged that Mary Huntley was guilty of adultery, had willfully deserted him, and was unfit to have custody of their children.

Carsena Huntley only had hearsay evidence for his accusations, and he may have felt desperate when he thought of Mary gaining control of his money through custody of the children. Judge Matthew Deady granted Carsena exclusive custody of the Huntleys' three living children—Ellen and Hellen, twins born in December of 1852, and Franklin, born in December of 1854. (Martin, the couple's first child, had died in 1852.)

After the divorce, Mary Avery Huntley had no access to her children, and she moved to Salem to live with her mother and stepfather. In an attempt to build a new life, she sought an education and attended classes at Willamette Institute. There, she met Cheston M. Sawtelle, also a Willamette student, and the two were married in Marion County, Oregon, in December of 1861.

For a number of years, the Sawtelles taught in various Oregon schools, including the Indian school at the Grand Ronde Reservation, and continued their studies at Willamette. Though they had three children, Sawtelle found time to lecture for women's rights and became an associate of Abigail Scott Duniway in equal suffrage work. Cheston Sawtelle, an opponent of organized religion, authored *Reflections on the Science of Ignorance, or the Art of Teaching Others What you Don't Know Yourself* (1868), in which he argued: "[A]s Science progresses, Christianity goes down" (48).

Apparently, Sawtelle continued to hold out hope of being reunited with the children of her first marriage. In 1868, the Sawtelles went to Roseburg, but their mission was not successful. Denied her children once again, Sawtelle decided to pursue her interest in medicine, an interest shared with her husband. In the summer of 1869, she enrolled as the first woman medical student at Willamette; however, she never received her diploma. She passed all her courses except for Anatomy.

Although she appealed and was given an opportunity to retake the exam, Sawtelle believed she would be failed again, simply because she was a woman. With her husband's encouragement, she transferred her credits to the Women's Medical College of New York, where she graduated with honors in 1872. A year later, Cheston Sawtelle received his medical degree from Willamette University.

Mary P. Sawtelle's name appeared frequently in early issues of Abigail Scott Duniway's newspaper, the *New Northwest*. While she was in New York, Sawtelle served as president of the New York Women's Real Estate Association, an organization established to "get a bill through Congress granting land for actual settlement by a colony of women on the public lands in Oregon" (*New Northwest*, 17 May 1872). She also convinced Senator Kelly of Oregon to introduce legislation to give unmarried women the right to hold property in their own names.

By the autumn of 1873, Dr. Mary P. Sawtelle was a practicing physician in Portland. When the Sawtelles moved to San Francisco, Sawtelle continued her efforts for women's health care, helped establish opportunities for women to gain medical degrees, and served as editor of the *Medico-Literary Journal*. Her only book, *The Heroine of '49*, was published in San Francisco in 1891.

In "Your Blows Have Divorced Us!," the title we have given to the following selections from *The Heroine of '49*, Sawtelle's opening comment is an indictment of abuses under the Donation Land Claim Act of 1850—the encouragement of hasty marriages of young girls to men several times their age. The Act gave 640 acres to men who arrived before 1850, provided they married within a year of enactment; settlers who arrived after 1850 received 320 acres if they were married. Under both circumstances, half of the land was in the husband's name and half in the wife's name. The remaining pieces follow the story's heroine Jean Ames in her early marriage to Cursica Miser, the birth of her first child, and her realization that she can no longer remain with Miser.

YOUR BLOWS HAVE DIVORCED US!

One of the noble features of the [Oregon] land law was that one-half of each grant was given to the women. No single man could hold more than three hundred and twenty acres of land, which placed all the marriageable women in the territory at par value immediately. Many an old bachelor brushed up his best suit of clothes, and hied him to see the fairest lady in the land. Like many other good laws, it could be turned to bad account. . . . Men, in order to hold the land claim they had staked out for themselves, would hunt for a wife pretty lively, or some other old bachelor could settle on one-half of his land claim. Girls of twelve and fourteen, and in some cases, only eleven years of age, were married in the years of '49 and '50, to men twice, and sometimes three times their own age. Now, to the great credit of the parents, and the men who contracted with these parents for these young girls for their wives, sometimes only the ceremony of marriage was enacted. By this arrangement, the girls secured the land, and then they were allowed to remain at home with their parents, sent to school, and grew to womanhood before the marriage rites were consummated.

Hazardous as this must have been to the future happiness of these fair young girls so entrapped, it was an infinitely better condition of affairs than the fate of those young girls who were taken by the marriage rites by these selfish men. . . . What man, building a home on such broad acres, did not need a slave to do his cooking, washing, general housekeeping, as also a wife, all in one and the same person? How convenient!

Mr. Miser . . . made an offer to Mrs. Murdstone for her daughter's hand in marriage, [and he] pressed his suit so fair and earnestly that Mrs. Murdstone wondered how she could have had a suspicion that he was not the soul of honor. She told Mr. Miser that if he could gain her daughter's consent, and wait two years for Jean, she would give him her consent. . . . Mrs. Murdstone admired the ardent style of the man's pleading, but could not reconcile her conscience to acquiescing in Jean's marriage at this tender age; she soothed her troubled fears, nevertheless, by thinking "two years is some time. Jean will be sixteen, and she may refuse the man. Why should I feel so badly. After all, something may occur to interfere." And thus she allowed herself to be deluded, and so drifted down the smooth stream of time.

Now that the adroit Mr. Miser had removed all resistance, with his strong will, coupled with Mr. Murdstone's, they had swept away every objection, and instead of waiting two years, in less than two months, Jean Ames was Mrs. Miser.

Jean thought her heart would burst. She was alone in the old wagon. . . . [S]he wished her husband to speak to her. He walked silently beside the dumb cattle; only the death-like stillness reigned. She tried to think how she would arrange her household. She could think of nothing but this nameless horror. . . .

They are at the cabin [on French Prairie]. Mr. Miser pulls a buckskin string, and the clapboard door swings back with an ominous creaking on its wooden hinges; and the old wood rat that had made its nest in the corner, the squirrels that are frisking over the roof, the blue-jay that is digging out some of the acorns that he laid away for his winter use, all scamper and fly the invasion. . . .

Jean's mother, with the consent of Mr. Murdstone, had loaned her one of the wagon covers to make a house lining in the corner of the cabin where the bed was to stand. This would serve as a protection to the sleepers from the strongest draft of wind, and also prevent the keen-eyed savages from peering in; but more than all, prevent the easy access to the bed, of the bugs, worms and spiders whose hiding place was behind the dead bark of the logs that composed the cabin. She fastened a tester sheet to this lining at the back and head of the bed. In front, and at the foot of the bed, she fastened drapery of well-ironed sheets, whose snowy folds fell nearly to the floor. Around the bottom of the bedstead she placed a valance of blue and white broad-checked gingham, which was a shiny accessory to the bed, and looked almost as much out of place in the cabin as she herself. When she had made the bed, with its snowy sheets and plump pillows, it looked good enough for a palace. The bedstead was made of Oregon curly maple, by a cabinet-maker, and given her by her mother—the only real piece of furniture in the hut.

Mr. Miser said, "It looks charming now, but after a few gusts of smoke from my patent fire-place it will present a very different appearance." . . .

Mr. Miser had utilized some of the puncheon boards to construct a table, by putting the ends of the boards through the crack
between the logs of the cabin, and two legs and a cross-piece to
hold up the front of the table. Jean covered it with a snowy table-
cloth, and set a very comfortable meal that she had brought cooked,
from her mother's. . . . The meal being over, she busied herself
clearing away the dishes, arranging them on their little clapboard
shelves, that Mr. Miser had fastened to the wall, and called a
cupboard. She took a kitchen apron which she fastened to the
back of the shelves, and at the front of these rough boards she
tacked some narrow ruffling, then she set away the few pieces of
crockery, tin cups and plates; the knives, forks and spoons she put
in a covered box, and all the food in the iron bake-kettle for security. By deft and shrewd management, constant and eternal
vigilance, she kept herself from being eaten or eating any of the
bugs, worms or spiders that inhabited the hut along with herself
and husband.

She had become accustomed to Miser's one peculiar phrase that
she had not as much sense as a "yaller dog." He was so constantly
planning villainy against his neighbors, that he did not dare to
speak before Jean for fear of disclosing his plans. When he entered the house, it was his habitual custom to hang his hat on a
peg, put his fingers through his hair, and, with the remark that his
"nerves were shottered," lie down on the bench, one hand under
his head for a pillow, the other shading his eyes. This was his
attitude during every moment spent in the house. Any woman
who has passed through the perils of maternity must know how
Jean longed for a little sympathy as her time of trial drew near—
a little tenderness. It never came in word or look. After three days
of agony, at the very verge of death, after praying that she might
never breathe again, and thus be relieved of this terrible torture,
she lay for weeks before she was conscious that a little puny life—
a feeble, wailing thing—was by her side, and that her mother was
hovering over her with the tears falling like rain in the blessed joy
that Jean knew her again. . . . And when Mr. Miser said he wished
Jean and the baby were both dead and out of the way, some words
escaped Mrs. Murdstone's lips that she thought afterwards she
should not have spoken. They were the dawning of truth and justice in her mind. She did not recognize them as such. They were
these: "If Jean were at home again, she should remain there until

she was a woman." Will Ames [Jean's brother], with rebellion in
his heart, said, "It's a shame! They are two babies together." And
Jean's soul was riveted to his, though she lay there so helpless.
Her first conscious grief, after returning to life, was that Mr. Miser never came near nor looked at the baby, and her next great
disappointment was that a pleasant morning caller apprized her
of the fact that her home was sold and she was to move one hundred and fifty miles from her mother and her present home—no
family living within fifty miles of the new habitation.

[After the move] Miser grew more and more tyrannical and abusive. Having no critical neighbors near by, no check-reins of any
kind, he was ruled alone by his masterly qualities of cruelty, mi-
serliness, and treachery. When there were no workmen about, he
starved Jean and Will almost to death, and put on his own plate
and devoured like a wild animal what he required for his own
sustenance, telling Jean that as she was not earning anything, she
could live on limited rations.

The family were seated at the breakfast table, which was set in the
middle of the cabin floor. . . . The little twin girls sat opposite Jean
and her baby boy. Mr. Miser, at the head of the table, was swal-
lowing his breakfast like a ravenous wolf, when his son and heir
to his vast estates espied the breakfast disappearing so rapidly,
and not being old enough to express himself, made desperate efforts to make himself understood by violent kicks and gestures,
signifying that he wanted an equal amount of food, whereupon
Jean gave him an egg. But he wanted more, and she gave him
another. It was clear that the ambition of the young man knew no
bounds. He wanted everything on the table put on his plate. His
mother, Jean, was trying with firm though gentle tones to quell
the disturbance.

Mr. Miser arose unceremoniously, put on his hat, and left the
room. Jean supposed he had gone to his business. The baby boy
was now quietly finishing his breakfast. Mr. Miser returned looking like a demon, with a tough, thrifty hazel three-quarters of an
inch thick and five feet long. He walked hastily to the baby, snatch-
ing him from his chair and holding him by one arm a foot or two
from the floor, and after a few withes on the back of the baby,
Jean, not being able to stop him, and knowing the child would die

in Miser's hands, she bent over it to protect it from the blows, and the fierce strokes that fell on her neck and shoulders made her thankful in her heart that she could shield her child from such agony. Each blow from the infuriated monster was like a knife thrust. When the stick had been beaten to splinters, he stopped and not till then; and when Jean could recover her breath to speak, she said: "Your blows have divorced us!" And no truer words did her lips ever utter. . . .

She . . . cut the child's clothes from his arms, and hastily dressed his wounds. She as quickly tore off her own blood-stained clothes and hid them away, as though she were the murderer and had done this brutal deed. . . .

She told Miser, on his return, to occupy another room, away from her and the children, which he did without one word ever passing between them on the subject. They were divorced. She still lived under the same roof, but found life much more endurable since the beating than it had ever been while she was the monster's wife.

She remained in the cabin a year and a half in daily fear of her life, thanking God for the privilege of caring for her children. She trembled as one standing over an earthquake, knowing full well there must come an end to her present life.

Abigail Scott Duniway
1834-1915

Writing "always *was* our forte," Abigail Scott Duniway announced in the first issue of the *New Northwest,* her weekly "human rights" newspaper, published in Portland, Oregon. She added, "[A]nd if we had been a man, we'd have had an editor's position and handsome salary at twenty-one" ("About Ourself," *New Northwest,* 5 May 1871).

Undoubtedly, Duniway was thinking of advantaged males such as her younger brother, Harvey Scott, who was the influential and eventually affluent editor of the Portland *Oregonian.* In contrast to what she saw as her brother's privileged position, Duniway had to cope with a number of constraints. In 1871, when she established the *New Northwest,* Duniway was thirty-six, the mother of six children, and the wife of a semi-invalid husband. Throughout her life, she felt constrained by gender prescriptions, very little formal education, family responsibilities, and limited financial resources.

Despite these constraints, Duniway became one of the most active and prolific public rhetors the Pacific Northwest has known. For over forty years, both as writer and speaker, she was a public advocate for women's rights, and the record of her tireless efforts is remarkable.

As an example of her work for woman suffrage, Duniway told the National Woman Suffrage Association Convention in Washington, D.C., in February of 1884, that "she had divided her time about equally between Oregon and Washington and had lectured in each about seventy times a year for twelve and one-half years" (T. A. Larson, "The Woman Suffrage Movement in Washington" 53). She reported giving 181 lectures in 1886 and 219 lectures the previous year. During 1886, she traveled, "in season and out of season, three thousand miles, going by stage steamer, buggy, buckboard and afoot." And, in the same year, she wrote "the MSS for over four hundred original columns of printed matter for this and other papers." In every town Duniway visited, she had "personally canvassed" for subscriptions and renewals to the *New Northwest,* a "labor requiring more irksome and fatiguing effort than all the rest of the work put together" ("Editorial Correspondence," *New Northwest,* 16 December 1886).

Although her health sometimes failed her, Duniway felt "impelled to go on and on." For a ten-day period when she was ill, Duniway wrote: "[I] have given four lectures, organized one suffrage society, visited a dozen families, done one day sewing, written two chapters of the serial story, and ever so much other MSS and yet we see no stopping place, although *compelled* to forgo much that voice and pen are tingling to attempt" ("Editorial Correspondence," *New Northwest,* 12 March 1875).

One of the most interesting and frequently overlooked records of Duniway's work is found in her "Editorial Correspondence" for the *New Northwest,* a chronicle of her travels and lectures on behalf of equal suffrage. To represent Duniway's commitment to carry her arguments to every corner of the Pacific Northwest, we have included selections from her Editorial Correspondence in this volume.

In contrast to her brother, Duniway was essentially self-taught. In a letter describing her education, Duniway wrote that she was "never a strong or healthy child" and attended school for less than a year in Tazewell County, Illinois, where she was born and lived for the first seventeen years of her life. After her father, John Tucker Scott, brought the family to Oregon in 1852, Abigail gained her real education through teaching school, first at Eola and later at Lafayette and Albany. Along with teaching and millinary experience, Duniway said she was "equipped with a tolerably good English education, and much practical experience, more varied than falls to the lot of almost any other woman I have known" (Letter to Barbara Booth, 11 April 1914).

While she was teaching in Eola, Abigail Scott met her "matrimonial fate"—Benjamin C. Duniway, a young rancher. The two were married in August of 1853. Although Scott was not a convert to woman's rights at the time of her wedding, she insisted that the word "obey" be deleted from their marriage vows. The Duniways settled on Ben Duniway's donation claim in Clackamas County, where the first two of their six children were born, and they later moved to a farm in Yamhill County. In 1862, the Yamhill farm was sold after a flood swept away the harvest, and interest on promissory notes signed by Ben Duniway could not be paid.

After a move to Lafayette, they faced another crisis: a runaway team of horses knocked Ben down, and a wagon rolled over him. He suffered permanent injury to his chest and could do only light work. Thus, Abigail Scott Duniway became breadwinner as well as bread baker for the family. In Lafayette, and later in Albany, she opened a private school and took in boarders, rising at three in the summer and four in the winter to care for her household before the day of teaching.

Married women in Oregon did not have full rights to their own property, businesses, and wages until the legislature adopted a sole trader bill in 1872 and a married woman's property bill in 1880. However, in 1865, with characteristic determination, Duniway enlisted financial assistance from a wealthy Portland wholesaler, Jacob Mayer, and opened a millinery business in Albany.

As a businesswoman, Duniway observed and grew to know women from all walks of life who had no financial independence, were not educated to support themselves and their families, and were subject to the authority—sometimes abuse—of their husbands. She learned of the tragedies of "grass widows" (women who were separated or divorced from their husbands) and she realized that "there was no Canada for fugitive wives to flee to," a metaphor that appears frequently in her writing.

During this period, she was evidently undergoing a conversion to the cause of woman's rights and woman suffrage; however, the conversion did not come easily. In "Personal Reminiscences," Duniway wrote: "I was not a willing convert to belief in equal rights for women. Blessed with a kind father and a sober, upright husband, I grew up from childhood imbued with the teaching that it was a woman's lot to engage in a lifetime of unpaid servitude and personal sacrifice; and, whether occupied with the wash tub, the churn dash, the cook stove, the kitchen sink, the mop handle, my own often infirmities or those of the ailing baby or older children, I schooled myself to imagine that I was filling my Heaven-appointed sphere, for which final recompense awaited me in the land of souls" (56). Duniway credited her "sensible" husband, Ben, with finally convincing her that conditions never would improve for women until they had the right to vote.

Duniway soon found a way to help support her family *and* serve the cause of woman's rights. The Duniways moved to Portland with their five sons and one daughter, and Abigail Scott Duniway began her own newspaper, the *New Northwest*. In the first issue, she wrote: "We have served a regular apprenticeship at working—washing, scrubbing, patching, darning, ironing, plain sewing, raising babies, milking, churning and poultry raising. We have kept boarders, taught school, taught music, wrote for the newspapers, made speeches and carried on an extensive millinery and dress-making business. . . . Now, having reached the age of thirty-six, and having brought up a family of boys to set the type and a daughter to run the millinery store [in Portland], we propose to edit and publish a newspaper; and we intend to establish it as one of the permanent institutions of the country" ("About Ourself," *New Northwest,* 5 May 1871).

During the same year that Duniway began the *New Northwest,* she conducted lecture tours in the Pacific Northwest. For two months during the fall of 1871, Duniway traveled with Susan B. Anthony on a tour of Oregon, the Washington Territory, and British Columbia. With Duniway serving as Anthony's business manager, the two women went by stagecoach, steamer, wagon, carriage, and rail to face hostile and friendly audiences in churches, schools, hotels, public halls, stores, and homes.

By the conclusion of their tour, Duniway and Anthony were friends and established an association that lasted until Anthony's death. In 1872, with Susan B. Anthony's invitation and encouragement, Duniway began attending conventions of the National Woman Suffrage Association (NWSA). In 1884, she was elected one of five vice-presidents-at-large of the NWSA. Five years later, she was appointed to the NWSA committee to negotiate the merger of the National Woman Suffrage Association, led by Elizabeth Cady Stanton and Susan B. Anthony, with the American Woman Suffrage Association, led by Lucy Stone and Henry Blackwell.

Although Duniway had found a place in the woman's rights movement, she became a controversial figure. Her refusal to combine temperance and prohibition issues with efforts for woman suffrage severed some of her ties with Woman's Christian Temperance Union members and displeased national suffrage leaders such as Susan B. Anthony and Anna Howard Shaw. She also disagreed with some of the Eastern organizers about campaign strategies. But despite her differences with various movement leaders, Duniway established a notable record in the woman's rights struggle.

In Oregon, which held more referenda on woman suffrage than any other state, Duniway witnessed five defeats—1884, 1900, 1906, 1908, and 1910—before final victory in 1912 with a close margin of 4,162 votes. In the Washington Territory, she campaigned, rejoiced in the 1883 victory, and mourned the territorial supreme court's reversal of woman suffrage in 1887. (In 1910, under the leadership of Emma Smith DeVoe, the state of Washington approved woman suffrage.) In the Idaho Territory, Duniway campaigned and celebrated Idaho's victory in 1896 with a serialized novel, *Bijah's Surprises,* which addressed that success. Another serialized novel, *Judge Dunson's Secret,* included an extended debate on suffrage at an Oregon woman suffrage convention.

Although scholars have underscored Duniway's role as the leader of the woman suffrage movement in the Pacific Northwest, relatively little attention has been given to the scope of her writing. Unlike the vast majority of women writers of the period, Duniway had her own publication outlets, first in the *New Northwest,* which she edited and published for sixteen years, and later in Frances Gotshall's *Pacific Empire,* which Duniway edited for three years in Portland. In these roles, she could address gender and power issues in a direct and forceful manner. Although she was constantly plagued by financial worries, Duniway had relative freedom to print what she wanted to print, including criticisms of Harvey Scott's anti-suffrage editorials in the *Oregonian.* Always dedicated to the improvement of "woman's condition," she opened the pages of the *New Northwest* to other Pacific Northwest writers such as Frances Fuller Victor, Belle Cooke, Minnie Myrtle Miller, Bethenia Owens-Adair, and Mary P. Sawtelle.

Duniway's own writing career began at an early age, and she became one of the most prolific writers in the Pacific Northwest. At the age of seventeen, she maintained the Scott family's journal during their 1852 overland trip from Illinois to Oregon Territory. Her first and last novels, both drawn from the overland journey, were published in book form: *Captain Gray's Company* (1859) and *From the West to the West* (1905). Duniway's earliest newspaper articles, which reflected her thinking as "a farmer's wife," were published in the Oregon City *Argus* and the *Oregon Farmer.* In addition to serialized novels and short stories, she published two volumes of poetry. Duniway's autobiography, *Path Breaking: An Autobiographical History of the Equal Suffrage Movement in Pacific Coast States,* was published in 1914, one year before her death.

The bulk of Duniway's writings, particularly her serialized novels, short stories, and editorials for the *New Northwest,* addressed issues of gender and equal rights. In keeping with the cultural expectations of nineteenth-century reform novels and women's fiction, her serialized novels were a combination of advocacy, verisimilitude, didacticism, and entertainment.

Finally, in her "Editorial Correspondence" for the *New Northwest,* Duniway published what we consider to be some of her most interesting and overlooked writing. These entertaining reports of travel on behalf of equal suffrage informed readers of her unflagging efforts, provided rich descriptions of people, places, and events throughout the Pacific Northwest, and revealed her sense of humor and indomitable character. From these writings, we have chosen five representative pieces published between 1875 and 1886. To the best of our knowledge, this is the first time these pieces have been reprinted since their original publication in the *New Northwest.*

The selections in "On the Road" illustrate Duniway's intent to persuade, as well as inform and entertain, her readers. Her encounters with overworked country women are more than interesting bits of social history: these sketches serve as data to support Duniway's claim that women are not supported and protected by men, and therefore must be given the vote—the key to their rights. Her descriptions of the travel hardships she endures are more than entertaining vignettes. These accounts enhance her ethos; they are testimony to her commitment to communicate the exigence for equal suffrage and evidence of the sacrifices she makes. Thus, through enactment, the example of self, Duniway seeks to empower other women to become agents of change. With good humor and seeming composure, Duniway reports on coping with a multitude of challenges—uncomfortable and dangerous travel, primitive lodgings, a collapsed lecture floor, and even a stagecoach robbery.

ON THE ROAD

The Women of Junction

[We reached] Junction before two o'clock where we were welcomed first at Berry's Hotel and afterward at the pleasant abode of brilliant, little Miss Roach, who entertained us hospitably and . . . fed us like any preacher, upon the best of chicken fixings, sweet pickles and cream.

Two fine audiences greeted us here, also a good number of new subscribers. Junction is improving rapidly. . . . But how the country women toil and drudge. Look upon the street at any hour, and

you will see a bowed and careworn object of man's protecting gentleness, in scant calico dress and ample sunbonnet, lugging a load of butter and eggs from the wagon to the store, to exchange for saleratus, concentrated lye, fruit cans, coffee, denims, calico, bed-bug exterminator, candle moulds, bedquilt materials, crockery, wash-boards, carpet-warp, etc., etc., everything she buys only adding to her means of toil while her sickly baby frets in the lap of an older child, and her rich husband's favorite brood mare roams at will in the September shades of the great farm pasture, "raising a blooded colt." Talk to one of these horny-handed, hopeless, weary women about the *New Northwest* and she'll sigh or sneer, owing to her mood, and shake her head and find fault with you, because you appear to be wealthier and more hopeful than herself. Get her out to a lecture though, and you have her. Once let her even dream there is a balm in Gilead, and her eyes will brighten and languid step grow quick; and then she'll "wish she *could* get the paper; but he must have tobacco; and *he takes several papers,* and the children need so many things and she can't afford it." But she grasps our hand at parting and says, "God bless and speed you," as she mounts the high seat in the great wagon and takes the baby in her lap and the little girl beside her; and while her husband touches the well-kept horses with an elegant whip, she ties up her sunken jaws to keep her decaying teeth from the draught, and we watch them till the rising dust enshrouds and hides them, and then walk on, repeating to ourself the hollow, mocking words we so often hear, "Women are protected and supported by men."
September 24, 1875

Oregon Mud

Saturday morning was ushered in by a drizzling rain. But the clouds coquetted with the sun and gave a half promise to retire before ten o'clock, and sundry picnicers, our liege with Clyde, Ralph, and self included, started by train for New Era. . . . We embarked in an open boat for Thomas Backman's farm, three miles up the river, on the Delectable Mountains, where all parties retired at a late hour, with the skies as clear as crystal, giving promise of a nipping frost. But morning brought, instead, another blinding, driving rain. What could be done? We had to go home; but how? A bright idea struck our liege. He would go back to New Era in the small boat and take the morning train, and ourself and the boys would hail the "Fannie Patton" at ten o'clock.

Now, good lady reader, if you want more fun than you can ever pay for, just try running down a slippery side hill for a quarter of a mile in a pouring rain, the mud over your shoes at every step, while you clutch your Sunday clothes with both hands and let your best hat catch the storm. Then, when you're over the worst of it, and turn to look after the boat, and find yourself sprawling in the mud, with your head downwards and your body at an angle of forty-five degrees, and you pick yourself up and go blundering on, while your smallest boy in following falls flat also and raises a pitiful cry for the aid you can't give him—if you don't think a circus is tame forever after, you've a poor appreciation for enjoyment, that's all.

June 1, 1877

A Lecture at Palouse City, Idaho

Palouse City sits on a hill, hard by the river whose name it bears, and presents even a newer appearance than Colfax, with its numerous box-houses, unfinished and yet occupied, not the least being a hotel, where we found primitive accommodations with an obliging landlord and capable landlady, who partitioned us a bedroom with carpets, up-stairs among the stars, and gave us food as nicely cooked as in the Palmer House of Chicago, at the low price of twenty-five cents per meal.

The dining room of the hotel was chosen for the lecture, and the people had gathered in from every direction and filled it densely, and the speech was fairly begun when *crash* went the floor, and *smash* went the benches, and *down* went the people into the cellar below, leaving the under-signed well-braced against a tottering partition to prevent it knocking her on the head. Luckily nobody was hurt, but the confusion was indescribable. The fallen and frightened crowd after a while emerged from the cellar through the *debris,* somebody lifted the partition from the burdened shoulders of the speaker, and we all repaired to another room, where the lecture was resumed amid a general feeling of thankfulness that nobody had been injured. By morning the break was repaired and everybody was happy.

November 30, 1877

Robbery on the Stagecoach

At 1 P.M. we started for Lewiston. By three o'clock we were out beyond the snow, and bowling up and down the dusty roads. Later, and we descended a long, steep and winding grade, on the "rough lock," and at anything but "double quick." Then we came into the valley of the Alpowa, a little river, along which reside several Indian farmers, who have renounced their tribal relations and builded themselves comfortable homes. The stage road crosses the Alpowa eleven times within a few miles, and the scenery on either hand is decidedly picturesque and wild.

Our stage had crossed the river for the last time, and we had come within four miles of the Snake River ferry, when we saw, to the right, and running along a bend in the creek, a man carrying a gun. The thought of robbers crossed our brain for an instant, but there were two wagons near with drivers, and two Indians farther on, and so we supposed the man was only after a bird or other small game. The fellow came up in front of the stage and crossed the road, and still we thought nothing of it. But when he came up to the team, and pointing a needle-gun at the driver and the undersigned, so close that we both looked down the barrel and almost into eternity, and when he ordered a halt, as though the institution belonged to him, we saw at once that the game he was after was of considerable proportions.

"Stop!" he cried earnestly, and what his word didn't accomplish was finished up by that glittering "persuader."

We stopped.

"Put out that box!" he exclaimed, with a feint at taking aim.

The driver, an honest and worthy denizen of Dayton, W.R. Dixon by name, put on the brake, gave the lines a twist, and went for the express box with alacrity. But it was not under the front seat, and he had to dismount and fish it out from under the back seat, on which a frightened Chinaman and his asthmatic wife sat like statues. The robber followed the driver with his "persuader" and kept him covered with it so closely that there was no chance for dodging.

Once the fellow looked at us with a sort of comical expression, as though the situation was ludicrous, and we should have begun a sparring conversation then and there, only there was too much cash in our side pocket for us to risk a joke with a highwayman. He taught us one lesson, however. We'll never go staging again with cash about us in any quantity worth stealing.

While the driver was getting the box for the bandit, we took another square look at the fellow, and are sure we'd know him anywhere. He was about five feet eight inches in height, would weigh about 150 pounds, was square-featured, intelligent, smooth-shaven, comfortably dressed and handsome. He had partly covered his face with dust from the roadside, but did not conceal his features nor try to avoid detection.

The men in the wagons sat by in a sort of daze while the robbery was going on.

The box once in the robber's possession, he demanded the express packet, but took the driver's word that there was none along unless it was in the box. . . .

When the driver mounted the stage again and took the ribbons to "travel," he was panting like a quarter horse at the end of a mile heat. He drove on a few yards, when we said, laughingly:

"That fellow'll get caught. I've marked him so well that I'd know him if I was coasting and should meet him in Kamtschatka."

"Schse-se-se! Don't talk!" he exclaimed, in a nervous whisper, and we then realized that we ought to have been frightened a little, too.

December 4, 1879

Stage Coach from Lakeview to Ashland; A Horse Stealer

We had the Sheriff of Jackson County for company all the way from Lakeview to Linkville, and in his charge was a prisoner in manacles, accused of horse-stealing, on his way to the lock-up. The crime of horse- or cattle-stealing is considered a much greater one in all border countries than girl-stealing, or even seduction or rape. In the latter cases, the perpetrator frequently gets off with a fine or reprimand. A marriage or a joke; but woe to the miscreant who is caught on the back of a "borrowed" horse or in the act of branding a stray "slick-ear." And yet the chivalrous feeling with which men of the borders regard the liberty of women is remarkable. The entire Southern Oregon country gave the Woman Suffrage Amendment a large vote, and the people heartily promise to double it when asked. They argue that in social crimes against unmarried women men are only half responsible, since women must consent to a wrong before they can become its victim. But they generally overlook the fact that the stolen girl is usually a mere child, to whom marriage is a fraud, because she does not comprehend it; and the victims of the other crimes are, in spite of alleged consent, as innocent of voluntarily shouldering the responsibilities that ensure as is the stolen broncho or branded heifer. . . .

During that [next] day's ride we passed a deserted mountain ranch, and the driver related a tragedy connected with the place that made the Sheriff of Jackson County fairly boil with honest indignation, while the prisoner gritted his teeth and clanked his chains, and your correspondent listened, shivering. A family of Germans, husband, wife and seven children had settled there; and after building a cabin, that had only a dirt floor, and fencing in a few acres with logs and sowing it to barley, the husband wandered off aimlessly somewhere, leaving the wife to manage as best she could without him. The wife harvested the barley by pulling it up with her hands. She did the family washing in a leaky box, and cooked their food in the most primitive way. One day the husband came home and saw a cow stealing from the barley stack, a fact which so enraged him because his wife had not prevented the theft, although she did not see it, that he knocked out her front teeth and then whipped her with a knotted rope. The act of "ruling over her" accomplished, the husband went away again and remained three weeks. The wife took to her poor miserable bed, not to leave it again till after the birth of a dead child, which the husband returned in time to bury. There was no action taken against the man, though the driver said there was much indignation over the affair, and he would have been glad indeed to have joined a company to treat him to tar and feathers.

"What a pity 'twas that, instead of maltreating his wife and murdering his baby, he hadn't stolen a horse or branded a "slick-ear," we couldn't help exclaiming as the prisoner clanked his chains.

The German in question removed shortly to another locality, and all trace of him is lost in the precinct, save his wife's abandoned barley field and his own recorded vote against the equal suffrage amendment.

November 18, 1886

Minnie Myrtle Miller (Theresa Dyer)
1845-82

❀

Theresa Dyer, who took the pen name of "Minnie Myrtle," was once called the "Poetess of the Coquille," but today's students of literature may know her only as "Minnie Myrtle Miller," one of the wives of renowned Oregon poet Joaquin Miller. Minnie Myrtle's life was marked, not only by her talent as a writer, but by a troubled first marriage to Miller, their controversial separation and divorce in 1870, and her early death. On May 15, 1882, at the age of thirty-seven, the Poetess of the Coquille died of pneumonia and consumption in the New York Infirmary for Women and Children. Her gravestone in Brooklyn's Evergreen Cemetery, far distant from the Dyer family home in Curry County, Oregon, bore the simple inscription: "Minnie Myrtle."

Those who read of Myrtle's death in Oregon newspapers were reminded of the scandal that surrounded her divorce and her attempts to explain the circumstances. Woman suffrage leaders, particularly Abigail Scott Duniway, had urged her to argue her case publicly in terms of women's rights—to present herself as the wronged wife of a Poet Lothario. Although she was attracted initially to women's rights and equal suffrage, Myrtle was reluctant to turn her private misfortune into a public affair. But, when the divorce became grist for journalists in 1871 and her former husband sought ways to improve his public image, Myrtle felt compelled to make a public response.

We have selected two of Myrtle's prose pieces for this volume— "Miss Anthony's Lectures—Observanda" and "A Communication to the Public from Mrs. M. M. Miller," both published in Abigail Scott Duniway's *New Northwest* in 1871. The first represents Myrtle's introduction to woman suffrage issues, and the second is her rhetorical appeal for "a truce to charges and accusations" related to her divorce.

Although details about Theresa Dyer's early life are sketchy and no collection of her poetry and prose was published, we know that she was born in Brookville, Indiana, on May 2, 1845, the daughter of Judge George M. and Sarah Dyer. She traveled to Oregon with her parents in 1859, and the Dyer family settled on a farm in Curry County, not far from the town of Port Orford. Dyer submitted her writing to Oregon newspapers under the name of "Minnie Myrtle" and, although she became best known as a poet, some prose pieces were also published.

On September 12, 1862, after a whirlwind courtship of less than a week, Myrtle married Cincinnatus Hiner Miller (1837?-1913), who later became famous as Joaquin Miller, "Poet of the Sierras." Miller had been attracted by her poetry and, after sending a picture of himself and exchanging letters with her, he arrived from Eugene City to meet the beautiful "Poetess of the Coquille." In his *Memorie and Rime*, published after her death, he recalled their romance: "Tall, dark and striking in every respect, this first Saxon woman I had ever addressed, had it all her own way at once. She knew nothing at all of my life, except that I was an expressman and country editor. . . . I arrived on Thursday. On Sunday next we were married! Oh, to what else but ruin and regret could such romantic folly lead" (214)?

Although he was not recognized as a poet until after his marriage to Minnie Myrtle, Miller's public writing career began in 1862 with editorship of Eugene City's *Democratic Register*. Years later, the Eugene City *Guard* reprinted a piece from the Albany *Democrat*, condemning Joaquin Miller for putting his name on plagiarized serials for the *Register* and for being "a first-class bilk" who had "filched" writings from Minnie Myrtle and published them as his own ("Such Is Fame," *Guard*, 12 August 1871).

In the spring of 1863, the Millers traveled to California but, as Miller later noted, they found "neither fortune nor friends" in California and returned to Oregon. They lived in Grant County for about five years, and then their "romantic folly" came to an end.

In *Memorie and Rime*, Miller wrote his version of their separation and divorce. Myrtle took their two children to visit at her mother's home in Port Orford. She was gone intermittently in 1868, and then they were separated for a year. When he arrived in Portland for the Democratic Convention in the spring of 1870, he discovered that "[t]he poor, impatient lady, impulsive always, and angry that I should have kept so long away, had forwarded papers . . . praying for a divorce" (218).

Miller made no reference in *Memorie and Rime* to particulars of the divorce proceedings in April of 1870, and details were not reported in the press. Records in the Oregon State Library Archives show that, in early April, Myrtle filed suit for divorce in the circuit court of Coos County, and the case was later moved to Lane County, where Miller's family resided. Myrtle stated in her divorce petition that she had borne three children by Joaquin Miller. Her claim was that Miller "wholly neglects to provide for the support and maintenance of said children,"

Drawing of Minnie Myrtle Miller by Bernard Hinshaw

and she asked for custody of the children and a cash settlement to care for them.

She was not present when Miller, several of his friends, and his father testified in Lane County on April 18, 1870. Miller did not consider Myrtle's "mind or judgment sufficient to rear and control all the children." Furthermore, he had "not treated her as a wife for one year past" and had knowledge of her association with "a man named Hill." William Brown of Eugene City testified that Myrtle had come and gone frequently from the Renfrew Hotel with the "man named Hill," who once bragged that "he had slept with her often." The third child was not, according to Miller's testimony, his child: "I do not claim to be the father of nor do I desire the custody of the youngest child." He requested custody of the two older children, who could be placed with Myrtle's widowed mother, and he offered to pay $200 per year for their care.

On April 19, 1870, the court granted a divorce. Myrtle was given care of Henry, the youngest child, whose paternity had been questioned. Her mother was given custody of the other two, who were to live with her for four years. Miller was to pay $200 annually for support of Maud and George, and he could place them in schools of his choice after four years. Apparently, there was no investigation of Miller's property holdings and income; the court held he "had no money" and did not award a cash settlement.

Not long after the divorce, Miller left Oregon, traveled to San Francisco and New York, and then sailed for Scotland and England in August of 1870. He had sold the Canyon City property, collected income due him as a county judge, given his father a thousand dollars, and paid his own travel costs. The London publication of *Songs of the*

Sierras (1871) brought him overnight fame, and his successful and prolific writing career was launched. He lived at various times in San Francisco, New York, Washington, D.C., and Oakland, California. He died in 1913.

While Miller was making his way in English society in 1870 and 1871, Myrtle found herself impoverished and frequently ill. She was helped by Belle W. Cooke, a Salem poet and equal suffrage advocate, and Abigail Scott Duniway. Duniway published a number of Myrtle's writings, enlisted her to canvas for the *New Northwest*, and began a campaign in the summer of 1871 for this deserted wife and children of "an inconstant lord."

With the success of Miller's *Songs of the Sierras*, the divorce became public knowledge, and Miller's friends in Oregon defended him through attacks on Myrtle. Duniway was quick to defend her in the pages of the *New Northwest*. For the rest of the year, the newspaper included numerous pieces by and about Minnie Myrtle Miller.

In "A Communication to the Public from Mrs. M. M. Miller," which we have included in this volume, Myrtle wrote that she felt obliged "to say a few words in . . . behalf" of her former husband. The piece, which was published in several Oregon newspapers in early November of 1871, prior to Miller's return to Oregon, created a stir. Duniway published the open letter but found Myrtle "entirely too lenient in her judgment" of Miller (*New Northwest*, 10 November 1871). Duniway contended that the high price paid for Joaquin Miller's fame was "marital and parental neglect."

With her name frequently before the public, Myrtle was encouraged by Duniway and others to begin a lecture career for women's rights. Her first lecture, "Behold, the Woman!," was given at Portland's Oro Fino Hall, on November 25, 1871. In a few weeks, Myrtle and Duniway planned a lecture tour together in the Willamette Valley.

Myrtle continued to lecture, but her position on women's rights changed substantially and she assumed an anti-suffrage position in her public discourse. From the lecture platform in 1872, she argued that women should cling to the "right not to vote"; women who wanted the vote would "pass away, as did the Amazons of old" ("Mrs. Miller's New Departure," *New Northwest*, 8 March 1872).

Woman suffrage was no longer Myrtle's cause. In San Francisco, in November of 1872, she turned her attention to popular lectures on "Joaquin Miller, the Poet and the Man." The *Chronicle* reported that her "delicate satire" and "vein of wit" kept her audience "in continual smiles and good humor" (quoted in Powers, *History of Oregon Literature* 232). Toward the end of 1872, Duniway published little by or about Minnie Myrtle, but sent her a terse public reminder: "M.M.M., Salem, your subscription [to the *New Northwest*] will expire with No. 43" (*New Northwest*, 27 December 1872).

Minnie Myrtle married T.E.L. Logan in 1877, separated from him within two years, and moved to San Francisco. Although very little is known about Logan, press reports linking him with Maud, Minnie Myrtle's daughter, suggest he may well have been "a shiftless fellow," as claimed by Duniway.

Myrtle's final months were not happy ones. Duniway wrote that she "was wandering through the East at the time of her death, on a lecturing tour that brought her little recognition and less recompense" ("A Thwarted Life," *New Northwest*, 22 June 1882). Other sources suggest also that Myrtle had gone East in the hope of seeing her daughter, Maud, and persuading her not to become a nun. Miller said that Myrtle sent for him when she fell ill in New York, and he permitted Maud to see her before she died.

Early in their marriage, Myrtle and Miller pledged to write well of each other after death, and Miller attempted to fulfill his pledge. He had questioned Minnie Myrtle's virtue in 1871 and persuaded the divorce court that she was an unfit mother, but none of this was mentioned in *Memorie and Rime*. "[N]o man or woman can put a finger on any stain in this woman's whole record of life, so far as truth and purity go," he wrote (217). He was less willing to give unqualified praise to her writing. "[M]uch that she wrote—and may be this is not great praise—was better than any writing of mine," he admitted. "But she lacked care and toil and sustained thought" (220). As part of his testimony during the divorce proceedings, Joaquin had claimed: "All her literary productions of any account in the last seven years I wrote for her." Minnie Myrtle entrusted "all her papers" to Joaquin before her death, but "the half a trunk full of papers" apparently never surfaced again.

The selections below represent two contrasting, yet related, rhetorical turns in Minnie Myrtle Miller's life: advocating for woman suffrage and attesting to the character of her former husband. In both pieces, the question arises of where "blame" should fall for woman's condition and, within the short period of less than two months, she gives two different answers. In the public context, "blame" is assigned generically to all men who subscribe to and perpetuate patriarchy; in the more private context, Myrtle shares "the blame" for her dissolved marriage.

After her divorce, her work for woman suffrage gave Myrtle both place and identity, and Susan B. Anthony's first lecture tour in the

Pacific Northwest probably heightened her understanding of women's rights. In "Miss Anthony's Lectures—Observanda," published in the *New Northwest* on September 29, 1871, the first selection below, Myrtle combined two rhetorical strategies: she used humor to focus on reactions from male audience members, most of whom were uncomfortable with Anthony's call for woman suffrage and, as if inspired by Anthony, she moved beyond these observations to her own arguments from justice and expediency.

The question of "blame" is far more complex for Myrtle in the second selection, "A Communication to the Public," published in the *New Northwest*, November 10, 1871. Within the totality of her essays, poetry, and lectures in late 1871, her open letter is a compromise response to a demand from Miller for a signed, public denial of rumors about him. But it was more than this. Myrtle was already distancing herself from woman suffrage with endorsement of woman's "right not to vote," and poems, such as "To a Poet," suggest that her love for Miller had not been extinguished.

Constrained by what she believed she could and should say in an open letter, Myrtle suggested that Miller's questionable behavior might be attributed to literary talent and artistic temperament. The fault, however, was not his alone; she made her own rhetorical apologia and accepted her "full share" of the blame. Ultimately, within the cultural prescriptions of the time, her own ethos was enhanced, and she emerged as a woman who refused to blemish the reputation of a man. Her public persuasive purpose was to end the "charges and accusations," but her private purpose may well have been to hold out her hand to Miller, if not for romance at least for the future security of her children and herself.

MISS ANTHONY'S LECTURES—OBSERVANDA

The first night of Miss Anthony's lectures [in Salem] my attention was entirely taken up with watching the speaker, for, be it known, the first, last and only time I ever heard a woman speak in public was in the "meeting' house," lang syne, when Aunt Tribulation Fear-the-Lord arose and through her tears, nose and handkerchief told her "experience."

So the first evening I had eyes and ears only for Miss A.

The following evening I gave her my ears, but managed to bestow my eyes furtively upon her audience.

What I took most interest in observing was the countenances of the gentlemen, who had lain aside that evening their important business matters and come to Miss Anthony's lecture like *lambs to the slaughter*. That my attention should have been bestowed almost exclusively upon the gentlemen may not seem natural; but when I tell you that I had never yet beheld a set of faces so mobile and expressive, so beaming, smiling and scowling, with all the variable and intense emotions of wrought-up manhood, you will not wonder.

The women were as cooly radiant as though the Suttee had never been performed. They were as serene and unruffled as a Quaker's night-gown. It was not their *funeral*.

But the men!

Here sat one along-side of his wife. She had towed him in. He was a very reluctant-looking man. It seemed as though if it had not been for the name of it he would rather have stayed at home. He was continually shifting his position, meanwhile casting glances at his wife to see the effect of everything upon her. She looked as happy as a cat with her first kitten.

I have not yet reached the point where I take delight in human suffering (now, if the typos print those two last words *woman suffrage*, I might as well give up). This man's apparent discomfiture made me unhappy, and I wanted to speak in a voice like Mrs. Winslow's syrup and say, "You shall not be hurted," for I could fancy I saw him dodging imaginary blows; he seemed momentarily expecting that Miss Anthony was going to box his ears.

A phlegmatic old gentleman sat behind me, with his chin resting upon his breast and his eyes closed. *His* play was to be oblivious when Miss Anthony made a point. But cats and old gentlemen are not always asleep when their eyes are closed.

Further on sat a great benevolent-looking fellow, with his head thrown back and his mouth open, staring as never man stared before. This individual interested me, and calling up all my physiognomical and psychological faculties, I essayed to read his thoughts. He heard the truth sublime, as truth ever is; he knew it was the truth and recognized it as such, but behind him sat a set of cynical old stoics of the old school, and to-morrow he must go out with them and canvass and discuss Miss Anthony's lecture, and they will ask him what he thinks of such sophistry as *that*, and *can* he say that what he heard was to him logical, forcible and conclusive? and that he believed that glorious woman to be devoted to the true interests of men and women, and laboring to institute a reform which would make men nobler and more successful, women happier and consequently better, and children nearer in the image of Him whose ambassador is fearless and eternal Truth? Will he have the courage to say this to those who scoff? Nay, nay. I read it on his fine, emotional face and weak intellect; but when he meets them in solemn conclave on the street corner he will muster the courage to say if he dies for it, "She is a fine figure of a woman."

Another style sat bolt upright, never moving a muscle of his body, contenting himself with blinking slowly and mildly at a neighboring chignon as much as to say: "Can these things be and not overcome us?" etc. Considering the conflict that must have been going on in his mind I felt that this behavior was very decorous and subdued.

But there were a goodly manner of happy men there—men who seemed jolly, whole-souled and willing to accept the truth.

Before me sat two of these sensible men, and their attention and evident satisfaction and appreciation won me; and when the lecture was ended said one of them, with a good-natured laugh: "Let's give her a dollar and tell her to send that book," referring to a valuable pamphlet which Miss Anthony was endeavoring to circulate, and he gave it, and I made a note of it as I passed out of Reed's Opera House, giving to an invisible angel who shifted by me the "God bless you" that was on my lips for Miss Anthony.

In the afternoon following Miss Anthony's first lecture she addressed, privately, the mothers, widows, wives and daughters of this place.

At the close of Miss Anthony's lecture a large proportion of these ladies placed their names upon a paper, which will be sent to Washington. These names will signify that these women desire to be allowed the right of suffrage. These women were among the best and most sensible in the city [Salem]. They did this act because they thought it about time that the spirit of woman should arise and assert itself.

Holding in ourselves the nature, physical, mental and moral of every human being that is to be born into the world, we feel that there ought to be some earnest thought among women; and even as there is a proscribed sphere for us in the moral and physical world, so is there a sphere which can only be filled by us in the scientific and metaphysical world. There are things in life never dreamed of in man's philosophy.

You say that we may develop ourselves in the science of matter and in the science of mind without ever being allowed to vote, legislate or hold office. In the first place, since we have set out to have some thought and responsibility, we want to be *"allowed"* to do anything we choose to do. And, after all, what is your chivalry worth if you are not going to give us what we want *when we ask for it*? You grant everywhere to woman the right to think for herself, and you say, standing in your superior height, that if she wants anything off the shelf of legislation you will hand it down to her. She has asked, plaintively, for the right of suffrage; you refuse to hand it down to her, and if in the righteous struggle to attain your eminence she grasps at whatever may help her up the steep ascent, thus piercing her hands and soiling her womanhood, *you are to blame.*

We fully relied upon your politeness, your gallantry, your chivalry; and when we said we wanted to vote with you if it would be agreeable, smiling tenderly all the while, we looked for you to take off your hat and bow acquiescence; but no such thing. You tell us just to keep still and quiet and go home and wash the children's faces, and when we *want* anything just to *say so*.

Salem, September 17, 1871

A Communication to the Public from Mrs. M. M. Miller

As Joaquin Miller is now expected to arrive in Portland, I deem it my duty to say a few words in his behalf to the people of Oregon. I have received many letters from different sources requesting me to disclose as much of his conduct towards his children as I will. Although I feel that these things concern no one on the face of the earth but my children and me, still he belongs to the world now, and I have remained silent until remarks have been carried so far as to make my children the subjects of idle gossip, and deem it right to now ask a truce to charges and accusations and request of you to behold the poet, and receive him in a manner that will give due tribute to his genius and success.

Mr. Miller has earned a fame, and an appreciation of his efforts should be awarded him. He is a man of literary culture and research; he has read constantly, industriously, and has command of the very best of literature, ancient and modern. It has been his sole ambition for years to go to Europe and acquire a literary fame. He felt, and justly, that he was gifted, and his mind being of a fine poetic structure, and his brain very delicately organized, the coarse and practical duties of providing for a family, and the annoyance of children conflicted with his dreams and literary whims. So, when he wrote to me that he would be absent in Europe five or six years, and, in the meantime, I need not expect to hear from him often, as he would be very busy, I asked for and obtained a divorce in the Courts of Lane County, and your singer was loosed and free and no longer chained to the annoying cares of a family; he could give his whole attention to his poems. I, myself, sympathize with him in his desire to have time and money to "tamper with the Muses" and cultivate his taste and talent for literature; and I feel that all poets and authors will also sympathize with him.

I did not intend that my misfortunes should be publicly known. Illness overtook me in Portland, and by irregularities of the mails, and accidents, we were cut off for a time from communication with our friends. My youngest brother was with me, and I did not ask for assistance; but by accident my friends found me. I must ever remain grateful to them for their timely and generous assistance, but they can bear me witness that I made no public complaint, and the charges made against Mr. M. were not made with my knowledge. I was as much surprised to see them as any one.

If, in five years of labor and complete isolation from my relatives, and the world, I worked with him, and not even my nearest neighbor or dearest friend heard one complaint or murmur from my lips; if, through that long winter in Portland, I sewed humbly, day after day, and day after day, as long as I was able; passed the offices and residences of our mutual friends, who were leading and wealthy people, and chose rather to let my babes come upon the verge of starvation than to blemish his reputation by letting my circumstances be known, it is not likely that after the day of hope came, and all was over, I should publicly make known what I had tried so hard to conceal. As I said before, Mr. Miller felt that he had gifts of mind, and if his system of economy was rigid and hard to endure, it was at least a success; and if he needed all his money to carry out his plans, I am satisfied that he thus used it. The bitter experience of the past cannot come again. My babes lived through all, and I am more than satisfied; I am grateful, and all is well.

The absurd statement of the Eugene *Journal,* that I had indignantly returned money that Mr. M. sent me, is incorrect; and its informers are as economical of truth as they are of affection for their own flesh and blood. It would be a sad time to show indignation toward a father when his babes were suffering for the necessaries of life. Joaquin Miller does not claim that he has ever sent a dollar to his children, or provided anything for them in any way from the time of his leaving Oregon until about two months ago, when he sent me twenty-five dollars. He has since sent fifty dollars to Mrs. B. [Belle] Cooke, for my little girl, and twenty-five to my mother who has the care of my younger children. He will doubtless make explanations, which will be satisfactory to those interested, when he returns.

It is true that I had a home with my widowed mother, but the place was dreary and secluded, and there was not a church or a school-house within fifty miles of my mother's home. So I did not deem it a proper place to educate my children, and I came away, bringing them with me, which was contrary to the decree of the Court which gave them to my mother. As I brought them away he was released by law for caring for them, and I have no reason to complain, nor can anyone have, justly. Two hundred dollars a year alimony was allowed, but as it was not secured, you will readily see that Mr. M. was entirely released from any obligations.

The marital relations between Mr. Miller and myself are dissolved, but that does not prevent our holding our precious babes in mutual love and protection; and, although there are many false sentiments in society in regard to these things, I beg the privilege of exercising my own judgment in regard to my duty towards the father of my children, and my children.

As we are both mortals, it would be affectation in me were I to profess to take upon myself all the blame, but I ask to bear my full share. The many who feel an interest in him are of more consequence than the few who know and love me; and henceforth I would have you deal with him only as a poet and author. Pronounce your judgment upon his books; know him by his epic heroes. No mortal man can go beyond himself in any conception; when he attempts to he only strikes against the border of his imagination; and rebounds further back. And when man attempts to image a god he takes a step back, and puts upon the shoulders of his god wings which belong to the lower order of creation. Good sometimes comes of evil; the most deadly pistil exhales a delicate perfume; and our separation and sorrows produced the poems of "Myrrh" and "Even So". If I have, after all, recovered my health, and sometimes smile, as others do, I feel that I have some kind of apology. If I am not today the shadowy, faded woman that might be expected, I beg your pardon; and if, as a facetious editor writes, I must go down the stream of life alongside of Lady Byron, Mrs. Bulwer, and the obstreperous wife of the author of "Boz", let that be my punishment.

M. M. Miller
Salem, November 5, 1871

Sarah Winnemucca (Hopkins)
1844-91

❖

Thocmetony (Shell Flower) was her Indian name, but she was best known as Sarah Winnemucca. During the latter half of the nineteenth century, Sarah Winnemucca, a direct descendant of Northern Paiute leaders, became the most publicized Indian woman of the Pacific Coast. From lecture platforms, in petitions and letters, and through the pages of her autobiography, *Life among the Piutes: Their Wrongs and Claims* (1883), Winnemucca emerged as a controversial spokesperson for Indian rights, specifically the rights of the Northern Paiute (also called the Numa—"the people").

Because of her familiarity with both Northern Paiute and Euro-American cultures, Sarah Winnemucca tried to serve as a cultural mediator, endeavoring to build bridges of understanding between peoples. In this role, however, she was often caught between cultures—criticized by the Northern Paiute for not accomplishing enough and condemned by government officials for being a troublemaker. The fact that she was an Indian woman in an essentially white man's world also made her vulnerable to racist and sexist attacks.

Sarah Winnemucca could easily be represented in all four sections of this volume. But, because she devoted the majority of her life to attempts for cultural understanding and to rhetorical acts for justice, we have elected to include her in this final section on communicating. In the selection we have titled "They Take Sweet Care of One Another," taken from Winnemucca's autobiography, she not only informs the reader of the traditional teachings, customs and ceremonies of the Northern Paiute but challenges the greed and passions of Euro-Americans who threatened the life of the gentle Numa. Winnemucca's unstated conclusion is that *all* peoples should "take sweet care of one another."

The authority with which Sarah Winnemucca could write and speak about the Northern Paiute culture was grounded in the first six years of her childhood. She was born about 1844, at the Humboldt Sink, later part of Nevada. Her father was Old Winnemucca, also called Poito, and Sarah was his second daughter and the fourth of his nine children. Her mother was Tuboitonie, one of the wives of Old Winnemucca and the daughter of Captain Truckee, who helped guide early immigrants across the Great Basin and served with expeditions under General John C. Frémont. Both Truckee and Old Winnemucca were leaders of Northern Paiute bands.

As a young child, Sarah lived in a *nobee,* a rounded hut woven of rushes and cattails, and she learned the traditional ways of the Northern Paiute culture. Composed of nomadic bands who hunted and gathered food in the seasonal round, the Northern Paiute were people of the high desert country of Western Nevada, Southeastern Oregon, and Northeastern California. Their survival depended on an ability to move freely from place to place, always in synchrony with seasonal turns of climate and nature's food supply.

When Sarah was about six, she had her first introduction to the world outside the Paiute culture. Grandfather Truckee took thirty of his people, including Sarah and her mother, to the San Joaquin Valley, where they worked on ranches to receive horses in payment. Additional trips and domestic work in California homes expanded Sarah's world view, and she also learned to speak Spanish and English.

When she was thirteen, Sarah and her sister Elma were placed in the home of Major William Ormsby, who was a friend of Grandfather Truckee and conducted the stage stop at Genoa, Utah Territory. The Winnemucca sisters did household chores, helped with stage passengers, and were companions to Major Ormsby's daughter Lizzie. With the Ormsbys, Sarah improved her use of English and became even more familiar with Euro-American culture.

The influx of Euro-Americans to the West threatened the traditional life and very survival of the Northern Paiute. The Numa were exposed to deadly diseases, such as typhus and smallpox, and the lands they had roamed were carved by emigrant roads, ranches, settlements, gold and silver mines, and eventually railroads.

Frederick Dodge, the first U.S. Indian agent assigned exclusively to the western section of the Utah Territory, was sympathetic to the plight of the Northern Paiute. In a communication to the Commissioner of Indian Affairs, dated November of 1859, Dodge requested establishment of reservations at Pyramid Lake and Walker River. "The Indians of my agency linger about the graves of their ancestors— 'but the game is gone,'" Dodge wrote, "and now, the steady tread of the white man is upon them. The green valleys too, once spotted with game are not theirs now" (quoted in Canfield, *Sarah Winnemucca* 20). Dodge, who was considered by some government officials as "too easy" on the Indians, was unable to realize his goals for the Northern Paiute and died in the Civil War.

Grandfather Truckee had faith in the ultimate goodwill of the white man and, in compliance with his dying wish in 1860, Sarah and Elma were sent to a convent school in San Jose, California. Sarah later gave conflicting accounts of exactly where and for how long they were enrolled; however, she was consistent in saying that, as the only Indian girls in attendance, the Winnemucca sisters were asked to leave when white parents complained.

Evidently, Sarah Winnemucca was not with her people when the strained peace with white settlers was broken. The conflict erupted in 1860, before a treaty was made to establish reservation lands. Two young Paiute girls, who had been missing for some time, were discovered in the cellar of Williams Station, a whiskey shop on the Carson River. The girls had been allegedly raped by two white men, and the event triggered retaliation by some of the Paiute bands. The warfare extended to battles at Pyramid Lake, a stronghold for the Numa. Major Ormsby, with whom Sarah and Elma Winnemucca had lived, was one of the eighty or so whites who died in the conflict.

After the Pyramid Lake battles of 1860, the Paiute were ordered to the Pyramid Lake Reservation, which was established north of what later became Reno, Nevada. The reservation system was marked by corruption and exploitation of the Numa. Food was scarce, and Numa who attempted to follow the seasonal round were looked upon with suspicion by white settlers, particularly when they traveled in bands for hunting expeditions or for the annual gathering of pine nuts.

When Sarah was reunited with the Numa, her knowledge of Euro-American culture and her linguistic facility in five languages—English, Spanish, and three native tongues—proved useful. Although her formal education was limited, Winnemucca's multilingual ability was important in her roles as interpreter, cultural mediator, teacher, public speaker, and author.

Winnemucca complained to officials, but no improvements were made. Hundreds of starving Paiute left the Pyramid Lake Reservation for assistance at Camp McDermit, where Winnemucca served as post interpreter from about 1868 to 1871, and as hospital matron in 1872. In April of 1870, she sent a letter to Ely Samuel Parker, Commissioner of Indian Affairs in Washington, D. C. "It is enough to say that we were confined to the reserve [Pyramid Lake] and had to live on what fish we could catch in the river," she wrote. "If this is the kind of civilization awaiting us on the reserve, God grant that we may never be compelled to go on one as it is more preferable to live in the mountains and drag out an existence in our native manner" (quoted in P. Stewart, "Sarah Winnemucca" 25). She urged "a permanent home" for her people "on their own native soil," without the encroachment of "white neighbors."

At the Malheur Reservation, established in Southeastern Oregon in 1872, Sarah Winnemucca served in 1875 as interpreter for trusted Indian agent Samuel B. Parrish, and she assisted with the agency school. When Parrish was replaced in 1876, the Numa mourned, and many left the Malheur Reservation when they learned of the policies of his replacement, W. V. Rinehart.

In the Bannock War of 1878, Winnemucca helped rescue her father and members of his band from a Bannock camp, and she was guide, scout and interpreter for General Oliver O. Howard. After the Bannock War, when some Paiutes were ordered to the Yakama Reservation in Washington Territory, she joined them and taught school there.

The public learned of Sarah Winnemucca through her speaking, publication of her autobiography, and press reports of her activities. As early as 1864, when she was twenty, Winnemucca made her debut on the public platform with her sister Elma and her father. In an attempt to educate the public about the culture and needs of the Northern Paiute, the Winnemuccas appeared on stages in Virginia City and San Francisco, with Sarah acting as interpreter. In 1880, Sarah Winnemucca, her father, and her brother Natchez were part of a four-person Numa delegation to Washington, D. C. The delegation asked Secretary of Interior Carl Schurz to remove the Northern Paiute from intolerable conditions at the Yakama Reservation and allow them to return to Malheur, which had been closed. Although Schurz promised his support, he and the other members of the Hayes administration failed to act. The proposal was successfully opposed by Father Wilbur, then head of the Yakama agency. Wilbur argued that white settlers would be disturbed if the Paiute left the Yakama Reservation, and he banned Sarah Winnemucca from the reservation as a troublemaker. In the eyes of some of her people, Winnemucca had given false hope and failed them.

Embittered by the broken promises of government officials, as well as the corruption and abuse in the reservation system, Sarah Winnemucca wrote an article entitled "The Pah-Utes," which was published in the July-December, 1882, issue of *The Californian, A Western Monthly Magazine.* "Once the Indians possessed all this beautiful country; now they have none," she wrote. "Then they lived happily, and prayed to the Great Spirit. But the white man came, with his cursed whisky and selfishness and greed, and drove out the poor Indian, because he was more numerous and better armed and knew more knowledge. I see very well that all my race will die out."

The next year, 1883, still convinced of the justice of her cause, Sarah Winnemucca once again took her protests to Washington, D. C. This time she was assisted in her efforts by two sisters: Elizabeth Peabody Palmer and Mary Peabody Mann, widow of Horace Mann. Dressed in fringed buckskin and adorned with shells and beads, Sarah Winnemucca spoke to curious audiences in New York, Connecticut, Rhode Island, Maryland, Massachusetts, and Pennsylvania. Her autobiography, completed with the editorial assistance of Mary Mann, was sold at her public lectures to cover travel expenses and to raise funds for the destitute Northern Paiute.

At her lectures, Winnemucca circulated a petition asking that the Indians be given lands in severalty and citizenship rights. She presented her petition to Congress and appeared before the Senate Subcommittee on Indian Affairs in 1884. Her plea for the Northern Paiute was that land be given to each head of family and a new reservation established, administered by the military, whom she trusted more than the agents of the Indian Bureau. Although the House approved a bill including much of what Winnemucca sought, the Senate, in July of 1884, directed that, under the Secretary of Interior, the remaining bands of unsettled Numa be sent to the Pyramid Lake Reservation, where they would receive 160 acres of land for each head of family in severalty. For the Northern Paiute, this was not a satisfactory solution. They had nominally possessed the Pyramid Lake Reservation since 1860, but virtually all good land and fishing areas had been taken by non-Indians.

Later, under the General Allotment Act (Dawes Act) of 1887, Winnemucca's hopes for her people were frustrated by the exploitation of the Northern Paiute in an ill-conceived and poorly administered system. The Dawes Act authorized allotments of 160 acres to heads of Indian families in severalty; land titles and citizenship would be granted after 25 years. The Burke Act of 1906 eliminated the 25-year waiting period but, with citizenship and land titles, came the burdens of taxation. Moreover, once the allotments were made to Indians, remaining reservation lands were opened to white settlement. It was not until 1935, long after the death of Sarah Winnemucca, that the dwindling numbers of Paiute in Oregon were located on an 800-acre tract, northwest of Burns, in Harney County. Today, the Burns Paiute Indian Colony, established by Congress in October of 1972, survives as one of Oregon's five Indian reservations.

Sarah Winnemucca's personal life was also filled with disappointments. She apparently married at least four times. Her first marriage, to a German named Snyder, has not been confirmed but may have occurred about 1866 (P. Stewart 24). She may have been married to an Indian for a short time, before marrying Edward C. Bartlett, a first lieutenant from New York. The couple eloped to Salt Lake City, to avoid laws against miscegenation, and were married on January 29, 1871. Sarah spent only one month with Bartlett, who was a "drunkard," and they were finally divorced in 1876, with Sarah taking back the name of Winnemucca. She was married to Joseph Satwaller, of Grant County, Oregon, on November 13, 1878, at Canyon City, and this marriage also ended after a short time (Canfield 114). Her last recorded marriage, on December 5, 1881, was to Lewis H. Hopkins, from Virginia. Their marriage, although charged with problems created by Hopkins's excessive gambling, lasted until his death from tuberculosis, October 18, 1887. Richey suggests that Sarah Winnemucca probably chose not to bear children in these marriages: "[T]he Paiutes practiced a highly effective method of birth control, which they never divulged" ("Sagebrush Princess" 62).

Winnemucca's personal life became fodder for attempts by the press and government officials to undermine her credibility. Her enjoyment of gambling, including stud poker, the fact that she carried a knife for protection, her volatile nature, and her multiple marriages became press copy. Winnemucca was engaged in a rhetorical conflict to establish her own integrity as well as to secure a good life for her people. When her autobiography was published in 1883, appended letters spoke of her good character.

Her last working years were devoted to the future of Indian children. She established a Paiute school, called the Peabody School, at Lovelock, Nevada. When the Dawes Act of 1887 required that Indian children be removed from their tribes and families, to be educated in white, English-speaking schools, Winnemucca tried to begin an industrial training school, taught by and for Paiutes, but she could not secure funding.

Ill with tuberculosis, Winnemucca's final days were spent visiting her sister Elma at Henry's Lake, Montana. She died on October 17, 1891, at the age of forty-seven. The coroner reported that she had collapsed after eating a meal and drinking chokecherry wine. Although the *New York Times* of October 27, 1891, carried notice of her death and accomplishments, her simple grave remained unmarked.

In "They Take Sweet Care of One Another," our selection from her autobiography, Winnemucca develops a restorative argument through contrast of the past and the present—the traditional and the changed—Northern Paiute cultures. After the intrusion of Euro-Americans, the Numa's happiness, represented by Winnemucca's description of the Festival of Flowers, has faded, traditional gender relationships have been disrupted, and even the traditional concept of keeping time in rhythm with all of life's events is threatened.

They Take Sweet Care of One Another

Our children are very carefully taught to be good. Their parents tell them stories, traditions of old times, even of the first mother of the human race; and love stories, stories of giants, and fables; and when they ask if these last stories are true, they answer, "Oh, it is only coyote," which means that they are make-believe stories. Coyote is the name of a mean, crafty little animal, half wolf, half dog, and stands for everything low. It is the greatest term of reproach one Indian has for another. Indians do not swear,—they have no words for swearing till they learn them of white men. . . .

We are taught to love everybody. We don't need to be taught to love our fathers and mothers. We love them without being told to. Our tenth cousin is as near to us as our first cousin; and we don't marry into our relations. Our young women are not allowed to talk to any young man that is not their cousin, except at the festive dances, when both are dressed in their best clothes, adorned with beads, feathers or shells, and stand alternately in the ring and take hold of hands. These are very pleasant occasions to all the young people.

Many years ago, when my people were happier than they are now, they used to celebrate the Festival of Flowers in the spring. I have been to three of them only in the course of my life.

Oh, with what eagerness we girls used to watch every spring for the time when we could meet with our hearts' delight, the young men, whom in civilized life you call beaux. We would all go in company to see if the flowers we were named for were yet in bloom, for almost all the girls are named for flowers. We talked about them in our wigwams, as if we were the flowers, saying, "Oh I saw myself to-day in full bloom!" We would talk all the evening in this way in our families with such delight, and such beautiful thoughts of the happy day when we should meet with those who admired us and would help us to sing our flower-songs which we made up as we sang. But we were always sorry for those that were not named after some flower, because we knew they could not join in the flower-songs like ourselves, who were named for flowers of all kinds.

At last one evening came a beautiful voice, which made every girl's heart throb with happiness. It was the chief, and every one hushed to hear what he said to-day.

"My dear daughters, we are told that you have seen yourselves in the hills and in the valleys, in full bloom. Five days from to-day your festival day will come. I know every young man's heart stops beating while I am talking. I know how it was with me many years ago. I used to wish the Flower Festival would come every day. Dear young men and young women, you are saying, 'Why put it off five days?' But you all know that is our rule. It gives you time to think, and to show your sweetheart your flower."

All the girls who have flower-names dance along together, and those who have not go together also. Our fathers and mothers and grandfathers and grandmothers make a place for us where we can dance. Each one gathers the flower she is named for, and then all weave them into wreaths and crowns and scarfs, and dress up in them.

Some girls are named for rocks and are called rock-girls, and they find some pretty rocks which they carry; each one such a rock as she is named for, or whatever she is named for. If she cannot, she can take a branch of sage-brush, or a bunch of rye-grass, which have no flower.

They all go marching along, each girl in turn singing of herself; but she is not a girl any more,—she is a flower singing. She sings of herself, and her sweetheart, dancing along by her side, helps her sing the song she makes.

I will repeat what we say of ourselves. "I, Sarah Winnemucca, am a shell-flower, such as I wear on my dress. My name is

Thocmetony. I am so beautiful! Who will come and dance with me while I am so beautiful? Oh, come and be happy with me! I shall be beautiful while the earth lasts. Somebody will always admire me; and who will come and be happy with me in the Spirit-land? I shall be beautiful forever there. Yes, I shall be more beautiful than my shell-flower, my Thocmetony! Then, come, oh come, and dance and be happy with me!" The young men sing with us as they dance beside us.

Our parents are waiting for us somewhere to welcome us home. And then we praise the sage-brush and the rye-grass that have no flower, and the pretty rocks that some are named for; and then we present our beautiful flowers to these companions who could carry none. And so all are happy; and that closes the beautiful day.

My people have been so unhappy for a long time they wish now to *disincrease*, instead of multiply. The mothers are afraid to have more children, for fear they shall have daughters, who are not safe even in their mother's presence.

The grandmothers have the special care of the daughters just before and after they come to womanhood. The girls are not allowed to get married until they have come to womanhood; and that period is recognized as a very sacred thing, and is the subject of a festival, and has peculiar customs. The young woman is set apart under the care of two of her friends, somewhat older, and a little wigwam, called a teepee, just big enough for the three, is made for them, to which they retire. She goes through certain labors which are thought to be strengthening, and these last twenty-five days. Every day, three times a day, she must gather, and pile up as high as she can, five stacks of wood. This makes fifteen stacks a day. At the end of every five days the attendants take her to a river to bathe. She fasts from all flesh-meat during these twenty-five days, and continues to do this for five days in every month all her life. At the end of the twenty-five days she returns to the family lodge, and gives all her clothing to her attendants in payment for their care. Sometimes the wardrobe is quite extensive.

It is thus publicly known that there is another marriageable woman, and any young man interested in her, or wishing to form an alliance, comes forward. But the courting is very different from the courting of the white people. He never speaks to her, or visits the family, but endeavors to attract her attention by showing his horsemanship, etc. As he knows that she sleeps next to her grandmother in the lodge, he enters in full dress after the family has retired for the night, and seats himself at her feet. If she is not awake, her grandmother wakes her. He does not speak to either young woman or grandmother, but when the young woman wishes him to go away, she rises and goes and lies down by the side of her mother. He then leaves as silently as he came in. This goes on sometimes for a year or longer, if the young woman has not made up her mind. She is never forced to marry against her wishes. When she knows her own mind, she makes a confidant of her grandmother, and then the young man is summoned by the father of the girl, who asks him in her presence, if he really loves his daughter, and reminds him, if he says he does, of all the duties of a husband. He then asks his daughter the same question, and sets before her minutely all her duties. And these duties are not slight. She is to dress the game, prepare the food, clean the buckskins, make his moccasins, dress his hair, bring all the wood,—in short, do all the household work. She promises to "be himself," and she fulfills her promise. Then he is invited to a feast and all his relatives with him. But after the betrothal, a teepee is erected for the presents that pour in from both sides.

At the wedding feast, all the food is prepared in baskets. The young woman sits by the young man, and hands him the basket of food prepared for him with her own hands. He does not take it with the right hand; but seizes her wrist, and takes it with the left hand. This constitutes the marriage ceremony, and the father pronounces them man and wife. They go to a wigwam of their own, where they live till the first child is born. This event also is celebrated. Both father and mother fast from all flesh, and the father goes through the labor of piling the wood for twenty-five days, and assumes all his wife's household work during that time. If he does not do his part in the care of the child, he is considered an outcast. Every five days his child's basket is changed for a new one, and the five are all carefully put away at the end of the days, the last one containing the navel-string, carefully wrapped up, and all are put up into a tree, and the child put into a new and ornamented basket. All this respect shown to the mother and child makes the parents feel their responsibility, and makes the tie between parents and child very strong. The young mothers often get together and exchange their experiences about the attentions of their husbands; and inquire of each other if the fathers did their duty to their children, and were careful of their wives' health. . . .

[T]he Piutes, and other tribes west of the Rocky Mountains, are not fond of going to war. I never saw a war-dance but once. It is always the whites that begin the wars, for their own selfish purposes. The government does not take care to send the good men; there are a plenty who would take pains to see and understand the chiefs and learn their characters, and their good will to the whites. But the whites have not waited to find out how good the Indians were. . . .

My people teach their children never to make fun of any one, no matter how they look. If you see your brother or sister doing something wrong, look away, or go away from them. If you make fun of bad persons, you make yourself beneath them. Be kind to all, both poor and rich, and feed all that come to your wigwam, and your name can be spoken of by every one far and near. In this way you will make many friends for yourself. Be kind both to bad and good, for you don't know your own heart. This is the way my people teach their children. It was handed down from father to son for many generations. I never in my life saw our children rude as I have seen white children and grown people in the streets.

The chief's tent is the largest tent, and it is the council-tent, where every one goes who wants advice. In the evenings the head men go there to discuss everything, for the chiefs do not rule like tyrants; they discuss everything with their people, as a father would in his family. Often they sit up all night. They discuss the doings of all, if they need to be advised. If a boy is not doing well they talk that over, and if the women are interested they can share in the talks.

If there is not enough room inside, they all go out of doors, and make a great circle. The men are in the inner circle, for there would be too much smoke for the women inside. The men never talk without smoking first. The women sit behind them in another circle, and if the children wish to hear, they can be there too. The women know as much as the men do, and their advice is often asked. We have a republic as well as you. The council-tent is our Congress, and anybody can speak who has anything to say, women and all. They are always interested in what their husbands are doing and thinking about. And they take some part even in wars. They are always near at hand when fighting is going on, ready to snatch their husbands up and carry them off if wounded or killed.

One splendid woman that my brother Lee married after his first wife died, went out into the battle-field after her uncle was killed, and went into the front ranks and cheered the men on. Her uncle's horse was dressed in a splendid robe made of eagles' feathers and she snatched it off and swung it in the face of the enemy, who always carry off everything they find, as much to say, "You can't have that—I have it safe"; and she staid and took her uncle's place, as brave as any of the men.

It means something when the women promise their fathers to make their husbands *themselves*. They faithfully keep with them in all the dangers they can share. They not only take care of their children together, but they do everything together; and when they grow blind, which I am sorry to say is very common, for the smoke they live in destroys their eyes at last, they take sweet care of one another. Marriage is a sweet thing when people love each other.

Sui Sin Far (Edith Maud Eaton)
1865-1914

"**M**y mother's race is as preju-
diced as my father's," wrote Edith Maud Eaton. "Only when the
whole world becomes one family will human beings be able to see
clearly and hear distinctly."

Writing under the pen name of Sui Sin Far, Edith Maud Eaton was
expressing both disappointment with the present and a rhetorical
vision for the future in her autobiographical essay, "Leaves from the
Mental Portfolio of an Eurasian," published in the *Independent*,
January 21, 1909. While living in Seattle, Washington, she drafted her
autobiography and reflected on her role as an Eurasian author.
"Fundamentally, I muse," she wrote, "all people are the same. . . . I
believe some day a greater part of the world will be Eurasian. I cheer
myself with the thought that I am but a pioneer" ("Leaves" 129).

Sui Sin Far was "a pioneer," not only as a Eurasian woman in a
predominantly white culture, but also in her role as cultural mediator
between the Chinese culture of her mother and the Anglo culture of
her father. Throughout her adult life as a self-described "very serious
and sober-minded spinster," Far sought ways to bridge the distance
between cultures. "I give my right hand to the Occidentals and my left
to the Orientals," she wrote, "hoping that between them they will not
utterly destroy the insignificant 'connecting link'" ("Leaves" 132). In
her fiction and essays, Sui Sin Far's rhetorical objective was cultural
understanding, and she addressed questions of race, class, and gender,
both between and within cultures.

Far was an unusual rhetor for her time. She had the courage to
select a Chinese pen name and emphasize her Chinese background at a
time when the Chinese were considered inferior and clearly discrimi-
nated against in the United States. She also had the courage to give
honest portrayals of the weaknesses, as well as the strengths, of the
Chinese with whom she associated in Pacific Coast cities.

In her story "The Americanizing of Pau Tsu," which we have
chosen for this volume, Sui Sin Far communicates her sensitivity to
assimilation issues within the Chinese-American community. The story
is set in Seattle, where Sui Sin Far spent ten of her most important
years as a writer. When she arrived in the Pacific Northwest in 1900,

Far joined Seattle's small Chinese community of less than five hundred persons. Because she did not appear to be Chinese and did not speak the language, Far sometimes had to convince doubters in Seattle, as well as in California, that she was, in fact, of Chinese ancestry. In Seattle, where she worked as a stenographer and journalist, Far taught English to Chinese people, assisted in a Baptist mission, and collected material for her articles and fiction.

A number of Far's short stories, which were published in major periodicals, were set on the Pacific Coast, particularly in the Chinatowns of Seattle and San Francisco. A collection of her short fiction, *Mrs. Spring Fragrance*, in which "The Americanizing of Pau Tsu" appeared, was published in 1912, two years before Far's death in Montreal, Canada. When we first examined *Mrs. Spring Fragrance*, we were struck by the appearance as well as the contents of the book. The design of the cover and pages suggests a stylized image of traditional Chinese femininity. The gray-green pages bear soft images of a flowering plum branch and a crested bird on a branch of bamboo, accompanied by the Chinese characters for Happiness, Prosperity and Longevity. Against this delicate backdrop, Far's writing, which addresses the harsh realities of racism and sexism, is foregrounded.

Limited biographical information is available on Sui Sin Far, but our understanding of her life has been informed by Far's brief autobiography, her sister Winnifred Eaton's fictionalized autobiography, and by the work of researchers listed in the bibliography. In particular, we are indebted to Amy Ling and Annette White-Parks for their studies of Far and her works.

Sui Sin Far was born in England on March 15, 1865, as Edith Maud Eaton, the eldest daughter of sixteen children born to Edward Eaton and Grace (Lotus Blossom) Trefusius Eaton. By the age of four, Sui Sin Far knew she was "something apart and different from other children" ("Leaves" 125). As she grew older, she realized that some children were forbidden to play with her because "her mamma is Chinese," and she was taught in her English school that China was "a heathen country, being civilized by England."

When Sui Sin Far was six years old, the Eatons moved from England to the United States, a move evidently prompted by the disapproval of Edward Eaton's parents of his marriage (Ling, "Pioneers" 26). With the exception of their mother, whom Far described as "English bred with English ways and manner of dress," the Eaton children had never seen a Chinese person. In Hudson City, New York, Far and her brother Charlie saw their first Chinese men. Far wrote in her autobiography: "The two men within the store are uncouth specimens of their race, drest in working blouses and pantaloons with queues hanging down their backs. I recoil with a sense of shock" (126). White children who knew that Grace Eaton was Chinese followed the Eaton children down the street and began to chant: "Chinky, Chinky, Chinaman, yellow-face, pig-tail, rat-eater," and soon a fight began, the first of many such confrontations.

Ridicule and ill health took their toll on Sui Sin Far's sensitive nature. Throughout her life, she suffered from rheumatic fever. As an adult, when she weighed only eighty-four pounds and walked with a limp, she was "ordered beyond the Rockies by the doctor, who declares that I will never regain my strength in the East" ("Leaves" 130). She died at the age of forty-nine.

Poverty also marked Far's life. Fourteen of the sixteen children born to the Eatons lived to adulthood, and it was difficult to provide for such a large family on the income produced by sales of Edward Eaton's landscape paintings. "I tramp around and sell my father's pictures," Far wrote, "also some lace which I make myself" ("Leaves" 128). Eventually, Far learned shorthand and helped supplement the family income with her earnings, a responsibility she evidently carried throughout her life as a journalist and author.

Although the Eaton family experienced poverty, eight of the nine daughters became "professional" women (Sam Solberg, "Sui" 86).

Edith and Winnifred were both journalists and then became authors. Sara and Mae were artists; Grace became the first Chinese-American lawyer in Chicago (Ling, "Pioneers" 27). Another sister took up nursing, one was a teacher of French, and another became a secretary (Solberg, "Sui" 86).

Edith and Winnifred Eaton shared interests in writing, though their lives and careers diverged. Edith never married; Winnifred married more than once and had children. Edith wrote articles and short fiction; Winnifred published "nearly two dozen books, the majority of which were best-sellers," and she became "chief scenarist for Universal Studios in Hollywood" (Ling, "Pioneers" 27). Both could pass for white, but neither chose to emphasize her Anglo ancestry.

The pseudonyms the two sisters chose represented their differences. Edith selected Sui Sin Far (Chinese Lily or Narcissus), a Chinese pen name, while Winnifred, ten years younger, chose Onoto Watanna, a pen name that sounded Japanese, and created the fiction of an exotic Japanese ancestry, including a Japanese noblewoman as a mother. Winnifred's decision was most probably based on knowledge of persistent stereotypes and prejudices. Negative views of the Chinese, who were brought to the United States as cheap labor for the mines in the 1850s and to build railroads in the 1860s, were fired by fictions of the sinister "Yellow Peril" and culminated in the Chinese Exclusion Act of 1882, which was made perpetual in 1902 and not repealed until 1943. In contrast, the Japanese were seen as the elite of the Far East. In the 1880s, a craze for westernization had swept through Japan, and the country came of age as a modern, major imperialist power with successes in the Sino-Japanese War of 1894-95 and the Russo-Japanese War of 1904-1905. Sui Sin Far wrote, "[A] Japanese Eurasian does not appear in the same light as a Chinese Eurasian" ("Leaves" 131).

The complications of marital relationships appear in several of the short stories in *Mrs. Spring Fragrance*. In two of these stories—"The Americanizing of Pau Tsu," set in Seattle, and "The Wisdom of the New," set in San Francisco—Sui Sin Far empathizes with the plight of Chinese wives who are expected by their Chinese merchant husbands to become Americanized. However, for the Chinese women, becoming "Americanized" is a fate worse than death.

In "The Americanizing of Pau Tsu," which appears below, Sui Sin Far provides a critique of gender relationships within and between Chinese and Anglo cultures. Eager to be appreciated and rewarded in his quest for upward mobility, Wan Lin Fo is flattered by the attentions of Adah Raymond, his well-positioned benefactress. But, as Raymond eventually points out, while Wan Lin Fo has cleverly adapted to American ways, he has remained "a thorough Chinaman" in his relationship with Pau Tsu, his wife.

Raymond is Far's cultural interpreter in this short story, but she also represents a relatively uninformed white culture. She is entertained by Wan Lin Fo and adopts him and his "little bride." Although she senses that Pau Tsu is suffering, Raymond does not realize until the end of the story that she has unwittingly contributed to Pau Tsu's agony.

THE AMERICANIZING OF PAU TSU

I

When Wan Hom Hing came to Seattle to start a branch of the merchant business which his firm carried on so successfully in the different ports of China, he brought with him his nephew, Wan Lin Fo, then eighteen years of age. Wan Lin Fo was a well-educated Chinese youth, with bright eyes and keen ears. In a few years' time he knew as much about the business as did any of the senior partners. Moreover, he learned to speak and write the American language with such fluency that he was never at a loss for an answer, when the white man, as was sometimes the case, sought to pose him. . . . [N]ow and again Lin Fo would while away an evening at the Chinese Literary Club, . . . New Year's Day, or rather, Week, would also see him business forgotten, arrayed in national costume of finest silk, and color "the blue of the sky after rain," visiting with his friends, both Chinese and American, . . .

It was on the occasion of one of these New Year's visits that Wan Lin Fo first made known to the family of his firm's silent American partner, Thomas Raymond, that he was betrothed. . . . One of the young ladies of the house, who was fair and frank of face and friendly and cheery in manner, observing as she handed him a cup of tea that Lin Fo's eyes wore a rather wistful expression, questioned him as to the wherefore:

"Miss Adah," replied Lin Fo, "may I tell you something?"

"Certainly, Mr. Wan," replied the girl. "You know how I enjoy hearing your tales."

"But this is no tale. Miss Adah, you have inspired in me a love—"

Adah Raymond started. Wan Lin Fo spake [sic] slowly.

"For the little girl in China to whom I am betrothed."

"Oh, Mr. Wan! That is good news. But what have I to do with it?"

"This, Miss Adah! Every time I come to this house, I see you, so good and so beautiful, dispensing tea and happiness to all around, and I think, could I have in my home and ever by my side one who is also both good and beautiful, what a felicitous life mine would be!"

"You must not flatter me, Mr. Wan!"

"All that I say is founded on my heart. But I will speak not of you. I will speak of Pau Tsu."

"Pau Tsu?"

"Yes. That is the name of my future wife. It means a pearl."

"How pretty! Tell me all about her!"

"I was betrothed to Pau Tsu before leaving China. My parents adopted her to be my wife. As I remember, she had shining eyes and the good-luck color was on her cheek. Her mouth was like a red vine leaf, and her eyebrows most exquisitely arched. As slender as a willow was her form, and when she spoke, her voice lilted from note to note in the sweetest melody."

Adah Raymond softly clapped her hands.

"Ah! You were even then in love with her."

"No," replied Lin Fo thoughtfully. "I was too young to be in love—sixteen years of age. Pau Tsu was thirteen. But, as I have confessed, you have caused me to remember and love her."

Adah Raymond was not a self-conscious girl, but for the life of her she could think of no reply to Lin Fo's speech.

"I am twenty-two years old now," he continued. "Pau Tsu is eighteen. Tomorrow I will write to my parents and persuade them to send her to me at the time of the spring festival. My elder brother was married last year, and his wife is now under my parents' roof, so that Pau Tsu, who has been the daughter of the house for so many years, can now be spared to me."

"What a sweet little thing she must be," commented Adah Raymond.

"You will say that when you see her," proudly responded Lin Fo. "My parents say she is always happy. There is not a bird or flower or dewdrop in which she does not find some glad meaning."

"I shall be so glad to know her. Can she speak English?"

Lin Fo's face fell.

"No," he replied, "but,"—brightening—"when she comes I will have her learn to speak like you—and be like you."

II

Pau Tsu came with the spring, and Wan Lin Fo was one of the happiest and proudest of bridegrooms. The tiny bride was really very pretty—even to American eyes. In her peach and plum colored robes, her little arms and hands sparkling with jewels, and her shiny black head decorated with wonderful combs and pins, she appeared a bit of Eastern coloring amidst the Western lights and shades.

Lin Fo had not been forgotten, and her eyes under their downcast lids discovered him at once, as he stood awaiting her amongst a group of young Chinese merchants on the deck of the vessel.

The apartments he had prepared for her were furnished in American style, and her birdlike little figure in Oriental dress seemed rather out of place at first. It was not long, however, before she brought forth from the great box, which she had brought over seas, screens and fans, vases, panels, Chinese matting, artificial flowers and birds, and a number of exquisite carvings and pieces of antique porcelain. With these she transformed the American flat into an Oriental bower, even setting up in her sleeping-room a little chapel, enshrined in which was an image of the Goddess of Mercy, two ancestral tablets, and other emblems of her faith in the Gods of her fathers.

The Misses Raymond called upon her soon after arrival, and she smiled and looked pleased. She shyly presented each girl with a Chinese cup and saucer, also a couple of antique vases, covered with whimsical pictures, which Lin Fo tried his best to explain.

The girls were delighted with the gifts, and having fallen, as they expressed themselves, in love with the little bride, invited her through her husband to attend a launch party, which they intended giving the following Wednesday on Lake Washington.

Lin Fo accepted the invitation in behalf of himself and wife. He was quite at home with the Americans and, being a young man, enjoyed their rather effusive appreciation of him as an educated Chinaman. Moreover, he was of the opinion that the society of the American young ladies would benefit Pau Tsu in helping her to acquire the ways and language of the land in which he hoped to make a fortune.

Wan Lin Fo was a true son of the Middle Kingdom and secretly pitied all those who were born far away from its influences; but there was much about the Americans that he admired. He also entertained sentiments of respect for a motto which hung in his room which bore the legend: "When in Rome, do as the Romans do."

"What is best for men is also best for women in this country," he told Pau Tsu when she wept over his suggestion that she should take some lessons in English from a white woman.

"It may be best for a man who goes out in the street," she sobbed, "to learn the new language, but of what importance is it to a woman who lives only within the house and her husband's heart?"

It was seldom, however, that she protested against the wishes of Lin Fo. As her mother-in-law had said, she was a docile, happy little creature. Moreover, she loved her husband.

But as the days and weeks went by the girl bride whose life hitherto had been spent in the quiet retirement of a Chinese home in the performance of filial duties, in embroidery work and lute playing, in sipping tea and chatting with gentle girl companions, felt very much bewildered by the novelty and stir of the new world into which she had been suddenly thrown. She could not understand, for all Lin Fo's explanations, why it was required of her to learn the strangers' language and adopt their ways. Her husband's tongue was the same as her own. So also her little maid's. It puzzled her to be always seeing this and hearing that—sights and sounds which as yet had no meaning for her. Why also was it necessary to receive visitors nearly every evening?—visitors who could neither understand nor make themselves understood by her, for all their curious smiles and stares, which she bore like a second Vashti—or rather, Esther. And why, oh! why should she be constrained to eat her food with clumsy, murderous looking American implements instead of with her own elegant and easily manipulated ivory chopsticks?

Adah Raymond, who at Lin Fo's request was a frequent visitor to the house, could not fail to observe that Pau Tsu's small face grew daily smaller and thinner, and that the smile with which she invariably greeted her, though sweet, was tinged with melancholy. Her woman's instinct told her that something was wrong, but what it was the light within her failed to discover. She would reach over to Pau Tsu and take within her own firm, white hand the small, trembling fingers, pressing them lovingly and sympathetically; and the little Chinese woman would look up into the beautiful face bent above hers and think to herself: "No wonder he wishes me to be like her!"

If Lin Fo happened to come in before Adah Raymond left he would engage the visitor in bright and animated conversation. They had so much of common interest to discuss, as is always the way with young people who have lived any length of time in a growing city of the West. But to Pau Tsu, pouring tea and dispensing sweetmeats, it was all Greek, or rather, all American.

"Look, my pearl, what I have brought you," said Lin Fo one afternoon as he entered his wife's apartments, followed by a messenger-boy, who deposited in the middle of the room a large cardboard box.

With murmurs of wonder Pau Tsu drew near, and the messenger-boy having withdrawn Lin Fo cut the string, and drew forth a beautiful lace evening dress and dark blue walking costume, both made in American style.

For a moment there was silence in the room. Lin Fo looked at his wife in surprise. Her face was pale and her little body was trembling, while her hands were drawn up into her sleeves.

"Why, Pau Tsu!" he exclaimed, "I thought to make you glad."

At these words the girl bent over the dress of filmy lace, and gathering the flounce in her hand smoothed it over her knee; then lifting a smiling face to her husband, replied: "Oh, you are too good, too kind to your unworthy Pau Tsu. My speech is slow, because I am overcome with happiness."

Then with exclamations of delight and admiration she lifted the dresses out of the box and laid them carefully over the couch.

"I wish you to dress like an American woman when we go out or receive," said her husband. "It is the proper thing in America to do as the Americans do. You will notice, light of my eyes, that it is only on New Year and our national holidays that I wear the costume of our country and attach a queue. The wife should follow the husband in all things."

A ripple of laughter escaped Pau Tsu's lips.

"When I wear that dress," said she, touching the walking costume, "I will look like your friend, Miss Raymond."

She struck her hands together gleefully, but when her husband had gone to his business she bowed upon the floor and wept pitifully.

III

During the rainy season Pau Tsu was attacked with a very bad cough. A daughter of Southern China, the chill, moist climate of the Puget Sound winter was very hard on her delicate lungs. Lin Fo worried much over the state of her health, and meeting Adah Raymond on the street one afternoon told her of his anxiety. The kind-hearted girl immediately returned with him to the house. Pau Tsu was lying on her couch, feverish and breathing hard. The American girl felt her hands and head.

"She must have a doctor," said she, mentioning the name of her family's physician.

Pau Tsu shuddered. She understood a little English by this time.

"No! No! Not a man, *not* a man!" she cried.

Adah Raymond looked up at Lin Fo.

"I understand," said she. "There are several women doctors in this town. Let us send for one."

But Lin Fo's face was set.

Chinese woman and children, Portland, Oregon

"No!" he declared. "We are in America. Pau Tsu shall be attended to by your physician."

Adah Raymond was about to protest against this dictum when the sick wife, who had also heard it, touched her hand and whispered: "I do not mind now. Man all right."

So the other girl closed her lips, feeling that if the wife would not dispute her husband's will it was not her place to do so; but her heart ached with compassion as she bared Pau Tsu's chest for the stethoscope.

"It was like preparing a lamb for slaughter," she told her sister afterwards. "Pau Tsu was motionless, her eyes closed and her lips sealed, while the doctor remained; but after he had left and we two were alone she shuddered and moaned like one bereft of reason. I honestly believe that the examination was worse than death to that little Chinese woman. The modesty of generations of maternal ancestors was crucified as I rolled down the neck of her silk tunic."

It was a week after the doctor's visit, and Pau Tsu, whose cough had yielded to treatment, though she was still far from well, was playing on her lute, and whisperingly singing this little song, said to have been written on a fan which was presented to an ancient Chinese emperor by one of his wives:

> "Of fresh new silk,
> All snowy white,
> And round as a harvest moon,
> A pledge of purity and love,
> A small but welcome boon.
>
> While summer lasts,
> When borne in hand,
> Or folded on thy breast,
> 'Twill gently soothe thy burning brow,
> And charm thee to thy rest.
> But, oh, when Autumn winds blow chill,
> And days are bleak and cold,
> No longer sought, no longer loved,
> 'Twill lie in dust and mould.
> This silken fan then deign accept,
> Sad emblem of my lot,
> Caressed and cherished for an hour,
> Then speedily forgot."

"Why so melancholy, my pearl?" asked Lin Fo, entering from the street.

"When a bird is about to die, its notes are sad," returned Pau Tsu.

"But thou art not for death—thou art for life," declared Lin Fo, drawing her towards him and gazing into a face which day by day seemed to grow finer and more transparent.

IV

A Chinese messenger-boy ran up the street, entered the store of Wan Hom Hing & Co. and asked for the junior partner. When Lin Fo came forward he handed him a dainty, flowered missive, neatly folded and addressed. The receiver opened it and read:

DEAR AND HONORED HUSBAND,—Your unworthy Pau Tsu lacks the courage to face the ordeal before her. She has, therefore, left you and prays you to obtain a divorce, as is the custom in America, so that you may be happy with the Beautiful One, who is so much your Pau Tsu's superior. This, she acknowledges, for she sees with your eyes, in which, like a star, the Beautiful One shineth. Else, why should you have your Pau Tsu follow in her footsteps? She has tried to obey your will and to be as an American woman; but now she is very weary, and the terror of what is before her has overcome.
Your stupid thorn,
Pau Tsu

Mechanically Lin Fo folded the letter and thrust it within his breast pocket. A customer inquired of him the price of a lacquered tray. "I wish you good morning," he replied, reaching for his hat. The customer and clerks gaped after him as he left the store.

Out on the street, as fate would have it, he met Adah Raymond. He would have turned aside had she not spoken to him.

"Whatever is the matter with you, Mr. Wan? she inquired. "You don't look yourself at all."

"The density of my difficulties you cannot understand," he replied, striding past her.

But Adah Raymond was persistent. She had worried lately over Pau Tsu.

"Something is wrong with your wife," she declared.

Lin Fo wheeled around.

"Do you know where she is?" he asked with quick suspicion.

"Why, no! exclaimed the girl in surprise.

"Well, she has left me."

Adah Raymond stood incredulous for a moment, then with indignant eyes she turned upon the deserted husband.

"You deserve it!" she cried, "I have seen it for some time: your cruel, arbitrary treatment of the dearest, sweetest little soul in the world."

"I beg your pardon, Miss Adah," returned Lin Fo, "but I do not understand. Pau Tsu is heart of my heart. How then could I be cruel to her?"

"Oh, you stupid!" exclaimed the girl. "You're a Chinaman, but you're almost as stupid as an American. Your cruelty consisted in forcing Pau Tsu to be—what nature never intended her to be—an American woman; to adapt and adopt in a few months' time all our ways and customs. I saw it long ago, but as Pau Tsu was too sweet and meek to see any faults in her man I had not the heart to open her eyes—or yours. Is it not true that she has left you for this reason?"

"Yes," murmured Lin Fo. He was completely crushed. "And some other things."

"What other things?"

"She—is—afraid—of—the—doctor."

"She is!"—fiercely—"Shame upon you!"

Lin Fo began to walk on, but the girl kept by his side and continued:

"You wanted your wife to be an American woman while you remained a Chinaman. For all your clever adaptation of our American ways you are a thorough Chinaman. Do you think an American would dare treat his wife as you have treated yours?"

Wan Lin Fo made no response. He was wondering how he could ever have wished his gentle Pau Tsu to be like this angry woman. Now his Pau Tsu was gone. His anguish for the moment made him oblivious to the presence of his companion and the words she was saying. His silence softened the American girl. After all, men, even Chinamen, were nothing but big, clumsy boys, and she didn't believe in kicking a man after he was down.

"But, cheer up, you're sure to find her," said she, suddenly changing her tone. "Probably her maid has friends in Chinatown who have taken them in."

"If I find her," said Lin Fo fervently, "I will not care if she never speaks an American word, and I will take her for a trip to China, so that our son may be born in the country that Heaven loves."

"You cannot make too much amends for all she has suffered. As to Americanizing Pau Tsu—that will come in time. I am quite sure that were I transferred to your country and commanded to turn myself into a Chinese woman in the space of two or three months I would prove a sorry disappointment to whomever built their hopes upon me."

Many hours elapsed before any trace could be found of the missing one. All the known friends and acquaintances of little Pau Tsu were called upon and questioned; but if they had knowledge of the young wife's hiding place they refused to divulge it. Though Lin Fo's face was grave with an unexpressed fear, their sympathies were certainly not with him.

The seekers were about giving up the search in despair when a little boy, dangling in his hands a string of blue beads, arrested the attention of the young husband. He knew the necklace to be a gift from Pau Tsu to the maid, A-Toy. He had bought it himself. Stopping and questioning the little fellow he learned to his great joy that his wife and her maid were at the boy's home, under the care of his grandmother, who was a woman learned in herb lore.

Adah Raymond smiled in sympathy with her companion's evident great relief.

"Everything will now be all right," said she, following Lin Fo as he proceeded to the house pointed out by the lad. Arrived there, she suggested that the husband enter first and alone. She would wait a few moments.

"Miss Adah," said Lin Fo, "ten thousand times I beg your pardon, but perhaps you will come to see my wife some other time—not today?"

He hesitated, embarrassed and humiliated.

In one silent moment Adah Raymond grasped the meaning of all the morning's trouble—of all Pau Tsu's sadness.

"Lord, what fools we mortals be!" she soliloquized as she walked home alone. "I ought to have known. What else could Pau Tsu have thought?—coming from a land where women have no men friends save their husbands. How she must have suffered under her smiles! Poor, brave little soul!"

Ella (Rhoads) Higginson
1862-1940

In a letter to Alfred Powers, dated May 11, 1935, Ella Higginson wrote: "What caused me to become a writer? Nothing but the consuming desire to write. It is the only thing I ever really wanted to do." In the same letter, she also told him, "I love the twin states of the Northwest next to God and my country; and if either should cease to claim me as one of her writers my heart would be broken." Higginson's desire to communicate her love of the extravagant beauty of the Pacific Northwest and the lives of its predominantly poor, working-class inhabitants—particularly its women—provided material for the vast majority of her writing. She wanted the natural beauty of the land to be treasured and protected, and she wanted the emotional and moral dilemmas of those who daily struggled with hard times and cultural isolation to be examined and understood.

Ella Higginson is claimed as a writer by both Oregon, where she lived from infancy until after her marriage, and Washington, where she spent the last forty-seven years of her life. She was born in Council Grove, Kansas, and traveled overland to Oregon in the early 1860s with her parents, Charles and Mary Rhoads, and her much older sister and brother. The date of Higginson's birth is unclear as she adamantly refused to provide it to biographers, but it appears to have been 1862, and she would have been a very small child when she came west. The Rhoads family originally settled in Eastern Oregon's Grand Ronde Valley. In 1870, they moved to Portland, and then to a farm near Milwaukie.

By the time Ella was about eleven years old, the family was living in Oregon City, where she attended public school. Ella Higginson said that her childhood and girlhood in Oregon influenced her work "more than anything else" (Letter to Powers, 11 May 1935). She began writing when she was eight and, at fourteen, published a love poem in the Oregon City paper. At sixteen, Higginson went to work for the Oregon City newspaper, where she learned everything from typesetting to editorial writing. She continued to write, and a few stories were published. Her writing was encouraged by her mother and her beloved older sister, Carrie Blake Morgan, who was also a writer.

In 1885, Ella married Russell Carden
Higginson, a pharmacist from New York. After
their marriage, the Higginsons lived in La Grande,
Oregon, for two years. In 1888, the couple moved
to Bellingham, Washington, where Russell
Higginson was the proprietor of a drugstore. He
died in 1909, and Ella Higginson remained at their
home in Bellingham. The Higginsons had no
children.

It was in Bellingham, in 1890, that Higginson's
literary career began in earnest. For a short time
she edited a column, "Fact and Fancy," for
Portland's *West Shore* and, after the journal's
demise, she began contributing poetry and short
stories to national magazines. Her work appeared
regularly in the *Overland Monthly, Atlantic,
Lippincott's, McClure's, Harper's, Short Stories,*
and many other magazines for the next 25 years.
She built a solid national and international reputation as a Pacific Northwest poet and short story
writer.

Her first volume of poetry, *A Bunch of Western
Clover*, was published in 1894 by Edson and Irish
of New Whatcom, Washington. Two years later,
her first book of short stories was issued by the
Calvert Company of Seattle. This book, *The Flower That Grew in the
Sand and Other Stories*, was quickly purchased by the Macmillan
Company and reprinted in 1897 with a new title—*From the Land of
the Snow Pearls*. Critics lauded the work. Several other works, including poetry, short stories, a novel, and a travel book about Alaska,
followed over the years, and all were critically well received. Yet
today, Higginson's body of work is largely unfamiliar to all but the
few Pacific Northwest historians of literature or anthologists who
concern themselves with early writers of the region.

Relatively little is known about Higginson's life. She left no diaries,
and only a few letters to Alfred Powers are included in the manuscript
collection at the Oregon Historical Society. She was extremely reticent
about autobiographical details.

Our first selection from Higginson's work, "Esther's 'Fourth,'" was
published in *From the Land of the Snow Pearls*. The setting is
Oregon's Grand Ronde Valley, Ella Higginson's first western home.
Like many of Higginson's female protagonists, Esther is from a poor

family and, though very young, she exhibits an innate spiritual connection with nature. In addition to economic deprivation, many protagonists of Higginson's stories suffer from isolation and loneliness, exacerbated by those who heap ridicule on the poor and working class and consider them unacceptably provincial. The antagonists are those who value having the right kind of shoes or dress or education above anything else, including, in this particular story, compassion for a child "with a beautiful faith."

Higginson's ambivalence about "Eastern" values and culture was played out many times in her work, but it is explored most fully on the larger canvas of her novel, *Mariella; of Out-West*. Mariella Palmer is the daughter of poor, uneducated, and overworked farming parents. She is willful and independent, close to nature, and she scorns pretension in all its forms. She is not intimidated by the Easterners who come in the "boom years" and consider her pitiable because of her lack of cultural refinement. Mariella is able to eventually combine what is best in her native Western character with the best attributes of the cultivated East, as exemplified by her childhood teacher, Leaming, whom she eventually, and significantly, marries. Thus she retains her reverence for nature, her innate spirituality, her lack of slavishness to convention, her sense of honor and fairness—and she leaves behind stubborn willfulness, ignorance, and small-mindedness through the tempering process of education. When, at the end of the novel, Mariella marries Leaming and they move to England, the reader can be sure that she is in no danger of losing her individuality, and that she will teach as much as she learns. The excerpt we have chosen from *Mariella; of Out-West* is a scene from Mariella's adolescence that we have titled "Isaphene's White Hat," wherein Mariella struggles with her "wickedness."

ESTHER'S "FOURTH"

It was the fourth day of July, and the fourth hour of the day. Long, beryl ribbons of color were streaming through the lovely Grand Ronde valley when the little girl awoke—so suddenly and so completely that it seemed as if she had not been asleep at all.

"Sister!" she cried in a thin, eager voice. "Ain't it time to get up? It's just struck four."

"Not yet," said the older girl drowsily. "There's lots o' time, Pet."

She put one arm under the child affectionately and fell asleep again. The little girl lay motionless, waiting. There was a large cherry tree outside, close to the tiny window above her bed, and she could hear the soft turning of the leaves, one against the other, and the fluttering of the robins that were already stealing the cherries. Innocent thieves that they were, they continually betrayed themselves by their shrill cries of triumph.

Not far from the tiny log-cabin the river went singing by on its way through the green valley; hearing it, Esther thought of the soft glooms under the noble balm trees, where the grouse drummed and butterflies drifted in long level flight. Esther always breathed softly while she watched the butterflies—she had a kind of reverence for them—and she thought there could be nothing sweeter, even in heaven, than the scents that the wind shook out of the balms.

She lay patiently waiting with wide eyes until the round clock in the kitchen told her that another hour had gone by. "Sister," she said then, "oh, it must be time to get up! I just *can't* wait any longer."

The older girl, with a sleepy but sympathetic smile, slipped out of bed and commenced dressing. The child sprang after her. "Sister," she cried, running to the splint-bottomed chair on which lay the cheap but exquisitely white undergarments. "I can't hardly wait. Ain't it good of Mr. Hoover to take me to town? Oh, I feel as if I had hearts all over me, an' every one of 'em beating so!"

"Don't be so excited, Pet." The older sister smiled gently at the child. "Things never are quite as nice as you expect them to be," she added, with that wisdom that comes so soon to starved country hearts.

"Well, this can't help bein' nice," said the child, with a beautiful faith. She sat on the strip of rag carpeting that partially covered the rough floor, and drew on her stockings and her copper-toed shoes. "Oh, sister, my fingers shake so I can't get the strings through the eyelets! Do you think Mr. Hoover might oversleep hisself? It can't help bein' nice—nicer'n I expect. Of course," she added, with a momentary regret, "I wish I had some other dress besides that buff calico, but I ain't, an' so—it's reel pretty, anyways, sister, ain't it?"

"Yes, Pet," said the girl gently. There was a bitter pity for the child in her heart.

"To think o' ridin' in the Libraty Car!" continued Esther, struggling with the shoe strings. "Course they'll let me. Paw knows the storekeeper, and Mr. Hoover kin tell 'em who I am. An' the horses, an' the ribbons, an' the music—an' all the little girls my age! Sister, it's awful never to have any little girls to play with! I guess maw don't know how I've wanted 'em, or she'd of took me to town sometimes. I ain't never been anywheres—except to Mis' Bunnell's fun'ral, when the minister prayed so long," she added, with a pious after-thought.

It was a happy child that was lifted to the back of the most trustworthy of the plow-horses to be escorted to the celebration by "Mr. Hoover," the hired man. The face under the cheap straw hat, with its wreath of pink and green artificial flowers, was almost pathetically radiant. To that poor little heart so hungry for pleasure, there could be no bliss so supreme as a ride in the village "Libraty Car"—to be one of the states, preferably "Oregon!" To hear the music and hold a flag, and sit close to the little girls of her own age who would smile kindly at her and, perhaps, even ask her name shyly, and take her home with them to see their dolls.

"Oh," she cried, grasping the reins in her thin hands, "I'm all of a tremble! Just like maw on wash days! Only I ain't tired—I'm just glad."

There were shifting groups of children in front of the school house. Everything—even the white houses with their green blinds and neat dooryards—seemed strange and over-powering to Esther. The buoyancy with which she had surveyed the world from the back of a tall horse gave way to sudden timidity and self-consciousness.

Mr. Hoover put her down in the midst of the children. "There, now," he said cheerfully, "play around with the little girls like a nice body while I put up the horses."

A terrible loneliness came upon Esther as she watched him leading away the horses. All those merry children chattering and shouting, and not one speaking to her or taking the slightest notice of her. She realized with a suddenness that dazed her and blurred everything before her country eyes that she was very, very different from them—why, every one of the little girls was dressed in pure, soft white, with beautiful sash and bows, all wore pretty slippers. There was not one copper-toed shoe among them!

Her heart came up into her thin, little throat and beat and beat there. She wished that she might sit down and hide her shoes, but then the dress was just as bad. *That* couldn't be hidden. So she stood awkwardly in their midst, stiff and motionless, with a look in her eyes that ought to have touched somebody's heart.

Then the "Liberty Car" came, drawn by six noble white horses decorated with flags, ribbons and rosettes, and stepping out oh, so proudly in perfect time with the village band. Esther forgot her buff calico dress and her copper-toed shoes in the exquisite delight of that moment.

The little girls were placed in the car. Each carried a banner on which was painted the name of a state. What graceful, dancing little bodies they were, and how their feet twinkled and could not be quiet! When "Oregon" went proudly by, Esther's heart sank. She wondered which state they would give to her.

The band stopped playing. All the girls were seated; somehow there seemed to be no place left for another. Esther went forward bravely and set one copper-toed shoe on the step of the car. The ladies in charge looked at her; then, at each other.

"Hello, Country!" cried a boy's shrill voice behind her suddenly. "My stars! She thinks she's goin' in the car. What a jay!"

Esther stood as if petrified with her foot still on the step. She felt that they were all looking at her. What terrible things human eyes can be! A kind of terror took hold of her. She trembled. There seemed to be a great stillness about her.

"Can't I go?" she said to one of the ladies. Her heart was beating so hard and so fast in her throat that her voice sounded far away to her. "My paw knows Mr. Mallory, the store-keeper. We live down by the river on the Nesley place. We're poor, but my paw alwus pays his debts. I come with Mr. Hoover; he's gone to put up the horses."

It was spoken—the poor little speech, at once passionate and despairing as any prayer to God. Then it was that Esther learned that there are silences which are harder to bear than the wildest tumult.

But presently one of the ladies said, very kindly—"Why, I am so sorry, little girl, but you see—er—all the little girls who ride in the car must—er—be dressed in white."

Esther removed her foot heavily from the step and stood back.

"Oh, look!" cried "Oregon," leaning from the car. "She wanted to ride *in here*! In a yellow calico dress and copper-toed shoes!"

Then the band played, the horses pranced and tossed their heads, the flags and banners floated on the breeze, and the beautiful car moved away.

Esther stood looking after it until she heard Mr. Hoover's voice at her side. "W'y, what a funny little girl! There the car's gone, an' she didn't go an' git in it, after all! Did anybody ever see sech a funny little girl? After gittin' up so airly, an' hurryin' everybody so for fear she'd be late, an' a-talkin' about ridin' in the Libraty Car for months—an' then to go an' not git in it after all!"

Esther turned with a bursting heart. She threw herself passionately into his arms and hid her face on his breast.

"I want to go home," she sobbed. "Oh, I want to go home!"

ISAPHENE'S WHITE HAT

Mariella sat out in the clover with the baby in her lap. The immaculate, unfreckled Isaphene [Mallory] sat beside her with folded hands, her dress spread out stiffly to prevent wrinkles. Two or three smaller Mallorys were sitting up primly in the grass. They were not above getting into mischief. They were merely making acquaintance with their surroundings and awaiting large opportunities.

Mariella had a look of suffering on her face. As a rule she loved babies, but not a Mallory baby. She hated all children with fat legs and no freckles. Most of all she hated the spotless Isaphene, with her smooth curls and perpetual smile of friendliness; her unwrinkled dress and her white chip hat which she had worn all summer without getting so much as a fly-speck on it; her pretty legs—which she never "braided" as Mariella did hers—and her well-behaved elbows which never got out at right angles to her plump little body.

As Mariella devoured her with her eyes, and listened with a kind of fierce patience to her small talk about her dolls and her dresses and her new organ, a black thought came into her mind and stayed there. O, that it were spring, and the Maydukes hung red and juicy in the big tree above them, and she might climb the tall ladder and entice her unsuspecting guest up behind her, and then turn and squeeze a big cherry, drop after drop, drop after drop, upon that chaste chip hat!

It was a horrible, sinful thought; and she repulsed it with shudders. But it returned. She tried to think of something else. She told herself that there were no cherries; that the stains would never come out; that she was wicked, and God would never love her again for thinking of such a thing; she talked about the new pigs, dwelling upon the "little white runt" with the black tail; about the bumblebees that would climb down into the crimson holly-hocks; about the little russet pears that lay so thick under the trees that you couldn't step for them; she even gave her finger to the baby and tried to force herself to kiss him—and failed. And when her strength gave out, lo, there was the same thought, just as black and just as firmly fixed in her mind as before.

She got up suddenly, almost rolling the baby out of her lap. "Do you like currants?" she asked. Her eyes glowed at Isaphene out of a pale, frightened face. Her heart hammered her throat as she awaited the answer.

"What is it?" asked Isaphene, in her thin, polite tone.

"Do you like currants?"

"What is it?"

"I say, do you like currants? *Currants!* Do you like currants?"

"I like 'em in spring."

"There's some on the vines now. Great big, juicy ones. Don't you want some?"

"I don't mind." Isaphene arose daintily. "Mother says they ain't got any flavor when they hang on so. What makes 'em hang on so? She says they never hung on so in Ioway."

"I don't know. Here, they're down this way. You sit on the clover, and I'll pick some and drop them down to you."

The unsuspecting guest obeyed, lifting her dress precisely as her mother would have done. Mariella, torn in that eternal con-flict between right and wrong which makes us all kin, stood over her. The currants were in her hand. The juice was in the currants, waiting to be squeezed out by those firm fingers—and oh, the soft whiteness of the hated hat! And yet—

Slowly she drew back her hand. The beating in her throat ceased. She drew a long breath of relief. The hat was all but saved when the unfortunate Isaphene did the one thing that could fire Mariella's most furious passion. She stretched out her plump legs and smoothed her stockings up over her dimpled knees. "Mariella," she said, wonderingly, "what makes your legs so thin?"

"I don't know," said Mariella, frigidly. "God, I guess."

A crimson splash descended swiftly upon the white hat.

Louise Gregg Stephens ("Katharine")
1843-1912

"**W**ill you, by kindly reading the accompanying MSS., ascertain if it be worthy a place in your columns? It is possessed of at least one merit—that of being a real experience." So read a note dated September 24, 1902, received and later published by the Sunday editor of the Portland *Oregonian*. The author of the note, Louise G. Stephens, continued, "I have found this life so novel and eventful that, thinking others might be interested, have thought of a series of letters descriptive of the trials and triumphs of inexperienced ranchmen" (*Oregonian*, 14 June 1903).

The editor read the manuscript, agreed that readers would, indeed, be interested and ran the "letters" in the pages of the Sunday *Oregonian* during the following months under the *nom de plume* of "Elizabeth." The descriptive letters were written as though to an old friend back East named "Nell," and they described with enormous charm and wit the adventures of the narrator, her husband Tom, and a second couple ("the Stanhopes"), who sold their homes in the city, bundled their household possessions into freight cars, and relocated on a ranch in rainy Western Oregon—all at a stage of life when most would have been looking forward to quiet retirement rather than adventure.

"But who *is* 'Elizabeth'?" readers of the *Oregonian* wanted to know. For months they had been charmed by her "letters" in the Sunday paper, but with no idea who she really was, how old she was, where she lived, or whether the happenings they were reading about were inventions or facts. A June 14, 1903, feature in the *Oregonian*, tantalizingly captioned "Who 'Elizabeth' Is," suggested the answers to these questions would be revealed.

In an attempt to gain further information, the Sunday editor of the *Oregonian* had written a letter to "Elizabeth" and asked for directions to her home. The idea was that a reporter would come around, interview her, get a picture of her house, and "her portrait to use as a vignette with it." Below is part of her reply, as quoted within the June 14, 1903, article:

Your letter of the 11th, received on the 18th, has murdered my sleep for the past two nights—not the complimentary part, but that talk of the "sending of a bright reporter for a story of 'Elizabeth' and picture of her home and herself." Ye gods! I can hardly think "on it and live." If this be "the penalty of success," then give me failure, age, even death. Truly, Mr.———, nothing in all this world could be more distasteful to me, and you would believe me if you knew my natural timidity and horror of publicity. But for the shelter of a nom de plume, I could never have written a line. . . .

Elizabeth as a "vignette." Heavens! How could I sleep under the shadow of such a possibility? I had to look up "vignette" in the dictionary—"a picture which vanishes gradually at the edge." I liked the vanishing feature; only when you make mine, please start the vanishing effect from the center.

Needless to say, the reporter was not dispatched. The *Oregonian* article concluded by saying, "And now the readers . . . know as much about 'Elizabeth' as those who publish and pay for her contributions, except her name—which doesn't matter."

Her name was Louise Gregg Stephens. She was born in 1843, and so was in her late fifties when she and her husband and the second couple, probably her brother and his wife, packed up and boarded the train for Oregon, about 1901. The ranch where the foursome took up their adventure was in the Coast Range near Philomath. In addition to Stephens' aversion to publicity, it is clear from reading her work that she was well educated, well read, and articulate, besides having a delicious sense of humor.

In later years, Louise and her husband, F. E. Stephens, the local agent for the *Oregonian*, moved to Corvallis. In 1905, the letters Stephens had published in the Portland newspaper were printed in book form as *Letters From An Oregon Ranch*; the book was reprinted in 1916 as *From An Oregon Ranch*. The author's pseudonym on both editions is not "Elizabeth" but "Katharine."

According to Wilma Waggoner, a friend of Stephens, it was the noted Oregon author, Eva Emery Dye, who encouraged Stephens to publish in book form. The intrepid Dye became interested in the "letters," secured Stephens' address from the Oregonian and wrote to her, urging publication. In a letter dated May 31, 1916, Waggoner wrote, "Mrs. S., who was very modest regarding her writing, answered that she did not think a publisher could be found. Mrs. Dye then asked her to send the clippings from the paper to her and she would take up the matter." Not long afterwards, A. C. McClurg & Company—Dye's publisher—forwarded a contract to Stephens.

Waggoner said the nom de plume "Elizabeth" was changed by McClurg to "Katharine"—"on account of the book *Elizabeth and her German Garden,* which was then much in vogue."

Louise G. Stephens died at age 69, on November 6, 1912, at her home in Corvallis. Her obituary in the *Daily Gazette Times* noted that she had been in poor health for over a year, and suffered from "a lingering illness with creeping paralysis" (8 November 1912). She was described as a "well known writer and journalist," and the article suggested she had also published in the *Ladies Home Journal,* but we have been unable to confirm this. Perhaps a third *nom de plume?*

Although Stephens insisted upon writing under the cloak of anonymity, she sought a public readership with which to communicate her experiences. She had a gift for writing humor and for portraying beauty, and she had much to tell that was worth sharing with readers—the adventures and misadventures of starting a new life under comparatively primitive conditions in her late fifties, her warm rapport with her husband, and her sense of awe as she discovered Oregon's natural beauty. *Letters From An Oregon Ranch* is a small treasure; the writing is skillful, witty, often very funny, and sometimes very beautiful.

Choosing one excerpt from this book was difficult—so we chose two. The first is a brief sample of Stephens' descriptive prose that we have called "I Am A Believer Now." The second selection, "Our Feathered Folk," takes place after months of "egg famine" have concluded with the acquisition of some hens. Once the hens at last begin to lay, and the taste for eggs is sated, the latter-day pioneers, Katharine and Tom, look forward to raising some chickens.

I Am a Believer Now

There was a time when I was rather skeptical of the existence of a "beauty that intoxicates," but that was before coming to Oregon. I am a believer now, and already half inebriated through the charm of this latest revelation. For a long time I have been sitting on an old stump—one of the decorative features of our woodland lawn—looking over this wonderland and regretting the years lost in finding it.

For the first and only time in my life, I am happy and content in my environment. . . . Such a sky as we have here today—blue as a harebell, and much the shape of one, its rim just resting upon this crown of dark firs; crawling up its western edge, a low line of white wreathing clouds, as if the sea, rolling high, were dashing its foam here. A luminous flood of sunshine is in the air, soft, caressing, and sweet with the aromatic breath of the fir trees; brooding over all is "Nature's own exceeding peace," a hush unusual even in this land of silence. . . . The only sounds that come to me in this peaceful Eden are those of softly rippling invisible waters, the low murmur of insects, the occasional dropping of the tiny brown cones of the alders, and a faint rustle of falling leaves. Nothing more. . . .

But we have a visitor who has brought his voice with him. He has but lately come to us, from out of the reeds and rushes of the lowlands—a meadow lark. Every morning comes floating up to us from this little glen a melody so divine that the angels above must fold their wings to listen. . . . Tears fill my eyes as I listen. . . .

All about me the dandelions are lifting high in air their gauzy white balloons. They are quite different from ours at home, which were low growers; and if one rashly attempted to cut down one of the white-headed veterans, his head fell off and blew away. Here they are nearly two feet high, and that hollow starry globe of lacework is a wonderful stayer. Nearly a month ago, tempted by the beauty of these delicate transparencies, I cut a few of the slender stems and stuck them in a pot of growing ferns, not expecting them to last more than a few hours; and here they are today, those fairy balloons just lifted above the green, fully inflated and tugging at their guy ropes. . . .

Farmers may despise the thistle, but I'm sure the butterflies love it. Oh, the beauties I have seen this day—not the delicately tinted butterflies of summer, but living, glowing jewels, fluttering always above the thistles! One rested for a long time upon a purple bloom quite near me, opening and closing his exquisite wings of black and gold, sun-illumined, like dainty, gauzy Japanese fans.

I must . . . tell you of the beauty of that towering hill directly in front of us. . . . We had quite forgotten the many maple trees growing upon its slopes, the green of their foliage in the summertime being lost in that of the firs. Though we forgot, autumn remembered; and, grieved that her favorites should remain unrecognized in that monotony of green, she stole softly into the shadowy forest, traced up the lost Cinderellas, and then, with the gorgeous dyes of Turner and the brush of an impressionist, splashed all their broad leaves with that ineffable glory which is the distinctive badge of the maple family. . . .

Such a blaze of beauty so near the sky seems passing strange to me coming from a level country, seems alien to this world, and I half believe it to be a celestial landslide. I look, and look and am thrilled through every fiber of my being. I feel such excitement, buoyancy, exultation, I want to absorb it all, to catch the luminous picture with its wavering lights, its tremulous shadows, and fold it away in memory as a sort of sacred amulet, a charm to be brought from its hiding place when the dull days come, as come they must in every human life.

Our Feathered Folk

One day I was out raking the yard when Tom, coming up the walk, said: "Brace yourself for painful news. This very day two hens belonging to those shameless Stanhopes were set—or sat— which would you say?"

Two fowls, dusting themselves under a rose bush near us, apparently overheard this talk; one of them sprang up and really did seem to say, quite sharply, "What's that?"

"I said, madam," answered Tom, "that the Stanhopes have two hens set; and I ask, 'Why stand ye here all the day idle?' You are a Plymouth dame, and should have the Plymouth conscience." . . .

Whether or not our hens were influenced by this talk will probably never be definitely known, but a couple of weeks later the setting craze broke out among them, raging as fiercely as the Egyptian plague. Clucking hens were everywhere, some setting in the most ludicrous places, others in their proper boxes, often two and sometimes even three on the same nest. The non-setters persisted in depositing their eggs with the setters, which resulted in noisy vituperations, with scratchings from sharp claws and jabbings from vicious beaks. . . .

Meanwhile the demand for eggs grew strenuous. We could not get half enough to supply the emergency call. Everywhere were hens setting on nothing. One in the woodhouse, with imbecile credulity, was placidly brooding a broken doorknob. . . . Out of pity for their needs, I urged Tom to "take to the hills" for supplies. . . .

Returning about dark with a full basket, obtained with difficulty from various sources, he hastened to visit the home of each feathered recluse and furnish it with supplies; after which this good Samaritan sank in exhaustion upon a convenient log, . . .

This was only the beginning of trouble. Two obstinate hens were holding the fort in one barrel; neither would give up. With great sagacity, as I thought, I advised putting another barrel there with a nest in it, and the removal of Miss Flite thereto. "You know, her brain is a little muddled," I added, "and she won't know one barrel from the other."

"Don't fool yourself!" was the ominous reply, as my plans were being executed.

The next morning he came in, saying, "Just as I expected! Both those hens are again on the same nest."

After due deliberation, the oracle thought it quite probable that Miss Flite was the original owner of the nest, and was holding it by right of discovery.

"Why not try Mrs. Pardiggle on the other?"

"It's no use, she won't stay; but I'll chuck her in."

And he was right; she would have none of it, but flounced out in high dudgeon as often as put in. Tom then fell back on "common sense" and his mythical experience at "Uncle Jim's," placing a partition in the barrel with a nest on each side of it—an arrangement which seemed satisfactory to both parties. All went well for about a week, when it was found that the straw had sunk below the partition, and, the avoirdupois of Mrs. Pardiggle being the greater, the eggs had all rolled into her nest. She was sitting on twenty-six, while poor Miss Flite had none; but as the latter seemed blissfully unconscious of any deficit, while the former, owing to her voluminous foliage, could easily cover all the eggs, we thought it best to leave their tranquility undisturbed.

Thirteen chickens were the result of this co-operative incubation. Tom happened to be at the barn when the triumphant Pardiggle, with loud maternal cluckings, sailed out of it with the entire brood of fledglings at her heels. It seemed to him that a light suddenly shone in upon the befogged intellect of Miss Flite; for, screaming maniacally, she dashed from her compartment and flew into the midst of the brood, making frantic efforts to secure a fair division of the spoils.

"I hope you gave her some of them," I said to Tom when he had finished his narration.

"Yes, six; though feeling that I was foolishly sentimental in doing it."

"No, Tom, it was right and just—a merited reward for twenty-one days of inefficient faithfulness."

I am grieved to relate that Mrs. P., with unscrupulous pertinacity, through bribes and blandishments, lured all those chickens back except two, which Miss Flite continued "to have and to hold" until they grew into a beautiful and independent young pullethood.

If it surprises you that our mania for names is carried into poultrydom, just observe fowls closely for a time, and you will discover that not only are they possessed of marked individuality, but also of many of the characteristics of people you have known. For instance, a dapper glossy black hen had a topknot like a high silk hat, and grotesquely long wing feathers resembling a frock coat, which gave her such a look of masquerading in male attire that "Dr. Mary Walker" seemed the only possible name for her. "The Doctor" is an impulsive, self-willed creature. Observing her friends going, one by one, "into the silence," she apparently reasoned that the social whirl was over, that it would probably be dull in the yard for a time, and so concluded to go into the setting business herself. Looking the quarters over, she found a desirable flat; and though the rooms were all taken, she arrogantly ousted a timid, dark-complexioned tenant of Spanish descent, taking immediate possession of her home, her goods and chattels. The evicted one hung about her old home, lamenting bitterly; and though frequent efforts were made to reinstate her, all were futile. No matter how often or how violent "The Doctor's" removal, an hour later she would be found back in the same place. Losing patience at last, Tom said in disgust: "Well, stay there, then you confounded old trespasser! You look ridiculous enough, perched up there, with your hat on and your coat-tails hanging over that box. You have just taken this up as a fad, and you'll mighty soon be sick of it!"

If "The Doctor" heard, she made no sign, but continued to gaze steadfastly toward the Pacific Ocean, and never turned a feather. Having won the battle, she settled down to business in a resolute way; and we thought that perhaps, after all, she wasn't so flighty as she looked.

A week later Tom said, "You can't guess whom I saw in the woods today."

"Robin Hood?"

"No."

"Friar Tuck?"

"No; one more guess and you're out."

After deep thought I hazarded, "Countess Irma and her little wood-carver."

"Oh, you're away off! It was Dr. Mary Walker."

"Good gracious! What was she doing away up there?"

"Sauntering along the brook, with a gay bevy of friends, picking up pebbles and grasses, seemingly quite care-free and joyous."

After this she was seen every day stalking over the fields. Great was our surprise when we found she really had hatched seven chickens. But having hatched them, she apparently didn't want them, or know what to do with them. She just stood in a far corner of the coop and eyed them gloomily, making no effort to feed, amuse, or instruct them. She evidently never told them a word about hawks, and the very first day they were allowed to go out for exercise two were carried off, and the next day another; the following morning she came straight to the house with the remaining four, threw them on my hands, walked off among the tall ferns, and never came back to them. The little dew-bedraggled things stood in a shivering huddle, peeping for their mother, until my nerves could no longer endure it. I brought them in, fed, and wrapped them up warmly; but still came those anxious cries, shrill and incessant. . . . Looking around for a weight that would "feel like the hen," an inspiration seized me. I took the fluffy feather duster, warmed it slightly, and placed it over them, and was instantly rewarded by hearing a soft, gentle twittering—"the low beginnings of content," which soon ended in perfect quiet. . . .

After that, whenever an ailing chicken was brought to me for treatment, I usually clapped the duster over it and let nature take its course. Sometimes, it is true, when I lifted the duster to take a look at the patient, the patient was dead; but then it was quiet, and that's something. I feel a great pride in being the discoverer of the feather-duster mother, and am quite sure that no other poultry preserve in the United States has as yet realized its possibilities.

Lydia Taylor
1873-?

From the perspective of almost twenty years as a prostitute, Lydia Taylor wrote her autobiography, *From under the Lid: An Appeal to True Womanhood* (1913), both as a progressive argument for social change and as an explanation for how she became entrapped in prostitution. Taylor's book was published in the same year as the *Report of the Portland [Oregon] Vice Commission,* one of many vice reports issued across the country during the Progressive era, and her rhetorical purpose was clearly in harmony with the reform movement. In the Preface to *From under the Lid,* Lydia Taylor wrote: "The great moral wave throughout the country prompts me to lay open my past; show the cause, effect, and prove to the public that much of the harm and immorality in this old world has its inception in the home."

With the details of her life as data for her claims, Taylor argued that women, specifically prostitutes, should not be blamed for their position in society. Instead, she cast prostitutes as the victims of poverty, abuse, and men's hypocrisy. To assure a better life for other women, Taylor called for social reform and appealed directly to mothers, urging them to protect their daughters from men who preyed on young girls, within and outside the home, and to instruct them about the sexual appetites of men and the evils of prostitution.

At age seventeen, when she entered her first marriage, in Stillwater, Minnesota, Taylor was armed only with three years of schooling, nine months of training as an apprenticed dressmaker, her beauty, and her wits. She carried the knowledge that her parents were not married; in later years, she also learned that her father had abandoned his lawful wife and four children to run away with Taylor's mother, who was only sixteen at the time.

Lydia Taylor's first marriage ended when she discovered that her husband was "a shiftless thing, who was scarcely able to support himself, not to mention a wife" (*From under the Lid* 23). She escaped to an alliance with a man who promised to protect and teach her, "the only human being who has ever shown me any consideration and kindness." From this man, Taylor learned about books, culture, and what it meant "to be a lady." When he died, Taylor mourned the loss of her scholar gentleman—"my best and the only friend I ever had" (24).

At the age of twenty, Taylor was in Minneapolis, where she and her sister Eliza tried to survive as dressmakers. But, in Taylor's words, "the die was cast" when Eliza introduced Taylor to the dazzle and glitter of a Minneapolis brothel. From there, Taylor began twenty years of wandering to "every state in the west, but one, from Canada to Mexico" (27). At times she worked as a prostitute, at other times as a dressmaker.

Three other marriages occurred in fairly rapid succession. Taylor's second marriage was in Anaconda, Montana, and she traveled for a time "with a theatrical company, winding up in a variety show" (32). She "soon tired of that life," settled in Butte, and eventually obtained a divorce. Her third marriage, in Baker City, Oregon, was to a saloon keeper. Within a period of about two years, the couple "drifted apart" and were divorced. Her fourth marriage was in Oregon City, Oregon, in 1912, the year preceding publication of her autobiography.

Lydia Taylor captioned this photograph from her book From under the Lid: "A smile that the egoists see more in than it conveys."

Taylor was not unlike the majority of prostitutes interviewed for eight studies published from 1911 to 1916 and summarized by historian Ruth Rosen in *The Lost Sisterhood: Prostitution in America, 1900-1918*. Like the women in the studies, Taylor appears to have entered prostitution due to "bad home conditions" and "economic need" (Rosen 146). She, too, "slipped in and out of prostitution as economic need required" (150). And, not unlike other prostitutes of her era, Taylor sought escape from prostitution but found herself caught in a mesh of male sexual exploitation and patriarchal sexual values. But Taylor, unlike the vast majority of prostitutes, left a published record. Rosen has questioned the authenticity of extant personal memoirs which might not have been written by prostitutes but "by reformers anxious to point out the dangers that led young women to prostitution" and, in a specific reference to Taylor's book, she wrote that it "appears to be from the hand of a zealous reformer, who may or may not have based it on facts" (202).

The authenticity of Taylor's story appears to be established in public records, however. For example, our search of the Clackamas County, Oregon, records revealed that, as stated by Taylor, her fourth marriage, to a man named "Roy," occurred on October 22, 1912, in Oregon City, at the home of friends. The marriage certificate shows that Roy B. Taylor and Lydia Starr were married on that date by a county judge at the Oregon City residence of Mr. and Mrs. W. B. Hunsaker.

To determine the authenticity of Taylor's claim that, prior to her 1912 marriage to "Roy," she was a prostitute in Baker City, Oregon, and married and divorced a "saloon keeper" (*From under the Lid* 36), we turned to the census records. We were aware that census records rarely include prostitutes, but our search proved surprisingly fruitful.

A *Lillian* Starr, identified as white, divorced, and a prostitute, appeared in the original schedules of the U.S. Thirteenth Census, 1910, for Baker County, Oregon, and we believe that this is probably Lydia Starr Taylor. Prostitutes commonly changed their first names when they moved to new locations, a practice defined by Rosen as "an interesting initiation rite" in which the new name "made a new claim on the individual's loyalties to her past through the purposeful elimination of an older identity" (102).

Lillian Starr of Baker City was listed without children, head of household, and living alone in a rented house on Auburn Avenue, in a neighborhood of twenty prostitutes on Auburn Avenue and Horseshoe Alley. Three of the twenty prostitutes were identified as Japanese and two as mulattoes. Four, including Starr, were listed as divorced, three as married, and two as widowed. Five had borne children. The average recorded age was just under twenty-six, and all but two could read and write. All were employed as prostitutes on their "own account" (self-employed).

In her autobiography, Taylor wrote of living in Baker City in 1910, "next door to girls, some of whom were not over twenty, if that old" (62). Moreover, she clearly disapproved of racially mixed transactions between clients and prostitutes along her street, probably Auburn Avenue, and "over in the alley," probably a reference to Horseshoe Alley.

Lillian Starr's age was recorded in the census as twenty-two. Age was a sensitive issue for prostitutes, and Taylor may have wanted clients and officials alike to think she was twenty-two, not her actual age of thirty-seven. Youth and personal appearance were the prostitute's currency; both would fade, and life expectancy was short. Taylor, however, at the age of forty, expressed pride in her appearance and longevity: "They tell me that statistics prove the average life of a fast woman is limited to five years, so if the old-time saying holds good, and statistics show it to be the case, I must be a rare specimen of bric brac" (86).

To confuse matters more, the census taker recorded France as Lillian Starr's place of birth, 1905 as the year of her arrival in the country—but her language as English, not French. Perhaps this reflects Taylor's longing for a romantic French identity rather than her rural Kansas roots. We know she felt a special connection to France, for she wrote that her ambition was "to study French, and go abroad, and find out for my own satisfaction if the same conditions exist in other countries as here" (100).

But what of Taylor's claim that she had married a "saloon keeper" in Sumpter, Baker County, and later divorced him? A 1905 census of Baker County listed Charles W. Starr, age forty, as a single "saloon man" in North Sumpter and also in South Sumpter. Henry Starr, age thirty, was a single "saloon man" in South Sumpter. Although no records have yet been located, we think it likely that Lydia/Lillian Starr married and divorced either Charles or Henry Starr between 1905 and 1910.

Contrary to Rosen's suspicion that Taylor's autobiography was not based on fact but was, instead, the work of a "zealous reformer," our research has convinced us that Taylor was what she said she was—a prostitute working in Oregon at around the turn of the century—and that she was making an appeal for social change by telling of her own experiences. To represent Taylor's exigence for reform, we have selected excerpts from her autobiography, which we have titled "The Die Was Cast."

What Taylor most desired—a stable "home, sweet home"—had never been within her reach, either as a child or an adult. She had coped with the realities of an impoverished and abusive childhood, only to struggle in an adulthood marked by prostitution, loss of savings and valuables to various men, and four failed marriages. In childhood and adulthood, "grand, beautiful nature" was Lydia Taylor's one constant source of comfort and inspiration.

THE DIE WAS CAST

From my earliest recollection, from about the age of four until I grew to womanhood, I lived in daily fear of the constant quarrels and continual bickerings in the home life. How often, oh, how often, have I listened to the heart-rendering cries and screams from my mother that would echo and re-echo through the house. Cursing, swearing, crashing of furniture, smashing of dishes and windows, banging of doors, tables and chairs overturned, all of this an almost daily occurrence. Many a time have we seen father bending over mother prostrate on the floor, choking her into an unconscious condition, his eyes glaring with a murderous look as he did so. A pleasant (?) home, was it not?

Oftimes we children would run and hide until all was quiet, fearing and hesitating to return for fear of seeing the lifeless, mutilated body of our mother. As years dragged on their quarrels became even more frequent. . . .

At the age of ten my father sold the farm and declared his intention of going to the southern part of the state. . . .

Mother had been making preparations for the long trip and finally the day arrived for our departure. Father hitched up the two old nags, Dick and Jim, to the covered wagon, and drove up to the door and loaded on only what we would actually need on a trip of that kind. The load comprised a feather bed, a few pieces of pieced calico quilts, blankets, one trunk, and a few cooking utensils. Then we all "piled" in, presenting a picture for Puck; but I could scarcely suppress a sob, as father started off leaving my poor dog, who looked up at me with almost human-life intelligence shining in his eyes, wagging his tail, begging in a brute way to go along—my only companion that had followed for several years at my heels, lightening my burden by rounding up the stock that had strayed from the herd. He had been faithful to a fault, and now was cast aside. . . .

For days and days, especially in the darkness of the night, I could hear ringing in my ears the mournful howl and cry of my poor dog as we drove away. . . .

Once father kicked me down stairs, and I was picked up by my mother, unconscious, remaining so for several hours.

At another time a stray cat visited the farm; father set the dog on the poor thing, and for hours they fought until she was scarcely recognizable, nothing left but a mass of flesh and broken bones. . . .

At the age of seventeen I was married to a man of twenty, a bookkeeper by profession, who had been born and raised in Stillwater. My mother rushed the marriage along by saying I had gone with him long enough, and if I did not get married I must leave home. So we were married; he leaving the next day for Great Falls, Mont., and I did not hear from him for six weeks. In the meantime I continued sewing by the day, as he had left me no money. After he had been gone ten days, and finding out he had not written, mother heaped insults and curses upon me, saying I had disgraced the family, and to get out, which I did. . . .

When I got to Minneapolis, my oldest sister joined me. We rented a room, a front one, in a lodging house and put out a dressmaking sign, but we had little work to do, scarcely enough to pay room rent and our two meals a day, part of the time eating cold lunches in our room. My sister seemed to be getting very down hearted and discouraged. The world, you know, looks entirely different to those who eat porterhouse steaks and those who have to live on cold lunches. To the one, the world is bright and gay, to the other, life is as cold as the food they eat. Sister dressed to go out one afternoon, refusing to say where she was going. She did not return that night, and not until late in the afternoon the following day did she come in. After returning she commenced packing up her meager belongings, telling me to do likewise; nor would she tell me where we were going until nearly there. But she had given me confidence, and I had no intention then of turning back, although the thoughts of going to such a place were revolting. However, the die was cast. The wind had blown the good fates to one side, and the victims of vice had two more souls added to their number on that day. Just two more girls, hungry and destitute, seeking for food and shelter, and despite our vaunted Christian civilization, having to go to hell to get them. Just two more victims to pander to the vice of man. Man, the so-called protector of woman, but always the destroyer of them, was not there to warn us of the thorny path that we were to tread, but on the other hand, they were there with their licentiousness and animal dispositions, apparently full of glee that they could have for new companions in their depravity some who were younger than some of the others.

I was then twenty years old, and, perhaps, somewhat attractive. The house where we went was large, richly and elaborately furnished. Rich tapestry, expensive rugs on more carpets, in fact all that perfect taste and skill could do; every thing had been done for the sole object of lulling the mind away from care and into a dream of forgetfulness. 'Twas like a fairy land to my poor starved soul. Picture for yourself the great change from a poorly furnished room in a third rate rooming house to a place furnished with all the gorgeousness and richness that money could buy. The dazzling chandeliers of richly tinted lights which at night sent a glow throughout the rooms that seemed to beckon me on. A ballroom, where I was to take my first lesson in dancing. Scattered around on divans and lounges were courtesans, lightly clad, reposing in tempting ease to stir and tempt the vulgar, amorous blood of the masculine frequenters. It was the beauty of my surroundings that marked the course and held me a willing captive ever after in the downward life that knows no pause.

We stayed there long enough to get a few evening robes, silk undergarments, and other necessary articles of wearing apparel known to those in this life. For many years after entering that place the humiliation of my past was forgotten. I had schooled myself, not to care—not to think. It is only in late years, as I have grown older, and, I trust, wiser, that my past comes up like a specter to haunt me. But no one cares—the world doesn't care. I, alone, must bear the brunt of my own folly, and pay the penalty. . . .

I was introduced to my last "affinity" ["Roy"] through a respectable, honorable family, and this is said in all sincerity, who had known him for eight years. He was well spoken of, and coming from that source it carried weight. As it was, after a short courtship, we were married in Oregon City, Ore., October 22, 1912, at my lady friend's apartments, and I don't think I was ever so happy and contented. I was so thoroughly satisfied, that to be with him alone, apart from any other enjoyment was sufficient in itself. Just in a few weeks my whole life had changed, even my hideous past seemed to fade away in the distance; even my dislike for the human race would melt in sympathy in his presence. I was like a child again, and I felt that to be with him I could have overcome the bitterness engendered through years of experience. My whole heart and soul were wrapped up in my husband, and the little four-room apartment we had furnished. I paid out of my own bank account one hundred and fifty dollars for silverware, steak set, salad set, pearl handle carving set, individual butter knives, three sets of dainty individual pepper and salt shakers, creamer spoon, berry spoon, and many other pieces of silver. What they did not have in stock I put in an order for. Each piece of silverware was engraved with an old English "T." I also bought a few pieces of cut glass, vinegar cruet, oil bottle and water jug. My table linen was of the best, and I was very proud of everything, as my husband complimented me on my taste.

The day after we were married we went over to Portland to do a little shopping, also to get a thousand dollars out of the bank for my husband, that amount he claimed would put him out of debt to his partner and $400 to put in the bank over there to our credit.

The next day he took "French leave"—skipped out, taking some of his partner's money, and, of course, mine. When twelve o'clock came and he did not return, I became worried and started out to look for him, expecting to meet him then on his way home, but I didn't, and, as his place of business was closed, I returned and awakened his partner, who was living in apartments in the same building. He then handed me an envelope, the contents of which are still engraven on my memory. My heart was broken. From that moment I lost all faith and every remnant of hope. . . .

Just think. Married and deserted in three days! . . .

It is my one desire now to be left alone. I am through with men, and hope, after perusing the pages of what I have written it will be a protection against them. I don't believe any real sensible man would want me, knowing my past. I hardly think time will ever efface the painful events I have just passed through, nor will I ever again allow my fancy to soar, as I have found, at bitter cost, my judgment to be entirely unreliable. . . .

Portland is now supposed to have closed the "lid" down real tight, but I have been here off and on for five years, and it never was so ROTTEN. At the present time I am rooming at a lodging house two blocks from Washington street, and to my knowledge there are eight or ten women, all of whom are entertaining men in their rooms. Men are coming up all hours of the night asking for girls, and they are shown to the rooms. The clerk is supposed to get his tip out of the amount the man spends.

Some of these women hang around the Fittsburg Grill, a tough resort, where drinks are sold with lunches, chili con carni, stale sandwiches, and food of a various nature, unfit to eat, is in display.

Most of these girls are living with parasites. In the spring of the year 1911 I was housekeeper in a resort on North Seventh street.

The landlady was on a visit to California. During her absence we all had notice to close. After the place had been closed for a week an officer, a plainclothes man, dropped in and asked me if I was doing anything. I told him I was not. He then said I was foolish; that if I put up some money I would be able to run on the Q.T., and informed me that the other houses were doing business. Those houses are closed now, but the dives in the lower part of town are still in existence. It looks like the Governor started something he couldn't finish. . . .

Nature, grand, beautiful nature, when all else fails, is my one and only friend. . . .

She gives me beautiful thoughts and inspirations which carry me beyond my home (the city's garbage dump or sewerage troughs), and, indeed, without that all overpowering love for nature and her wonderful works, I would long ago have fallen by the wayside, or have drowned by the filth of the sewer pipes, to be washed down and out, and thrown upon the shore, unfit, even for the buzzards to peck at.

Hazel Hall
1886-1924

❖

Although Hazel Hall spent twenty-six years in a wheelchair, she once confided to a friend, "I am not unmindful of my advantage." Hall's instinctive wisdom, imagination, and aesthetic sensibility enabled her not only to cope with her handicap, but to transform the mundane and communicate symbolically through her art what she found within the silence of her solitude. Hall's poetry was her means of coping, of self-empowerment, and the legacy she left behind at the end of her brief life. "The facts of my sister's life were few," wrote Ruth Hall. "They were only a framework upon which was hung so much that found no words except in her poetry. Reality, to her, was so impersonal and diffused, that it made insignificant the tragic or seemingly tragic conditions of her existence" (quoted in introduction, Hazel Hall, *Cry of Time* 12).

Hazel Hall was born February 7, 1886, in St. Paul, Minnesota, but came to Portland with her family as a small child. Her parents were Mary Garland Hall and Montgomery G. Hall, and she had two sisters, Ruth and Lulie. Hall's childhood was apparently normal until the age of twelve, when she lost her ability to walk, either due to an accident or an attack of scarlet fever. She remained unable to walk until her death at age thirty-eight.

In 1917, the family moved to 52 Lucretia Street (now 104 Northwest 22nd Place), and Hall spent the rest of her life in that Portland home (Franklin, *A Tribute to Hazel Hall* 14). Unable to attend public school beyond fifth grade, she educated herself through reading and through close observation of the lives of others. Her sister, Ruth, said: "I have never known a better educated person, in the richest sense of the word. She browsed where she wanted to . . . and with a broad intuitive sense, she grasped facts quickly in their entirety" (quoted in Saul, *Quintet* 22). Some of her favorite authors were Edna St. Vincent Millay, Elinor Wylie, Emily Dickinson, Robert Frost, Lytton Strachey, Katherine Mansfield, and Virginia Woolf (Franklin 30).

Hazel Hall's days were spent sitting at her window reading or doing fine embroidery for bridal linens and christening gowns, while she observed the people who passed her house in the changing light of sun and shadow. These were the experiences and observations from which

she formed her poetry, which was crafted as meticulously as her needlework. Hall's eyes were her most arresting feature, large, luminous, unforgettable, even in photographs. But, during her last few years, her eyesight began to fail, forcing her to give up the intricate needlework with which she had occupied her time and earned money. Her artistic vision, however, grew stronger, as she turned more and more to her poetry when no longer able to sew. When she combined the two occupations in her "needlework" poems, she produced work which is unique and unparalleled.

Hazel Hall was thirty years old when her first published poem appeared in the *Boston Transcript* in 1916. Before her death, eight years later, she had published two volumes of poetry—*Curtains* in 1921 and *Walkers* in 1923—and she was preparing a third. This third volume, *Cry of Time*, which contains poems written only days before Hall's death, was collected by her sister, Ruth Hall, and published in 1928. In addition to the three books, approximately seventy-five poems by Hall were published between 1919 and 1925 in such periodicals as *New Republic, Outlook, Nation, Century, Sunset, Yale Review, Bookman,* and *Touchstone* (Franklin 24-27).

Although Hazel Hall is anthologized as a western poet, her work is not typically regional; place or landscape are not significant features of her poetry. When Hall writes of nature, it is of the grass, flowers, and

trees visible from her window, and they are used symbolically. At its
best, her poetry displays exquisite precision, certainty, and economy of
phrasing. Her poems are quiet; her touch is calm and sure. And we
agree with Louise Townsend Nicholl, who said of Hall's work: "They
are women poems. . . . The consciousness of a man, in that same
unveiled contact with reality, would be a different thing. It is not any
poet speaking—it is a woman poet, poet woman" (introduction, *Cry
of Time* 14). These lines from "Inheritance" are illustrative:

> But sorrow does not die, sorrow only gathers
> Weight about itself—a clay that bakes to stone.
> When your own share of sorrow has worn itself to slumber
> Then every woman's sorrow is your own.

Hazel Hall died at her mother's home at 52 Lucretia Street on May
11, 1924. Though the cause of her death, like the cause of her invalidism, remains unclear, Ruth Hall said, "The doctors called it heart
failure . . . She died quietly, without pain" (quoted in Saul 23). She
was survived by her mother and sisters.

Ruth Hall emphasized that invalidism was not what Hall would
have wanted stressed: "When anyone speaks of my sister as crippled, I
always feel rebellious, because she gave the impression of such abundant health. She enjoyed living immensely—her days were never long
enough for all the activities she wished to press into them. Except that
she did not walk, she was in good health until about six weeks before
her death" (quoted in Franklin 43).

One of the great joys for us as we prepared this anthology was in
discovering the unique, undisguised, female sensibility of Hazel Hall's
poetry. Her work is compassionate, personal, and yet coolly objective;
her subjects and metaphors are commonplace, and yet her artistry
gives them universal significance. When the common intimacies of life,
which most of us take as the touchstones of reality, were denied her,
Hall looked ever deeper inside her own mind—"fashioned as it were
by solitude," and in her poetry she left us the gift of what she found.

We quote Ruth Hall one last time: "Since my sister was fond of
silence and its larger meanings, she heartily disliked discussions of
herself as an individual. Rather she would want her poetry to speak of
herself—to represent her to those who might be interested in following
the flight of her mind" (quoted in Franklin 15).

We have chosen selections from each of Hazel Hall's three volumes.
The ellipses in these poems are Hall's and do not denote any omission.

INSTRUCTION

My hands that guide a needle
In their turn are led
Relentlessly and deftly
As a needle leads a thread.

Other hands are teaching
My needle; when I sew
I feel the cool, thin fingers
Of hands I do not know.

They urge my needle onward,
They smooth my seams, until
The worry of my stitches
Smothers in their skill.

All the tired women,
Who sewed their lives away,
Speak in my deft fingers
As I sew today.

From *Curtains*, 1921

A Baby's Dress

It is made of finest linen—
Sheer as wasp-wings;
It is made with a flowing panel
Down the front,
All overrun with fagot-stitched bow-knots
Holding hours and hours
Of fairy-white forget-me-nots.

And it is finished.
To-night, crisp with new pressing,
It lies stiffly in its pasteboard box,
Smothered in folds of tissue paper
Which envelop it like a shroud—
In its coffin-shaped pasteboard box.

To-morrow a baby will wear it at a christening;
To-morrow the dead-white of its linen
Will glow with the tint of baby skin;
And out of its filmy mystery
There will reach
Baby hands. . . .

But to-night the lamplight plays over it and finds it cold.
Like the flower-husk of a little soul,
Which, new-lived, has fluttered to its destiny,
It lies in its coffin-shaped pasteboard box.

To-morrow will make it what hands cannot:
Limp and warm with babyness,
A hallowed thing,
A baby's dress.

From *Curtains*, 1921

MONOGRAMS

I am monogramming
Seven dozen napkins,
With tablecloths to match,
For a bride.

Ninety-one times my needle shall trace
The leaf-like scrolls that interlace
Each other; up the padded side
Of the monogram my eye shall guide
For ninety-one days where the stitches run;
And every day one more is done.

She is tall and fair,
She will be married
In June. . . .

The linen is fine as satin is fine;
Its shining coolness flaunts design
Of death-white poppies, trailing ferns
Rioting richly from Grecian urns.

Ghost-flowers.
Cold, cold . . .

All these patterned splendours fade
Before the crest my hands have made;
In the lifeless flax my stitches cry
With life my hands may not put by.

June . . .
Real flowers,
Moist and warm to touch,
Like flesh . . .

And by and by with all the rest
Of intimate things in her bridal-chest,
Gentle muslins and secret lace,
Something of mine will have a place;
Caught in these scrolls and filigrees
There will be that which no eye sees,
The bulk of a season's smothered wonder,
My ninety-one days stitched under and under.

They will be decking an altar
With white roses,
And lacing an aisle
With white ribbon. . . .

From *Curtains*, 1921

TWO SEWING

The wind is sewing with needles of rain.
With shining needles of rain
It stitches into the thin
Cloth of earth. In,
In, in, in.
Oh, the wind has often sewed with me.
One, two, three.

Spring must have fine things
To wear like other springs.
Of silken green the grass must be
Embroidered. *One and two and three.*
Then every crocus must be made
So subtly as to seem afraid
Of lifting colour from the ground;
And after crocuses the round
Heads of tulips, and all the fair
Intricate garb that Spring will wear.
The wind must sew with needles of rain,
With shining needles of rain,
Stitching into the thin
Cloth of earth, in
In, in, in,
For all the springs of futurity.
One, two, three.

From *Curtains*, 1921

THE LISTENING MACAWS

Many sewing days ago
I cross-stitched on a black satin bag
Two listening macaws.

They were perched on a stiff branch
With every stitch of their green tails,
Their blue wings, yellow breasts and sharply
       turned heads,
Alert and listening.

Now sometimes on the edge of relaxation
My thought is caught back,
Like gathers along a gathering thread,
To the listening macaws;
And I am amazed at the futile energy
That has kept them,
Alert to the last stitch,
Listening into their black satin night.

From *Curtains*, 1921

MADE OF CRÊPE DE CHINE

A needle running in white crêpe de chine
Is not the frail servant of utility
It was designed to be;
It is an arrow of silver sunlight
Plunging with a waterfall.

And hands moving in white crêpe de chine
Are not slaves of the precedent
That governs them;
They are the crouching women of a fountain,
Who have sprung from marble into life
To bathe enthusiastically
In the brimming basin.

From *Curtains*, 1921

Summary

They are always looking for what they never find.
With eyes eager for sky they look ahead,
Mirroring for a moment the color of space.

They are always seeking a road to vividly wind
Out of the ways that have tamed and hurt their tread.
It is always before them like wind that brushes the face.

I am always looking for what I never find;
Peering and crying into my heart, I seek
The breath that is made of fire which shall fulfill.

I am always hungering for the undefined
Taste of a word I have not learned to speak.
My breath is wasted flame, my lips are still.

We are always seeking, and when we do not find,
One by one, we see the symbol of things
In the sky's illusion of light, in the wind's rebuff.

One by one, in the refuge of the mind,
We strive to give the understanding wings
And to make the brilliant flight of it enough.

From *Walkers*, 1923

WHITE BRANCHES

I had forgotten the gesture of branches
Suddenly white,
And I had forgotten the fragrance of blossoms
Filling a room at night.
In remembering the curve of branches
Who beckoned me in vain,
Remembering dark rooms of coolness
Where fragrance was like pain,
I have forgotten all else; there is nothing
That signifies—
There is only the brush of branch and white breath
Against my lips and eyes.

From *Cry of Time*, 1928

INHERITANCE

Over and over again I lose myself in sorrow;
Whatever I have borne I bear again tenfold.
The death of sorrow is a sleep; a newer sorrow
Wakes into flame from ashes of the old.

They said that sorrow died and that a sorrow buried
Made your mind a dear place like a grave with grass,
Where you might rest yourself as in a willow's shadow,
And cold and clean, might feel the long world pass.

But sorrow does not die, sorrow only gathers
Weight about itself—a clay that bakes to stone.
When your own share of sorrow has worn itself to slumber
Then every woman's sorrow is your own.

From *Cry of Time*, 1928

Epilogue

When we began our collection of writings and oral narratives by Pacific Northwest women in the nineteenth and early twentieth centuries, we were unaware of how rich and diverse the resources are. Nor did we have any presuppositions about what we would find. After exploring the lives and words of over two hundred women, thirty of whom appear in this volume, patterns began to emerge, and we identified the four major themes discussed and illustrated in this volume—connecting with nature, coping with difficult circumstances, caregiving to family and community, and communicating for self and others. When we then looked at how these themes function within the lives and writings of the women, we discovered the thesis which guided our thinking about sources of empowerment—*no woman in this volume writes or speaks from a position devoid of the authority or capacity to act.*

How are we to define what "being liberated" meant for western women during the period covered by this volume? For some feminist historians, liberation has been defined as political equity. This is one measure, but only one, and is probably not the most significant gauge. Our interpretations of women's empowerment have led us to agree, once again, with Glenda Riley, who writes: "To assume that women could be significant only when they expanded, or fled from, the domestic realm is to impute powerlessness to women, power to men. But women were already empowered and esteemable in their own world; women's contributions were worthy and satisfying in their own right" (*A Place to Grow* 4). Our sample of thirty women is representative, but clearly more work needs to be done to test the validity of autonomy-based and connection-based empowerment within the lives of women *and* men in the Pacific Northwest, as well as in other regions.

How did the experiences of men in the Pacific Northwest in this period compare with those of women? How did the region affect men's sense of autonomy-based and connection-based empowerment? Susan Armitage has suggested that when the real lives of western women are discovered female stereotypes of "the lady, the helpmate, and the bad woman" will be destroyed *as well as* "the male myths of adventure, individualism, and violence" (*The Women's West* 17). The marital partnerships described by Sarah Cummins, Susanna Ede, Esther Selover Lockhart, and Emma J. Ray suggest that men, as well as women, in the Pacific Northwest were empowered through connection, as well as autonomy.

How do men's lives and writings relate to the themes of nature, coping, caregiving, and communicating that we found in women's experiences? Did Pacific Northwest men, like the men in Christiane Fischer's study of the territories of California, Nevada, and Arizona, show "a much greater readiness in adjusting to the new environment" than the women (*Let Them Speak for Themselves* 14)? Our readings of the texts in this volume indicate that this was not the case in the Pacific Northwest.

How did being born in the early Pacific Northwest shape women's expectations and experiences? Were second-generation women empowered in different ways than first-generation women? The lives and writings of Susanna Ede, Bethenia Owens-Adair, and Emily Inez Denny suggest this may have been the case. And what of the experiences of second-generation women of color? What were the themes in their lives, and how were they empowered or disempowered? Regardless of which generation or ethnic group we are exploring, however, we must expect to find diversity and avoid what Glenda Riley refers to as "the trap of 'colonizing' types of women—older, single, religious, lesbian, women of color" (*A Place to Grow* 2).

The patterns or themes we discover in the Pacific Northwest should be viewed from as many angles of vision as possible, and in comparison with other regions. More defined and complete regional studies will permit valuable comparisons of how place affected women's and men's lives in the American West; questions about cross-regional differences and similarities in women's and men's empowerment can then be addressed.

Before regional comparisons can be made, however, we must learn how best to define region. Julie Roy Jeffrey, who examined the "frontier experiences" of two hundred white women in the trans-Mississippi West, did not fully distinguish by region (*Frontier Women*); Christiane Fischer, who looked at the experiences of twenty-four white women and one Indian woman in California, Nevada and Arizona, found these were "three adjoining territories which presented a great diversity of conditions" (*Let Them Speak for Themselves* 16). Clearly, to understand the role of place in shaping western experiences, "adjoining territories" is not always the best way to define region.

Emily Inez Denny

The concept of region as externally mapped land areas of geographical proximity ignores factors of internal significance to the people of the region. Although diversity of conditions will be found within any western region, we should expect to see more commonalities than differences in natural resources, climate, accessibility to and from areas outside the region, and ease of travel by land and water within the region. Other critical identifiers for western regions include cultures of oral tradition, arrival of competing systems of religious belief, and the introduction of the concept of property ownership with consequent conflicts over land division and land rights. In the region we have defined as the Pacific Northwest, these commonalities and identifiers are clear.

The recovery and interpretation of women's experiences in the Pacific Northwest is an ongoing process much like the creation and mending of a patchwork quilt—a quilt with no predetermined pattern, color, or even size. Each patch carries a woman's memories of specific times, places, and events. Some swatches have faded with time, and others are vibrant with color. Some fabrics are treasured remnants of fine silk, and others are simple homespun. Some are as fragile as gossamer lawn; others as enduring as pliable buckskin. The piecing of these patches requires patience, close stitches, and careful knotting. Sometimes the stitches must be taken out and redone; sometimes the quilting frame must be readjusted to accommodate the size and shape of the growing quilt. Our work is one piece toward identifying the patterns in the diverse experiences of Pacific Northwest women.

Bibliography

Margaret Jewett (Smith) Bailey

Selected Writings

Bailey, Margaret Jewett [Ruth Rover]. *The Grains; or, Passages in the Life of Ruth Rover, with Occasional Pictures of Oregon, Natural and Moral.* 2 vols. Portland: Carter and Austin, 1854. Rpt. edited and with an introduction by Evelyn Leasher and Robert J. Frank. Corvallis: Oregon State University Press, 1986.

———. "Affliction" [poem]. *Oregon Spectator* 4 March 1846.

———. "It Charms Me That I Hope to Live" [poem]. *Oregon Spectator* 22 July 1847.

———. "Ladies Department" [column; poems and short stories by R. R.]. *Oregon Spectator*, 12 May - 16 June 1854.

———. "Love" [poem]. *Oregon Spectator* 5 Feb. 1846.

———. "May Morning in Oregon" [poem]. *Oregon Spectator* 28 May 1846.

———. "New Columbia" [poem]. *Oregon Spectator* 26 Nov. 1846.

———. "Slander" [essay]. *Oregon Spectator* 19 Aug. 1847.

Selected Other Sources

Bingham, Edwin R. Foreword to reprint of *The Grains; or, Passages in the Life of Ruth Rover* by Margaret Jewett Bailey. Corvallis: Oregon State University Press, 1986.

Duncan, Janice K. "'Ruth Rover'—Vindictive Falsehood or Historical Truth?" *Journal of the West* 12 (April 1973): 240-53.

Frost, O. W. "Margaret J. Bailey: Oregon Pioneer Author." *Marion County History* 5 (1959): 64-70.

Leasher, Evelyn, and Robert J. Frank. Introduction to reprint of *The Grains* by Margaret Jewett Bailey. Corvallis: Oregon State University Press, 1986.

Nelson, Herbert B. "First True Confession Story Pictures Oregon 'Moral.'" *Oregon Historical Quarterly* 45 (June 1944): 168-76.

———. "Ruth Rover's Cup of Sorrow." *Pacific Northwest Quarterly* 50 (July 1959): 91-98.

Reviews of *The Grains* by "Squills." *Oregonian* 5 Aug. 1854; 9 Sept. 1854.

Tabitha Moffat Brown

Writing

Brown, Tabitha. "Documents. A Brimfield Heroine—Mrs. Tabitha Brown." *Oregon Historical Quarterly* 5 (June 1904): 199-205.

Selected Other Source

Smith, Jane Kinney. "Recollections of Grandma Brown." Ed. H. S. Lyman. *Oregon Historical Quarterly* 3 (Sept. 1902): 287-95.

Susie Revels Cayton

Selected Writings

Cayton, Susie Revels. "Black Baby Dolls" [speech to the Baptist Literary Society]. *Cayton's Weekly* [Seattle] 4 Jan. 1919: 3.

———. "A Brief Sketch of Hyram [sic] R. Revels." n. d. [1937?], item 188, Hiram R. Revels Papers. Schomburg Center for Research in Black Culture, New York Public Library.

———. "A Daughter of Solomon" [column]. *Cayton's Weekly* [Seattle] 11 May 1918; 25 May 1918; 1 June 1918.

———. "Licker" [unpublished, 3-page, typewritten short story], 1880 [?]. Susie Revels Cayton File, Cayton Papers, Vivian G. Harsh Collection, Chicago Public Library.

———. "Negroes at the Atlanta Exposition." *Seattle Republican* 4 Jan.1896.

———. "The Negro's Handicap: An Excuse or a Spur?" *Seattle Republican* 7 Feb. 1908: 2.

———. "Our Heroic Women." *Seattle Republican* 22 May 1908: 8.

———. "Sallie the Egg-Woman." *Seattle Post-Intelligencer* 3 June 1900: 33.

———. "The Storm." n.d. Susie Revels Cayton File, Cayton Papers, Vivian G. Harsh Collection, Chicago Public Library.

Selected Other Sources

Bell, S. Leonard. "Seattle's First Black Journalist." *Seattle Post-Intelligencer*, 1 Sept. 1968, *Northwest Today*: 11.

Borome, Joseph H. "The Autobiography of Hiram Rhodes Revels together with Some Letters by and about Him." *Midwest Journal* 5 (Winter 1952-53): 79-92.

Cayton, Horace R. [Jr.]. *Long Old Road*. Seattle: University of Washington Press, 1963. Rpt. New York: Trident Press, 1965.

Cayton, Horace R. [Sr.]. *Cayton's Year Book—Seattle's Colored Citizens*. Seattle: Horace R. Cayton and Son, New Year, 1923.

———. Special New Year's Issue. *Seattle Republican* 4 Jan. 1896.

Hobbs, Richard S. "The Cayton Legacy: Two Generations of a Black American Family, 1859-1976." PhD Diss. University of Washington, 1989.

———. "Horace Cayton—Seattle's Black Pioneer Publisher." *Seattle Times Magazine* 26 Feb. 1978: 9-10.

"Horace Cayton Passes at 81." *Seattle Post-Intelligencer* 18 Aug. 1940: 22.

Mumford, Esther Hall. *Seattle's Black Victorians, 1852-1910*. Seattle: Ananse Press, 1980.

Thompson, Julius Eric. "Hiram R. Revels, 1827-1901: A Biography." PhD Diss. Princeton University, 1973.

Stripling, Sherry. "Our Black Settlers." *Seattle Times* 3 Feb. 1984: D1.

Sarah J. Lemmon Walden Cummins

Writing

Cummins, Sarah J. Lemmon Walden. *Autobiography and Reminiscences*. La Grande, OR: La Grande Printing Co., 1914. Rpt. Fairfield, WA: Ye Galleon Press, 1968; 1987.

Emily Inez Denny

Selected Writings

Denny, Emily Inez. *Blazing the Way; or, True Stories, Songs, and Sketches of Puget Sound and other Pioneers*. Seattle: Ranier Printing Co., 1909. Rpt. with an introduction by Susan J. Torntore. Seattle: Seattle/King County Historical Society, 1984.

──────. *A Rare Wild Flower of Washington* [poetry]. San Francisco: n. p., 1893.

──────. "Sealth and Angeline." *The Souvenir of Western Women*. Ed. Mary Osborn Douthit. Portland, OR: Anderson & Duniway, 1905. 70-71.

Selected Other Sources

Denny, Arthur A. *Pioneer Days on Puget Sound*. 1908. Rpt. Fairfield, WA: Ye Galleon Press, 1979.

Torntore, Susan J. Introduction to reprint of *Blazing the Way, or, True Stories, Songs and Sketches of Puget Sound and Other Pioneers* by Emily Inez Denny. Seattle: Seattle/King County Historical Society, 1984.

Abigail Scott Duniway

Selected Writings and Oral Narratives

Duniway, Abigail Scott. "About Ourself." *New Northwest* 5 May 1871.

──────. *Captain Gray's Company, or; Crossing the Plains and Living in Oregon*. Portland: S. J. McCormick, 1859.

──────. *David and Anna Matson* [poetry]. New York: S. R. Wells & Co., 1876.

──────. "Editorial Correspondence" [column]. *New Northwest*, 1871-1887.

──────. "A Few Recollections of a Busy Life." *The Souvenir of Western Women*. Ed. Mary Osborn Douthit. Portland: Anderson & Duniway, 1905. 9-12.

──────. *From the West to the West: Across the Plains to Oregon*. Chicago: A. C. McClurg, 1905.

──────. "How I Became a Literary Woman." *The Western Lady*. Portland: n.p., 1904. 3.

──────. "Journal of a Trip to Oregon." Ed. David C. Duniway. Vol. 5 of *Covered Wagon Women: Diaries and Letters from the Western Trails, 1840-1890*. Ed. Kenneth L. Holmes and David C. Duniway. Glendale, CA: Arthur H. Clark Company, 1986. 21-172.

──────. "Mrs. Duniway's Reminiscences: How I Became a Suffragist." *Woman's Journal* [Boston] 31 Dec. 1898.

──────. *My Musings* [poetry]. Portland: Duniway Publishing Co., 1875.

──────. "The Pacific Northwest" [speech]. *The Congress of Women*. Ed. Mary Kavanaugh Oldham Eagle. Chicago: International, 1895. 90-96.

──────. *Path Breaking: An Autobiographical History of the Equal Suffrage Movement in Pacific Coast States*. Portland: James, Kerns & Abbott Co., 1914. Rpt. New York: Schocken Books, 1971.

──────. "Personal Reminiscences of a Pioneer." Vol. 3 of *Portland: Its History and Builders*. Ed. Joseph Gaston. Chicago: Clarke, 1911. 52-60.

──────. "Susan B. Anthony's Visits to Oregon." *The Souvenir of Western Women*. Ed. Mary Osborn Douthit. Portland: Anderson & Duniway, 1905. 36-37.

──────. "'Women's War with Whisky.'" *New Northwest* 11 Sept. 1874.

──────. Newspapers.

New Northwest [Portland, Oregon]. Edited by Abigail Scott Duniway, 1871-1887.

Pacific Empire [Portland, Oregon]. Edited by Abigail Scott Duniway, 1895-
1898.

————. Serialized Novels in the *New Northwest*:

Judith Reid: A Plain Story of a Plain Woman, 12 May 1871 to 22 Dec. 1871.

Ellen Dowd, the Farmer's Wife, part one, 5 Jan. 1872 to 26 Apr. 1872, and
part two, 1 July 1873 to 26 Sept. 1873.

Amie and Henry Lee; or, The Spheres of the Sexes, 29 May 1874 to 13 Nov.
1874.

The Happy Home; or, The Husband's Triumph, 20 Nov. 1874 to 14 May
1875.

Captain Gray's Company; or, Crossing the Plains and Living in Oregon, 21
May 1875 to 29 Oct. 1875.

One Woman's Sphere; or, The Mystery of Eagle Cove, 4 June 1875 to 3 Dec.
1875.

Madge Morrison, the Molalla Maid and Matron, 10 Dec. 1875 to 28 July 1876.

Edna and John: A Romance of Idaho Flat, 29 Sept. 1876 to 15 June 1877.

Martha Marblehead: The Maid and Matron of Chehalem, 29 June 1877 to 8
Feb. 1878.

Her Lot; or, How She Was Protected, 1 Feb. 1878 to 19 Sept. 1878.

Fact, Fate and Fancy; or, More Ways of Living than One, 26 Sept. 1878 to 15
May 1879.

Mrs. Hardine's Will, 20 Nov. 1879 to 26 Aug. 1880.

The Mystery of Castle Rock, a Story of the Pacific Northwest, 2 Mar. 1882 to
7 Sept. 1882.

Judge Dunson's Secret: An Oregon Story, 15 Mar. 1883 to 6 Sept. 1883.

Labane McShane: A Frontier Story, 13 Sept. 1883 to 6 Mar. 1884.

Dux: A Maiden Who Dared, 11 Sept. 1884 to 5 Mar. 1885.

The De Launcy Curse; or, The Law of Heredity—A Tale of Three Generations,
10 Sept. 1885 to 4 Mar. 1886.

Blanche Le Clerq: A Tale of the Mountain Mines, 2 Sept. 1886 to 24 Feb.
1887.

————. Serialized Novels in the *Pacific Empire*:

Shack-Locks: A Story of the Times, 3 Oct. 1895 to 26 Mar. 1896.

'Bijah's Surprises, book one, 2 Apr. 1896 to 26 Sept. 1896, and book two, 1
Oct. 1896 to 31 Dec. 1896.

The Old and the New, 7 Jan. 1897 to 30 Dec. 1897.

Selected Other Sources

Bennion, Sherily Cox. *Equal to the Occasion: Women Editors of the Nineteenth-
Century West*. Reno: University of Nevada Press, 1990.

————. "The *New Northwest* and *Woman's Exponent*: Early Voices for Suffrage."
Journalism Quarterly 54 (Summer 1977): 286-92.

Duniway, David Cushing. "Abigail Scott Duniway, Path Breaker." *With Her Own
Wings: Historical Sketches, Reminiscences, and Anecdotes of Pioneer Women*.
Ed. Helen Krebs Smith. Portland, OR: Beattie and Co., 1948. 123-26.

Edwards, G. Thomas. *Sowing Good Seeds: The Northwest Suffrage Campaigns of
Susan B. Anthony*. Portland: Oregon Historical Society Press, 1990.

Johnson, L.C. "Abigail Jane Scott Duniway." *Notable American Women, 1607-
1950*. Vol. I. Ed. Edwart T. James. Cambridge: Harvard University Press, 1971.
531-33.

Kessler, Lauren. "A Siege of the Citadels: Access of Woman Suffrage Ideas to the Oregon Press, 1884-1912." PhD Diss. University of Washington, 1980.

Morrison, Dorothy Nafus. *Ladies Were Not Expected: Abigail Scott Duniway and Women's Rights.* New York: Atheneum, 1977.

Moynihan, Ruth Barnes. "Abigail Scott Duniway of Oregon: Woman Suffragist of the American Frontier." PhD Diss. 2 vols. Yale University, 1979.

———. *Rebel for Rights: Abigail Scott Duniway.* New Haven: Yale University Press, 1983.

Smith, Helen Krebs. *Presumptuous Dreamers: A Sociological History of the Life and Times of Abigail Scott Duniway.* Vol. I. Lake Oswego, OR: Smith, Smith, and Smith Publishing Co., 1974.

Ward, Jean M. "The Emergence of a Mentor-Protegé Relationship: The 1871 Pacific Northwest Lecture Tour of Susan B. Anthony and Abigail Scott Duniway." *Proceedings of the 1982 Northwest Women's Heritage Conference.* Seattle: University of Washington, 1984. 120-45.

———. "Women's Responses to Systems of Male Authority: Communication Strategies in the Novels of Abigail Scott Duniway." PhD Diss. 2 vols. University of Oregon, 1989.

Susanna M. Slover McFarland Price Ede

Oral Narrative

Ede, Susanna Maria Slover McFarland Price. "Pioneer Woman in Southwestern Washington Territory: The Recollections of Susanna Maria Slover McFarland Price Ede." Ed. Barbara Baker Zimmerman and Vernon Carstensen. *Pacific Northwest Quarterly* 67 (Oct. 1976): 137-50.

Sui Sin Far (Edith Maud Eaton)

Selected Writings

Far, Sui Sin [Edith Maud Eaton]. "The Americanizing of Pau Tsu." *Mrs. Spring Fragrance.* Chicago: A. C. McClurg, 1912. 144-61.

———. "A Chinese Ishmael." *Overland Monthly* 34 (July 1899): 43-48.

———. "Chinese Workmen in America." *Independent* 75 (3 July 1913): 56-58.

———. "Its Wavering Image." *Rediscoveries: American Short Stories by Women, 1832-1916.* Ed. Barbara H. Solomon. New York: Penguin, 1994. 608-13.

———. "Leaves from the Mental Portfolio of an Eurasian." *Independent* 66 (21 Jan. 1909): 125-32. Rpt. *Chinese America: History and Perspectives 1987.* San Francisco: Chinese Historical Society of America, 1987. 169-87.

———. *Mrs. Spring Fragrance.* Chicago: A. C. McClurg, 1912.

———. "Spring Impressions: A Medley of Poetry and Prose." *Dominion Illustrated* 7 June 1890.

———. *The Spring of Chinese North American Literature: Collected Writings of Sui Sin Far.* Ed. Amy Ling and Annette White-Parks. Urbana: University of Illinois Press, 1995.

Selected Other Sources

Ammons, Elizabeth. "Audacious Words: Sui Sin Far's *Mrs. Spring Fragrance.*" *Conflicting Stories: American Women Writers at the Turn into the Twentieth Century.* By Ammons. New York: Oxford University Press, 1992. 105-120.

Dong, Lorraine, and Marlon K. Hom. "Defiance or Perpetuation: An Analysis of Characters in *Mrs. Spring Fragrance.*" *Chinese America: History and Perspectives 1987.* San Francisco: Chinese Historical Society of America, 1987. 139-68.

Doyle, James. "Sui Sin Far and Onoto Watanna: Two Early Chinese-Canadian Authors." *Canadian Literature* No. 140 (Spring 1994): 50-58.

Eaton, Winnifred [Onoto Watanna]. *Me, A Book of Remembrance*. New York: Century Co., 1915.

"Edith Eaton Dead: Author of Chinese Stories under the Name of Sui Sin Far." *New York Times* 9 Apr. 1914: 11.

Ling, Amy. "Edith Eaton: Pioneer Chinamerican Writer and Feminist." *American Literary Realism* 16 (Autumn 1983): 287-98.

———. "Pioneers and Paradigms: The Eaton Sisters." *Between Worlds: Women Writers of Chinese Ancestry*. By Ling. New York: Pergamon Press, 1990. 21-55.

———. "Winnifred Eaton: Ethnic Chameleon and Popular Success." *MELUS* 11 (3): 5-15.

———. "Writers with a Cause: Sui Sin Far and Han Suyin." *Women's Studies International Forum* 9 (1986): 411-19.

"Literary Notes." Review of *Mrs. Spring Fragrance*. *Independent* 73 (15 Aug. 1912): 388.

"A New Note in Fiction." Review of *Mrs. Spring Fragrance*. *New York Times* 7 July 1912.

Solberg, Sam E. "Sui Sin Far/Edith Eaton: First Chinese American Fictionist." *MELUS* 8 (Spring 1981): 27-39.

———. "Sui, the Storyteller: Sui Sin Far (Edith Eaton), 1867-1914." *Turning the Shadows into Light: Art and Culture of the Northwest's Early Asian/Pacific Community*. Ed. Mayumi Tsutakawa and Alan Chong Lau. Seattle: Young Pine Press, 1982. 85-87.

White-Parks, Annette. "Introduction to 'The Wisdom of the New' by Sui Sin Far." *Legacy: A Journal of Nineteenth-Century American Women Writers* 6 (Spring 1989): 34-37.

———. *Sui Sin Far/Edith Maud Eaton: A Literary Biography*. Urbana: University of Illinois Press, 1994.

———. "Sui Sin Far: Writer on the Chinese-Anglo Borders of North America, 1885-1914." PhD Diss. Washington State University, 1991.

Emeline L. Trimble Fuller

Writing
Fuller, Emeline L. (Trimble). *Left by the Indians; Story of My Life*. Mt. Vernon, Iowa: Hawk-Eye Steam Print, 1892. New York: E. Eberstadt, 1936. Rpt. The Garland Library of Narratives of North American Indian Captivities, Vol. 96. New York: Garland Publishing Co., 1978. Rpt. Fairfield, WA: Ye Galleon Press, 1988.

Selected Other Sources
Adams, Glen C. Introduction to reprint of *Left by the Indians* by Emeline L. Fuller. Fairfield, WA: Ye Galleon Press, 1988.

Shannon, Donald H. *The Utter Disaster on the Oregon Trail: The Utter and Van Ornum Massacres of 1860*. Caldwell, ID: Snake Country Publications, 1993.

Hazel Hall

Selected Writings
Hall, Hazel. *Cry of Time*. New York: E. P. Dutton & Co., 1928.

———. *Curtains*. New York: John Lane Co., 1921.
———. *Selected Poems by Hazel Hall*. Ed. Beth Bentley and O. Burmaster. Boise, ID: Ahsahta Press, Boise State University, 1980.
———. *Walkers*. New York: Dodd, Mead and Co., 1923.

Selected Other Sources
Braithwaite, William Stanley, ed. *Anthology of Magazine Verse for 1921*. Boston: Small, Maynard & Co., 1921.
Bright, Verne. "Hazel Hall." *With Her Own Wings: Historical Sketches, Reminiscences, and Anecdotes of Pioneer Women*. Ed. Helen Krebs Smith. Portland, OR: Beattie and Co., 1948. 196-97.
Franklin, Viola Price. *A Tribute to Hazel Hall*. Caldwell, ID: Caxton, 1939.
Matthews, Eleanor H. "Hazel Hall." *An Anthology of Northwest Writing: 1900-1950*. Ed. Michael Strelow. Eugene, OR: Northwest Review Books, 1979. 98-103.
Saul, George Brandon. "Wasted Flame?—A Note on Hazel Hall and Her Poetry." *Quintet: Essays on Five American Women Poets*. The Hague, Netherlands: Mouton & Co., 1967. 21-29.

Elizabeth Sager Helm
Oral Narrative
Helm, Elizabeth Sager. Autobiographical Narrative in Fred Lockley's "Observations and Impressions of the *Journal* Man," *Oregon Journal*, July 23-27, Sept. 4-6, 1923. Rpt. *The Lockley Files: Conversations with Pioneer Women*. Comp. & ed. Mike Helm. Eugene, OR: Rainy Day Press, 1981. 44-63.

Selected Other Sources
Delaney, Matilda Jane Sager. "Mathilda [sic] Jane Sager Delaney." Autobiographical Narrative in Fred Lockley's "Impressions of the *Journal* Man," *Oregon Journal*, 24 Dec. and 25 Dec. 1921. Rpt. *The Lockley Files: Conversations with Pioneer Women*. Comp. and ed. Mike Helm. Eugene, OR: Rainy Day Press, 1981. 5-11.
———. *A Survivor's Recollections of the Whitman Massacre*. Spokane, WA: Esther Reed Chapter, Daughters of the American Revolution, 1920.
Lansing, Ronald B. *Juggernaut: The Whitman Massacre Trial, 1850*. Portland, OR: Ninth Judicial Circuit Court Historical Society, 1993.
Pringle, Catherine Sager. *Across the Plains in 1844*. 2nd ed., Portland, OR, 1905. Rpt. Fairfield, WA: Ye Galleon Press, 1989.
———. "Christmas with the Whitman Captives 1847." Ed. Henry M. Majors. *Northwest Discovery* 1 (Dec. 1980): 361-64.
Sager, Catherine, Elizabeth and Matilda. *The Whitman Massacre of 1847*. Ed. L. L. Dodd. Fairfield, WA: Ye Galleon Press, 1986.
Saunders, Mary. *The Whitman Massacre*. Rpt. Fairfield, WA: Ye Galleon Press, 1978.

Ella (Rhoads) Higginson
Selected Writings
Higginson, Ella Rhoads. *Alaska: The Great Country*. New York: Macmillan, 1908. New ed., 1917.
———. *A Bunch of Western Clover* [poetry]. New Whatcom, WA: Edson & Irish, Publishers, 1894.

———. "Esther's 'Fourth.'" *From the Land of the Snow Pearls; Tales from Puget Sound*. New York: Macmillan, 1897, 1902. Rpt. Freeport, NY: Ayer Co., Books for Libraries Press, 1970.

———. *The Flower that Grew in the Sand, and other Stories*. Seattle: The Calvert Co., 1896. Rpt. Freeport, NY: Books for Libraries Press, 1970.

———. *A Forest Orchid and other Stories*. New York: Macmillan, 1897.

———. *Four-Leaf Clover: A Little Book of Verse*. Bellingham, WA: Edson & Irish, 1901.

———. *From the Land of the Snow Pearls; Tales from Puget Sound*. New York: Macmillan, 1897. Rpt. Freeport, NY: Ayer Co., Books for Libraries Press, 1970.

———. *Mariella; of Out-West* [novel]. New York: Macmillan, 1902. Rpt. Tacoma, WA: P. K. Pirret & Co., 1924.

———. "The New West: The Other Side" [essay]. *Overland Monthly* 19 (Jan. 1892): 107-109.

———. *The Snow-Pearls* [poetry]. Seattle: Lowman & Hanford, 1897. Rpt. New York: Macmillan, 1902.

———. *The Vanishing Race and other Poems*. Bellingham, WA: C. M. Sherman, Press of S. B. Irish and Co., 1911.

———. *The Voice of April-Land* [poetry]. New York: Macmillan, 1906.

———. *When the Birds Go North Again* [poetry]. New York: Macmillan, 1898.

Selected Other Sources
Bright, Verne. "Ella Higginson." *With Her Own Wings: Historical Sketches, Reminiscences, and Anecdotes of Pioneer Women*. Ed. Helen Krebs Smith. Portland, OR: Beattie and Co., 1948. 194-95.
Goodman, Susan. "*Legacy* Profile: Ella Rhoads Higginson." *Legacy: A Journal of Nineteenth-Century American Women Writers* 6 (Spring 1989): 59-63.
Horner, John B. "Mrs. Ella Higginson." *Oregon Native Son* 1 (Sept. 1899): 5.
Koert, Dorothy. *The Lyric Singer: A Biography of Ella Higginson*. Bellingham, WA: Center for Pacific Northwest Studies & Fourth Corner Registry, 1985.
Powers, Alfred. "Ella Higginson." *History of Oregon Literature*. Portland, OR: Metropolitan Press, 1935. 415-40.
Reynolds, Helen Louise. "Ella Higginson, Northwest Author." MA Thesis. University of Washington, 1941.
Ward, Jean M. "Ella Rhoads Higginson." *American Women Writers*. Vol. 2. Ed. Lina Mainiero. New York: Ungar, 1980. 296-98. Rpt. in *American Women Writers*. Abr. ed. Vol. 1. Ed. Langdon Lynne Faust. NewYork: Ungar, 1983. 310-11.

Amanda Gardener Johnson
Oral Narrative
Johnson, Amanda Gardener. Autobiographical Narrative in Fred Lockley's "Observations and Impressions of the *Journal* Man," *Oregon Journal* 23 Oct. 1921. Rpt. *The Lockley Files: Conversations with Pioneer Women*. Comp. and ed. Mike Helm. Eugene, OR: Rainy Day Press, 1981. 208-11.

Selected Other Sources
Davenport, T. W. "Slavery in Oregon." *Oregon Historical Quarterly* 9 (Sept. 1908): 189-253.

Obituary of Amanda Johnson. *Albany Democrat Herald* 28 March 1927.

Richard, K. Keith. "Unwelcome Settlers: Black and Mulatto Oregon Pioneers." Two Parts. *Oregon Historical Quarterly* 84 (Spring/Summer1983): 29-55; 173-205.

Stanard, Everett Earle. "Aunt Amanda Johnson." Interview with Amanda Gardener Johnson, 1924, Albany, Oregon. Published in *Albany Democrat Herald*, 1924. Albany Public Library, Linn County Vertical Files.

Mother Joseph of the Sacred Heart, S. P. (Esther Pariseau)

Selected Writings

Mother Joseph of the Sacred Heart, S.P. Letters and Papers in Sisters of Providence Archives, Seattle, Washington.

Selected Other Sources

Bergamini, Rita, S. P., and Loretta Swolak Greene, comps. *Mother Joseph of the Sacred Heart: A Bibliography*. Seattle: Sisters of Providence, 1985.

Dean, Lucille, S. P. "Mother Joseph of the Sisters of Providence." Seattle: Sisters of Providence, 1980.

James, Mary, S. P. *Providence; A Sketch of the Sisters of Charity in the Northwest, 1856-1931*. Seattle: Sisters of Charity of Providence, 1931.

Lentz, Dorothy, S. P. *The Way It Was in Providence Schools*. Montreal, Canada: Sisters of Providence, 1978.

Lucia, Ellis. *Magic Valley: The Story of St. Joseph Academy and the Blossoming of Yakima*. Seattle: Sisters of Providence, 1976.

McCrosson, Mary, S. P. *The Bell and the River*. Seattle: Sisters of Providence, 1957. Rpt. 1986.

McDonald, Lucile. "Mother Joseph." *Women Who Made the West*. By Western Writers of America. Garden City, NY: Doubleday & Co., 1980. 120-29.

Sisters of Providence. *The Sisters of Providence in Oregon*. Vol. 5 of *The Institute of Providence*. Montreal, Canada: Providence Mother House, 1949.

Anna Maria Pittman Lee

Writing

Lee, Anna Maria Pittman. *Life and Letters of Mrs. Jason Lee, First Wife of Rev. Jason Lee of the Oregon Mission*. Ed. Theressa Gay. Portland: Metropolitan Press, 1936.

Selected Other Sources

Brosnan, Cornelius J. *Jason Lee: Prophet of the New Oregon*. New York: Macmillan, 1932.

Carey, Charles H., ed. "Mission Record Book of the Methodist Episcopal Church, Willamette Station, Oregon Territory, Commenced 1834." *Oregon Historical Quarterly* 23 (1922): 230-66.

Loewenberg, Robert J. *Equality on the Oregon Frontier: Jason Lee and the Methodist Mission, 1834-1843*. Seattle: University of Washington Press, 1976.

Mattson, Sylvia. *Missionary Foot Paths: The Story of Anna Maria Pittman (Mrs. Jason Lee)*. Salem, OR: Mission Mill Museum Association, 1978.

Caroline C. Leighton

Selected Writings

Leighton, Caroline C. *Intimations of Eternal Life*. Boston: Lee and Shepard, 1892.
————. *Life at Puget Sound, with Sketches of Travel in Washington Territory, British Columbia, Oregon and California, 1865-1881*. Boston: Lee and Shepard, 1883; New York: Charles T. Dillingham, 1884. Rpt. Fairfield, WA: Ye Galleon Press, 1980.
————. *A Swiss Thoreau: Henry Frederick Aniel* [30-page booklet]. 1890.

Selected Other Sources

Adams, Glen C. "A Lady Travels Our Region—The Northwest in 1865." *The Pacific Northwesterner* 24 (Summer 1980): 33-40.
Bredeson, Robert C. "Landscape Description in Nineteenth Century American Travel Literature." *American Quarterly* 20 (Spring 1968): 86-94.

Esther M. Selover Lockhart

Selected Writings

[Lockhart, Esther M. Selover]. *Destination, West! A Pioneer Woman on the Oregon Trail*. Comp. Agnes Ruth Lockhart Sengstacken. Portland, OR: Binfords and Mort, 1942; 2nd ed. 1972.
————. "Recollections of Early Days." *With Her Own Wings: Anecdotes and Reminiscences about Pioneer Women and Life in the Oregon Territory*. Ed. Helen Krebs Smith. Portland, OR: Beattie and Co., 1948. 123-26.
————. "Recollections of Early Days by Mrs. Esther M. Lockhart." *Pioneer History of Coos and Curry Counties*. By Orvil Dodge. [Coos County]: Coos-Curry Pioneer Historical Association, 1898. 349-56. 2nd ed. with errata, Bandon, OR: Western World Publishers-Printers, 1969.

Selected Other Sources

Dodge, Orvil. *Pioneer History of Coos and Curry Counties*. 1898. 2nd ed. Bandon, OR: Western World for the Coos-Curry Pioneer and Historical Association, 1969.

Minnie Myrtle Miller (Theresa Dyer)

Selected Writings

Miller, Minnie Myrtle [Theresa Dyer]. "A Communication to the Public from Mrs. M. M. Miller, Salem, Oregon, Nov. 5, 1871" [letter]. *New Northwest* 10 Nov. 1871.
————. "Day Dreams" [prose]. Albany *Oregon Democrat* 9 Apr. 1861.
————. "A Few Words for the Men" [essay]. *New Northwest* 3 Nov. 1871.
————. "Lang Syne" [prose]. Albany *Oregon Democrat* 3 Dec. 1861.
————. "Miss Anthony's Lectures—Observanda" [essay]. *New Northwest* 20 Sept. 1871.
————. "My Boys" [poem]. *New Northwest* 1 Mar. 1872.
————. "To a Poet" [poem]. *New Northwest* 24 Nov. 1871.
————. "Sacrifice Impetro" [poem]. *New Northwest* 4 Aug. 1871; 25 Aug. 1871.
————. "A Woman's Reply" [essay]. *New Northwest* 1 Sept. 1871.

Selected Other Sources

Duniway, Abigail Scott. "A Few Facts about 'Joaquin' Miller." *New Northwest* 28 July 1871.

———. "'Joaquin' Miller." *New Northwest* 20 Oct. 1871.

———. "'Joaquin' Miller." *New Northwest* 8 Dec. 1871.

———. "Mrs. Miller's Lecture." *New Northwest* 22 March 1872.

———. "Mrs. Miller's New Departure." *New Northwest* 8 March 1872.

———. "Mrs. Miller's Triumph." *New Northwest* 15 March 1872.

———. "A Thwarted Life." *New Northwest* 22 June 1882.

Frost, O. W. *Joaquin Miller.* New York: Twayne, 1967.

Haight, Mary M. "Joaquin Miller in Oregon, 1852-54 and 1854-70." PhD Diss. University of Washington, 1936.

Lawson, Benjamin S. *Joaquin Miller.* Boise, ID: Boise State University Western Writers Series, 1980.

Miller, Joaquin. *Memorie and Rime.* New York: Funk and Wagnalls, 1884.

———. *My Own Story.* Chicago: Belford-Clarke Co., 1890.

———. *Songs of the Sierras.* Boston: Roberts Brothers, 1871. Rpt. New Jersey: Literature House/Gregg Press, 1970.

Peterson, Martin Severin. *Joaquin Miller: Literary Frontiersman.* Stanford, CA: Stanford University Press, 1937.

Powers, Alfred. "Minnie Myrtle Miller." *History of Oregon Literature.* Portland, OR: Metropolitan Press, 1935. 247-77.

Thompson, H.C. "Reminiscences of Joaquin Miller and Canyon City." *Oregon Historical Quarterly* 45 (1944): 326-36.

Anne Shannon Monroe

Selected Writings

Monroe, Anne Shannon. *Behind the Ranges* [novel]. Garden City, NY: Doubleday, Page & Co., 1925.

———. *Eugene Norton: A Tale of the Sagebrush Land* [novel]. Chicago: Rand, McNally and Co., 1900.

———. *Feelin' Fine! Bill Hanley's Book.* Garden City, NY: Doubleday & Co., 1930.

———. *God Lights a Candle: It Illumines Your Way to Happiness.* Garden City, NY: Doubleday, Doran and Co., 1933.

———. *Happy Valley: A Story of Oregon* [novel]. Chicago: A. C. McClurg, 1916. Rpt. with an introduction by Karen Blair. Corvallis: Oregon State University Press, 1991.

———. *Hearth of Happiness.* Garden City, NY: Doubleday, Doran and Co., 1929.

———. *Making a Business Woman.* New York: Henry Holt and Company, 1912.

———. "Memories of Edwin Markham: Oregon's Poet-Laureate." *Sunday Oregonian* 27 June 1937.

———. *Singing in the Rain.* New York: The Sun Dial Press, 1926.

———. *Sparks from Home Fires.* New York: Doran and Co., 1940.

———. *Walk with Me Lad.* Garden City, NY: Doubleday, Doran and Co., 1934.

———. *The World I Saw* [autobiography]. Garden City, NY: Doubleday, Doran and Co., 1928.

———, and Elizabeth Lambert Wood. *Mansions in the Cascades* [novel]. New York: The Macmillan Co., 1936.

Selected Other Sources

Blair, Karen. Introduction to reprint of *Happy Valley: A Story of Oregon* by Anne Shannon Monroe. Corvallis: Oregon State University Press, 1991. vii-xxxii.

Kirkland, Winifred Margaretta, and Frances Kirkland. "Anne Shannon Monroe, Who Sees and Hears the Out-of-Doors." *Girls Who Became Writers.* New York: Harper, 1933. Rpt. Freeport, NY: Ayer Co., Books for Libraries Press, 1971. 80-91.

Story, Elizabeth Monroe. "Anne Shannon Monroe." *With Her Own Wings: Historical Sketches, Reminiscences, and Anecdotes of Pioneer Women.* Portland, OR: Beattie and Co., 1948. 200-201.

Mourning Dove (Christine Quintasket)

Selected Writings and Oral Narratives

Mourning Dove [Humishuma; Christine Quintasket] (Okanogan). *Co-Ge-We-A, the Half-Blood: A Depiction of the Great Montana Cattle Range.* Boston: Four Seas, 1927. Rpt. with an introduction by Dexter Fisher. Lincoln: University of Nebraska Press, 1981.

———. *Coyote Stories.* Ed. Heister Dean Guie. Caldwell, ID: Caxton Printers, Ltd., 1933.

———. Interview. Spokane *Spokesman Review* 19 Apr. 1916.

———. *Mourning Dove: A Salishan Autobiography.* Ed. Jay Miller. Lincoln: University of Nebraska Press, 1990.

———. *Tales of the Okanogans.* Ed. Donald M. Hines. Fairfield, WA: Ye Galleon Press, 1976.

Selected Other Sources

Ammons, Elizabeth. "Art: Willa Cather, the Woman Writer as Artist, and Humishuma [Mourning Dove]." *Conflicting Stories: American Women Writers at the Turn into the Twentieth Century.* By Ammons. New York: Oxford University Press, 1992. 121-39.

Ault, Nelson, ed. *The Papers of Lucullus Virgil McWhorter.* Pullman, WA: Friends of the Washington State University Library, 1959.

Brown, Alanna Kathleen. "*Legacy* Profile: Mourning Dove (Humishuma), 1888-1936." *Legacy: A Journal of Nineteenth-Century American Women Writers* 6 (Spring 1989): 51-56.

———. "Looking through the Glass Darkly: The Editorialized Mourning Dove." *New Voices in Native American Literary Criticism.* Ed. Arnold Krupat. Washington, D.C.: Smithsonian Institution Press, 1993. 274-90.

———. "Mourning Dove, an Indian Novelist." *Plainswoman* 11 (1988): 3-4.

———. "Mourning Dove's Canadian Recovery Years, 1917-1919." *Canadian Literature* No. 124/125 (Spring/Summer 1990): 113-22.

Fisher, Alice Poindexter [Dexter]. "The Transportation of Tradition: A Study of Zitkala Sa and Mourning Dove, Two Transitional American Indian Writers." PhD Diss. City College of New York, 1979.

Fisher, Dexter [Alice Poindexter]. Introduction to reprint of *Cogewea: The Half-Blood* by Mourning Dove (Humishuma). Lincoln: University of Nebraska Press, 1981.

Miller, Jay. "Mourning Dove: The Author as Cultural Mediator." *Being and Becoming Indian: Biographical Studies of North American Frontiers.* Chicago: Dorsey Press, 1989. 160-82.

Obituary of Mourning Dove. Spokane *Spokesman Review* 15 Aug. 1936: 3.

Ryker, Lois. "Hu-mi-shu-ma: Mourning Dove Was the Sweet Voice of the Indians of Eastern Washington." *Seattle Times* 18 Feb. 1962.

Bethenia Owens-Adair

Selected Writings

Owens-Adair, Bethenia A. *Dr. Owens-Adair: Some of Her Life Experiences.* Portland: Mann & Beach, Printers, 1906.

———. *The Eugenic Marriage Law and Human Sterilization; The Situation in Oregon.* Salem, OR: n.p., 1923.

———. "Heredity." *New Northwest* 28 Feb. 1884.

———. *Human Sterilization: It's [sic] Social and Legislative Aspects.* Portland: Metropolitan Press, 1922.

———. "Sarah Damron Adair [Owens], Pioneer of 1843." *Oregon Pioneer Transactions, 1900*: 65-82.

———. *A Souvenir: Dr. Owens-Adair to Her Friends, Christmas 1922.* Salem, OR: *Statesman* Publishing Co., 1922.

Selected Other Sources

Bingham, Edwin R. "Bethenia Owens-Adair." *Notable American Women, 1607-1950.* Vol. II. Ed. Edward T. James. Cambridge: Harvard University Press. 657-59.

Lockley, Fred. "Bethenia Owens-Adair." *With Her Own Wings: Historical Sketches, Reminiscences, and Anecdotes of Pioneer Women.* Ed. Helen Krebs Smith. Portland, OR: Beattie and Co., 1948. 212-14.

Ward, Jean M. "Bethenia Owens-Adair." *American Women Writers.* Vol. 3. Ed. Lina Mainiero. New York: Ungar, 1981. 328-30.

Young, F. C. Review of *Dr. Owens-Adair: Some of Her Life Experiences. Oregon Historical Quarterly* 5 (Dec. 1906): 437.

Alice Day Pratt

Selected Writings

Pratt, Alice Day. *Animal Babies.* Boston: Beacon Press, 1941.

———. *Animals of a Sagebrush Ranch.* New York: Rand McNally, 1931.

———. *A Homesteader's Portfolio.* New York: Macmillan, 1922. Rpt. with an introduction by Molly Gloss. Corvallis: Oregon State University Press, 1993.

———. *Three Frontiers.* New York: Vantage Press, Inc., 1955.

Selected Other Sources

Allen, Barbara. *Homesteading the High Desert.* Salt Lake City: University of Utah Press, 1987.

Brimlow, George F. *Harney County, Oregon, and Its Range Land.* Portland: Binfords & Mort, 1951.

Gloss, Molly. Introduction to reprint of *A Homesteader's Portfolio* by Alice Day Pratt. Corvallis: Oregon State University Press, 1993. vii-lvi.

Silver, Clarine. "The Old Maid of Friar Butte [Alice Day Pratt]." Eugene *Register-Guard* 23 Apr. 1972.

Emma J. Ray

Writing

Ray, Emma J. *Twice Sold, Twice Ransomed: Autobiography of Mr. And Mrs. L. P. Ray.* Chicago: The Free Methodist Publishing House, 1926. Rpt. Freeport, NY: Ayer Co., Books for Libraries Press, 1971.

Selected Other Sources

Davis, Elizabeth Lindsay. *Lifting As They Climb*. Chicago: National Association of Colored Women, 1933.

Mumford, Esther Hall. *Seattle's Black Victorians, 1852-1910*. Seattle: Ananse Press, 1980.

Mary P. Avery Sawtelle

Writing

Sawtelle, Mary Priscilla. *The Heroine of '49; a Story of the Pacific Coast*. San Francisco: n.p., 1891.

Selected Other Sources

Bakken, Lavola J. *Lone Rock, Free State: A Collection of Historical Adventures and Incidents in Oregon's North Umpqua Valley, 1850-1910*. Myrtle Creek, OR: The Mail Printers, 1970.

———. Mary P. Sawtelle. Unpublished ts.

Sawtelle, Cheston M. *Reflections on the Science of Ignorance, or the Art of Teaching Others What You Don't Know Yourself*. Salem, OR: Waite & Denlinger, Printers, 1868.

Louise Gregg Stephens ("Katharine")

Selected Writings

Stephens, Louise Gregg ["Elizabeth" and "Katharine"]. *Letters from an Oregon Ranch*. [by Katharine]. Chicago: A. C. McClurg Co., 1905. Rpt. *From an Oregon Ranch* [by Katharine]. Chicago: A. C. McClurg Co., 1916.

Selected Other Sources

Dye, Eva Emery. "Review of *Letters from an Oregon Ranch*." *Oregon Historical Quarterly* 7 (1906): 435.

Obituary of Louise Gregg Stephens. Corvallis *Daily Gazette Times*. 8 Nov. 1912.

Waggoner, Wilma. Letter of 31 May 1916, from Lebanon, Oregon, to Miss Cornelia Marvin, State Librarian, Oregon State Library, re. Louise Gregg Stephens. Oregon State Library Archives, Salem, Oregon.

"Who 'Elizabeth' Is." Portland *Oregonian* 14 June 1903.

Lydia Taylor

Writing

Taylor, Lydia. *From under the Lid: An Appeal to True Womanhood*. [Portland, OR]: Mrs. Lydia Taylor, 1913.

Selected Other Sources

Connelly, Mark Thomas. *The Response to Prostitution in the Progressive Era*. Chapel Hill: University of North Carolina Press, 1980.

Jones, W. R. "Prostitution in Seattle." *Northwest Medicine* 17 (1918): 239-42.

Lubove, Roy. "The Progressives and the Prostitute." *Historian* 24 (1962): 308-30.

Portland Vice Commission. *Report of the Portland [Oregon] Vice Commission to the Mayor and City Council of the City of Portland*. Portland, OR, 1913.

"To Rehabilitate Portland Prostitutes." *Survey* 31 (1913): 176.

Frances Auretta Fuller Victor

Selected Writings

Victor, Frances Auretta Fuller. "All about Looking-Glasses" [essay]. *New Northwest* 25 Aug. 1871.

———. *All Over Oregon and Washington*. San Francisco: John H. Carmany & Co., 1872.

———[Frances Auretta Fuller]. *Anizelta, the Guajira; or, the Creole of Cuba* [novel]. Boston: "Star Spangled Banner" Office, 1848.

———. *Atlantis Arisen; or, Talks of a Tourist about Oregon and Washington*. Philadelphia: J. B. Lippincott, Company, 1891.

———. "Autobiographical Sketch." Salem *Oregon Statesman* 16 June 1895.

———. "The Bancroft Historical Library." *The Californian* Dec. 1882.

———. "Bancroft's Histories." *Oregonian* 8 July 1900.

———. "Did Dr. Whitman Save Oregon?" *The Californian* Sept. 1880.

———. "Dr. Marcus Whitman . . . an Exhaustive Examination . . . of all the Points in the So-Called Whitman Controversy." *Oregonian* 6 Nov. 1884.

———. *The Early Indian Wars of Oregon, Compiled from the Oregon Archives and other Original Sources, with Muster Rolls*. Salem, OR: F. C. Baker, 1894.

———. *East and West; or the Beauty of Willard's Mill* [novel]. New York: Beadle and Adams, 1862.

———. *Eleven Years in the Rocky Mountains and Life on the Frontier; also a History of the Sioux War, and a Life of General George A. Custer with Full Account of His Last Battle*. Hartford: Columbian Book Company, 1877.

———. "The First Oregon Cavalry." *Oregon Historical Quarterly* 3 (1902): 123-63.

———. *History of California*. Vols 6 and 7. San Francisco: The History Publishing Co., 1890. [See Bancroft]

———. *History of Nevada, Colorado and Wyoming, 1540-1888*. San Francisco: The History Publishing Co., 1890. [See Bancroft]

———. *History of Oregon 1832-1847*. San Francisco: The History Publishing Co., 1886. [See Bancroft]

———. *History of Oregon 1848-1888*. San Francisco: The History Publishing Co., 1888. [See Bancroft]

———. *History of Washington, Idaho and Montana, 1845-1889*. San Francisco: The History Publishing Co., 1890. [See Bancroft]

———. "How Jack Hastings Sold His Mine" [short story]. *New Northwest* 7 Nov. 1873.

———. *Judith Miles, or What Shall Be Done with Her?* Serialized novel in 23 chapters in the *New Northwest*, 5 Dec. 1873 to 8 May 1874.

———. *The Land Claim: A Tale of The Upper Missouri* [novel]. New York: Beadle and Adams, 1862.

———. "Letter from Miss Fuller." *Monthly Hesperian and Odd-Fellows Literary Magazine* (Detroit) II (Aug. 1851): 87-88.

———. "Letter from Mrs. Victor." *New Northwest* 5 Sept. 1873.

———. "Literature of Oregon." *West Shore* (Jan. 1876): 2-3.

———. "Manifest Destiny in the West." *Overland Monthly* (Aug. 1869):158.

———. "Mr. Thornton's Review of *The River of the West*." Portland *Pacific Christian Advocate* 21 May 1870.

———. *The New Penelope and Other Stories and Poems*. San Francisco: A. L. Bancroft & Co., 1877.

———. "The Oregon Indians." *Overland Monthly* Oct. 1871.

———. *Poems.* Author's ed.: 1900.

———. *The River of the West.* Hartford: R. W. Bliss & Company, 1870.

———. *"The River of the West* Vindicated: Reply of Mrs. Fuller to Judge Thornton; Important Original Documents Furnished." *Oregonian* 14 July 1870; 15 July 1870.

———. "A Short Stay in Acapulco." *Overland Monthly* (March 1871): 214-16; 222.

———. "Some Thoughts about Ourselves." *New Northwest* 27 Feb. 1874.

———. "A Stage Ride in Oregon and California." *The American Publisher* [Hartford, CT] I (Aug. 1871) and II (Sept. 1871).

———. "Suffrage and Religion." *New Northwest* 28 Aug. 1874.

———. "Summer Wanderings." *Oregonian* June 27; July 2, 7, 27; August 1, 2, 6, 10, 1870.

———. "Talk with a Woman Who Writes Poems." Portland *Evening Telegram* 11 Sept. 1900.

———. "A Voyage up the Columbia River." San Francisco *Evening Bulletin* 2 Sept. 1865.

———. [Dorothy D.] "Wanted: A Divorce." San Francisco *Call* 6 June 1875.

———. "Wayside Pictures from Oregon." San Francisco *Evening Bulletin* 14 July 1865.

———. "The Webfoot History." Salem *Oregon Statesman* 24 Feb. 1895.

———. "A Winter Trip to Victoria and Portland." San Francisco *Evening Bulletin* 20 Jan. 1865.

———. *The Women's War with Whisky; or, Crusading in Portland.* Portland: G. H. Himes, 1874.

———[Frances Auretta Fuller], and Metta Victoria Fuller. *Poems of Sentiment and Imagination, with Dramatic and Descriptive Pieces.* New York: A. S. Barnes and Co., 1851.

Selected Other Sources

Johannsen, Albert. *The House of Beadle and Adams and Its Dime and Nickel Novels, the Story of a Vanished Literature.* Norman: University of Oklahoma Press, 1950. 2 vols.

Martin, Jim. *A Bit of a Blue: The Life and Work of Frances Fuller Victor.* Salem, OR: Deep Well Publishing Co., 1992.

Mills, Hazel Emery. "The Emergence of Frances Fuller Victor—Historian." *Oregon Historical Quarterly* 62 (Dec. 1961): 309-36.

———. "Francis Fuller Victor: Historian and Traveler of the Oregon Country." *The Western Shore: Oregon Country Essays Honoring the American Revolution.* Ed. Thomas Vaughan. Portland: Oregon Historical Society, 1975. 270-80.

Morris, William Alfred. "Historian of the Northwest: A Woman Who Loved Oregon." *Oregon Historical Quarterly* 3 (Dec. 1902): 429-34.

———. "The Origin and Authorship of the Bancroft Pacific States Publications: A History of a History." *Oregon Historical Quarterly* 4 (Dec. 1903): 287-364.

Powers, Alfred. "Frances Fuller Victor." *History of Oregon Literature.* By Powers. Portland, OR: Metropolitan Press, 1935. 305-16.

———. "Scrapbook of a Historian—Frances Fuller Victor." *Oregon Historical Quarterly* 42 (Dec. 1941): 325-31.

Taylor, William R. "Metta Victoria Fuller Victor." *Notable American Women, 1607-1950.* Vol. III. Ed. Edward T. James. Cambridge: Harvard University Press, 1971. 519-20.

Victor, Metta Victoria Fuller. *Fashionable Dissipations*. New York: United States Book Co., 1853.

————. *Mormon Wives: A Narrative of Facts Stranger than Fiction*. New York: Derby & Jackson; Cincinnati: H. W. Derby, 1856.

————. *The Senator's Son: or the Maine law; a last refuge; a story dedicated to the lawmakers*. Cleveland: Tooker & Gatchel, 1851.

Walker, Franklin. "Frances Auretta Fuller Victor." *Notable American Women, 1607-1950*. Vol. III. Ed. Edward T. James. Cambridge: Harvard University Press, 1971. 518-19.

————. *San Francisco's Literary Frontier*. New York: Knopf, 1939.

Narcissa Prentiss Whitman

Selected Writings

Whitman, Narcissa Prentiss. *The Coming of the White Women, 1836, as Told in the Letters and Journal of Narcissa Whitman*. Comp. T. C. Elliott. Portland: Oregon Historical Society, 1937.

————. *The Letters of Narcissa Whitman*. Fairfield, WA: Ye Galleon Press, 1986.

————. *My Journal*. Ed. Lawrence Dodd. Fairfield, WA: Ye Galleon Press, 1982.

Selected Other Sources

Drury, Clifford M. *First White Women over the Rockies: Diaries, Letters, and Biographical Sketches of the Six Women of the Oregon Mission Who Made the Overland Journey in 1836 and 1838*. 3 vols. Glendale, CA: Arthur H. Clark Co., 1963-66.

————. *Marcus and Narcissa Whitman and the Opening of Old Oregon*. Glendale, CA: Arthur H. Clark Co., 1973.

Elliott, T. C. "The Coming of the White Women, 1836." Parts I-V. *Oregon Historical Quarterly* 37 and 38 (1936 & 1937): 87-101; 171-91; 275-90; 44-62; 205-23.

Jeffrey, Julie Roy. *Converting the West: A Biography of Narcissa Whitman*. Norman: University of Oklahoma Press, 1991.

Wilkins, Thurman. "Narcissa Prentiss Whitman." *Notable American Women, 1607-1950*. Vol. III. Ed. Edward T. James. Cambridge: Harvard University Press, 1971. 595-97.

Sarah Winnemucca (Hopkins)

Selected Writings

Winnemucca, Sarah (Hopkins) (Paiute). *Life Among the Piutes: Their Wrongs and Claims*. Ed. Mrs. Horace Mann. Boston: Cupples, Upham & Co.; New York: Putnam's Sons, 1883. Rpt. Bishop, CA: Chalfant Press/Sierra Media, Inc., 1969.

————. "The Pah-Utes." *The Californian* 6 (July-Dec. 1882): 252-56.

Selected Other Sources

Brimlow, George F. "The Life of Sarah Winnemucca: The Formative Years." *Oregon Historical Quarterly* 53 (June 1952): 103-34.

Canfield, Gae Whitney. *Sarah Winnemucca of the Northern Paiutes*. Norman: University of Oklahoma Press, 1983.

Fowler, Catherine S. "Sarah Winnemucca (Hopkins), Northern Paiute." *American Indian Intellectuals*. Ed. Margot Liberty. St. Paul: West Publishing Co., 1978.

Gehm, Katherine. *Sarah Winnemucca*. Phoenix: O'Sullivan, Woodside, 1975.

Georgi-Findlay, Brigilte. "Frontiers of Native American Women's Writings: Sarah Winnemucca's *Life among the Paiutes*." *New Voices in Native American Literary Criticism*. Ed. Arnold Krupat. Washington, D.C.: Smithsonian Institution Press, 1993. 222-52.

Morrison, Dorothy Nafus. *Chief Sarah: Sarah Winnemucca's Fight for Indian Rights*. New York: Atheneum, 1980.

Peabody, Elizabeth P. *The Piutes: Second Report of the Model School of Sarah Winnemucca*. Cambridge: John Wilcox & Son, 1887.

———. *Sarah Winnemucca's Practical Solution of the Indian Problem*. Cambridge: John Wilcox & Son, 1886.

Richey, Elinor. "Sagebrush Princess with a Cause: Sarah Winnemucca." *American West* 12 (Nov. 1975): 30-33; 57-63.

Stewart, Patricia. "Sarah Winnemucca." *Nevada State Historical Society Quarterly* 14 (Winter 1971): 23-38.

Thorp, Louise Hall. *The Peabody Sisters of Salem*. Boston: Little, Brown & Co., 1950.

Wilkins, Thurman. "Sarah Winnemucca [Hopkins]." *Notable American Women, 1607-1950*. Vol. III. Ed. Edward T. James. Cambridge: Harvard University Press, 1971. 628-30.

Nancy Perkins Wynecoop

Writing

Wynecoop, Nancy Perkins, and N. Wynecoop Clark. *In the Stream: An Indian Story*. Spokane, WA: N. Wynecoop Clark, 1985.

Selected Other Sources

Wynecoop, Nancy Perkins (Spokane). "Nancy Winecoop [sic]." WPA Interview and Autobiographical Narrative. *Told by the Pioneers: Reminiscences of Pioneer Life in Washington*. Vol I. Olympia: State of Washington, 1938. 114-19.

Special Manuscript Collections

Jesse Applegate Letters. Oregon Historical Society, Portland, Oregon.

Margaret Jewett Bailey. Miscellaneous Papers. Oregon Historical Society, Portland, Oregon.

Cayton Family Papers. Vivian G. Harsh Collection. Chicago Public Library.

Horace R. Cayton Collection. Bancroft Library, University of California, Berkeley.

Horace R. Cayton Collection. George Arents Research Library, Syracuse University.

Matthew P. Deady Collection. Oregon Historical Society Library, Portland, Oregon.

Abigail Scott Duniway. Letter to Barbara Booth (11 April 1914) and copy of the *Coming Century* 1 (2 December 1891), Special Collections, The Library, University of Oregon, Eugene, Oregon.

Abigail Scott Duniway Papers. Special Collections, The Library, University of Oregon, Eugene, Oregon.

Duniway Family Papers. David C. Duniway Private Collection. Salem, Oregon.

Duniway Publishing Company Ledgers. Oregon Historical Society, Portland, Oregon.

Elwood Evans Collection. Oregon Historical Society, Portland, Oregon.

Ella Higginson Papers. Bellingham Public Library, Bellingham, Washington.

Mother Joseph of the Sacred Heart, S. P. [Esther Pariseau]. Letters and Papers in Sisters of Providence Archives, Seattle, Washington.

Mourning Dove [Humishuma; Christine Quintasket]. Letters included in Lucullus V. McWhorter Papers. Holland Library, Washington State University Archives, Pullman, Washington.

Oregon State Equal Suffrage Association Papers. Oregon Historical Society, Portland, Oregon.

Alfred Powers Collection. Oregon Historical Society, Portland, Oregon.

Frances Fuller Victor Letter to Elwood Evans, 15 Nov. 1865. Microfilm copy at Oregon State Library, Salem, Oregon.

Frances Fuller Victor and Oliver C. Applegate Correspondence. Special Collections, The Library, University of Oregon, Eugene, Oregon.

Nancy Perkins Wynecoop Papers. Eastern Washington State Historical Society Library, Spokane, Washington.

Special Newspaper Collections

(Not all runs are complete.)

Cayton's Monthly [Seattle, Washington]. 1921. University of Washington, Seattle, Washington. Microfilm.

Cayton's Weekly [Seattle, Washington]. 1917-1921. University of Washington, Seattle, Washington. Microfilm.

New Northwest [Portland, Oregon]. 1871-1887. Oregon Historical Society. Portland, Oregon. Microfilm.

Pacific Empire [Portland, Oregon]. 1895-1898. Multnomah County Library, Portland, Oregon. Bound volumes contain: 16 Aug. 1895; 3 Oct. 1895 to 11 Feb. 1897; 10 March 1898 to 23 June 1898. Oregon Historical Society, Portland. Unbound issues include: 3 Oct. 1895 to 11 Feb. 1897; 2 Sept. 1897 to 7 July 1898.

Seattle Republican [Seattle, Washington]. 1894-1913. University of Washington, Seattle, Washington. Microfilm.

Other Books and Articles

Abbott, Marian Redington. "Marian Redington Abbott on Her Turn-of-the-Century Camping Trip." *Oregon Historical Quarterly* 88 (Summer 1987): 196-203.

Adams, Emma Hildreth. *To and Fro, Up and Down in Southern California, Oregon and Washington Territory, with Sketches in Arizona, New Mexico, and British Columbia.* Chicago: Cranston, 1888.

Adams, Harriet L. *A Woman's Journeyings in the Northwest.* Cleveland: B-P Printing Co., 1892.

Adams, Roy William. "The Oregon Style." MA Thesis. University of Oregon, 1958.

Adamson, Thelma. *Folk-Tales of the Coast Salish.* New York: G. E. Stechert & Co. for the American Folk-Lore Society, 1934. Rpt. New York: Kraus Reprint Co., 1969.

Additon, Lucia H. Faxon. *Twenty Eventful Years of the Oregon Woman's Christian Temperance Union, 1880-1900, Statistical, Historical, and Biographical.* Portland: Gotshall Printing Co., 1904.

Aikens, C. Melvin, and Marilyn Couture. "The Great Basin." *The First Orego-nians*. Ed. Carolyn C. Buan and Richard Lewis. Portland: Oregon Council for the Humanities, 1991. 21-35.

Allen, Eleanor Waggoner. *Canvas Caravans; Based on the Journal of Esther Bells McMillan Hanna, Who, with Her Husband, Rev. Joseph A. Hanna, Brought the Presbyterian Colony to Oregon in 1852*. Portland: Binfords & Mort, 1946.

Aloysia, Mary, S. N. D. *Notice sur la territoire et sur la mission de l'Oregon, suivie de quelques lettres des Soeurs de Notre Dame établie a St. Paul de Willamette*. Bruxelles, Belgium: Bibliotheque d'education, 1847.

Ammons, Elizabeth. *Conflicting Stories: American Women Writers at the Turn into the Twentieth Century*. New York: Oxford University Press, 1992.

Anderson, Ada Woodruff. *The Heart of the Red Firs: A Story of the Pacific Northwest*. Boston: Little, Brown & Co., 1908.

———. *The Rim of the Desert*. Boston: Little, Brown & Co., 1915.

———. *The Strain of White*. Boston: Little, Brown & Co., 1909.

Anderson, Lorraine, ed. *Sisters of the Earth: Women's Prose and Poetry about Nature*. New York: Random House/Vintage, 1991.

Anderson, Martha E. *Black Pioneers of the Northwest, 1800-1918*. n.p.: Martha E. Anderson, 1980.

Applegate, Shannon. *Skookum: An Oregon Pioneer Family's History and Lore*. New York: William Morrow, 1988.

———, and Terence O'Donnell, eds. *Talking on Paper: An Anthology of Oregon Letters and Diaries*. The Oregon Literature Series, Vol. VI. A Project of the Oregon Council of Teachers of English. Corvallis: Oregon State University Press, 1994.

Armitage, Susan H. Foreword to reprint of *A Pioneer's Search for an Ideal Home* by Phoebe Goodell Judson. Lincoln: University of Nebraska Press, 1984.

———, and Elizabeth Jameson, eds. *The Women's West*. Norman: University of Oklahoma Press, 1987.

———, Helen Bannan, Katherine G. Morrissey, Vicki L. Ruiz, eds. *Women in the West: A Guide to Manuscript Sources*. New York: Garland Publishing, Inc., 1991.

Atwood, Albert. *Glimpses of Pioneer Life on Puget Sound*. Seattle: Denny-Coryell Co., 1903.

Azuma, Eiichiro. "A History of Oregon's Issei, 1880-1952." *Oregon Historical Quartlery* 94 (Winter 1993-94): 315-67.

Bagley, Clarence Booth. *In the Beginning; A Sketch of Some Early Events in Western Washington While It Was Still a Part of 'Old Oregon.'* Seattle: Lowman & Hanford, 1905.

———. *Early Catholic Missions in Old Oregon*. 2 vols. Seattle: Lowman & Hanford, 1932.

———. *History of King County, Washington*. 3 vols. Chicago: The S. J. Clarke Publishing Co., 1929.

———. *History of Seattle*. 3 vols. Chicago: The S. J. Clarke Publishing Co., 1916.

Bancroft, Hubert Howe. *History of Oregon, 1834-1848. The Works of Hubert Howe Bancroft*. Vol. 29. San Francisco: The History Publishing Co., 1886. [See Frances Fuller Victor]

———. *History of Oregon, 1848-1888. The Works of Hubert Howe Bancroft*. Vol. 30. San Francisco: The History Publishing Co., 1888. [See Frances Fuller Victor]

————. *History of Washington, Idaho, and Montana, 1845-1889.* San Francisco: The History Publishing Co., 1890. [See Frances Fuller Victor]

————. *Literary Industries.* San Francisco: The History Publishing Co., 1890.

Banta, Martha. *Imaging American Women: Ideas and Ideals in Cultural History.* New York: Columbia University Press, 1987.

Barclay, Wade Crawford. *History of Methodist Missions.* 2 Vols. New York: Board of Missions and Church Extension of the Methodist Church, 1949-50.

Bashford, Herbert. "The Literary Development of the Far Northwest." *Overland Monthly* 33 (Apr. 1899): 316-20.

Bataille, Gretchen M., and Kathleen M. Sands. *American Indian Women: A Guide to Research.* New York: Garland Publishing, Inc., 1991.

————. *American Indian Women: Telling Their Lives.* Lincoln: University of Nebraska Press, 1984.

Bates, Josephine (White). *Bunch-Grass Stories.* Philadelphia: Lippincott, 1895.

Baun, Carolyn M., and Richard Lewis, eds. *The First Oregonians: An Illustrated Collection of Essays on Traditional Lifeways, Federal-Indian Relations, and the State's Native People Today.* Portland: Oregon Council for the Humanities, 1991.

Baym, Nina. *Novels, Readers and Reviewers: Responses to Fiction in Antebellum America.* Ithaca, NY: Cornell University Press, 1984.

————. *Woman's Fiction: A Guide to Novels by and about Women, 1820-1870.* Ithaca, NY: Cornell University Press, 1978.

Bearce, Stella E. "Suffrage in the Pacific Northwest: Old Oregon and Washington." *Washington Historical Quarterly* 3 (1908): 106-14.

Beckham, Stephen Dow. "Federal-Indian Relations." *The First Oregonians.* Ed. Carolyn M. Buan and Richard Lewis. Portland: Oregon Council for the Humanities, 1991. 39-54.

————, ed. *Many Faces: An Anthology of Oregon Autobiography.* The Oregon Literature Series, Vol. 2. A Project of the Oregon Council of Teachers of English. Corvallis: Oregon State University Press, 1993.

Belenky, Mary Field, Blythe McVicker Clinchy, Nancy Rule Goldberger, and Jill Mattuck Tarule. *Women's Ways of Knowing: The Development of Self, Voice, and Mind.* New York: Basic Books, 1986.

Bell, Polly McKean. "A Pioneer Woman's Reminiscences of Christmas in the Eighties." *Oregon Historical Quarterly* 49 (1948): 284-96.

Bennett, Robert A., ed. *We'll All Go Home in the Spring: Personal Accounts and Adventures as Told by the Pioneers of the West.* Walla Walla, WA: Pioneer Press Books, 1984.

Benstock, Shair, ed. *Feminist Issues in Literary Scholarship.* Bloomington: Indiana University Press, 1987.

Berquist, James M. "The Oregon Donation Land Act and the National Land Policy." *Oregon Historical Quarterly* 58 (Mar. 1957): 17-35.

Bingham, Edwin R. "Pacific Northwest Writing: Reaching for Regional Identity." *Regionalism and the Pacific Northwest.* Ed. William G. Robbins, Robert Frank, and Richard Ross. Corvallis: Oregon State University Press, 1983.

————, and Glen A. Love, eds. *Northwest Perspectives: Essays on the Culture of the Pacific Northwest.* Seattle: University of Washington Press, 1979.

Binheim, Max, ed. *Women of the West.* Los Angeles: Publishers Press, 1928.

Blair, Karen, ed. *Women in Pacific Northwest History: An Anthology.* Seattle: University of Washington Press, 1988.

Blankenship, Georgiana, ed. *Early History of Thurston County, Washington: Tillicum Tales of Thurston County*. Olympia: n.p., 1914.

Bledsoe, Lucy Jane. "Adventuresome Women on the Oregon Trail, 1840-1867." *Frontiers* 7 (1984): 22-29.

Bliss, Beatrice L. *Mary Vowell Adams: Reluctant Pioneer*. Portland: Metropolitan Press, 1972.

Boas, Franz. "Traditions of the Tillamook Indians." *Journal of American Folklore* 11 (1898): 23-38; 133-51.

———, ed. *Chinook Texts*. Bureau of American Ethnology Bulletin 20 (1894).

Bowden, Angie Burt. *Early Schools of Washington Territory*. Seattle: Lowman & Hanford, 1935.

Bowen, William A. "The Oregon Frontiersman: A Demographic View." *The Western Shore: Oregon Country Essays Honoring the American Revolution*. Portland: Oregon Historical Society, 1975. 181-97.

———. *The Willamette Valley: Migration and Settlement on the Oregon Frontier*. Seattle: University of Washington Press, 1978.

Boyd, Robert. "The Pacific Northwest Measles Epidemic of 1847-1848." *Oregon Historical Quarterly* 95 (Spring 1994): 6-47.

Brewalter, David, and David Buerge, eds. *Washingtonians: A Biographical Portrait of the State*. Seattle: Sasquatch Books, 1988.

Brier, Warren J. "A History of Newspapers in the Pacific Northwest, 1846-1896." PhD Diss. State University of Iowa, 1957.

Broderick, Therese [Tin Schreiner] *The Brand, a Tale of the Flathead Reservation*. Seattle: Alice Harriman, 1909.

Brooks, Virginia [Washburne]. *Tilly from Tillamook: Her Temptation and Triumph*. Portland: A. E. Kern & Co., 1925.

Brown, Arthur J. "The Promotion of Emigration to Washington, 1854-1909." *Pacific Northwest Quarterly* 36 (Jan. 1945): 3-17.

Brown, Clara Spaulding. *Life at Shut-in Valley, and Other Pacific Coast Tales*. Franklin, OH: Editor Publishing Co., 1895.

Brown, Dazie M. (Stromstadt). *Metlakahtla*. Seattle: H. M. Hill Co., 1907.

Brown, Dee. *The Gentle Tamers: Women of the Old Wild West*. Lincoln: University of Nebraska Press, 1958.

Buan, Carolyn M., and Richard Lewis. *The First Oregonians: An Illustrated Collection of Essays on Traditional Lifeways, Federal-Indian Relations, and the State's Native People Today*. Portland: Oregon Council for the Humanities, 1991.

Budlong, Caroline D. *Memories: Pioneer Days in Oregon and Washington Territory*. Eugene: Picture Press Printers, 1949.

Bugley, Clarence B. "The Mercer Immigration: Two Cargoes of Maidens for the Sound Country." *Oregon Historical Quarterly* 5 (March 1904): 1-24.

Butler, America E. Rollins. "Mrs. Butler's 1853 Diary of Rogue River Valley." Ed. Oscar Osburn Winther and Rose Dodge Galey. *Oregon Historical Quarterly* 41 (Dec. 1940): 337-66.

Butler, Anne M. *Daughters of Joy, Sisters of Misery: Prostitutes in the American West, 1865-1890*. Urbana: University of Illinois Press, 1985.

———. "The Tarnished Frontier: Prostitution in the Trans-Mississippi West, 1865-1890." PhD Diss., University of Maryland, 1979.

Butrille, Susan G. *Women's Voices from the Oregon Trail*. Boise, ID: Tamarack Books, Inc., 1993.

Cameron, F. Marie. *Voices of the Wild*. Seattle: Peace Pipe Press, 1910.

Cameron, Mabel Ward, comp. *Biographical Cyclopedia of American Women*. New York: Harvard Publishing Co., 1924.

Campbell, Helen (Stuart). *White and Red; a Narrative of Life among the Northwest Indians, by Helen C. Weeks*. New York: Hurd & Houghton, 1869.

Carey, Charles H. *General History of Oregon through Early Statehood*. Portland: Binfords & Mort, 1971.

———. *History of Oregon*. 3 Vols. Chicago: The Pioneer Historical Publishing Co., 1922.

Carpenter, Cecilia Smith (Nisqually). *They Walked Before: The Indians of Washington State*. Washington State Historical Society Ethnic Series. Tacoma: The Washington State American Bicentennial Committee, 1977.

Caughey, Mildred. *Through the Eyes of a Child* [Connell, Washington, 1906-1920]. Fairfield, WA: Ye Galleon Press, 1979.

Champney, Elizabeth Williams. *All Around a Palette*. Boston: Lockwood, Brooks, 1878.

———. *Anneka*. New York: Dodd, 1900.

———. *Margarita*. New York: Dodd, 1902.

Chinese Historical Society of America. *Chinese America: History and Perspectives 1987*. San Francisco: Chinese Historical Society of America, 1987.

Clark, Malcolm H., Jr. "The War on the Webfoot Saloon." *Oregon Historical Quarterly* 58 (Mar. 1957): 48-62.

Clark, Robert Carlton. *History of the Willamette Valley, Oregon*. Chicago: The S. J. Clarke Publishing Co., 1927.

———, Robert H. Down, and George V. Blue. *A History of Oregon*. Chicago: Row, Peterson, 1925.

Clayson, Edward. Sr. *Historical Narratives of Puget Sound*. Seattle: Davis Printing Co., 1911.

Cleland, Mabel Goodwin. *Early Days in the Fir-Tree Country*. Seattle: Washington Printing Co., 1923.

———. *Little Pioneers of the Fir-Tree Country*. Boston: Houghton, 1924.

Coe, Alice Rollit. *Lyrics of Fir and Foam*. Seattle: Harriman, 1908.

Coggeshall, William T. *The Poets and Poetry of the West; with Biographical and Critical Notices*. Columbia, OH: Follet, Folster & Co., 1860.

Coleman, Rufus A., ed. *Western Prose and Poetry*. New York: Harper, 1932.

Collins, Martha Elizabeth Gilliam. "Reminiscences of Mrs. Frank Collins, née Martha Elizabeth Gilliam." Ed. Fred Lockley. *Oregon Historical Quarterly* 17 (1916): 358-72.

Conant, Roger. *Mercer's Belles: The Journal of a Reporter*. Ed. Lenna A. Deutsch. Pullman: Washington State University Press, 1992.

Conray, Michael S. "Blacks in the Pacific West, 1850-1860: A View from the Census." *Nevada Historical Society Quarterly* 28 (Summer 1985): 90-121.

Cooke, Belle [Susan Isabella Walker]. "A Letter from Mrs. Belle W. Cooke, Salem, Oregon." *New Northwest* 30 June 1871.

———. "Letter from Mrs. Belle W. Cooke." *New Northwest* 18 Aug. 1871.

———. *Tears and Victory and Other Poems*. Salem, OR: Waite, 1871.

———. "Who Gets Breakfast?" *New Northwest* 12 Apr. 1872.

———. *Willow Grange: A Story of Life in Eastern Oregon*. Serialized novel in the *New Northwest*, 16 Sept. 1880 to 10 Mar. 1881.

Corant, Roger. *Mercer's Belles*. Seattle: University of Washington Press, 1960.

Corbett, P. Scott, and Nancy Parker Corbett. "The Chinese in Oregon, c. 1870-1880." *Oregon Historical Quarterly* 78 (March 1977): 73-85.

Corning, Howard McKinley, ed. *Dictionary of Oregon History*. Portland: Binfords & Mort, 1956.

Crane, Florence R. *Faithful Indians of St. Ignatius, by Redfeather, daughter of White Buffalo*. n.p.[WA]: n.p., 1907.

Cross, Mary Bywater. *Treasures in the Trunk: Quilts of the Oregon Trail*. Nashville: Rutledge Hill Press, 1993.

Daugherty, James. *Marcus and Narcissa Whitman, Pioneers of Oregon*. New York: Viking Press, 1953.

Davies, Mary Carolyn. *The Skyline Trail*. New York: The Bobbs-Merrill Co., 1924.

Davis, Lenwood G. "Sources for History of Blacks in Oregon." *Oregon Historical Quarterly* 73 (1972): 197-211.

———. "Sources for History of Blacks in Washington State." *Western Journal of Black Studies* 2 (March 1978): 60-64.

Deady, Matthew P. *Pharisee among Philistines: The Diary of Judge Matthew P. Deady, 1871-92*. 2 vols. Ed. Malcolm Clark, Jr. Portland: Oregon Historical Society, 1975.

Dearborn, Mary. *Pochahontas's Daughters, Gender and Ethnicity in American Culture*. New York: Oxford University Press, 1986.

Debow, Samuel P., and Edward A. Pitter, eds. *Who's Who in Religious, Fraternal, Social, Civic and Community Life on the Pacific Coast, State of Washington*. Seattle: Searchlight Publishing Co., 1926-1927.

Degler, Carl. N. "What Ought to Be and What Was: Women's Sexuality in the Nineteenth Century." *American Historical Review* 79 (1975): 1476-90.

DeGraaf, Lawrence B. "Race, Sex and Regions: Black Women in the American West, 1850-1920." *Pacific Historical Review* 49 (May 1980): 285-313.

Dickinson, Charlotte Humphrey. "Diary of a Voyage to Oregon." Ed. Mary K. Lightfoot and Priscilla Kmeth. *Oregon Historical Quarterly* 84 (1983): 243-56.

Dodds, Gordon B. *Oregon: A Bicentennial History*. New York: Norton, 1977.

———, ed. *Varieties of Hope: An Anthology of Oregon Prose*. The Oregon Literature Series, Vol. 3. A Project of the Oregon Council of Teachers of English. Corvallis: Oregon State University Press, 1993.

Donovan, Lynn. "Women's History: A Listing of West Coast Archival and Manuscript Sources." *California Historical Quarterly* 55 (Spring/ Summer 1976): 74-83; 170-85.

Douglas, Jesse. "Origins of the Population of Oregon in 1850." *Pacific Northwest Quarterly* 41 (April 1950): 95-108.

Douthit, Mary Osborn, ed. *Souvenir of Western Women*. Portland: Anderson & Duniway, 1905.

Drury, Clifford M. *Elkanah and Mary Walker, Pioneers Among the Spokanes*. Caldwell, ID: Caxton Printers, Ltd., 1940.

———, ed. *Nine Years with the Spokane Indians: The Diary, 1838-1848, of Elkanah Walker*. Glendale, CA: Arthur H. Clark Co., 1976.

Dunlop, Richard. *Doctors of the American Frontier*. Garden City, NY: Doubleday, 1965.

Dye, Eva Emery. *The Conquest: The True Story of Lewis and Clark*. Chicago: A. C. McClurg and Co., 1902.

———. *McDonald of Old Oregon: A Tale of Two Shores*. Chicago: A. C. McClurg and Co., 1906.

———. *McLoughlin and Old Oregon: A Chronicle.* Chicago: A. C. McClurg, 1900.

———. *The Soul of America: An Oregon Iliad.* New York: The Press of the Pioneers, 1934.

———. *Stories of Old Oregon.* Vol. 7 of the Western Series of Readers. San Francisco: The Whitaker & Ray Co., 1900.

———. "Woman's Part in the Drama of the Northwest." *Transactions of the 23rd Annual Reunion of the Oregon Pioneer Association for 1894.* Portland: George H. Himes and Co., 1895.

Edson, Christopher J. *Chinese in Eastern Oregon, 1860-1890.* San Francisco: R and E Research Association, 1974.

Edwards, G. Thomas, and Carlos A. Schwantes, eds. *Experiences in a Promised Land: Essays in Pacific Northwest History.* Seattle: University of Washington Press, 1986.

Ellis, Salone. *The Last Wilderness.* Boston: Small & Maynard, 1925.

———. *The Logger.* Boston: Small & Maynard, 1924.

Engle, Flora A. P. "The Story of the Mercer Expeditions." *Washington Historical Quarterly* 6 (Oct. 1915): 225-37.

Evans, Elwood. *History of the Pacific Northwest: Oregon and Washington.* 2 vols. Portland: North Pacific History Co., 1889.

Feldman, Egol. "Prostitution, the Alien Woman, and the Progressive Imagination, 1910-1915." *American Quarterly* 30 (Summer 1967): 192-206.

Fetterley, Judith. *The Resisting Reader: A Feminist Approach to American Fiction.* Bloomington: Indiana University Press, 1978.

———, and Marjorie Pryse, eds. *American Women Regionalists, 1850-1910, A Norton Anthology.* New York: W. W. Norton, 1992.

Fischer, Christiane, ed. *Let Them Speak for Themselves: Women in the American West, 1849-1900.* New York: E.P. Dutton, 1978.

Flexner, Eleanor. *Century of Struggle: The Woman's Rights Movement in the United States.* New York: Atheneum, 1974. Rev. ed. Cambridge: Belknap Press of Harvard University Press, 1975.

Foote, Mary Hallock. *A Picked Company; a Novel.* Boston: Houghton, 1912.

Fowler, William W. *Woman on the American Frontier: A Valuable and Authentic History of the Heroism, Adventures, Privations, Captivities, Trials, and Noble Lives and Deaths of the "Pioneer Mothers of the Republic."* Chicago: C. B. Beach & Co., 1877.

Friedman, Ralph. *The Other Side of Oregon.* Caldwell, ID: Caxton, 1993.

———. *In Search of Western Oregon.* Caldwell, ID: Caxton, 1990.

———. *Tracking Down Oregon.* Caldwell, ID: Caxton, 1978.

Gaston, Joseph. *The Centennial History of Oregon, 1811-1912.* 4 vols. Chicago: The S. J. Clarke Publishing Co., 1912.

——— *Portland, Oregon; Its History and Builders.* 3 vols. Chicago: The S. J. Clarke Publishing Co., 1911.

Gatke, Robert Moulton. *Chronicles of Willamette: The Pioneer University of the West.* 2 vols. Portland: Binfords & Mort, 1943.

———, ed. "A Document of Mission History, 1833-43." *Oregon Historical Quarterly* 36 (1935): 71-94; 163-81.

Geiger, Susan N. G. "Women's Life Histories: Method and Content." *SIGNS: Journal of Women in Culture and Society* 11 (1986): 334-51.

Gilbert, Frank T. *Historic Sketches of Walla Walla County*. Portland: A. G. Walling, 1882.

Gill, John. *Gill's Dictionary of the Chinook Jargon*. 17th ed. Portland: J. K. Gill Co., 1933.

Gilligan, Carol. *In a Different Voice: Psychological Theory and Women's Development*. Cambridge: Harvard University Press, 1982.

Gilliss, Julia Stellwagen. *So Far from Home: An Army Bride on the Western Frontier, 1865-1869*. Portland: Oregon Historical Society Press, 1993.

Goldenweiser, Alexander. "Culture of the Indian Tribes of the Pacific Northwest." *Oregon Historical Quarterly* 41 (June 1940): 137-46.

Graulich, Melody. "Violence Against Women in Literature of the Western Family." *Frontiers* 7 (1984): 14-20.

Gray, Dorothy. *Women of the West*. Millbrae, CA: Les Femmes, 1976.

Gray, William H. *A History of Oregon 1792-1849, Drawn from Personal Observation and Authentic Information*. Portland: Harris & Holman, 1870.

Green, Rayna (Cherokee). *Native American Women: A Contextual Bibliography*. Bloomington: Indiana University Press, 1983.

———. "Review Essay: Native American Women." *Signs: Journal of Women in Culture and Society* 6 (1980): 248-67.

Grissom, Irene Welch. *A Daughter of the Northwest*. Boston: The Cornhill Publishing Co., 1918; 1923.

———. *The Superintendent*. New York: Harriman, 1910.

Griswold, Rufus Wilmot. *The Female Poets of America*. Philadelphia: Carey & Hart, 1849.

Haeberlin, Hermann, and Erna Gunther. *The Indians of Puget Sound*. Seattle: University of Washington Press, 1930.

Halvorsen, Helen Olson, and Lorraine Fletcher. "Nineteenth Century Midwife: Some Recollections." *Oregon Historical Quarterly* 70 (Mar. 1969): 39-49.

Hamilton, Mrs. S. Watson. *A Pioneer of '53*. Introduction by J. B. Hoover. Albany, OR: The *Herald* Press, 1905.

Hanford, Cornelius Holgate, ed. *Seattle and Environs, 1852-1924*. 3 vols. Seattle: Pioneer Historical Publishing, 1924.

Hanley, Sharon, and Roslyn Terbor-Penn, eds. *The Afro-American Woman: Struggles and Images*. Port Washington, NJ: Kennikat Press, 1978.

Hargreaves, Sheba May. *The Cabin at the Trail's End*. New York: Harper & Brothers Publishers, 1928.

———. *Heroine of the Prairies: A Romance of the Oregon Trail*. New York: Harper & Brothers, Publishers, 1930.

Harriman, Alice. *Songs of the Olympics*. Seattle: Harriman, 1909.

———. *Songs of the Sound*. Seattle: Stuff Printing Co., 1906.

Harris, Susan K. *Nineteenth-Century American Women's Novels: Interpretive Strategies*. Cambridge: Cambridge University Press, 1990.

Hassell, Susan Whitcomb, comp. *A Hundred and Sixty Books by Washington Authors*. Seattle: Lowman & Hanford, 1916.

Hatton, Raymond R. *High Desert of Central Oregon*. Portland: Binford & Mort, 1977.

Hayden, Mary Jane Bean. *Pioneer Days*. San Jose: Murgotten Press, 1915.

Hayes, Ralph. *Northwest Black Pioneers: A Centennial Tribute*. Seattle: Ralph Hayes, 1987.

Hazard, Joseph Taylor. *Pioneer Teachers of Washington*. Seattle: Retired Teachers Association, 1955.

Henderson, Archie M. "Introduction of Negroes in the Pacific Northwest, 1788-1842." MA Thesis. University of Washington, 1949.

Higbee, Mrs. Blanche. *The Autobiography of a Pioneer Woman*. Spokane, WA: The Knapp Book Store, 1934.

Hildebrand, Lorraine. *Straw Hats, Sandals, and Steel: The Chinese in Washington State*. Tacoma: Washington State Bicentennial Commission, 1977.

Hill, D. G. "The Negro as a Political and Social Issue in the Oregon Country." *Journal of Negro History* 33 (April 1948): 130-45.

————. "The Negro in Oregon, A Survey." MA Thesis. University of Oregon, 1932.

Hine, Darlene Clark, ed. *Black Women in American History: From Colonial Times through the Nineteenth Century*. 4 vols. Brooklyn: Carlson, Publishing, Inc., 1990.

Hines, Gustavus. *Oregon: Its History, Condition, and Prospects: Containing a Description of the Geography, Climate and Productions, with Personal Adventures among the Indians during a Residence of the Author on the Plains Bordering the Pacific while Connected with the Oregon Mission: Embracing Extended Notes on a Voyage around the World*. Buffalo, NY: George H. Derby and Co., 1851.

Hines, Harvey Kimball. *An Illustrated History of the State of Oregon*. Chicago: Lewis, 1893.

————. *An Illustrated History of the State of Washington*. Chicago: Lewis, 1893.

————. *Missionary History of the Pacific Northwest*. Portland: n.p., 1899.

Hirata, Lucy Cheng. "Free, Enslaved, and Indentured Workers in Nineteenth Century Prostitution." *Signs: Journal of Women in Culture and Society* 5 (Fall 1979): 3-29.

Hitchman, Robert. *Place Names of Washington*. Tacoma: Washington State Historical Society, 1985.

Hoff, Benjamin, ed. *The Singing Creek Where the Willows Grow: The Mystical Nature Diary of Opal Whiteley: with a biography and an afterword*. New York: Penguin, 1988, 1994.

Holbrook, Stewart H. *The Columbia*. New York: Rinehart, 1956. Rpt. Sausalito, CA: Comstock Editions, 1991.

————. *Far Corner; a Personal View of the Pacific Northwest*. New York: Macmillan, 1952. Rpt. Sausalito, CA: Comstock Editions, 1987.

Holmes, Kenneth, ed. *Covered Wagon Women: Diaries and Letters from the Western Trails, 1840-1890*. 10 vols. Glendale: CA and Spokane, WA: The Arthur H. Clark Co., 1983-1991.

Hong, Maria, ed. *Growing up Asian American: An Anthology*. New York: William Morrow, 1993.

Horner, John B. *Oregon Literature*, 2nd ed. Portland: The J. K. Gill Co., 1902.

Horton, Emily McCowen. *My Scrapbook*. Seattle, WA: n.p., 1927.

Hughes, Agnes Alice Lockhart. *Told in the Garden*. Boston: n.p., 1902.

Hussey, John A. "The Women of Fort Vancouver." *Oregon Historical Quarterly* 92 (Fall 1991): 265-308.

Ichioka, Yuji. "Ameyuki-san: Japanese Prostitution in Nineteenth Century America." *Amerasia Journal* 4 (1977): 1-21.

Jackson, Philip, and A. Jon Kimerling, eds. *Atlas of the Pacific Northwest.* 8th ed. Corvallis: Oregon State University Press, 1993.

Jacobs, Melville. *The Content and Style of Oral Literature: Clackamas Chinook Myths and Tales.* Chicago: The University of Chicago Press, 1959.

———. *Coos Myth Texts.* University of Washington Publications in Anthropology 8 (1940): 127-260.

———. *Coos Narrative and Ethnological Texts.* University of Washington Publications in Anthropology 8 (1939): 1-125.

———. "The Fate of Indian Oral Literature in Oregon." *Northwest Review* 3 (Summer 1962): 90-99.

———. *Kalapuya Texts.* University of Washington Publications in Anthropology 11 (1945): Part 3.

———. *Nehalem Tillamook Tales.* Eugene: University of Oregon Books, 1959. Rpt. Corvallis: Oregon State University Press, 1990.

———. *Northwest Sahaptin Texts.* Part I. New York: Columbia University Press, 1934.

———. *The People Are Coming Soon: Analyses of Clackamas Chinook Myths and Tales.* Seattle: University of Washington Press, 1960.

———, and Elizabeth Derr Jacobs. *Texts in Chinook Jargon.* University of Washington Publications in Anthropology 7 (1936): 1-27.

James, Edward T., ed. *Notable American Women, 1607-1950: A Biographical Dictionary.* 3 vols. Cambridge: Harvard University Press, 1971.

Jameson, Elizabeth. "Women as Workers; Women as Civilizers; True Womanhood in the American West." *Frontiers* 7 (1984): 1-8.

Jeffrey, Julie Roy. *Frontier Women: The Trans-Mississippi West, 1840-1880.* New York: Hill and Wang, 1979.

Jelinek, Estelle C. *Women's Autobiography: Essays in Criticism.* Bloomington: Indiana University Press, 1980.

Jensen, Joan M. *With These Hands: Women Working the Land.* New York: The Feminist Press, 1981.

———, and Darlis A. Miller. "The Gentle Tamers Revisited: New Approach to the History of Women in the American West." *Pacific Historical Review* 49 (May 1980): 173-214.

Johansen, Dorothy. *Empire of the Columbia: A History of the Pacific Northwest.* 2d ed. New York: Harper, 1967.

Jones, Jacqueline. *Labor of Love, Labor of Sorrow: Black Women, Work and the Family from Slavery to the Present.* New York: Basic Books, 1985.

Jones, Suzi, and Jarold Ramsey, eds. *The Stories We Tell: An Anthology of Oregon Folk Literature.* The Oregon Literature Series, Vol. V. A Project of the Oregon Council of Teachers of English. Corvallis: Oregon State University Press, 1994.

Jones, W. R. "Seattle Prostitution from inside the Quarantine." *Northwest Medicine* 18 (1919): 184-87.

Josephy, Alivin M., Jr. *The Nez Perce Indians and the Opening of the Northwest.* New Haven: Yale University Press, 1965.

Judson, Katharine Berry. *Early Days in Old Oregon.* Chicago: A. C. McClurg, 1916.

———. *When the Forests Are Ablaze.* Chicago: A. C. McClurg, 1912.

Judson, Phoebe Goodell. *A Pioneer's Search for an Ideal Home, by Phoebe Goodell Judson, Who Crossed the Plains in 1853 and Became a Resident on Puget Sound before the Organization of Washington Territory.* Bellingham,

WA: Union Printing, Binding & Stationery Co., 1925. Rpt. with an introduction by Susan H. Armitage. Lincoln: University of Nebraska Press, 1984.

Katz, William Loren. *The Black West*. Seattle: Open Hand Publishing, 1987.

Kelley, Mary. *Private Woman, Public Stage: Literary Domesticity in Nineteenth-Century America*. New York: Oxford University Press, 1984.

———. "The Sentimentalists: Promise and Betrayal in the Home." *Signs: Journal of Women in Culture and Society* 4 (Spring 1979): 434-46.

Kennedy, David M. "Overview: The Progressive Era." *American Quarterly* 37 (1974-75): 453-68.

Kessler, Lauren. "The Ideas of Woman Suffragists and the Portland *Oregonian*." *Journalism Quarterly* 57 (Winter 1980): 597-605.

Ketcham, Rebecca. "From Ithaca to Clatsop Plains: Miss Ketcham's Journal of Travel." Ed. Leo M. Kaiser and Priscilla Knuth. *Oregon Historical Quarterly* 62 (Sept. & Dec. 1961): 237-87; 337-402.

King, Charles R. "The Woman's Experience of Childbirth on the Western Frontier." *Journal of the West* 29 (Jan.-Feb. 1990): 76-84.

Kirk, Ruth, and Carmela Alexander. *Exploring Washington's Past: A Road Guide to History*. Seattle: University of Washington Press, 1990.

Kirkland, Winifred Margaretta, and Frances Kirkland. *Girls Who Became Writers*. New York: Harper, 1933. Rpt. Freeport, NY: Ayer Co., Books for Libraries Press, 1971.

Knowles, Karen, ed. *Celebrating the Land: Women's Nature Writings, 1850-1991*. Flagstaff, AZ: Northland Publishing Co., 1992.

Kohl, Edith Eudora. *Land of the Burnt Thigh*. St. Paul: Minnesota Historical Society Press, 1986.

Kolodny, Annette. *The Land Before Her: Fantasy and Experience of the American Frontier, 1630-1860*. Chapel Hill: University of North Carolina Press, 1984.

———. *The Lay of the Land: Metaphor as Experience and History in American Life and Letters*. Chapel Hill: University of North Carolina Press, 1976.

Kraditor, Aileen S. *The Ideas of the Woman Suffrage Movement, 1890-1920*. New York: W.W. Norton, 1965. Rpt. 1981.

Krupat, Arnold. *For Those Who Come After: A Study of Native American Autobiography*. Berkeley: University of California Press, 1985.

———, ed. *New Voices in Native American Literary Criticism*. Washington, D.C.: Smithsonian Institution Press, 1993.

Lampman, Evelyn Sibley. "As It Was . . . [Dallas, OR]." *Oregon Historical Quarterly* 78 (June 1977): 158-73.

Lang, Herbert O., ed. *History of the Willamette Valley*. Portland: Himes & Lang, 1885.

Larsell, Olaf. *The Doctor in Oregon: A Medical History*. Portland: Binfords & Mort, 1947.

Larson, T. A. "Dolls, Vassals, and Drudges—Pioneer Women in the West." *Western Historical Quarterly* 3 (Jan. 1972): 1-16.

———. "The Woman Suffrage Movement in Washington." *Pacific Northwest Quarterly* 67 (Apr. 1976): 49-62.

Lee, L. L., and Merrill Lewis, eds. *Women, Women Writers, and the West*. Troy, NY: Whitson Publishing Company, 1979.

Lee, Mary Paik. *Quiet Odyssey: A Pioneer Korean Woman in America*. Seattle: University of Washington Press, 1990.

Lee, W. Storrs, ed. *Washington State: A Literary Chronicle*. New York: Funk and Wagnalls, 1969.

Lerner, Gerda. *The Majority Finds Its Past: Placing Women in History*. New York: Oxford University Press, 1979.

LeWarne, Charles. *Utopias on Puget Sound, 1885-1915*. Seattle: University of Washington Press, 1975.

Lewis, William S. *The Okanogan, Methow, Sanpoils, Nespelem, Colville, and Lakes Indian Tribes or Bands of the State of Washington*. Washington, D.C.: Government Printing Office, 1927.

Liestman, Daniel. "'To Win Redeemed Souls from Heathen Darkness': Protestant Response to the Chinese of the Pacific Northwest in the Late Nineteenth Century." *Western Historical Quarterly* 24 (March-May 1993): 179-201.

Limerick, Patricia Nelson. *The Legacy of Conquest: The Unbroken Past of the American West*. New York: W.W. Norton, 1987.

——, Clyde A. Milner II, and Charles E. Rankin, eds. *Trails: Toward a New Western History*. Lawrence: University Press of Kansas, 1991.

Lindsay, Batterman [Annie]. "Abandoned: A Tale of the Plains." *Atlantic* 78 (Oct. 1886): 538-42.

——. "Cusack's Ghost." *Overland Monthly* 28 (Sept. 1896): 281-85.

——. *Derelicts of Destiny [Being a Few Short Annals of a Vanishing People]*. New York: Neely Co., 1900. Ltd. ed. rearranged by Harry S. Stuff. Seattle: Ivy Press, 1901.

——. "Diamond Hunters of Boise." *Overland Monthly* 28 (Nov. 1896): 518-20.

——. "Extracts from Mrs. Lofty's Diary." *Overland Monthly* 23 (June 1894): 600-11; 24 (Oct. 1894): 425-32; 25 (Mar. 1895): 237-52; 25 (May 1895): 470-76; 26 (July 1895): 64-69; 26 (Nov. 1895): 502-13; 27 (June 1896): 611-15.

——. "How the Boys Resigned Judge Travers." *Overland Monthly* 28 (Oct. 1896): 391-92.

——. "Kwelth-Elite, The Proud Slave." *Overland Monthly* 33 (June 1899): 534-39.

——. "Riddle of the Sage-brush." *Overland Monthly* 26 (Aug. 1895): 172-82.

Ling, Amy. *Between Worlds: Women Writers of Chinese Ancestry*. New York: Pergamon Press, 1990.

Lockley, Fred. "Documentary: The Case of Robin Holmes vs. Nathaniel Ford." *Oregon Historical Quarterly* 23 (Mar. 1922): 111-37.

——. *History of the Columbia River Valley, from the Dalles to the Sea*. 3 vols. Chicago: The S. J. Clarke Publishing Co., 1928.

——. *The Lockley Files: Conversations with Pioneer Women*. Comp. and ed. Mike Helm. Eugene, OR: Rainy Day Press, 1981.

——. *The Lockley Files, Voices of the Oregon Country: Conversations with Bullwhackers, Muleskinners, Pioneers, Prospectors, 49ers . . . . and All Sorts and Conditions of Men*. Comp. and ed. Mike Helm. Eugene, OR: Rainy Day Press, 1981.

——, ed. *Oregon Folks*. New York: Knickerbocker Press, 1927.

——. *Oregon Trailblazers*. New York: Knickerbocker Press, 1929.

——. *Oregon's Yesterdays*. New York: Knickerbocker Press, 1928.

——. "Some Documentary Records of Slavery in Oregon." *Oregon Historical Quarterly* 17 (June 1916): 107-115.

Loewenberg, Robert J. *Equality of the Frontier: Jason Lee and the Oregon Mission 1834-1843*. Seattle: University of Washington Press, 1975.

———. "Saving Oregon Again: A Western Perennial?" *Oregon Historical Quarterly* 78 (Dec. 1977): 332-50.

Lohn, Agnette Midgarden. *The Voice of the Big Firs.* St. Paul, MN: Pioneer Co., 1918.

Lord, Elizabeth Laughlin. *Reminiscences of Eastern Oregon.* Portland: Irwin-Hodson, 1903.

Love, Glen A., ed. *The World Begins Here: An Anthology of Oregon Short Fiction.* The Oregon Literature Series, Vol. I. A Project of the Oregon Council of Teachers of English. Corvallis: Oregon State University Press, 1993.

Love, Helen Stewart. *Diary of Helen Stewart, 1853.* Eugene, OR: Lane County Pioneer Historical Society, 1961.

Lovejoy, Esther Clayson Pohl. "My Medical School, 1890-1894," *Oregon Historical Quarterly* 75 (Mar. 1974): 7-35.

Lowenstein, Steven. *The Jews of Oregon, 1850-1950.* Portland: Jewish Historical Society of Oregon, 1987.

Luchetti, Cathy, and Carol Olwell, eds. *Women of the West.* St. George, UT: Antelope Island Press, 1982.

"Luteshia Carson, Woman Slave in Missouri Brought to Oregon, Sues Estate of Master for Back Wages." Salem *Oregon Statesman* 17 Oct. 1854.

Lyman, William Denison. *An Illustrated History of Walla Walla Country.* San Francisco: W. H. Lever, 1901.

Lynch, Vera Martin. *Free Land for Free Men: A Story of Clackamas County.* Portland: Artline Printing, 1973.

MacColl, E. Kimbark. *The Growth of a City, Power and Politics in Portland, Oregon, 1915-1950.* Portland: Georgian Press Co., 1979.

———. *The Shaping of a City: Business and Politics in Portland, Oregon, 1885-1910.* Portland: Georgian Press Co., 1976.

Mackey, Thomas C. *Red Lights Out: A Legal History of Prostitution, Disorderly Houses and Vice Districts, 1870-1917.* New York: Garland Pub., Inc., 1987.

Mantle, Beatrice. *Gret; the Story of a Pagan.* New York: Century, 1907.

Masterson, Martha Gay. *One Woman's West: Recollections of the Oregon Trail and Settling the Northwest Country, 1838-1916.* 2nd ed. Ed. Lois Barton. Eugene, OR: Spencer Butte Press, 1990.

McArthur, Harriet Nesmith. "Recollections of the Rickreall." *Oregon Historical Quarterly* 30 (Mar.-Dec. 1929): 367-76.

McArthur, Lewis A. *Oregon Geographic Names.* 6th ed. Portland: Oregon Historical Society, 1992.

McLagan, Elizabeth. *A Peculiar Paradise: A History of Blacks in Oregon, 1788-1940.* The Oregon Black History Project. Portland: Georgian Press, 1980.

McNamee, Mary Dominica, S. N. D. *Willamette Interlude.* Palo Alto, CA: Pacific Books, 1969.

McWhorter, Lucullus Virgil. *Yellow Wolf: His Own Story.* Caldwell, ID: Caxton Printers, 1940.

Meany, Edmond Stephen. *History of the State of Washington.* New York: Macmillan, 1909.

Meier, Gary and Gloria. *Those Naughty Ladies of the Old Northwest.* Bend, OR: Maverick Publishers, 1990.

Merriam, Harold G. *Northwest Verse, an Anthology.* Caldwell, ID: Caxton Printers, 1931.

Miller, Jean Baker. *Toward a New Psychology of Women*. Boston: Beacon Press, 1976.

Mills, Hazel Emery, ed. *Who's Who Among Pacific Northwest Authors*. Salem, OR: Pacific Northwest Library Association, 1957.

——— and Nancy B. Pryor. *The Negro in the State of Washington: 1788-1969*. Olympia: Washington State Library, 1970.

Mock, Lucy Byrd. *The Maid of Pend d'Oreille, An Indian Idyl, by Le Moquer*. Siwash ed. Seattle: n.p., 1910.

Montgomery, James W. *Liberated Woman: A Life of May Arkwright Hutton*. Spokane, WA: Gingko Publishers, 1974.

Morgan, Carrie Blake. *The Path of Gold*. New Whatcom, WA: Edson & Irish, 1900.

Morris, Anna Van Rensselaer. *The Apple Woman of the Klickitat*. New York: Duffield & Co., 1918.

Moynihan, Ruth Barnes, Susan Armitage, and Christiane Fischer Dichamp, eds. *So Much to Be Done: Women Settlers on the Mining and Ranching Frontier*. Lincoln: University of Nebraska Press, 1990.

Mumford, Esther Hall. *Calabash: A Guide to the History, Culture and Art of African Americans in Seattle and King County, Washington*. Seattle: Ananse Press, 1993.

———. *Seven Stars and Orion: Reflections of the Past*. Seattle: Ananse Press, 1986.

Myres, Sandra L. *Westering Women and the Frontier Experience, 1800-1915*. Albuquerque: University of New Mexico Press, 1982.

"Negro Pioneers; Their Page in Oregon History." *Oregon Native Son* 1 (Jan. 1900): 432-34.

Nelson, Herbert B. *The Literary Impulse in Pioneer Oregon*. Oregon State Monographs, Studies in Literature and Language, No. 1. Corvallis: Oregon State University Press, 1948.

Nixon, Oliver W. *How Marcus Whitman Saved Oregon*. Chicago: Star Pub. Co., 1895.

Noland, Edward. *A Guide to the Manuscript Collections in the Eastern Washington State Historical Society*. Spokane: Eastern Washington State Historical Society, 1987.

Northwest Books. *Report of the Committee on Books of the Inland Empire Council of Teachers of English*. Portland: Binfords & Mort, 1942.

O'Donnell, Terence. *That Balance So Rare: The Story of Oregon*. Portland: Oregon Historical Society, 1988.

Oliphant, J. Orin. *On the Cattle Ranges of the Oregon Country*. Seattle: University of Washington Press, 1968.

O'Neill, William. *Divorce in the Progressive Era*. New Haven: Yale University Press, 1967.

———. *The Progressive Years: America Comes of Age*. New York: Dodd, Mead, 1975.

———, ed. *Echoes of Revolt: The Masses, 1911-1917*. Chicago: Quadrangle, 1966.

Owens, Narcissa (Cherokee). *Memoirs of Narcissa Owens*. Seattle: University of Washington, 1907.

Papshivily, Helen Waite. *All the Happy Endings: A Study of the Domestic Novel in America, The Women Who Wrote It, The Women Who Read It, In the Nineteenth Century*. Port Washington, NY: Kennikat, 1956.

Pascoe, Peggy. *Relations of Rescue: The Search for Female Moral Authority in the American West, 1874-1939*. New York: Oxford University Press, 1990.

———. "Western Women at the Cultural Crossroads." *Trails: Toward a New Western History*. Eds. Patricia Nelson Limerick, Clyde A. Milner, II, and Charles E. Rankin. Lawrence: University Press of Kansas, 1991. 40-58.

Patterson-Black, Sheryle, and Gene. *Western Women in History and Literature*. Crawford, NE: Cottonwood Press, 1978.

Peil, Alice Applegate. "Old Oregon School Days." *Oregon Historical Quarterly* 59 (June 1958): 196-207.

Perry, Maude Caldwell. *Tide House: A Novel*. New York: Harcourt, Brace & Company, 1929.

Personal Narratives Group, eds. *Interpreting Women's Lives: Feminist Theory and Personal Narratives*. Bloomington: Indiana University Press, 1989.

Peterson, Emil R., and Alfred Powers. *A Century of Coos and Curry*. Coquille, OR: Curry Pioneer and Historical Association, 1952.

Peterson, Jacqueline, and Jennifer S. H. Brown. *The New Peoples: Being and Becoming Métis in North America*. Manitoba Studies in Native History, I. Lincoln: University of Nebraska Press, 1985.

Petrick, Paula. "Capitalists with Rooms: Prostitution in Helena, Montana, 1865." *Montana, The Magazine of Western History* 31 (Apr. 1981): 28-41.

Pettibone, Anita. *The Bitter Country*. Garden City, NY: Doubleday, Page & Co., 1925.

Pioneer Ladies Club of Pendleton, comp. *Reminiscences of Oregon Pioneers*. [Pendleton]: Eastern Oregon Publishing Company, 1937.

Pollard, Lancaster, comp. "A Check List of Washington Authors," *Pacific Northwest Quarterly* 31 (Jan.-Oct. 1940): 3-96.

———. "A Checklist of Washington Authors: Additions and Corrections." *Pacific Northwest Quarterly* 35 (July 1944): 233-66.

———. *A History of the State of Washington*. 4 vols. New York: American Historical Society, 1937.

———. "Washington Literature: A Historical Sketch." *Pacific Northwest Quarterly* 29 (July 1938): 227-54.

Pottsmith, Marie M. Holst. "Pioneering Years in Hamlet, Oregon: A Finnish Community." *Oregon Historical Quarterly* 61 (1960): 4-45.

Poulton, Helen Jean. "The Attitude of Oregon Toward Slavery and Secession, 1843-1865." MA Thesis. University of Oregon, 1946.

Powers, Alfred. *History of Oregon Literature*. Portland: Metropolitan Press, 1935.

Prosser, William Farrand. *A History of the Puget Sound Country; Its Resources, Its Commerce, and Its People*. 2 vols. New York: Lewis Publishing Co., 1903.

Putnam, Rozelle Applegate. "The Letters of Roselle [sic] Putnam." Ed. Sheba Hargreaves. *Oregon Historical Quarterly* 29 (1928): 242-65.

Radner, Joan Newlon, ed. *Feminist Messages: Coding in Women's Folk Literature*. Urbana: University of Illionois Press, 1993.

Rees, Helen Guyton. "*Schoolmarms*." Portland: Binford & Mort, 1983.

Rice, Carrie Shaw. *In Childhood Straying*. Tacoma: Vaughan and Merrill, 1895.

———. *Where the Rhodedendrons Grow*. Tacoma: C. S. Rice, 1904.

———. *Windows that Shine*. Tacoma: Smith-Kinney, 1922.

Richey, Elinor. *Eminent Women of the West*. Berkeley, CA: Howell-North Books, 1975.

Riley, Glenda. *Divorce: An American Tradition*. New York: Oxford University Press, 1991.

————. *The Female Frontier: A Comparative View of Women on the Prairie and the Plains*. Lawrence: University Press of Kansas, 1988.

————. *A Place to Grow: Women in the American West*. Arlington Heights, IL: Harlan Davidson, Inc., 1992.

————. *Women and Indians on the Frontier, 1825-1915*. Albuquerque: University of New Mexico Press, 1984.

————. "Women in the West." *Journal of American Culture* 3 (Summer 1980): 311-29.

Robbins, William G., Robert Frank, and Richard Ross, eds. *Regionalism and the Pacific Northwest*. Corvallis: Oregon State University Press, 1983.

Roe, Virgie Eve. *The Heart of Night Wind: A Story of the Great Northwest*. New York: Grosset and Dunlap, 1913.

Rosen, Ruth. *The Lost Sisterhood: Prostitution in America, 1900-1918*. Baltimore: The Johns Hopkins University Press, 1982.

Rosenberg, Charles, and Carroll Smith-Rosenberg, eds. *The Prostitute and the Social Reformer*. New York: Arno, 1974.

Ross, Nancy Wilson. *Farthest Reach: Oregon and Washington*. New York: Alfred A. Knopf, 1941.

————. *Westward the Women*. New York: Aldred A. Knopf, 1945.

Ruby, Robert H., and John A. Brown. *Indians of the Pacific Northwest: A History*. Norman: University of Oklahoma Press, 1981.

Rudnick, Lois, and Adele Heller, eds. *The Cultural Moment: 1915*. New Brunswick: Rutgers University Press, 1991.

Sanders, Helen Fitzgerald. *Trails through Western Woods*. New York and Seattle: The Alice Harriman Co., 1910.

Sapir, Edward, ed. *Takelma Texts*. University of Pennsylvania Anthropological Publications from the University Museum 2 (1900): 1-267.

Sargent, Alice Applegate. "A Sketch of Rogue River Valley History." *Oregon Historical Quarterly* 22 (Mar. 1921): 1-11.

Saul, George Brandon. *Quintet: Essays on Five American Women Poets*. Vol. 17, Studies in American Literature. The Hague, Netherlands: Mouton & Co., 1967.

Savage, W. Sherman. "The Negro in the History of the Pacific Northwest." *Journal of Negro History* 8 (July 1928): 255-64.

————. "The Negro Pioneer in the State of Washington." *Negro History Bulletin* 21 (Jan. 1958): 93-95.

Schlissel, Lillian. *Women's Diaries of the Westward Journey*. New York: Schocken Books, 1992.

————, Byrd Gibbens, and Elizabeth Hampsten. *Far from Home: Families of the Westward Journey*. New York: Schocken Books, 1989.

————, Vicki L. Ruiz, and Janice Monk, eds. *Western Women: Their Land, Their Lives*. Albuquerque: University of New Mexico Press, 1988.

Schoffen, Elizabeth. *The "Demands of Rome"; Her Own Story of Thirty-one Years as a Sister of Charity of Providence of the Roman Catholic Church*. Portland, OR; n.p., 1917.

Schultz, John L. "Acculturation and Religion on the Colville Indian Reservation." PhD Diss. Washington State University, 1971.

Scott, Harvey Whitefield. *History of the Oregon Country*. 6 vols. Comp. Leslie M. Scott. Cambridge: Riverside Press, 1924.

————. *History of Portland, Oregon*. Syracuse, NY: Mason, 1891.

Seattle Public Library. *The Population of Seattle: Censuses and Estimates, Past, Present and Future*. Seattle: Seattle Public Library, 1929.

Sengstacken, Agnes Ruth (Lockhart). *A Legend of the Coos*. San Francisco: Philopolis Press, 1909.

Shaw, George C. *The Chinook Jargon and How to Use It: A Complete and Exhaustive Lexicon of the Oldest Trade Language of the American Continent*. Seattle: Ranier Printing Co., 1909.

Sherr, Lynn, and Jurate Kazickas. *The American Woman's Gazateer*. New York: Bantam, 1976.

Simmons, Alexy. *Red Light Ladies: Settlement Patterns and Material Culture on the Mining Frontier*. Corvallis: Oregon State University Department of Anthropology, Anthropology Northwest No. 4, 1989.

Sisters of Notre Dame de Namur [Sister Anthony, S. H.]. *In Harvest Fields by Sunset Shores; The Work of the Sisters of Notre Dame on the Pacific Coast by a Member of the Congregation; Diamond Jubilee Edition, 1851-1926*. San Francisco: Gilmartin Co., 1926.

Skiff, Frederick Woodward. *Adventures in Americana*. Portland: Metropolitan Press, 1935.

Smith, Charles Wesley. *Pacific Northwest Americana: A Check List of Books and Pamphlets Relating to the History of the Pacific Northwest*. 3rd ed. Rev. and extended by Isabel Mayhew. Portland: Binford & Mort, 1950.

Smith, Helen Krebs, ed. *With Her Own Wings: Historical Sketches, Reminiscences, and Anecdotes of Pioneer Women*. Portland: Beattie and Co., 1948.

Smith, Herndon, comp. *Centralia: The First Fifty Years, 1845-1900*. Centralia, WA: *Daily Chronicle* and F. H. Cole Printing Company, 1942.

Smith, Louisa (Umpqua). "The Story of Louisa Smith's Childhood." *Lower Umpqua Texts*. Ed. Leo J. Frachtenberg. New York: Columbia University, 1914.

Smith-Rosenberg, Carroll. *Disorderly Conduct: Visions of Gender in Victorian America*. New York: Oxford University Press, 1985.

———, and Charles Rosenberg. "The Female Animal: Medical and Biological Views of Woman and Her Role in Nineteenth-Century America." *Journal of American History* 110 (1973): 332-56.

Society of the Sisters of the Holy Names. *Gleanings of Fifty Years; the Sisters of the Holy Names of Jesus and Mary in the Northwest, 1859-1909*. Portland: Glass & Prudhomme, 1909.

Solomon, Barbara, ed. *Rediscoveries: American Short Stories by Women, 1832-1916*. New York: Penguin, 1994.

Soucie, Minerva T. "The End of a Way of Life: The Burns Paiute Indian Tribe." *The First Oregonians*. Ed. Carolyn C. Buan and Richard Lewis. Portland: Oregon Council for the Humanities, 1991. 70-76.

Spalding, Eliza Hart. "Diary of Mrs. Henry Hart Spalding." *Memories of the West: The Spaldings*. Ed. Eliza Spalding Warren. Portland: Marsh Printing Co., 1916. 54-71.

Steeves, Sarah Hunt. *A Book of Remembrances of Marion County Oregon Pioneers, 1840-1860*. Salem, OR: Berncliff Printers, 1927.

Stephens, Ann Sophia Winterbotham. *Esther: A Story of the Oregon Trail*. New York: Beadles' Dime Novels, 1862.

Strasser, Susan. *Never Done: A History of American Housework*. New York: Pantheon Books, 1982.

Strelow, Michael, ed. *An Anthology of Northwest Writing: 1900-1950*. Eugene, OR: Northwest Review Books, 1979.

Sunoo, Sonia S. "Korean Women Pioneers of the Pacific Northwest." *Oregon Historical Quarterly* 79 (Spring 1978): 51-63.

Swanson, Kimberly. "Eva Emery Dye and the Romance of Oregon History." *Pacific Historian* 29 (1985): 59-68.

Tamura, Linda. "Railroads, Stumps, and Sawmills: Japanese Settlers of the Hood River Valley." *Oregon Historical Quarterly* 94 (Winter 1993-94): 369-98.

Taylor, Quintard. "The Emergence of Black Communities in the Pacific Northwest, 1864-1910." *Journal of Negro History* 64 (Fall 1974): 342-54.

Tenney, W. A. "From Savagery to Civilization." *Overland Monthly* 34 (Sept. 1899): 141-49.

Terrell, John Upton, and Donna M. *Indian Women of the Western Morning*. New York: The Dial Press, 1974.

Thomas, David Charles. "Religion in the Far West: Oregon's Willamette Valley, 1830-1850." PhD Diss. Ohio State University, 1993.

Thornton, Jesse Quinn. "*The River of the West*." Portland *Pacific Christian Advocate* 21 May 1870.

Tisdale, Sallie. *Stepping Westward: The Long Search for Home in the Pacific Northwest*. New York: Henry Holt & Co., 1991.

Todd, Janet M. *Women's Friendship in Literature*. New York: Columbia University Press, 1979.

Tompkins, Jane P. *Sensational Designs: The Cultural Work of American Fiction, 1790-1860*. New York: Oxford University Press, 1985.

Trusky, A. Thomas, ed. *Women Poets of the West: An Anthology, 1850-1950*. Boise, ID: Ahsahta Press, 1979.

Tsutakawa, Mayumi, and Alan Chong Lau, eds. *Turning Shadows into Light: Art and Culture of the Northwest's Early Asian/Pacific Community*. Seattle: Young Pine Press, 1982.

Turnbull, George S. *History of Oregon Newspapers*. Portland: Binfords & Mort, 1939.

Uebelacker, Morris. *Time Ball: A Story of the Yakima People and the Land*. Toppenish, WA: The Yakima Nation, 1984.

Vaughn, Thomas, ed. *The Western Shore: Oregon Country Essays Honoring the American Revolution*. Portland: Oregon Historical Society, 1975.

Walsh, Mary Roth. *"Doctors Wanted: No Women Need Apply": Sexual Barriers in the Medical Profession, 1835-1975*. New Haven: Yale University Press, 1977.

Warren, Eliza Spalding. *Memoirs of the West; the Spaldings*. Portland: Marsh Printing Company, 1916.

Warren, Sidney. *The Farthest Frontier: The Pacific Northwest*. New York: The Macmillan Co., 1949.

Washington State Library, comp. *The Negro in the State of Washington, 1788-1967, a Bibliography*. Olympia: State of Washington, 1968.

Welter, Barbara. "The Cult of True Womanhood: 1820-1860." *American Quarterly* 18 (Summer 1966): 151-62; 173-74.

———. *Dimity Convictions: The American Woman in the Nineteenth Century*. Athens: Ohio University Press, 1976.

———. "She Hath Done What She Could: Protestant Women's Missionary Careers in Nineteenth-Century America." *American Quarterly* 30 (Winter 1978): 624-38.

Wendt, Ingrid, and Primus St. John, eds. *From Here We Speak: An Anthology of Oregon Poetry.* The Oregon Literature Series, Vol. 4. A Project of the Oregon Council of Teachers of English. Corvallis: Oregon State University Press, 1993.

West, Leoti L. *The Wide Northwest: As Seen by a Pioneer Teacher.* Spokane, WA: Shaw & Borden, Co., 1927.

Wheat, Margaret M. *Survival Arts of the Primitive Paiutes.* Reno: University of Nevada Press, 1967.

White, Beatrice L. Bliss. *Not on a Silver Platter: Settling the Willamette Valley and Salem, Oregon, 1858-1904.* Forest Grove, OR: Meredith L. Bliss, 1989.

Whiteley, Opal. *The Fairyland Around Us.* Los Angeles: O. S. Whiteley, 1918.

———. *The Flower of Stars.* Washington, D.C.: the author, 1923.

———. *The Story of Opal: The Journal of an Understanding Heart.* Boston: The Atlantic Monthly Press, 1920.

Whitney, March. *Notable Women.* Tacoma, WA: Tacoma *News Tribune*, 1977.

Wiggins, Myra Albert. *Letters from a Pilgrim.* Salem, OR: *Statesman* Pub. Co., 1904.

Wilbert, Deborah. "A History of Black Women in the Pacific Northwest." Olympia: Humanities Resource Service of the Washington Commission for the Humanities, nd.

Williams, Christina MacDonald McKenzie. "Reminiscences." *Washington Historical Quarterly* 13 (1922): 107-17.

Wilson, Elizabeth M. "From New York to Oregon, via the Isthmus of Panama, in 1851." *Proceedings of the Oregon State Historical Society.* Salem, OR: Oregon State Historical Society, 1901. 99-113.

Wong, Bertha D. *Sending My Heart Back Across the Years: Tradition and Innovation in Native American Autobiography.* New York: Oxford University Press, 1992.

Woody, Ozro. *Glimpses of Pioneer Life of Okanogan County, Washington.* Okanogan, WA: Okanogan Historical Society, 1983.

Works Progress Administration and Washington Pioneer Project. *Told by the Pioneers: Reminiscences of Pioneer Life in Washington.* 3 vols. Olympia: State of Washington, 1938.

Yasui, Barbara. "The Nikkei in Oregon, 1834-1940." *Oregon Historical Quarterly* 76 (Sept. 1975): 225-57.

Yung, Judy. *Chinese Women of America: A Pictorial History.* Seattle: University of Washington Press, 1986.

Acknowledgments

The creation of *Pacific Northwest Women, 1815-1925: Lives, Memories, and Writings* has been a labor of love that would not have been possible without the collaborative interest and support of many friends and colleagues. We thank them for their encouragement, suggestions, and sharing of materials and ideas. To historian Ruth Barnes Moynihan, we express our gratitude for planting the seed for this collection; to editor Jo Alexander and members of the Board of the Oregon State University Press, we express our appreciation for encouraging us to nurture and develop this volume.

The late David C. Duniway deserves special mention for his interest in this collection and his lasting contributions to Pacific Northwest history and literature. As in the past, the lives of future generations will be enriched by David Duniway's work as historian, author, and archivist for the state of Oregon. We recall David's enthusiastic recommendation that we consider Esther Selover Lockhart's story from *Destination, West!*, and we trust he would be pleased to see excerpts from his favorite narrative by a western woman included in *Pacific Northwest Women*.

We are also indebted to new friends from Washington who helped us find "disappeared" writings for this volume. Nettie (Janet) Beryl Wynecoop Clark of Spokane taught us about her Arrow Lake, Colville, and Spokane ancestry, and she shared her family's privately published story—*In the Stream: An Indian Story*, begun by her mother, Nancy Perkins Wynecoop, and completed by Clark. The first part of this manuscript, which is included in this collection, tells the story of Able-One, born about 1815, the grandmother of Nancy Wynecoop and the great-grandmother of Nettie Clark.

Historian Esther Hall Mumford of Ananse Press in Seattle helped us identify sources for a number of African-American women of the Pacific Northwest, including Emma J. Ray and Susie Revels Cayton, both of whom appear in this volume. Through Mumford, we were introduced to Susan Cayton Woodson of Chicago, the granddaughter of Susie Revels Cayton, and to Richard S. Hobbs, historian, biographer of the Cayton family, and regional archivist for the Eastern Washington Regional Archives at Eastern Washington University. The assistance of Woodson and Hobbs has been invaluable in interpreting the life and writings of Susie Revels Cayton.

Susan Armitage, director of the American Studies Program at Washington State University, suggested a number of fruitful avenues for research on Washington women writers. Loretta Zwolak Greene, archivist of the Sisters of Providence in Seattle, located and identified documents by Mother Joseph of the Sacred Heart, expanded our knowledge of Catholic mission history in the Pacific Northwest, and reviewed our introductory essay on Mother Joseph. Annette White-Parks, now at the University of Wisconsin-La Crosse, kindly put us in touch with L. Charles Laferriere, who provided us with a photo of Sui Sin Far (Edith Eaton), his great-aunt.

Our searches in Washington were expedited by the special assistance of the Spokane Tribal Council at Wellpinit and Ellen Levesque, librarian for Northwest Collections at the Washington State Library in Olympia. Also, we appreciate the research support given by staff at the Cheney Cowles Museum, Special Collections, Eastern Washington State Historical Society; the Fort Vancouver Regional Library; the Seattle Public Library; the Spokane *Spokesman's Review*; the University of Washington Library; and the Washington Historical Society.

In Oregon, a number of individuals were critical to the development of *Pacific Northwest Women*. Stephen Dow Beckham, the Robert B. Pamplin, Jr., Professor of History at Lewis & Clark College, shared materials from his extensive personal collection and introduced us to Lydia Taylor's *From under the Lid: An Appeal to True Womanhood*, the 1913 autobiography of a prostitute. Glenda Suklis of the *Albany Democrat-Herald*, and Kimberly S. Kuhn, library assistant for the City of Albany Public Library, located important material on Amanda Gardener Johnson and her husband Ben Johnson, both former slaves. Molly Gloss, Portland author and historian, shared her excellent research on the life and writing of homesteader Alice Day Pratt. Oregon author Shannon Applegate and Judy Rycraft Juntunen, assistant director/librarian of the Benton County Historical Museum, exchanged materials with us on the life and writings of Louise Gregg Stephens. Alden Moberg, Oregoniana information specialist for the Oregon State Library, located a 1916 letter about the elusive Louise G. Stephens, written by her friend, Mrs. Wilma Waggoner. Susan Seyl and Mikki Tint of the Oregon Historical Society Photographs Department helped locate many of the photographs that appear in this volume.

In addition, our research was aided immeasurably by Beverly B. Stafford, interlibrary loan librarian for the Aubrey Watzek Library at Lewis & Clark College, and her assistant Susan Sarah Strand. Deanna Cecotti, reference librarian of the Multnomah County Public Library, M. C. Cuthill of the Oregon Historical Society, and Judy Bieber, reference librarian of the Oregon City Library, were always willing to assist us. We also thank staff members at a number of other Oregon libraries and historical societies, in particular the Clackamas County Historical Society, the Genealogical Forum of Oregon, the Lake Oswego Library, the Newberg Public Library, the Oregon State

University Library, the University of Oregon Library, and the Washington County Museum.

We are deeply indebted to Lewis & Clark College for faculty research grants which helped support our research and photographic collection.

Finally, we express our appreciation to members of the Feminist Research Group at Lewis & Clark College—friends and scholars who believed in this project from the beginning, to the students from Lewis & Clark with whom we had wonderful discussions about this project, and to our husbands, Paul and Pat, who welcomed Pacific Northwest women into their lives.

Jean M. Ward and Elaine A. Maveety
Lewis & Clark College

Copyright Acknowledgments & Permissions
Text

Bailey, Margaret Jewett. Excerpts from *The Grains; or, Passages in the Life of Ruth Rover with Occasional Pictures of Oregon, Natural and Moral*, 1854; reprint by Oregon State University Press, 1986.

Brown, Tabitha Moffat. Excerpts from "Documents. A Brimfield Heroine—Mrs. Tabitha Brown," *Oregon Historical Quarterly* 5 (June 1904): 199-205. Reprinted by permission of Oregon Historical Society, Portland, Oregon.

Cayton, Susie Revels. Excerpts from "Sallie the Egg-Woman," *Seattle Post-Intelligencer*, 3 June 1900: 33.

Cummins, Sarah J. Excerpts from *Autobiography and Reminiscences*, 1914; reprint by Ye Galleon Press, 1968. Reprinted by permission of Ye Galleon Press, Fairfield, Washington.

Denny, Emily Inez. Excerpts from *Blazing the Way; or True Stories, Songs, and Sketches of Puget Sound and Other Pioneers*, 1909; reprint by Seattle/King County Historical Society, 1984.

Duniway, Abigail Scott. Excerpts from "Editorial Correspondence," *New Northwest*, 1875-1886.

Ede, Susanna. Excerpts from "Pioneer Woman in Southwestern Washington Territory: The Recollections of Susanna Maria Slover McFarland Price Ede," edited by Barbara Baker Zimmerman and Vernon Carstensen, *Pacific Northwest Quarterly* 67 (October 1976): 137-50. Reprinted by permission of *Pacific Northwest Quarterly*, Seattle, Washington.

Far, Sui Sin. Excerpts from "The Americanizing of Pau Tsu," in *Mrs. Spring Fragrance*, A. C. McClurg, 1912.

Fuller, Emeline. Excerpts from *Left by the Indians: Story of My Life*, 1892; reprint by Ye Galleon Press, 1993. Reprinted by permission of Ye Galleon Press, Fairfield, Washington.

Hall, Hazel. Poems from *Curtains*, John Lane Co., 1912.

Hall, Hazel. Poems from *Walkers*, Dodd, Mead & Co., 1923.

Hall, Hazel. Poems from *Cry of Time*. Copyright 1928 by E.P. Dutton. Used by permission of Dutton Signet, a division of Penguin Books USA Inc.

Helm, Elizabeth Sager. Excerpts from autobiographical narrative in *The Lockley Files: Conversations with Pioneer Women,* 1981, compiled and edited by Mike Helm. Reprinted by permission of Rainy Day Press, Eugene, Oregon.

Higginson, Ella. "I Am a Mossback to My Very Finger Ends," originally titled "The New West: The Other Side," *Overland Monthly,* January 1892: 107-109.

Higginson, Ella. "Esther's 'Fourth,'" from *The Flower that Grew in the Sand and Other Stories,* 1896, and *From the Land of the Snow Pearls: Tales from Puget Sound,* 1902.

Higginson, Ella. Excerpts from *Mariella; of Out-West,* MacMillan, 1902; reprint by P. K. Pirrett & Company, 1924.

Johnson, Amanda Gardener. Excerpts from autobiographical narrative in *The Lockley Files: Conversations with Pioneer Women,* 1981, compiled and edited by Mike Helm. Reprinted by permission of Rainy Day Press, Eugene, Oregon.

Mother Joseph of the Sacred Heart, S. P. Excerpts from the 1866 *Chronicles of the Sisters of Providence.* Permission to publish courtesy Sisters of Providence Archives, Seattle, Washington.

Lee, Anna Maria Pittman. Excerpts from *Life and Letters of Mrs. Jason Lee, First Wife of Rev. Jason Lee of the Oregon Mission,* edited by Theressa Gay, Metropolitan Press, 1936. Reprinted by permission of Binford & Mort Publishing, Portland, Oregon.

Leighton, Caroline C. Excerpts from *Life at Puget Sound, with Sketches of Travel in Washington Territory, British Columbia, Oregon and California, 1851-1881,* 1883; reprint by Ye Galleon Press, 1980. Reprinted by permission of Ye Galleon Press, Fairfield, Washington.

Lockhart, Esther M. Selover. Excerpts from *Destination, West! A Pioneer Woman on the Oregon Trail,* by Agnes Ruth Sengstacken. Binford & Mort, 1942; 2nd edition 1972. Reprinted by permission of Binford & Mort Publishing, Portland, Oregon.

Miller, Minnie Myrtle. Excerpts from "Miss Anthony's Lectures--Observanda," *New Northwest,* 29 September 1871.

Miller, Minnie Myrtle. "A Communication to the Public by Mrs. M. M. Miller," *New Northwest,* 10 November 1871.

Monroe, Anne Shannon. Excerpts from *The World I Saw.* Copyright 1928 by Doubleday, a division of Bantam Doubleday Dell Publishing Group, Inc. Used by permission of Doubleday, a division of Bantam Doubleday Dell Publishing Group, Inc.

Mourning Dove. Excerpts from the autobiography of Mourning Dove. Reprinted from *Mourning Dove: A Salishan Autobiography,* edited by Jay Miller, by permission of the University of Nebraska Press. Copyright © 1990 by the University of Nebraska Press.

Owens-Adair, Bethenia. Excerpts from *Dr. Owens-Adair, Some of Her Life Experiences,* 1906.

Pratt, Alice Day. Excerpts from *A Homesteader's Portfolio,* 1922; reprinted by Oregon State University Press, 1993.

Ray, Emma J. Excerpts from *Twice Sold, Twice Ransomed: Autobiography of Mr. and Mrs. L. P. Ray,* 1926; reprint by Books for Libraries Press, 1971. Reprinted with permission from Ayer Company Publishers, Inc., North Stratford, New Hampshire.

Sawtelle, Mary P. Excerpts from *The Heroine of '49; A Story of the Pacific Coast,* 2nd edition, 1891.

Stephens, Louise Gregg. Excerpts from *Letters from an Oregon Ranch, by Katharine*, A. C. McClurg, 1905; reprinted as *From an Oregon Ranch*, 1916.

Taylor, Lydia. Excerpts from *From under the Lid: An Appeal to True Womanhood*, 1913.

Victor, Frances Fuller. Excerpts from *Atlantis Arisen; or Talks of a Tourist about Oregon and Washington*, J. B. Lippincott Company, 1891.

Winnemucca, Sarah. Excerpts from *Life Among the Piutes: Their Wrongs and Claims,* 1883; reprint by Chalfant Press/Sierra Media Inc., 1969. Reprinted by permission of Chalfant Press/Sierra Media Inc., Bishop, California.

Whitman, Narcissa Prentiss. Excerpts from *The Letters of Narcissa Whitman,* published by Ye Galleon Press, 1986. Reprinted by permission of Ye Galleon Press, Fairfield, Washington.

Wynecoop, Nancy Perkins. Excerpts from *In the Stream: An Indian Story*, 1985. Reprinted by permission of N. Wynecoop Clark.

Photographs

page 1. Marie Holst Portsmith, Oregon schoolteacher, doing laundry in a wooden tub behind her home, 1908, courtesy Oregon Historical Society, #cn 014255.

page 4. Ka-Ki-Is-Il-Ma, Princess Angeline, daughter of Chief Sealth, after whom Seattle was named. She died in 1896, about age ninety. Johnson and Son, Seattle, Washington, photo, courtesy Oregon Historical Society, #OrHi 62654.

page 9. Arrival in Northeastern Washington, courtesy Oregon Historical Society, #cn 015512.

page 11. A country school at the Garrison, Cascades, Columbia River, 1867. Carlton E. Watkins stereo photo, courtesy Oregon Historical Society, #OrHi 38498.

page 17. Nancy Perkins Wynecoop, courtesy Nettie (Janet) Beryl Wynecoop Clark.

page 28. Emily Inez Denny, courtesy Museum of History and Industry, Seattle, Washington, #13,393.

page 40. Frances Fuller Victor, courtesy Oregon Historical Society, #OrHi 5463.

page 45. Stagecoach between Roseburg and Myrtle Point, Oregon, courtesy Oregon Historical Society, #cn 015542.

page 50. Alice Day Pratt, 1901, courtesy Crook County Historical Society, Prineville, Oregon.

page 65. Anna Maria Pittman Lee, courtesy Oregon Historical Society, #OrHi 11849.

page 72. Sarah J. Cummins, courtesy Ye Galleon Press, Fairfield, Washington.

page 79. Bethenia Owens-Adair, courtesy Oregon Historical Society,#OrHi 4062.

page 85. Unidentified family group with overturned covered wagon, probably in Eastern Oregon, courtesy Oregon Historical Society, #cn 023973.

page 97. Emeline L. Trimble Fuller, courtesy Ye Galleon Press, Fairfield, Washington.

page 108. Mother Joseph of the Sacred Heart, S. P., courtesy Sisters of Providence Archives, Seattle, Washington.

page 113. A Sisters of Providence begging tour, courtesy Sisters of Providence Archives, Seattle, Washington.

page 124. Anne Shannon Monroe at her home near Lake Oswego, Oregon, 1940, courtesy Oregon Historical Society, #OrHi 91137.

page 133. Emma J. Ray, from *Twice Sold, Twice Ransomed* (1926).

page 136. Seattle A.M.E. Woman's Christian Temperance Union Chapter. Emma J. Ray is fourth from left in back row. Photo from *Twice Sold, Twice Ransomed* (1926).

page 140. "Constance Crookham works in her kitchen," Oregon, circa 1910. Myra A. Wiggins photo, courtesy Oregon Historical Society, #cn 021461.

page 144. Narcissa Prentiss Whitman, Oliver W. Dixon drawing made after her death, courtesy Oregon Historical Society, #OrHi 1645.

page 152. Detail from photograph of Elizabeth Sager Helm, courtesy Oregon Historical Society, #OrHi 87392.

page 159. Tabitha Moffat Brown, courtesy Oregon Historical Society, #OrHi 53563.

page 167. Amanda Gardener Johnson, photo from *Albany Democrat-Herald*, 1924, courtesy Albany Public Library.

page 174. Susie Sumner Revels Cayton, *Seattle Republican* photo, 23 July 1909, courtesy Richard S. Hobbs.

page 175. Susie Sumner Revels Cayton, painted by Eldzier Cortor shortly before her death. Isadore Howard photo, courtesy Susan Cayton Woodson.

page 180. Mourning Dove picking huckleberries at Mt. Hood, 1932, courtesy Oregon Historical Society, #cn 011495.

page 183. Mourning Dove, courtesy Oregon Historical Society, #OrHi 87139.

page 191. Eva Emery Dye interviewing Se-Cho-Wa, Umatilla County, Oregon, circa 1900. Major Lee Moorehouse photo, courtesy Oregon Historical Society, #OrHi 4333.

page 201. Mary P. Avery Sawtelle, from *The Heroine of '49*, 2nd edition (1891).

page 210. Abigail Scott Duniway, 1871. W. H. Caterlin photo, editors' collection, courtesy David C. Duniway.

page 222. Minnie Myrtle Miller. Bernard Hinshaw drawing for *History of Oregon Literature*, courtesy Binford & Mort.

page 232. Sarah Winnemucca, courtesy Nevada Historical Society.

page 246. Sui Sin Far (Edith Maud Eaton), courtesy L. Charles Laferriere.

page 253. Chinese woman and children, from M. Douthit's *Souvenir of Western Women* (1905).

page 259. Ella (Rhoads) Higginson, 1924, courtesy Oregon Historical Society, #OrHi 91136.

page 275. Lydia Taylor, from *From under the Lid* (1913).

page 284. Hazel Hall, courtesy Oregon Historical Society, #OrHi 77466.

page 298. Emily Inez Denny, Boyd photo, courtesy Museum of History and Industry, Seattle, Washington, #10,791.

Photographs used on the book jacket: Emma J. Ray, "Nurse Emmy and the child who loved her," from *Twice Sold, Twice Ransomed* (1926); "Shared Moments," courtesy Washington County Museum, Portland, Oregon; woman on horseback in Jefferson County, Oregon, courtesy Oregon Historical Society, OrHi18527; and photographs acknowledged above also used on pages 191 and 246.

INDEX

❖

A

Able-One, 4, 8, 13, 14, 16-26
Adams, Glen, 34
Adaptation, *see* Coping
African Americans, 132-37, 140-41, 166-72, 173-79, 276: Oregon exclusion laws, 168; population in Oregon in 1860, 167; women, *see* Susie Sumner Revels Cayton, Amanda Gardener Johnson, Emma J. Ray
Albany Democrat-Herald (Albany, Oregon), 166, 167, 169, 170, 172, 221
Albany, Oregon, 141, 166, 168, 169, 171, 210, 211
Alki Point, Washington, 28
American Indian rituals: burial, 36-38; childbirth, 241; council meetings, 242; courtship and marriage, 240-41; Festival of Flowers, 238-40; initiation into womanhood, 240; Prairie Chicken Dance, 25; Song of the Generous Supply, 19-23; Women's Song of Fruitage, 20
American Indians, 4, 16-26, 36-39, 47, 141-42, 180-87, 232-43: birth control, 237; women, *see* Able-One, Mourning Dove, Sarah Winnemucca, Nancy Perkins Wynecoop. *See also* names of specific tribes
American Woman Suffrage Association (AWSA), 212
Androgyny, 62, 109, 117
Anthony, Susan B., 191, 212, 220, 223, 224-28
Applegate, Jesse, 44, 45, 46, 81, 159
Applegate, Oliver Cromwell, 44, 47
Applegate Trail, 46, 159

B

Argus (Oregon City, Oregon), 213
Armitage, Susan H., 2, 61, 296
Arrow Lake Indians, 16
Ashland, Oregon, 46, 218
Asian Americans, 244-57: women, *see* Sui Sin Far, Onoto Watanna
Astoria, Oregon, 80, 81, 82
Athena, Oregon, 51, 53
Autonomy, *see* Empowerment

Bailey, Margaret Jewett (Smith), 9, 189, 190, 193-99, 200
Bailey, William J., 193, 195, 196
Baker City, Oregon, 51, 275, 276
Baker County, Oregon, 276, 277
Bakken, Lavola J., 200-201
Bancroft, Hubert Howe, 40, 43
Bannock Indians, 96, 235
Bannock War of 1878, 235
Belenky, Mary Field, 12
Bellingham, Washington, 259
Bend, Oregon, 124
Bingham, Edwin, 193
Bingham, Jane Straight, 153
Blackwell, Henry, 212
Blair, Karen, 124
Blanchet, A.M.A. (Bishop of Nesqually), 109-10
Blue Mountains, Oregon, 159
Brown, Alanna Kathleen, 180-81, 182
Brown, Tabitha Moffat, 12, 140, 159-65
Burke Act of 1906, 236
Burns, Oregon, 237
Burns Paiute Indian Colony, 237